ROUTLEDGE LIBRARY EDITIONS: AGRIBUSINESS AND LAND USE

Volume 12

# STATE-ADMINISTERED RURAL CHANGE

# STATE-ADMINISTERED RURAL CHANGE

## Agricultural Cooperatives in Kenya

BJÖRN GYLLSTRÖM

LONDON AND NEW YORK

First published in 1991 by Routledge

This edition first published in 2024
by Routledge
4 Park Square, Milton Park, Abingdon, Oxon OX14 4RN

and by Routledge
605 Third Avenue, New York, NY 10158

*Routledge is an imprint of the Taylor & Francis Group, an informa business*



*British Library Cataloguing in Publication Data*
A catalogue record for this book is available from the British Library

ISBN: 978-1-032-48321-4 (Set)
ISBN: 978-1-032-47391-8 (Volume 12) (hbk)
ISBN: 978-1-032-47396-3 (Volume 12) (pbk)
ISBN: 978-1-003-38592-9 (Volume 12) (ebk)

DOI: 10.4324/9781003385929

**Publisher's Note**
The publisher has gone to great lengths to ensure the quality of this reprint but points out that some imperfections in the original copies may be apparent.

**Disclaimer**
The publisher has made every effort to trace copyright holders and would welcome correspondence from those they have been unable to trace.

# State-administered rural change

## Agricultural cooperatives in Kenya

Björn Gyllström

London and New York

First published 1991
by Routledge
11 New Fetter Lane, London EC4P 4EE

Simultaneously published in the USA and Canada
by Routledge
a division of Routledge, Chapman and Hall, Inc.
29 West 35th Street, New York, NY 10001



Typeset by J&L Composition Ltd, Filey, North Yorkshire
Printed and bound in Great Britain by
Billings & Sons Limited, Worcester



*British Library Cataloguing in Publication Data*

Gyllström, Björn, *1945–*
State administered rural change; agricultural cooperatives in Kenya.
1. Kenya. Agricultural industries. Policies of government
I. Title
338.186762

ISBN 0–415–04815–X

*Library of Congress Cataloging in Publication Data*

Has been applied for

# Contents

# List of tables

# List of figures

# Acknowledgements

This book is the second publication resulting from a pro-ject concerning Agricultural Marketing Cooperatives and Rural Development in Kenya (for the first book, see Hedlund, 1986). The project, which was started in 1983, could not have been carried through without the support of university bodies, government institutions and donor agencies.

I am grateful to the Council for Research in the Social Sciences and the Humanities (HSFR), Stockholm which provided both the fellowship support that made the research possible and financial resources. Financial support has also been received from the Swedish Agency for Research Cooperation with Developing Countries (SAREC) and from the Swedish Cooperative Centre (SCC).

To the many people in government bodies and cooperative organizations in Kenya who have contributed time, effort, advice and encouragement, I wish to extend my warmest thanks. I also wish to express my sense of debt to colleagues and associates in Sweden who have commented on drafts of the present work, and to Ms Maria Johansson for her invaluable editorial assistance.

For the cartographic work, including statistical mapping, SMILE® has been used, which is a PC-based program from Nogys AB, Lund (Sweden).

Björn Gyllström

Chapter one

# Introduction

This study focuses on the economic and social role of cooperative organizations in rural areas of Kenya. Its principal aim is to illuminate how the capacity of cooperatives as agents of change is influenced by the interplay between, on the one hand their organizational structure and institutional interdependencies and, on the other, the local environments in which they operate.

## 1.1 Background

In sub-Saharan Africa, small-scale agriculture is the major source of livelihood. The subsistence element constitutes an important feature, although its significance varies. Most smallholders have established exchange relations which to some extent connect them to a wider economic context. Small scale of production and high distance friction limit more regular movements and exchange transactions to the local umland.[1] This kind of predominantly vertically linked agricultural economy can be characterized as institutionally fragmented. It operates at a generally low level of technological development and surplus production is limited. The individual production units tend to replicate each other in terms of output mix. When differentiation occurs, it is due mainly to the ecological variations.

At the same time, agriculture supports the majority of the economically active population. Hence, it is bound to play a central role in national development strategies.[2] In that context, agriculture has to meet multiple, and conflicting demands, including (i) contributing to an adequate supply of food and raw materials (ii) earning foreign exchange (iii) providing resources required for capital formation outside agriculture.[3] The last mentioned aspect in particular readily comes into conflict with another national development objective, namely (iv) to raise income levels and improve living conditions in rural areas.

To meet these demands, there is a need for improved utilization of available human and physical resources, which, in turn, calls for a closer integration of smallholder agriculture with the national economy. It has to involve intensified exchange of goods and services as well as technology transfers that together enhance specialization, diversification and raised levels of productivity. Reductions of prevailing transaction and interaction costs are mandatory. Hence, investments in human capital and infrastructure are required. In addition, prices of agricultural produce, and of urban goods and services, have to be managed in such a way that the price system satisfies the need both for raising capital for non-agricultural investment and for providing incentives for increased agricultural production. These broadly defined types of measures can all be said to belong to a basic assortment of policy instruments which, in various mixtures, figure in economic and regional development strategies. In agriculture, more direct types of intervention are also common. These include land reforms, extension services and the establishment of institutionalized constructs intended to influence more directly critical commodity and service linkages between the national economy and the smallholder sector.

In that context, agricultural service cooperatives have attracted considerable attention. They have been seen as a feasible device for organizing collection, first-stage processing and marketing of agricultural produce and, increasingly, for channelling credit services and input supplies to smallholders. In addition to the perceived economic logic of this kind of arrangement, there also seems to have been a political rationale behind the appeal of cooperatives. In many instances they are perceived as compatible with 'African socialism' and its connotations with traditional communalism and populism.[4] Hence, they are expected to enhance local participation and cohesiveness in development. Although not openly admitted, cooperatives also offer the advantage of providing a network of communication in rural areas which facilitates both the transmission of ideological influence and political control.[5]

## *The cooperative mode of organization*

A pertinent feature of the 'model cooperative society' is that it is owned by its members, who are entitled to share in any profits made and who manage the society on a one-member one-vote basis. ILO Recommendation No. 127 defines a cooperative society as

> an association of persons who voluntarily joined together to achieve a common end through the formation of a democratically controlled organization, making equitable contributions to the capital required and accepting a fair share of the risks and benefits of the undertaking in which the members actively participate.
>
> (Copac 1983:3)

A society has to have a certain minimum number of members (generally seven or more) and the individual member has to have at least one share. The member has one vote irrespective of the number of shares held. The general meeting is the superior body of a society, in which members review/approve their society's operations and management, vote on basic policies and programmes, and elect members to the committee. Any surplus made by a society should be distributed to members in proportion to their volume of business with the society. Given the nature of this ideal type of cooperative organization, a common argument in favour of the promotion of cooperatives – voiced by both Third World governments and a range of donor agencies – is that they are particularly well suited for mobilization of small farmers and workers for both their own development and that of nations as a whole.

Although a cooperative society may endeavour to satisfy both economic and social aspirations of its members, it seems reasonable to assume that the main reason for a smallholder to join a society is to realize economic benefits that cannot be obtained on an individual basis.[6] The ability of a society to operate as an efficient business enterprise, in particular, can thus be expected to be of importance for the degree of member support and, hence, for its contribution to economic development.

Evidently, however, there is a principal difference between an ordinary commercial enterprise and a cooperative organization. A private enterprise operates in markets composed of actors other than the owners/shareholders. Generated profits will quite unequivocally reflect its performance.

A cooperative enterprise of the agricultural service society type, on the other hand, has commercial relations both with a 'neutral' market and its own members. As a business enterprise it has an overriding objective to operate for the maximum benefit of its members. This ability, however, is not necessarily reflected in the size of the surplus generated by a society. A large surplus may have been achieved by rendering poor services or by charging members high prices. Of central concern to smallholder households will thus be their society's level of efficiency *and* service quality. That the 'model society' provides its members with the relevant 'package' of services is warranted by the fact that this mix is decided by the members themselves or their elected representatives.[7] The democratic element, however, also results in a more complex decision-making process, usually comprising three levels, namely (i) the general membership, (ii) the elected committee and (iii) the management staff.[8] The complexity of this structure is magnified in a federative structure, that is, when primary societies establish secondary cooperatives and apex organizations to exploit further economies of scale and/or to handle specialized activities.

## 1.2 Agricultural cooperatives in sub-Saharan Africa

### *The colonial period*

Even in colonial times, governments made attempts, with various degrees of coercion, to introduce local organizations aimed at commercializing smallholder agriculture. In most French colonies in West and Equatorial Africa so-called 'Native Provident Societies' (Sociétés Indigènes de Prévoyance) were established at village level, along with the introduction of tax and labour obligations, to increase agricultural production.[9] The establishment of this kind of society, which started in 1910, received little local support. When it became apparent that very few farmers voluntarily joined the societies, membership became obligatory for every head of household.[10] Initially the main activities of these societies were to distribute seeds, fertilizers and agricultural equipment. From the early 1930s, they were given the right to buy and sell agricultural produce and also to carry out extension services. However, in spite of a number of changes in structure and activity orientation, the economic and social roles played by these quasi-governmental organizations remained limited. Their most significant impact seems to have been the perpetuation of social inequalities. Thus, most technical and financial assistance did rather systematically benefit local elites. Towards the end of the colonial period, special legislation for state-sponsored cooperatives was promulgated. In basic respects it resembled the 'British–Indian pattern of co-operation' (Münkner 1983:56).[11]

In the Portuguese colonies (Guinea Bissau, Angola and Mozambique) hardly any attempts were made to raise and/or commercialize peasant production. Portugal had limited capacity to administer her colonies and, as in the Belgian Congo, the priority task was to secure the labour and land required by the mining and plantation industries.[12]

In Anglophone Africa the establishment of cooperatives was derived from the legislation introduced in India by the British authorities in 1904. The law gave the government a supreme supervisory and controlling role *vis-à-vis* cooperative organizations. However, while cooperatives in India were focusing on providing credit services to smallholders, marketing became the predominant activity in the African colonies. The development of agricultural service societies first gained momentum in the 1930s. In Ghana and Nigeria, this development focused on societies involved in the collection and marketing of cocoa, in Mauritius on sugar cane, and in Tanzania and Uganda on cotton and coffee.

In Kenya and Northern and Southern Rhodesia (Zambia and Zimbabwe), the expansion of cooperatives was affected by substantial white settler communities and the protection of their particular interests. Although the first cooperatives were started as early as 1909 in S. Rhodesia and 1914 in N. Rhodesia, African farmers were barred from membership. The same applied to the first Cooperative Societies Act introduced in Kenya in 1931. In the latter half of the 1940s, this legislation was revised both in Kenya and N. Rhodesia. In S. Rhodesia this was first done in 1956 and the new Act was then modelled on the Ceylon Cooperative Ordinance of 1922.[13] In Botswana the first society was not registered until 1964, only three years before the country gained independence.

### *After independence*

In the early 1960s most countries in sub-Saharan Africa were either independent or in the process of decolonization. By this time agricultural cooperatives constituted a generally fragile and financially weak structure of limited or no consequence for most peasants. The main exceptions were limited to a few areas in western and eastern Africa where smallholders were involved in export-oriented cash crop production.

In Ghana about 400 service cooperatives were in operation (cocoa) as well as 11 national cooperative organizations providing various specialized services. A few years after independence, this structure collapsed. The present official position is that cooperative constructs derived from the Western mode of organization are incompatible with the type of cultural, social and economic environment that Ghana represents.[14] The kind of institution now given preference, *nnoboa* (community association), builds on traditional forms of organizing community activities.[15] A similar approach (*nam*) has been introduced in Burkina Faso.[16]

In Nigeria, the total estimated membership of agricultural cooperatives is around half a million. The individual societies are small both in terms of membership and turnover, and play a marginal role in the agricultural economy.[17] In Senegal as well as Niger attempts are being made to develop societies which each cover several villages and of which all households are members. In Cameroon, about 100,000 smallholders are members of service societies marketing coffee.[18] Since the collapse of the savings and credit societies,[19] the role of other types of cooperatives has been negligible.

The countries in southern Africa have been late in gaining political independence. In 1964, when Zambia became a sovereign state, about 200 societies were operating in the country with a registered membership of about 40,000. By 1984, the number of societies had increased to over 1,000 and the membership to about 150,000. The dominating activity of agricultural cooperatives is grain marketing (principally maize) although they also engage in other activities such as distribution of farm inputs and implements, credit services, retailing and milling.[20]

At the time of independence, in 1980, there were about 370 smallholder cooperatives in Zimbabwe with an estimated total membership of about 40,000. Most of them were economically and managerially weak. The post-independence period has seen a considerable increase in the number of registered societies, which in 1985 stood at 597 with a total membership of about 100,000. However, probably only around 400 of these societies were active.[21] Their typical activities include the collection of agricultural produce from their members and the organization of transport to local depots run by marketing boards. Some societies also operate stores for resale, for the supply of farm inputs and consumer goods.

Procurement and distribution of inputs, linked to a government-supported credit scheme, are the main activities of the cooperative unions. For the cooperative sector as a whole, managerial shortcomings remain a serious problem and so does their financial position. In addition to the service societies, about 260 collective agricultural societies had been registered by 1985. Of these, however, only 52 seem to have been resettled. Their total membership may be in the range of 3,000–4,000. Generally, the collectives have a record of poor performance.

In the early 1960s, agricultural cooperatives in East Africa shared certain basic characteristics in terms of organization and activity orientation. This period also saw a considerable growth in the membership and in the number of registered societies. Since the beginning of the 1970s, however, the national development trends have diverged. In Tanzania, the introduction of the Ujamaa policy meant a drastic reorganization of both settlement pattern and economic structure. Primary agricultural service societies as well as unions were dissolved in 1976, and most of their assets and functions were appropriated by government bodies. In 1982, however, the 'old type' of agricultural cooperatives was again revived, although the rebuilding of this structure as yet seems far from finalized.[22]

The main activities of agricultural cooperatives in Uganda were the marketing of cotton and coffee. During the political chaos that hit the country in the 1970s, the cooperative infrastructure collapsed. In the last years of the 1980s, efforts have again been made to render the cooperatives operational. In Kenya, about 450 agricultural cooperatives were in the register in 1962. The societies had a total estimated membership of around 300,000. As distinct from Tanzania and Uganda, the post-independence period has been characterized both by political stability and by the absence of radical shifts in agricultural and cooperative policies. Marketing of cash/export crops (coffee, pyrethrum, sugar cane, cotton, cashew), combined with credit and input supply services, dominate the activity pattern of societies and unions. Available information clearly indicates that Kenya's sector of agricultural service cooperatives is presently the largest in sub-Saharan Africa. The total number of *active* societies is around 800, with a total membership of about 750,000 (see Chapter five).

In post-revolutionary Ethiopia, the peasant association (PA) is the basic rural institution, functioning as a semi-official administrative unit at the grass-roots level. Geographically it usually covers an area of around 800 ha and 200–400 households. Clusters of three to ten PAs are served by a service cooperative (SC). These service cooperatives are not based on individual membership; instead each PA is represented by its chairman on the board of the SC. The SCs market grain and usually also run a shop for basic consumer goods. Many societies have also started supplying fertilizers and seeds on credit. There are some 4,500 SCs in Ethiopia.[23] In addition to the SCs, there are about 2,000 agricultural producers' cooperatives (PC) that practise collective farming. A PC can be created by a small group of peasants within a PA. In 1986, the total membership of PCs stood at around 130,000 or about 2 per cent of all peasant households.[24]

Considering the basic features of agricultural cooperatives in

*Table 1.1* Estimated membership of agricultural cooperatives sub-Saharan Africa, by region, 1979–84

| *Region* | *Membership (millions)* | *Estimated % total number of rural households* |
|---|---|---|
| West Africa[1] | 2.3 | 8 |
| Equatorial Africa[2] | 0.3 | 4 |
| Southern Africa[3] | 1.4 | 15–20 |
| Eastern Africa[4] | 7.4 | 34–45 |

*Sources:* ICA, Statistics of Affiliated Organizations, London 1982; Copac, Cooperative Information Notes, various issues, 1980–85; Internal documentation from national cooperative organizations and public bodies; World Bank, World Development Report 1987.

*Notes*

1 Guinea, Sierra Leone, Guinea Bissau, Mauritania, Ivory Coast, Gambia, Mali, Liberia, Ghana, Nigeria, Burkina Faso, Niger, Togo, Senegal.

2 Benin, Gabon, Congo, Zaire, Centr. African Republic, Chad, Rwanda, Burundi, Cameroon.

3 Angola, Botswana, Zambia, Zimbabwe, Malawi, Lesotho, Swaziland, Mozambique.

4 Tanzania, Kenya, Uganda, Somalia, the Sudan, Ethiopia.

sub-Saharan Africa, a few general observations may be made. First, it is evident that agricultural cooperatives still reach only a fraction of the total number of smallholder households (Table 1.1). The regional variations are however striking. While available information indicates that possibly over one-third of the smallholder households are linked to cooperatives in eastern Africa, 4–8 per cent are members of cooperatives in Equatorial and West Africa. Within each of these regions, in turn, we can observe large variations among individual nations.

Secondly, it is apparent that agricultural cooperatives in practically all nations are rife with problems of a managerial and financial nature. These characteristics have also been a recurrent theme in the debate of the actual and possible role of cooperatives as rural change agents. A third common feature is the decisive role played by both colonial and independent governments in the organization, the planning and promotion of cooperatives.

## 1.3 Conceptual framework

### *Performance and impact – a review*

The 'cooperative approach' has been criticized for having brought few dividends to the African farmer. Agricultural cooperatives have been blamed not only for a mediocre record in terms of economic performance but also for having failed to contribute towards the achievement of basic social objectives.[25] In the early

1970s, Guy Hunter argued that 'an obsession with cooperatives is one of the major impediments to agricultural development'.[26] In a UNRISD study on cooperatives of 1975, it is noted that,

> their activities have often had little effect on the existing patterns and trends of economic activity in the country, and their performance has usually had little relevance to the wider context of social and economic change and the general strategy of development.
>
> (UNRISD 1975:32)

Although most studies seem to be in basic agreement in this respect, the same cannot be said about the explanations of observed shortcomings, where two broad, partly overlapping, perspectives dominate. One pays attention primarily to the cooperative mode of organization in its local, *social* setting, and how this relation influences a society's behaviour, performance and impact characteristics. In the second category of studies, the perspective is extended to encompass also the vertical interdependencies between state and cooperatives.

The main body of studies, however, falls outside even this broad taxonomy. It lays emphasis on the management performance of cooperatives but takes the organizational and political framework largely as given. Thus, observed deficiencies, in terms of efficiency and service quality, are assumed to be due neither to the mode of organization nor to its social and economic connotations. Conventionally, they are instead seen as a result of various 'operational constraints' which, if removed, will release the development potential of cooperatives. To this assortment of deterrents usually belong factors such as uninformed members, shortage of appropriate manpower, deficient administrative systems, lack of production credit, shortage of vehicles, etc. This kind of 'instrumental' approach is generally of limited explanatory value. As it builds on system-belief it attends to ways of treating symptoms rather than to analyses of more basic societal determinants of observed anomalies.[27]

The first of the earlier mentioned categories of studies focuses on the relation between the management structure of the individual cooperative and the social environment at local level. Member households are seen as not only linked to their cooperative society but also as constituent parts of social constructs with inbuilt parochial elements. Individual behaviour is conditioned by value systems related to edifices such as kinship, age set groups and gender. These ties, it is argued, hinder the management of the cooperative to secure the measure of autonomy required for efficient and stable operations.[28] Patron–client relationships and other 'vertical' dependencies will penetrate the organization and limit both employees' and the ordinary members' ability to exercise any effective control of their societies.[29] Thus, according to Widstrand, 'these often self-contained social units become involved in factional warfare over the control of cooperative resources and their distribution. This means that parochial rather than technical or economic considerations tend to determine the outcome of management decisions.' (Widstrand 1972:18).

The second category of studies explicitly considers the fact also that the policies pursued by most African states have established strong interdependencies between national government bureaucracies and cooperatives. In his studies of cooperatives in East Africa, Hydén links the local environment of cooperative activities to the policy dimension and to its derivatives in the form of organizational blueprints and imposed government directives. The actual impact, however, is seen as not caused solely by the government-cooperative relation. In vital respects it is perceived also as a function of the local socio-political environment.[30] With reference to East Africa, and the situation in the 1960s, Hydén notes that,

> neither the regulatory nor the supporting activities of the Co-operative Departments in the three [East African] countries have eliminated the fundamental obstacles to a strong co-operative *movement*. Factionalism in the committees remains prominent. So does the tendency for already privileged people to become leaders of the co-operative societies and unions, thereby preventing the latter from developing into a front of poor peasants against wealthier groups, both inside and outside rural communities. There is also evidence that the government control measures have the effect of reducing the commitment of members and leaders alike to their organization. . . . The heavy load of duties imposed upon co-operatives by governments in East Africa also reduces the capacity to store and use information adequately.
>
> (Hydén 1972:76)

In a later study, Hydén argues that the cooperative is not the only modern institution to be a victim of the socio-political environment. Thus, more generally, when the culture embodied in the state and modern institutions is perceived as alien, i.e. newly introduced rules of social interaction do not conform to moral obligations based on prevailing cultural values, induced changes will tend to be largely unavailing.[31]

Hedlund also argues in favour of a wider interpretation of a society's social environment.[32] In a recent study of a coffee society in Kenya, Hedlund concludes that the price paid to growers for marketed produce is the critical determinant of the performance and stability of the local system, i.e. the cooperative and its members. It is also noted that, in this case, the local cooperative had developed sufficient strength to reduce at least part of the negative effects of fluctuating markets. Considerably less weight is assigned both to the influence of local, parochial relations and to the conditioning impact of government control and intervention.[33]

Apthorpe, like Hydén, bases his analysis on the relations of state–cooperative and cooperative–environment.[34] However, unlike Hydén, he argues for more economically oriented analyses of the local consequences of state-prescribed cooperative organizations. Thus, when cooperatives go wrong it is tempting to use the convenient 'social values philosophy' (Apthorpe 1972:217) and put the blame on culturally based 'peasant attitudes'.

As regards the economic impact of cooperatives, it seems to be widely held that cooperatives in Africa have been generally of limited positive consequence. Further, in those cases where they have played a more significant role in the local economy, they have tended to benefit the already affluent households, while leaving out the poor. However, some findings deviate from this general pattern. Thus, in a study referring to a densely populated smallholder area in western Kenya, it is argued that cooperatives have prevented increasing stratification of the local smallholder economy.[35]

### *Perspective*

In our view, the role of the societies' social environment has often been given attention at the expense of other conditioning forces. As pointed out by Peter Worsley,

> When we begin to list the factors which make for or inhibit success [of cooperatives] we begin to realize that to concentrate simply on the question of the nature of pre-existing social bonds is wrongly to isolate only one aspect of the problem.
>
> (Worsley 1971:37)

By consistently paying attention to one specific set of aspects, the explanatory value of a particular factor easily gets inflated, at the same time as its interdependencies with other social phenomena may be neglected. Thus while generalized judgements and opinions flourish as regards the incompatibility of the rural social structure and cooperative organizations, surprisingly few empirical studies exist that verify these claims. The empirical studies which have actually been carried out, are predominantly case studies. Hence, caution should still be taken before using them for induced generalizations.

As argued here, there is reason not to start off from the assumption that the performance and impact records of cooperatives singularly are caused by affections, loyalties and factionalism. Although this kind of social dynamism admittedly is a reality, it is obviously necessary to try to establish its relations to other societal conditions. This applies in particular to economic factors.

Low levels of technological development limit the means indigenously available to realize a more considerable acceleration of the utilization of available human and physical resources.[36] We support Apthorpe's observation that poverty and low productivity tend to be perceived as equivalent to backwardness, and hence, rather systematically have lured polity, planners and administrators to underestimate smallholders' ability to respond to economic incentives.[37] As a result, preference is given to more direct, administered means of 'inducing' change. However, as shown also by Bates, individual economic self-interest is a decisive cross-cultural force in social reproduction processes.[38] Efforts aimed at initiating a self-sustained process of increasing interaction, specialization, technological development and material well-being essentially have to build on this recognition.

In this perspective, cooperatives can be seen as instruments for joint efforts among individuals aiming at achieving some common purpose. The involvement, however, is conditional in the sense that the organization's contribution constitutes only part of a member's total purpose. Subsequently, if the organization cannot provide the necessary inducements, we can expect participation to be negatively affected and, hence, also the cooperative's role as change agent.[39] In many instances, cooperatives have been granted a monopoly position to provide specific services which, seemingly, solves the problem of member defection. However, if anything, this may perpetuate deficiencies in efficiency and service quality and, hence, negatively influence farm output.

For cooperatives to play a role in agricultural and rural development it is thus necessary for them to make sense economically to large strata of smallholders. This will only be the case when cooperatives are able to offer advantageous producer prices, low marketing commissions, competitive prices on inputs, production credit on reasonable conditions, and generally are able to ensure accessibility, timeliness and reliability of services provided. If these prerequisites are not met, they may instead constitute a mechanism which revives or perpetuates parochial social networks both locally and between the community level and the political and administrative superstructure. The occurrence of such anomalies may subsequently be a consequence of an already proven inability of cooperatives to establish the prerequisites and incentives required for deepened market integration and economic growth. As seen here, profound, but generally neglected, determinants of the ability of cooperatives to meet this kind of requirement are (i) the 'modern' institutional structure, of which they constitute part and (ii) the physical–technical characteristics of the local environment.

As regards the local environment, a range of conditions are of direct consequence for the farmers'/members' performance potential. To these belong agro-ecological conditions, access to arable land, level of development of transport, of communications and social infrastructure, and the degree of differentiation of the local economy. These conditions are of direct and indirect consequence for the transaction costs incurred by smallholders and, hence, influence costs of production and farm output. For a member, these transaction costs will be partly determined by the society's efficiency and service quality both of which, in turn, are likely to be affected by the same range of local conditions that impinge upon the member.[40] The relations between local conditions, as defined above, and the performance of cooperatives are of a complex nature. One reason is that they partly embody the on-farm performance of members and are partly operational in character. Another reason is that they are conditioned also by the cooperatives' organizational structure and external interdependencies.

This brings us to the organizational and institutional aspects. Many studies in Africa, and certainly in Kenya, convey the impression that agricultural cooperatives largely operate as conventional service societies. Hence it is also assumed that they principally act as autonomous establishments. This is not the case. As a matter of fact, it is generally the case that public bodies subjugate them to an inordinate range of regulations and rules, and to direct intervention in their administration and management. Although being widely acknowledged as significant, the relation of state and cooperatives has apparently not been judged as sufficiently important to attract much systematic, empirical research.[41] To understand the behaviour and performance of cooperatives, it is here seen as necessary to shift the focus of enquiry towards these interdependencies with a wider set of institutionalized power.[42] Friedman has defined the concept of power as,

> the ability of organizational and institutional actors, located in geographical space, to mobilize and allocate resources in geographical space (manpower, capital and information) and intentionally to structure the decision field of others (i.e. to constrain the decisions of others by policies, rules and commands). . . . Both kinds of power (governmental and private economic), I will assume, have the capacity to influence the location decisions of firms and households, the quantity, location and application of resources and the flow of innovations.
>
> (Friedman 1985:12)

State authority is encapsulated in a network of institutions and organizations at local, regional and national levels, of which some are sanctioned to prescribe and control directly the structure and behaviour of cooperatives. Also indirectly, cooperatives are influenced by a range of public institutions concerned with agricultural and rural policies. For example, there is often an elaborate structure of marketing boards, and as pointed out by G. Lamb,

> each with its own bureaucracy, each enjoying legally and administratively defined areas of predominance or monopoly, each standing in a particular relationship to peasant and other producers, to the international economy, and to the régime and its clients. There is the overwhelming presence of the administration in the rural areas, with the district commissioners wielding wide but sometimes unclear administrative and political power over other government agencies and over the rural population. And there are the technical ministries.
>
> (Lamb 1974:27)

Paradoxically enough, the official justification for government support and control is usually the social qualities of cooperatives. That is, the democratic–participative features of this organizational mode are perceived as making them particularly useful as rural change agents and, hence, also as targets of promotion. Having been assigned this role, however, most of their democratic features eventually get lost. Also donor agencies have rather consistently supported the state-sponsored 'change agent approach' to cooperative and agricultural development.

> Captivated by the idea that governmental structures seemed the only viable way of implementing development plans, development agencies poured more and more resources into building

> and strengthening government cooperative structures. Government employees became the most knowledgeable of cooperative principles and organization, most skilled in cooperative management, the instruments of cooperative training, the source of cooperative financing.
>
> (Copac 1984:2)

In conclusion, there is a need to examine more systematically (i) how government intervention patterns the activity orientation, administrative structure and management of cooperatives and (ii) the compatibility of these behavioural prescriptions with local conditions.

### *Approach*

Most social science studies, including those dealing with agricultural and rural development issues, only implicitly take in a geographical dimension. This convention is no doubt nurtured by the paucity and inadequacies of spatially defined statistics. Hence it is often necessary, not least in developing countries, to supplement this kind of information with special, and expensive, rounds of extraction or collection of data. Even so, an inbuilt treatment of geographical space is justified as it, in our view, considerably adds to the explanatory power of social studies. In the context of examining the role of agricultural service cooperatives as change agents in rural areas, aspects concerning their location (spread), performance and impact are of principal interest. Thus, which factors or circumstances have been of decisive importance as determinants of their geographical *location* (distribution)? Second, given the geographical distribution of service societies, to what extent are observed variations in *performance* a consequence of the local environment in which societies operate? Third, what are the contributions of cooperatives to production and income generation (*impact*)? Do they reveal spatial and social features that may contribute to more general conclusions regarding their scope and limitations as rural change agents?

#### Location (spread)

As indicated above, one issue of general interest is to clarify why activities (establishments) locate to, or develop in, some places to the exclusion of others. This is particularly true for establishments which may be seen as necessary, even if not sufficient, elements of an economic transformation of the economic landscape. In our context this applies to agricultural cooperatives with their perceived inherent qualities as change agents. Hence, is the specific geographical location of a cooperative society a consequence of the physical resource endowment, of specific political or social conditions, of local entrepreneurship, of a well-developed infrastructure, of access to markets or information? Or is it rather a combination of these factors? If so, which have been the decisive ones? What role has been played by 'invisible' forces and interdependencies such as the earlier discussed concept of institutional power?

In probing this issue, case studies have the advantage of allowing for detailed analysis of a wide range of circumstances. If not explicitly linked to a wider framework, however, there is the risk that induced generalizations are invalidated by features that are unique to a specific place. If, on the other hand, all establishments (societies) are included, there is a necessary loss of information. This disadvantage, however, is compensated for by the possibility of examining whether certain factors are playing a more general role in affecting the geographical distribution of societies. Further, the observed location pattern may in itself reveal patterns that offer additional explanations to reasons behind the registration of societies. This possibility is further enhanced if the temporal dimension is included, i.e. by analysing the succession of society registrations through time and geographical space. It facilitates identification of both process and pattern characteristics which, in turn, offer a basis for probing further into the aspects that here are seen as essential. These include the influence of regional characteristics and changes of the agricultural economy, agricultural/rural development policies, and policies and government intervention focusing on the cooperative sector. Hence, in this study of agricultural service cooperatives in Kenya, the empirical analysis covers all societies registered during the period 1946–83 (for further data specifications, see below).

### Performance

Generally it can be assumed that local conditions in decisive respects affect societal operations. These include agro-ecology, level of development of social and physical infrastructure, and degree of economic differentiation. The texture of the environment, and hence the relative importance of its constituent elements, are likely to vary geographically. Identified co-variation between spatially differentiated local conditions and the societies' performance ratings thus may assist in identifying environmental factors which, in decisive respects, affect societal operations.

However, performance is obviously not solely a function of environmental influences. The societies are far from identical objects in terms of activity orientation, organization and size. Further, they do not operate as autonomous establishments but are in different ways subjugated to other modern institutions. For these reasons their susceptibility to environmental influences will vary. Societies that operate in identical environments may display differences in performance ratings. We can thus perceive performance as a function of complex interplay between local environment and organizational features, where the latter in decisive respects are conditioned by external dependencies, primarily to the government bureaucracy and other public bodies. Also in this context, inclusion of the spatial dimension could assist in disentangling and identifying possible critical combinations of elements contained by the spheres environment–organization–external interdependencies.

The empirical analyses refer to both 'survival' and 'performance'. The former concept is here used as a primitive indicator of performance. Its inclusion is warranted by the fact that it makes it possible to consider the total population of cooperatives, i.e. the fate of all societies registered since 1946. The analysis of 'performance', on the other hand, has to be confined to the societies that are still in operation.

*Survival* The survival rate of societies (number of societies not liquidated/dormant in relation to the total number of societies registered) is examined in relation to local environment. To facilitate illumination of the influences of the local environments on survival rates, a taxonomy is evolved using 'environmental indicators' for the periods 1963–70 and 1971–83. Survival is also studied in relation to the societies' activity orientation and to institutional–organizational parameters. The latter refer mainly to policies and the nature and extent of direct government intervention in the cooperative sector (including donor-assisted support programmes)

*Performance* For unions and societies still active in 1983, selected performance indicators are examined in relation to type of local environment (using the taxonomy arrived at under 'survival'). Societies and unions, categorized by activity orientation, are analysed with regard to the interplay of environmental and organizational features. In the case of primary societies, gross value of marketed produce and payment rates are used as main performance indicators. Due to variations in the reliability of the data, the latter indicator is applied only to the major categories of societies. As regards unions, a broader range of performance indicators is used. Apart from turnover, account is also taken of the range of service activities provided, staffing, administrative overhead costs, viability and solidity.

Impact

To indicate the influence of cooperatives on production and living conditions of members/smallholders, three concepts have been used, namely (i) reach, (ii) functional participation and (iii) reflective participation. Reach simply denotes the extent to which cooperatives are linked to households within their respective areas of operation. Functional participation indicates the degree to which those reached by societies actually take part in their activities as economic actors. By reflective participation is meant the subordination of societal activities to members' conscious reflection and decision-making. Finally, the profile of the co-operative sector in these three respects is linked to the source of participation. Of three main categories – spontaneous, induced and coerced – the latter two are predominant in Kenya.

## 1.4 Data and field work

The approach is demanding in terms of data requirements as it requires access to information both about certain environmental conditions and about each individual organization (society). The advantages of the method first become apparent at the stages of data compilation and analysis. It then allows for considerable flexibility in choosing the level of aggregation and types of classification criteria, e.g. by taxonomizing the material according to environmental or organizational attributes.

A data base has been established which comprises all agricultural service societies and unions registered during the period 1932–83. For each of 1944-registered societies, the following information has been collected:

- registration number
- name
- primary or secondary society
- main activity
- year of registration
- present status (active/liquidated/dormant)
- year of liquidation (if applicable)
- period of dormancy

- area of operation (administrative location)
- district of operation
- geographical location (x- and y-coordinates)
- agro-ecological conditions.

This stage of data collection was started up in 1983 and finalized in 1985. A major portion of these data were retrieved from documentation at the Legal Section of the Ministry of Cooperative Development. However, information about the period of dormancy, area of operation and geographical location was collected through a nationwide survey. The statistics clerks at the district cooperative offices, with the assistance of other district staff, collected and compiled these pieces of information. In order to facilitate identification of the societies' geographical location, district maps were prepared for the use of all offices. In the few districts having no permanent MOCD-staff, information was gathered either at provincial or central level. After completion of the field exercise, the geographical information was transferred to a national map and cross-checked against information about the administrative locations in which societies were located. A national map on essential agro-ecological features was prepared (derived from maps prepared by IRS and IADPII) and on this basis, the agro-ecological 'status' of the societies was estimated. This information was cross-checked against information compiled by the district offices. Considerable efforts were made to ensure the reliability of the material. As a consequence, several rounds of data gathering were carried out, either to supplement or to correct collected information.

Although it has been a time-consuming and inordinately cumbersome procedure to define the geographical location of all societies by means of co-ordinates, the method offers obvious advantages at subsequent stages of the study. As the information is digitized, it facilitates analyses that manually would simply be too demanding. Thus, it expedites identification/analysis of spatial and temporal patterns in the incidence of registrations and liquidations, both for the whole population of societies and of particular segments, and their possible relation, for example to policy changes or to economic fluctuations. It also makes it possible to relate observed activity expansion/contraction patterns to various environmental characteristics.

According to official statistics, over 1,000 agricultural service societies were active in 1983. The survey findings, however, show that number is about 20 per cent lower, or 819 societies. It is this figure rather than the official one that is correct, i.e. although the survey material may still contain errors, the data have been so carefully controlled that we are in a position to claim that their reliability is superior to those of the Ministry of Cooperative Development.

As regards societies that were found to be active in 1983, two additional data collection exercises were carried out. Both were national in coverage and for each society the following information was collected with reference to the accounting year 1982/83 (in addition to the variables specified above):

- affiliation and, if so, which union
- number of members
- turnover
- main type of produce marketed, gross proceeds, gross payment to members, payment rate
- ditto, second main produce
- ditto, third main produce
- whether input supply services were provided
- if MT-system had been introduced
- if the society had permanent staff employed
- number of years since final accounts last were audited
- own accounting or centralized to union
- whether the society participated in any of the following credit schemes/programmes (CPCS, IADPI, IADPII, SPSCP, FISS, MIDP, SCIP, GASP, other)
- if credit section or not
- management performance (as judged by the District Cooperative Officer).

Again, the data collection exercise was carried out in collaboration with the MOCD and its district offices. Including a test survey and follow-ups, the field work covered most of 1984 and 1985.

The adjusted annual accounts for thirty-five unions were used as source for extraction of the following information:

- fixed assets
- stock of goods for resale
- other current assets
- members' debts and loans
- own capital
- medium- and long-term loans
- members' deposits
- current liabilities
- commissions
- turnover, goods for resale
- total union turnover

- total salaries/wages
- no. of staff employed
- surplus/loss.

In addition to these three general surveys, in-depth studies were carried out in four districts (Kirinyaga, Nyeri, Kisii and S. Nyanza). The field work, carried out in three phases during 1984–86, focused on providing a more detailed picture of the management and operations of twenty-five societies and unions. It included interviews of management committees (societies) and union managers. Three of these societies were also covered by anthropological studies.[43] Furthermore, according to the original design of the research project, agricultural economists at the Institute for Development Studies were to carry out surveys focusing on production and income characteristics of member and non-member households in each of these four districts. Although an agreement had been reached both with the IDS and the researchers concerned, it was not possible to secure the necessary financial support for this part of the project, which consequently had to be abandoned.

At central level, documentation at ministries and other government bodies constituted the main sources for collection of information pertaining to basic economic and 'infrastructural' characteristics at district level. Internal documentation at the MOCD as well as official publications have been used as sources for statistics on agricultural service cooperatives referring to the 1960s and 1970s.

A special data collection round was carried out in order to determine the development of central bodies directly linked to the cooperative sector in terms of their structure, staff, expenditure/turnover and operations. These were the Ministry of Cooperative Development, the Cooperative Bank of Kenya, the Cooperative Insurance Society, the Cooperative College, and the Kenya National Federation of Cooperatives. From the MOCD and the Cooperative Bank information was also collected about the loans issued to unions and primary societies and the debts outstanding at the end of 1983. This information is specified by society/union and type of loan/credit scheme.

The field work/data collection activities, which started in 1983, were finalized in early 1986. Compilation, coding and control of the data material, and the building-up of a digitized data base, which have constituted ongoing activities since 1984, were completed in 1987.

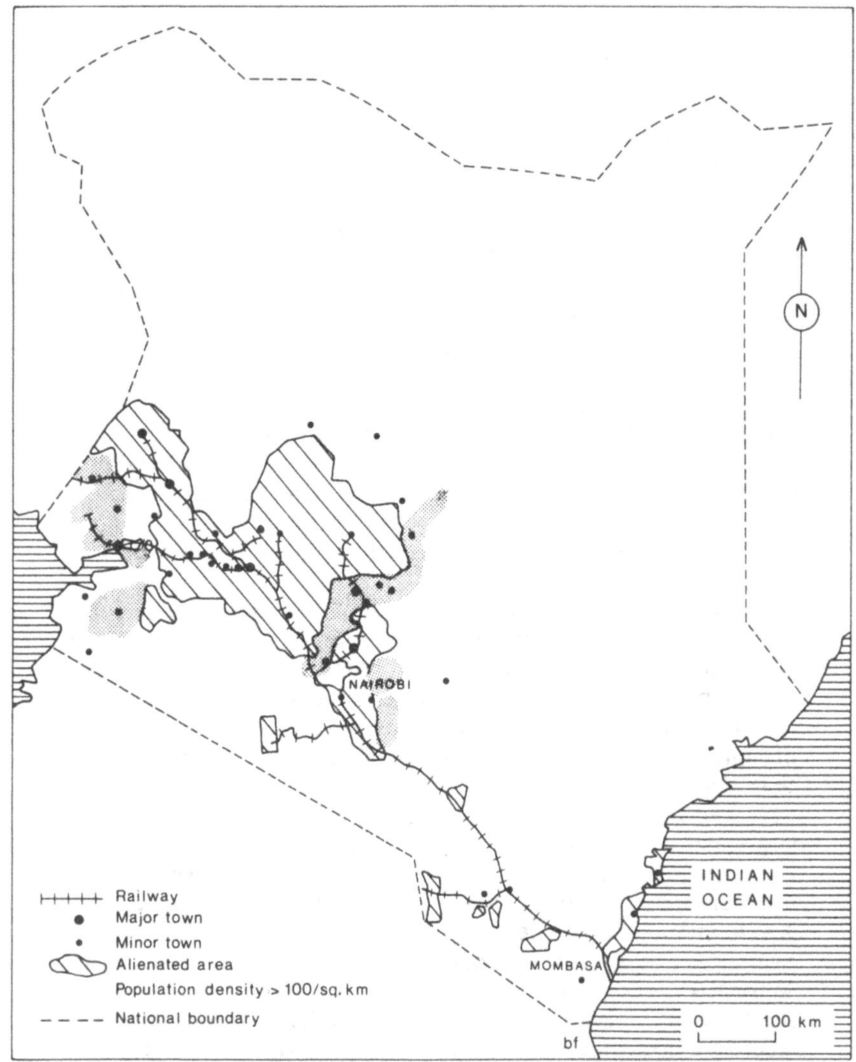


*Figure 1.1* Alienated land and major smallholder areas in the early 1960s

## 1.5 Organization of the study

Chapter two reviews policies and economic trends during the colonial era and the post-independence period, and how they have influenced smallholder agriculture and the location, *spread*, activity orientation and organizational structure of service cooperatives.

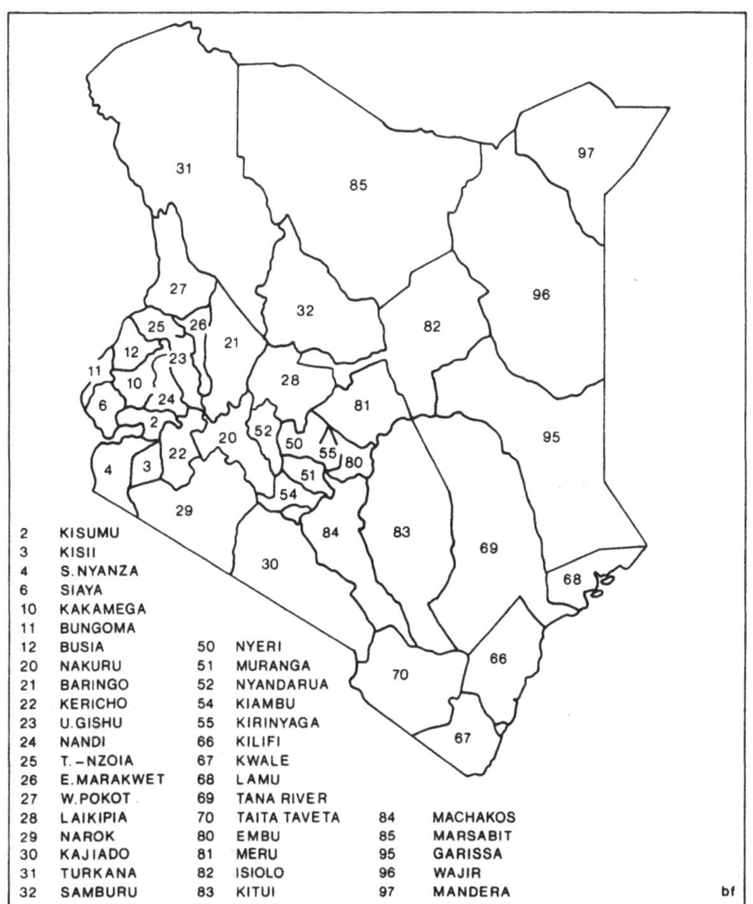


*Figure 1.2* Administrative districts, 1983

The *survival* characteristics of agricultural cooperatives are considered in Chapter three. Based on the argument that survival could be perceived as a basic performance indicator, the analyses aim at illuminating the extent to which liquidations/dormancies are consequences of the kind of local environment in which societies operate, their activity orientation, and organizational features. Three different periods are considered, namely 1946–62, 1963–70 and 1971–83.

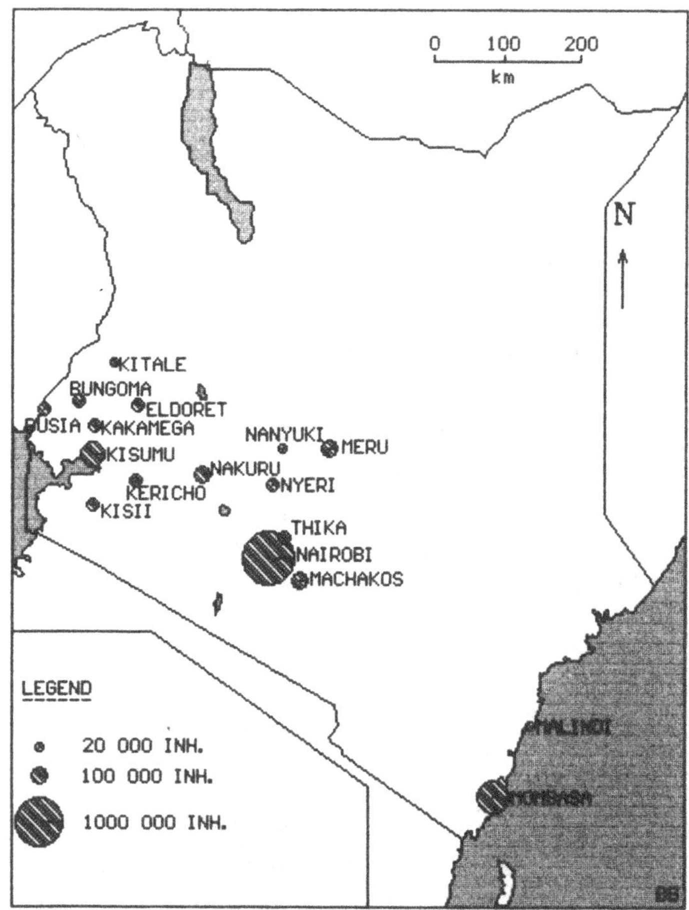


*Figure 1.3* Urban centres

In Chapter four, the analysis focuses on the *performance* of unions and primary societies, again with the aim of determining the nature and importance of influences generated by the local environment, activity orientation, and organizational arrangements and interdependencies.

With reference to basic features of the local and regional environments in which agricultural marketing and delivery services are performed, Chapter five considers basic social and economic *impact* characteristics.

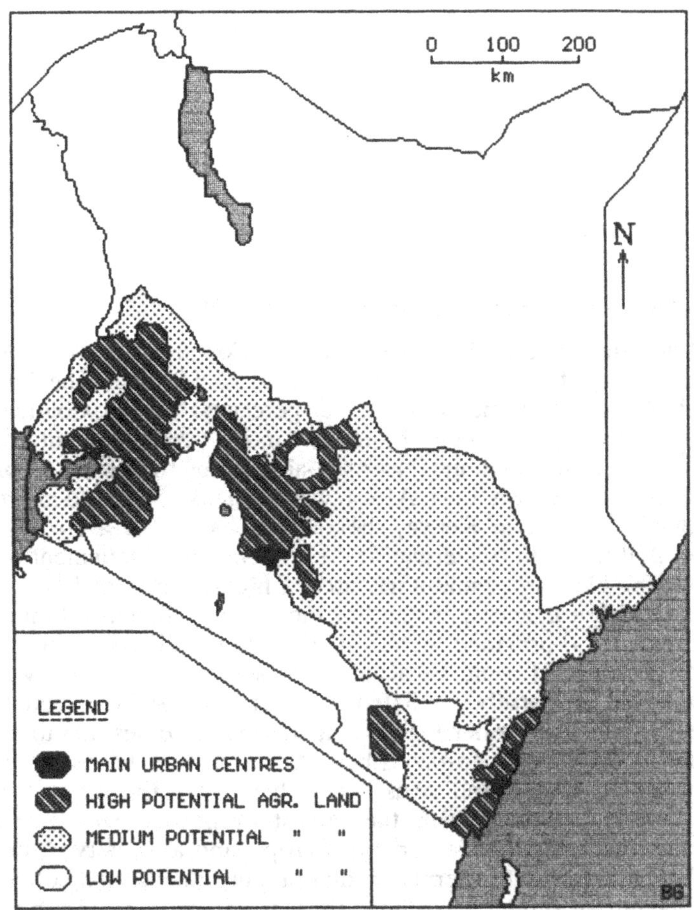


*Figure 1.4* Agricultural potential

Chapter two

# Spread

## 2.1 Submission separation and integration (1896–1945)

In 1896, the Imperial British East Africa Company initiated the construction of a railway from Mombasa to Uganda. The line reached Lake Victoria in 1901. As perceived by the Colonial Office, one way of turning the railway into a profitable venture, and also to terminate annual grant-in-aid paid by the Treasury for administering British East Africa, was to make the land more productive. Thus, in Kenya, the railway was to be a strongly influential factor in triggering off subsequent white settlement on something like three million hectares of high-altitude land.[1]

Two land ordinances, enacted by the colonial administration in 1902 and 1915, provided for the alienation of land and the terms under which land could be acquired by settlers. Some land was unoccupied or sparsely populated. In other cases land was sequestered or alienated under the pretext that buffer zones had to be established between hostile tribes. Africans were barred from owning land in alienated areas. About half of the European area was arable land of which the largest proportion was mixed farmland yielding a wide variety of crops, and also dairy cattle. Although important in terms of total output, ranches and coffee/tea plantations supported comparatively few Europeans. Instead it was the large-scale mixed farms which represented the majority of settlers and also constituted the political nexus of the colony.[2]

In the late 1930s, the total amount of alienated land amounted to about 27,000 sq. km which supported a total European farming population of less than 5,000. Areas defined as 'native reserves' comprised about 80,000 sq. km, while the remaining area of Kenya – about 460,000 sq. km – comprised arid and semi-arid lands. Over 80 per cent of the 2.6 million Africans lived in the native reserves. A majority lived in two large clusters of reserves along the eastern and western borders of the Highlands, in the Kikuyu (Central province) and Kavirondo (S. Nyanza and Western provinces) areas.[3]

With the development of large-scale agriculture in the White Highlands, there followed extensive investment in the infrastructure of communications and administration. Distant farming areas were connected by branch lines and interior nodes increased in size and importance. This applied in particular to Nairobi, which benefited not only from being the political and administrative centre, but also from a strategic position in the emerging transportation network, making it function as a gateway to the White Highlands. The Nairobi–Thika line was opened in 1913, Nakuru–Kitale in 1926, Gilgil–Thompson's Falls in 1929 and Nairobi–Fort Hall–Nyeri–Nanyuki in 1930. The railways, reinforced by subsequent investments in the road network and public and commercial services, established the pattern of urban development. By 1914, about 2,400 km of motorable roads had been built, primarily to serve growing settler areas. The 1920s were characterized by intensive road construction and by 1928 the road mileage exceeded 14,000 km, of which about 60 per cent was located in the African areas. The road construction in the reserves, which was intensified after 1923, was triggered off by the need for more effective administrative control and easier recruitment of labour. Links were established to Narok, Kajiado, Embu, Meru, Machakos, Kitui, Kakamega, Bungoma and Kisii. The period between 1930 and 1945 saw relatively little road construction.

Also telephone and postal services developed rapidly. In 1931, the mileage of telephone wires in exchange areas exceeded 9,000 km. By 1945, almost all major telephone exchanges were located in the White Highlands. The post services showed a similar pattern, having spread outwards from the railway with the growth of European settlement and having a poor service network in the reserves.[4]

Already by the 1920s, the settler economy was linked to fairly sophisticated systems of transportation, communication and administration which also supported urban centres supplying the settler economy with commercial services. This core of transmission and control facilities were necessary for the build-up, and subsequent expansion, of large-scale Western production technologies based on specialization and, accordingly, on exchange. At the same time, however, it is apparent that this economy hardly would have survived had it not, by means of repression and exploitation, been subsidized by a large segment of the colony's African population. As shown by Leo, Leys, Soja, van Zwanenberg and others, the colonial government applied a range of policies to assure this system of privilege.

## *Agriculture in the White Highlands*

During the first phase of settlement, lasting until 1908, land was alienated only around the railway towns and at other points along the line. The areas immediately north and northwest of Nairobi, claimed by the Kikuyu as traditionally their own, became the major centres of early settlement.[5] After 1908, some 280 South Africans arrived, most of them coming from the Transvaal. They established themselves on the Uasin Gishu Plateau where wheat farming had a large potential. This pocket of Boers were instrumental in starting the new town of Eldoret. The frontier now also expanded into the lowland country near Lake Victoria.

By 1915, 1.8 million hectares of land had been alienated on behalf of about 1,000 white settlers. Of the total area, about one-fifth was held by five individuals or groups. For several decades, these land speculators were very successful in lobbying for continued white settlement in Kenya.[6] In 1946, the number of settlers had increased to about 3,000 and the alienated acreage to 2.5 million hectares. At this time, the total European population was about 30,000.[7]

During the first decades, agriculture was to a large degree experimental. The settlers first concentrated on products with which they were familiar, such as wheat, maize, meat and dairy. To these were soon to be added coffee, sisal and tea. In 1930, maize was the major crop on about half of the total number of settler farms.

The alienation of land created land shortages, particularly in North Nyanza (presently Western province) and the southern parts of Central province. Many households owned little or no land in these densely populated areas. There was an abundance of land in the alienated areas and the European farmers were looking for cheap labour. For the settlers to be able to develop their large-scale farms, plantations and ranches, Africans had to be compelled to work. Initially this was achieved both by taxation and by force. It was soon realized that resident, and thus reliable, supplies of labour could be secured in return for allowing these households to use part of their uncleared land. In 1918, a law was passed which forbade squatting, unless the squatters had agreed with the landowners to be resident labourers. This meant that they had to work for a minimum of 180 days a year for the landowner in exchange for a plot of land and a small wage. According to estimates made by the colonial administration, some 70,000 resident labourers were employed on European farms. Over the following two decades this figure more than doubled. This would be equivalent to about 30–35 per cent of the recorded number of adult male taxpayers among the African population.[8]

As agriculture continued to develop, the economic advantages of the squatter system gradually diminished. The settlers began to demand more work from their squatters while at the same time trying to reduce their benefits. Thus, increasingly, squatters were banned from holding cattle and limits were also set on the size of their cultivation plots. In spite of this, it is estimated that the number of squatters grew from about 100,000 in the 1920s to about 200,000 by 1945, and in the 1930s it was estimated that the land used by squatters in alienated areas amounted to about half a million hectares.

During the early period of settlement, squatting was probably seen as an attractive option. Life on the large-scale farms included, in addition to land, some cash wages, taxation relief and the lifting of some other administrative restrictions imposed on the reserves. But as agriculture in the alienated areas continued to develop, the pressure on squatters increased. By the 1930s they were in a vulnerable position. With few having the option of getting land if returning to the overcrowded reserves, their bargaining position was extremely weak. As a consequence, most of them had to accept progressive reductions in their real income. For the majority it meant having to accept extreme poverty and the absence of schools and other basic services.

For some segments of the African population, tax obligations could be met by means other than wage labour. Urbanization and growth of the labour force in settler areas resulted in raised demand for staple food, and increasingly farmers in the reserves met their cash requirements through the sale of produce or cattle. This commercialization was encouraged by the colonial administration.[9] There was little opportunity for Africans to grow more profitable crops such as coffee, pyrethrum, sisal, tea, wheat and sugar. The colonial administration refused to grant them licences for coffee and pyrethrum cultivation, and for crops like tea and sugar they were prohibited by the large capital investments required.

## *Settler organizations*

The various privileges secured by the settlers were to a considerable degree a consequence of their forceful lobbying and organizational skills. Already around 1912–13, African farmers supplied most of the maize on the local market, and among European settlers measures were taken to secure markets for their less cost-efficient production. In 1916, they established the British East Africa Maize Growers' Association (BMG), which in 1919 changed its name to British East Africa Farmers' Association. The Association graded members' cereal crops and negotiated forward bulk export sales for each grade. This arrangement excluded African maize producers from the higher-priced export markets[10] and was accepted by the colonial government as a 'dual policy', under which no attempt was made to grade African crops for export.

In 1922, another marketing association developed – the Plateau Maize Growers' Association, which was formed by 113 settlers in the Uasin Gishu Plateau area. The following year, BMG changed its name to Kenya Farmers' Association (KFA) and registered as a company. It now also started importing farm requirements on behalf of its members. In 1927 it merged with the Plateau Maize Growers' Association. By this move KFA was in a position to represent most European maize growers *vis à vis* transporters, exporters and the government. After the passing of the first Cooperative Ordinance in 1931, the KFA was registered as a cooperative society (1932). As the organization already was registered as a company, it was given the status of being both a company and a cooperative. This legal peculiarity applied also to other nationwide organizations registered during the Thirties and Forties, such as the Kenya Cooperative Creameries Ltd. (KCC) and the Kenya Planters' Cooperative Union Ltd (KPCU).

In 1929, effects of the world depression started being felt in Kenya. Prices of agricultural produce fell. In 1935 the price of maize was one-third of the price paid in 1930. Also the prices of coffee, cotton and sisal deteriorated, although less dramatically. Many estates and mixed farms went bankrupt and between 1930 and 1936, the cultivated area on settler farms fell from 290,000 ha to 225,00 ha. The administration stepped in by forming a Land Bank which tied farm lending to crop diversification. In the late 1930s, KFA got actively involved in this scheme by handling government credit, acting through the Land Bank and other banks.

The settlers had already been granted a production monopoly of the most profitable crops. To save the settler economy, the administration now extended the settlers' control of the marketing system of temperate-zone foodstuffs such as wheat, dairy products and bacon. In 1930, the government introduced regulations which made it compulsory for farmers to sell their wheat through the KFA, which had been appointed as agent. Two years later, settlers formed the Kenya Pyrethrum Association and appointed KFA as its marketing agent. This agreement continued until 1938, when

KFA was appointed agent on behalf of the newly established Pyrethrum Board of Kenya.

As early as 1912, dairy farmers west of Nakuru started operating a creamery organized as a cooperative society (Lumbwa Coop. Society Ltd). Originally, the society was formed to cater for joint marketing of cereals. In 1924, Lord Delamere together with other dairy farmers organized a syndicate at Naivasha to coordinate dairy activities in the Rift Valley. In 1932 the group was incorporated and was registered under the Cooperative Societies Ordinance as the Kenya Cooperative Creameries Ltd (KCC). The KCC was the first organization in Kenya to be registered under the Ordinance and the KFA was the third.

Under the Coffee Act of 1933, the Coffee Board was established to supervise and regulate all sections of the coffee industry. The activities of the Board included licensing of producers, pulping factories and exporters; grading of all coffee; marketing and payment to growers; insurance and publicity. On behalf of the Coffee Board, the KPCU was appointed to take care of the hulling, grading and bagging of coffee. The KPCU was registered as a company in 1933 and under the Cooperative Ordinance in 1945.

The Cooperative Societies Ordinance of 1931, which was instrumental in institutionalizing these and other settler organizations during the 1930s and 1940s, did not permit the formation of cooperatives among Africans. If squatters in alienated areas had a surplus of produce to sell, it was common for their employer to purchase the products at prices set by him and later sell them through the settler cooperatives. In the reserves, farmers sold their produce to private traders.[11]

Legislation and subsequent formalization of the cooperative organizations were thus some of the strategies which aimed at either a monopoly in the domestic food market or centralized and cost-efficient marketing systems. By the end of 1945, seventeen cooperative organizations had been registered, of which six were secondary and had nationwide coverage, while the remaining eleven were primary societies handling produce such as pyrethrum, dairy and sugar.

In the 1930s, there was also the ambition to divert African low-cost production on to export markets. It was anticipated that this would increase the African contribution to export earnings. Hence, it would strengthen the administration's ability to subsidize the high-cost production of settler agriculture, particularly that of large-scale mixed farms.

This meant a policy shift, as it had to involve more active

support to African agriculture. Thus, zone development planning was introduced in 1932. It meant that, for each of five ecological zones, plans were drawn up for promotion of production, including introduction of new or improved crops. Although being only partially implemented, the programme probably was of importance in some regions.[12]

Initially, maize was not part of this strategy. It soon became clear, however, that African maize production was increasing rapidly. As there was no possibility of cartelizing production, an extended system for control of maize marketing was introduced. Thus, the Kenya Farmers' Association was appointed a purchaser in these markets and was expected to sell the produce at prices which would be profitable to the settlers. The intention was to keep the domestic price of maize above the export price, while channelling as much as possible of the African farmers' low-cost maize to the export market. There are reasons to doubt the effectiveness of these attempts to control maize marketing.[13]

During the Second World War, the KFA was appointed as agent to the government for all maize purchasing. The settlers' position now was further strengthened. They were given a monopoly of maize sales in the towns and also got the price announced before the planting season. The price obtained by the settlers was well above world market prices and almost twice the price paid to African farmers.

## *Developments in major smallholder areas west of Rift Valley*

The Kavirondo province then covered what at present is equivalent to Western and Nyanza provinces. Its total area was approximately 20,000 sq km. In the late 1920s, the total population was estimated at about one million and comprised three main ethnic groups; Abaluyhas in North Kavirondo (W. province), Luos in Central (Kisumu, Siaya) and Luos/Gusiis in South Kavirondo (S. Nyanza, Kisii).

In Central Kavirondo, the colonial administration introduced industrial crops like cotton and sesame and improved varieties of food crops such as maize and beans. To the local administration, increased commercialization had the advantage of ending the practice of paying taxes in livestock. One indication of the local response to these measures is that, during the period 1909–18, over 73,000 tons of maize and maize flour left Nyanza province.

Consequently trade expanded and it started filtering down to more outlying areas, such as Kisii.[14] Both the Gusii (Kisii) and the Abaluyha (N. Kavirondo) responded early to the opportunities offered by a growing internal market. The Gusii even transported their produce for sale in Kisumu.[15] This also affected the cultivating technology; in the Kisumu district report for 1913–14, it thus is mentioned that 30,000 'English hoes' had been sold.[16] In Northern Kavirondo (Western province), district records from 1910 and 1914 indicate that the colonial administration was quite successful in disengaging labour for work in the White Highlands, particularly in the densely populated areas (Kakamega district).[17]

In the early 1920s, expansion of the cultivated area was accompanied by increasing commercialization. In 1923, some 10,000 acres of cotton were planted in the Kisumu and Busia areas, although food crops accounted for a more steady expansion with surplus production and export of maize and beans continuing until 1930. According to the administration's records, about one-quarter of the total maize production in C. Kavirondo was then shipped outside the district, and part of it was exported. Still, by the end of the 1920s, agriculture in the reserves west of Rift Valley was commercialized only to a limited extent. Productivity levels per capita and acre were low, and considerably below those of Kikuyuland. North Kavirondo seems to have been the more developed area with an estimated 37 per cent of the cultivable land under crops, as compared to 18 per cent for Central Kavirondo and 8 per cent in South Kavirondo. In some areas, though, these figures were much higher. In densely populated parts of N. Kavirondo (Kakamega) almost 80 per cent of the arable land was either under crops or fallow in 1931. In the same year, nearly 700 tons of maize and beans were exported from Kisii.[18]

By the late 1930s, North Kavirondo was described as the 'granary of Kenya'. During the war period, the district's prominent position in maize production was further accentuated.[19] Even by this time, however, the northern and western lowland locations of the province were only marginally commercialized. A cotton campaign, started in the early 1930s, resulted in a considerable expansion of production. In spite of favourable prices relative to major food crops, the increase in output was not sustained. At least in South Kavirondo, the fall in production was caused by unfavourable soil and rainfall conditions.[20]

### *Central province*

As the major area of early settlement was located immediately north and northwest of Nairobi, the Kikuyus were the first to be affected by European immigration. The land alienated for settlers almost enclosed the most densely populated Kikuyu areas. Being in close proximity both to one of the major cores of settlement and to the colony's main urban centre soon led to considerable economic and social changes in the Kikuyu districts.[21]

As early as 1900, new crops such as potatoes and white maize were grown for the Nairobi market by farmers in Kiambu district. The rapid population increase that soon characterized this district was due both to alienation of land and to migration of Kikuyus from the districts to the north (Nyeri, Fort Hall). The District Commissioner in Kiambu reported as early as 1915–16 that shortage of land had become a problem, particularly in the low-lying, maize-producing areas.[22] By this time, the surplus production was large enough to provide a basis for Kikuyu-owned shops which traded consumer goods in exchange for food crops.

Also further north, in Nyeri district, maize production expanded mainly in response to the demand of white settler farms. The Fort Hall road had been extended to Nyeri before the end of the First World War. Also the construction of the Thika–Nyeri railway at Karatina in 1926 contributed to quite dramatic increases in production and sales of food crops. In addition to the conventional staple crops, farmers in Fort Hall now also began production of vegetables. This development was supported both by good prices and, in the highland areas, by generally good harvests. As pastoralists at the same time were badly affected by drought, livestock was traded for food crops on terms that were very favourable to the farmers. By the early 1930s, more than half of the cultivable area of Kiambu, Fort Hall and Nyeri was under crops. Kiambu still dominated in terms of sales of food crops. According to Kitching this, however, did not reflect differences in productivity but rather that farm households in Kiambu sold more of what they produced.[23]

Available evidence indicates that the marketed surplus of maize continued to grow in the 1930s, together with increased production of most other crops. However, geographically, production shifted towards less densely populated lowland locations. The main reason was that smallholders in high-altitude areas reduced their maize acreage in favour of wattle. The shift to wattle also reflected an increasing shortage of land and labour. In this situation, wattle was superior to maize in the highland areas. The value of output per acre was higher and it was also a non-labour-intensive crop. Furthermore, as a tree crop it could be used, or sold, both for building purposes and for burning of charcoal. The cultivation of wattle was actively promoted by the Department of Agriculture, in conjunction with a UK multinational. Between 1934 and 1935 the area under wattle in Central province increased dramatically from

20,000 to 45,000 hectares. Sales of dry bark jumped from 900 tons in 1929 to about 16,000 tons in 1938.[24]

By the latter half of the 1930s, Fort Hall was dominating commercial agricultural production in the province. The district accounted for 58 per cent of marketed wattle and 52 per cent of the maize (c. 50,000 bags). For the province as a whole, it is evident that production and trade of a range of produce increased, including bananas, onions, cotton, tobacco, poultry, eggs and pigs.

This process of commercialization was intensified after the outbreak of the Second World War. Prices developed favourably and the colonial administration encouraged African households to expand crop production. In spite of this, average household farm income probably was lower in 1948 than in 1931. Since the late 1930s, settler efforts to reduce the number of squatters had resulted in a massive migration of Africans back to their home areas in already densely populated reserves. In this period, Kiambu's population grew by 148 per cent and Nyeri's by 61 per cent. Households with the smallest landholdings and with production restricted to cereals with low yield and exchange value, increasingly diverted part of their labour time in wage labour on adjacent landholdings. Further, through Kiambu's proximity to Nairobi, many households responded by successively shifting production pattern towards high-value crops, in particular fruit, vegetables and wattle. One indication of the magnitude of this switch is that Kiambu now turned into a net importer of cereals.

## 2.2 Introduction of agricultural service cooperatives in African areas

By the end of the Second World War, distinct regional differences had emerged. Apart from the profound duality caused by the way European areas had been built up, there were, as earlier indicated, also considerable differences among African areas. Ecologically favoured and densely populated areas, in close proximity to the White Highlands, had not only been penetrated by the administration but also were linked to markets for labour, goods and services based on exchange transactions in money. Commercialization of agriculture had begun in the 1920s and then focused on cereals, mainly maize; during the 1930s were added cotton, wattle and vegetables. The subsequent expansion of the monetized economy in the more favoured districts (mainly Kisii, Bungoma, Kiambu, Muranga, Nyeri, Kirinyaga, Embu and Meru and Machakos) is indicated by the rapid growth of market centres. By 1946, Kisii district had twenty-four authorized markets. In the same year, the district administration received 1,600 applications for trading licences.[25] Similarly, in the 1943 District Report for Fort Hall (Muranga and part of Kirinyaga district), it is noted that the reserve had 384 retail outlets constructed in stone rather than the common wattle and daub.[26]

With few exceptions, African farmers were not permitted to grow more profitable cash crops such as coffee, tea and pyrethrum. The exception was a small number of farmers in Kisii, Embu and Meru, who had been granted coffee licences in 1933. This was done on a trial basis within a programme for agricultural production initiated by the colonial administration in 1930. The limited scope of this experiment can be illustrated by its implementation in Kisii. Here, a chief in Nyaribari location was the first to plant coffee and a pulping station was set up near his plot in 1934.[27] By 1946, the total area of land under coffee in the district was still not more than 80 hectares. Even when adding Embu and Meru, probably not more than about 140 hectares of coffee had been planted.[28] The total number of smallholders involved can be estimated at around 500. Permission to grow pyrethrum was limited to smallholders in Kiambu and Nyeri districts.

During the latter half of the 1940s, the colonial authorities more seriously began to encourage the expansion of African cash cropping. A main reason was the deteriorating living conditions in the reserves, not least in what today is Central province. Since the Second World War, the conditions for the white settler economy had been very favourable. As production and land under cultivation expanded, the squatters found themselves in an increasingly vulnerable position. To meet their growing needs for land, settlers evicted squatters, who were moved back to the reserves by the army and police. Most of these squatters had no land to return to.

The reserves already suffered from inequality of landownership, population pressure and ecological degradation, and thus had limited capacity to absorb the influx of refugees. As the economic pressure to which squatters and the population living in Kikuyuland were being subjected intensified, so did the political activity. The growing political opposition among the African population certainly furnished the incentives required for changing the attitude of the colonial administration in respect of African areas. Another contributing factor was the political changes that took place in Britain immediately after the war. A new government came to power in 1945 and instituted several measures in support of a more broadly based social and economic development in the colonies. They included passage of the Overseas Resources Development Act and establishment of the Colonial Development Corporation.

These changes were reflected in the colonial government's introduction of a plan for land rehabilitation in the reserves. Over a ten-year period, starting in 1946, about 120 million K.Sh. was to be spent on prevention of soil erosion. For the implementation of the plan, the African Land Utilization and Settlement Board (ALUS) was established. The Board, which soon was renamed ALDEV (African Land Development Programme), also administered a small rural credit scheme.[29] The same year a Department of Cooperative Development was established. The colonial government had enacted a new Cooperative Act (1945), replacing the Act of 1931, with the explicit aim of fostering marketing cooperatives among the African population. This step was clearly in line with the policy of the Colonial Office in London.[30]

### *Campaigns (1946–53)*

The Department was charged with the responsibility of promoting and controlling societies, and of educating the members and the public on the usefulness of cooperative efforts, with emphasis on rural areas. The Department was placed under the Ministry of African Affairs and headed by a Registrar of Cooperatives. Initially, the staff was composed of the Registrar, four inspectors and two clerks.[31]

Although handicapped by minute resources, the Department carried out campaigns among smallholders and traders to entice them to the cooperative idea. During the first few years the response was predominantly negative, in some cases even hostile. As observed by Karanja, these difficulties were enhanced by an administrative arrangement giving the Registrar the responsibility for promoting not only cooperatives but also African trade.[32] Most African businessmen being informed about the object and organization of cooperative societies saw them either as some kind of inferior 'herding' arrangement invented by the administration, or as a potential threat to their own position in the local economy. As these entrepreneurs usually constituted an influential segment of the elite at local level, their defiance of cooperatives effectively hampered the acceptance of them by smallholders in general.[33] As could be expected, these difficulties were particularly pronounced in Central province with its commercially more advanced economy. Another disappointment was the ex-soldiers, who returned home from the war in 1945, and had been perceived by the administration as a possible base for recruitment of cooperative staff. However, most of them were more interested in starting business enterprises on their own or in partnership.

*Table 2.1* Registrations by district, 1946–53

| *District* | *District No.* | *Frequency* | *%* | *Cum. %* |
|---|---|---|---|---|
| Kisumu | 2 | 38 | 11.4 | 11.4 |
| Kisii | 3 | 17 | 5.1 | 16.5 |
| S. Nyanza | 4 | 56 | 16.9 | 33.4 |
| Busia | 6 | 7 | 2.1 | 35.5 |
| Kakamega | 10 | 29 | 8.7 | 44.3 |
| Bungoma | 11 | 45 | 13.6 | 57.8 |
| Kericho | 22 | 10 | 3.0 | 60.8 |
| Uasin Gishu | 23 | 1 | 0.3 | 61.1 |
| Nyeri | 50 | 34 | 10.2 | 71.4 |
| Muranga | 51 | 6 | 1.8 | 73.2 |
| Kiambu | 54 | 53 | 16.0 | 89.2 |
| Kirinyaga | 55 | 3 | 0.9 | 90.1 |
| Taita/Taveta | 70 | 14 | 4.2 | 94.3 |
| Embu | 80 | 3 | 0.9 | 95.2 |
| Meru | 81 | 13 | 3.9 | 99.1 |
| Machakos | 84 | 3 | 0.9 | 100.0 |
| Total | | 332 | 100.0 | |

*Source:* survey data

As a result, not only was the number of cooperatives registered during the period 1946–49 quite small, but most societies were either located in less prosperous areas or dealt with produce for which the marketing arrangements were difficult to handle. Another common feature, in part being a consequence of the limited support gained from the local elite, was that they consisted of groups of farmers who knew little about managing their societies.

About half of the societies registered during these first years were located in Nyanza and Western provinces. They included thirty-nine societies in Kisumu and Kakamega which had been registered by women's groups to market eggs and poultry. The groups had been created during the war in response to the administration's wholesale procurement of these products. Central province accounted for about one-third of the societies registered during this period. In Muranga and Nyeri, a number of vegetable and dairy societies were established, and in Muranga there were also a considerable number of multiproduce societies. In terms of numbers of registrations, the dominance of the areas west of the Rift Valley continued during the first years of the 1950s. Between 1950 and 1953, two-thirds of the newly established societies were located in Nyanza or Western provinces. In South Nyanza and Kisumu were registered thirty-two dairy societies selling mainly ghee and cream to the Ghee Marketing Control Board. It is interesting to note that even then a difference in activity profile could be discerned between these areas and Central and Eastern provinces. In the former societies, the marketing of cereals, eggs/poultry and dairy produce were clearly most common, while societies in Kikuyuland more consistently dealt with new and remunerative crops such as coffee, pyrethrum, dairy produce and vegetables (Table 2.1–3, Figure 2.1).

*Table 2.2* Registrations by main activity, 1946–53

| *Activity* | *Dist. No.* | *Frequency* | *%* | *Cum. %* |
|---|---|---|---|---|
| Cereals | 11 | 21 | 6.3 | 6.3 |
| Coffee | 12 | 45 | 13.6 | 19.9 |
| Cotton | 13 | 1 | 0.3 | 20.2 |
| Vegetables | 14 | 26 | 7.8 | 28.0 |
| Pyrethrum | 15 | 6 | 1.8 | 29.8 |
| Dairy | 21 | 75 | 22.6 | 52.4 |
| Eggs/Poultry | 22 | 88 | 26.5 | 78.9 |
| Pigs | 23 | 9 | 2.7 | 81.6 |
| Multiproduce | 30 | 53 | 16.0 | 97.6 |
| Unions | 35 | 8 | 2.4 | 100.0 |
| Total | | 332 | 100.0 | |

*Source*: survey data

*Table 2.3* Registrations by district and main activity, 1946–53

| | *Activity* | | | | | | | | | | |
|---|---|---|---|---|---|---|---|---|---|---|---|
| District | 11 | 12 | 13 | 14 | 15 | 21 | 22 | 23 | 30 | 35 | Total |
| Kisumu | | | | | | 11 | 24 | | 3 | | 38 |
| Kisii | | 14 | | | | 1 | | | 1 | 1 | 17 |
| S. Nyanza | | | | | | 54 | | | 2 | | 56 |
| Siaya | | | | | | | 5 | | 2 | | 7 |
| Kakamega | 1 | | | | | 2 | 18 | | 8 | | 29 |
| Bungoma | 19 | 5 | 1 | | | | 10 | | 7 | 3 | 45 |
| Kericho | | | | | | | 10 | | | | 10 |
| Uasin Gishu | | | | | | | | | 1 | | 1 |
| Nyeri | | 3 | | 7 | 2 | 5 | | 9 | 5 | 3 | 34 |
| Muranga | | 3 | | 2 | | 1 | | | | | 6 |
| Kiambu | | 6 | | 14 | 4 | | 12 | | 17 | | 53 |
| Kirinyaga | | 3 | | | | | | | | | 3 |
| Taita/Taveta | | | | 3 | | 1 | 5 | | 5 | | 14 |
| Embu | | 2 | | | | | | | 1 | | 3 |
| Meru | | 8 | | | | | 4 | | | 1 | 13 |
| Machakos | 1 | 1 | | | | | | | 1 | | 3 |
| Total | 21 | 45 | 1 | 26 | 6 | 75 | 88 | 9 | 53 | 8 | 332 |
| % | 6.3 | 13.6 | 0.3 | 7.8 | 1.8 | 22.6 | 26.5 | 2.7 | 16.0 | 2.4 | 100.0 |

*Source:* survey data
*Activity codes*: (11) cereals, (12) coffee, (13) cotton, (14) vegetables, (15) pyrethrum, (21) dairy, (22) eggs/poultry, (30) multiproduce, (35) unions.

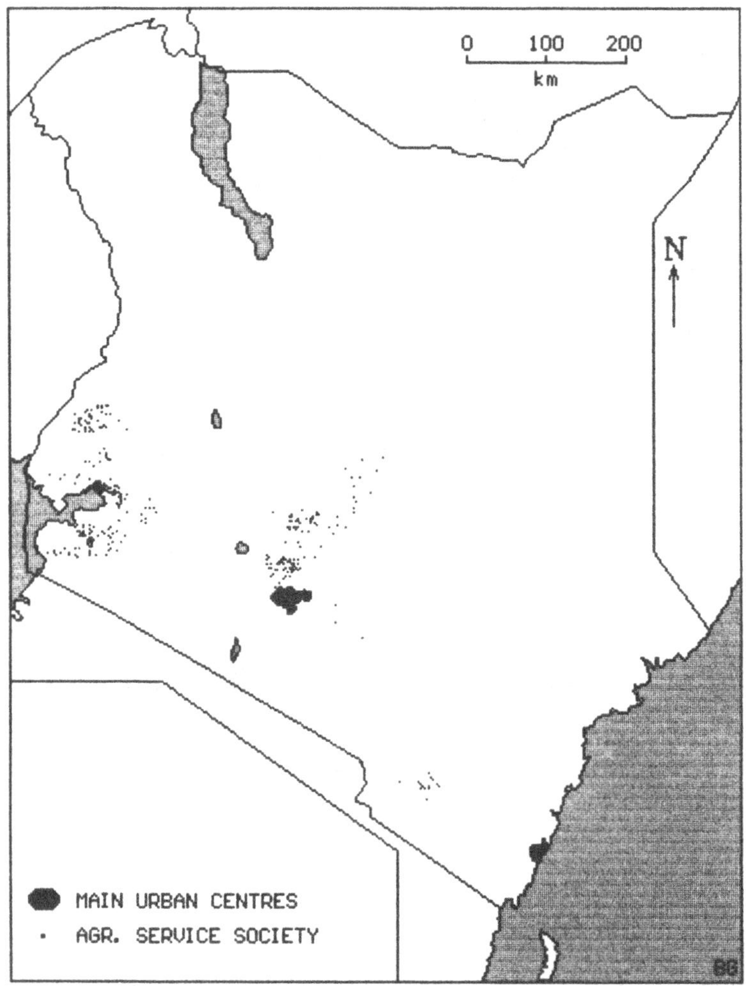


*Figure 2.1* Registrations of agricultural service societies, 1946–53
*Sources: survey data; MOCD*

## *Revolt and collusion (1954–62)*

The economic pressure the settler community put on squatters during the 1940s, in combination with its subsequent destructive effects on already difficult social and economic conditions in the Kikuyu reserves, escalated in stages into open revolt. It emanated from the Kikuyu reserve and soon spread to Embu and Meru, and gained support among resident labourers in the Rift Valley. The liberation fighters, usually called Mau Mau, referred to themselves as soldiers in the Land Freedom Army. The revolt having been sparked off as a reaction to increasing landlessness among the Kikuyus, soon evolved into warfare against colonial rule. In 1952, Kenya's Governor declared a state of emergency which would last until 1960. The civil war was cruel and meant severe hardships for most Kikuyus, particularly the poor. In 1955 at least 77,000 people were in detention. By 1956, over 13,000 Africans had been killed in the war as compared to less than 100 Europeans.

The Swynnerton Plan, launched in 1954, can be seen as a major attempt to influence the conditions in African areas, particularly in Kikuyuland. It also resulted in dramatic changes for some segments of the smallholder economy, particularly in ecologically favoured parts of Central, Eastern, Western and Nyanza provinces.[34] The plan recommended that all high-quality land should be surveyed and enclosed. This, it was argued, would make it possible for so-called progressive farmers to obtain credit. With title deeds would also follow security of tenure and incentives for development of the individual holdings. Furthermore, African farmers should have the right to grow cash crops (including coffee, tea and pyrethrum), to get technical assistance and to have access to existing marketing facilities. During the 1950s, the Land Registration programme had its most dramatic effects in Central province and then, ironically enough, mainly due to the extraordinary powers given the government after the declaration of an emergency in 1952.

Considering the changes introduced through the Swynnerton Plan, it is reasonable to expect that it would have had positive consequences for farmers' interest in cooperative marketing societies. However, in the Kenyan case, possible spontaneous responses were in important instances subordinated to institutional arrangements that established a direct relation between increased cash-crop production among smallholders and the expansion of cooperatives. The issue on marketing arrangements for coffee smallholders' crops had been discussed since the first allocations had been made to farmers in Kisii, Embu and Meru in the 1930s. After considerable deliberation, it was eventually decided that all marketing of the crop would be organized on a cooperative basis. To ensure that smallholders actually marketed their coffee through these institutions, they were only given permission to grow coffee if they were members of a primary cooperative society. Similar arrangements were also introduced for pyrethrum. Hence, about one-third of the societies registered during the period 1953–62 were a consequence of increased cultivation of these crops and not because smallholders had realized the importance of creating their own organizations for marketing, inputs supplies and production credit.

Throughout the 1920s and 1930s the local elites in Nyanza, Western, Central and Eastern provinces had demanded guaranteed land titles. Accumulation of land was a pertinent feature in Central province from the 1920s onwards, and often involved chiefs and headmen using coercion to plunder land from others. The local elites had also constituted the core of the first adopters of cash crops having been previously monopolized by Europeans. By 1953, forty-five coffee societies and six pyrethrum societies had been registered, the majority in Central province.

In the wake of the Swynnerton Plan, the expansion continued in the province in spite of the Mau Mau activities. Land consolidation and introduction of remunerative cash crops were seen as means of creating a middle class among African farmers willing to accept the prevailing political and economic order. In this respect, the Swynnerton Plan no doubt had a considerable impact on the social and economic reproduction process in Central province. Thus, the registration of coffee and pyrethrum societies continued seemingly unabated over the period 1954–62. Over eighty of these societies were registered in Central province (including Meru). New growers/members were initially limited to 100 trees each. This quota was raised to 280 trees in 1958,[35] seemingly because most members of these societies were loyal to the colonial administration and even actively assisted in reporting suspect rebels. The reasons behind this lay both in resultant material benefits and in the fact that the emerging rural elite included chiefs and other local officials who were part of the British system of indirect rule.

Outside Central province, the registration of coffee and pyrethrum was largely confined to the highland areas of Kisii, Bungoma and Machakos. Although not yet linked to a programme for land consolidation, the expansion of these crops was subject to similar stratification mechanisms as in Central province, though it was possibly less pronounced. In most of these highland areas, it resulted in the creation of cooperative organizations with a considerable economic leverage. One indication of this is that the total membership of coffee societies had reached 193,000 by independence in 1962.

However, about two-thirds of the total number of agricultural marketing societies registered during 1954–62 dealt with other types of produce than coffee and pyrethrum (Table 2.5). Nyanza and Western provinces accounted for most of these societies. In Nyanza, cotton, sugar, dairy and 'multipurpose' societies predominated, while in Western province it was cotton and maize. Very few societies were registered in Coast province or, for obvious reasons, in Rift Valley (Table 2.6).

Although the 1945 Cooperative Societies Ordinance did not mention secondary societies, the first union was established in 1949 in Nyeri district. By the end of 1962, fifteen unions had been formed. They were established mainly to serve as intermediaries for produce boards and their operations were quite limited.[36] A further element had been added to the cooperative structure in 1952, when the East African School of Cooperation was established in Nairobi.[37] The following year the school also started organizing

*Table 2.4* Registrations by district, 1954–62

| *District* | *Dist. No.* | *Frequency* | *%* | *Cum. %* |
|---|---|---|---|---|
| Kisumu | 2 | 26 | 5.7 | 5.7 |
| Kisii | 3 | 42 | 9.2 | 14.9 |
| S. Nyanza | 4 | 28 | 6.1 | 21.0 |
| Siaya | 6 | 9 | 2.0 | 23.0 |
| Kakamega | 10 | 45 | 9.8 | 32.8 |
| Bungoma | 11 | 58 | 12.7 | 45.5 |
| Busia | 12 | 12 | 2.6 | 48.1 |
| Nakuru | 20 | 1 | 0.2 | 48.3 |
| Baringo | 21 | 3 | 0.7 | 49.0 |
| Kericho | 22 | 6 | 1.3 | 50.3 |
| Uasin Gishu | 23 | 2 | 0.4 | 50.7 |
| Nandi | 24 | 6 | 1.3 | 52.0 |
| Elgeyo/Marakwet | 26 | 6 | 1.3 | 53.3 |
| W. Pokot | 27 | 2 | 0.4 | 53.7 |
| Narok | 29 | 2 | 0.4 | 54.1 |
| Kajiado | 30 | 3 | 0.7 | 54.8 |
| Nyeri | 50 | 23 | 5.0 | 59.8 |
| Muranga | 51 | 29 | 6.3 | 66.2 |
| Kiambu | 54 | 35 | 7.6 | 73.8 |
| Kirinyaga | 55 | 4 | 0.9 | 74.7 |
| Kilifi | 66 | 6 | 1.3 | 76.0 |
| Kwale | 67 | 4 | 0.9 | 76.9 |
| Tana River | 69 | 1 | 0.2 | 77.1 |
| Taita/Taveta | 70 | 5 | 1.1 | 78.2 |
| Embu | 80 | 5 | 1.1 | 79.3 |
| Meru | 81 | 47 | 10.3 | 89.5 |
| Kitui | 83 | 2 | 0.4 | 90.0 |
| Machakos | 84 | 46 | 10.0 | 100.0 |
| Total | | 458 | 100.0 | |

*Source:* survey data

*Table 2.5* Registrations by activity, 1954–62

| *Activity* | *Act. No.* | *Frequency* | *%* | *Cum. %* |
|---|---|---|---|---|
| Cereals | 11 | 54 | 11.8 | 11.8 |
| Coffee | 12 | 111 | 24.2 | 36.0 |
| Cotton | 13 | 15 | 3.3 | 39.3 |
| Vegetables | 14 | 8 | 1.7 | 41.0 |
| Pyrethrum | 15 | 44 | 9.6 | 50.6 |
| Sisal | 16 | 1 | 0.2 | 50.8 |
| Sugar Cane | 17 | 10 | 2.2 | 53.0 |
| Other crops | 18 | 17 | 3.7 | 56.7 |
| Dairy | 21 | 25 | 5.5 | 62.2 |
| Eggs/poultry | 22 | 17 | 3.7 | 65.9 |
| Pigs | 23 | 22 | 4.8 | 70.7 |
| Other animals | 26 | 4 | 0.9 | 71.6 |
| Multiproduce | 30 | 122 | 26.6 | 98.3 |
| Unions | 35 | 8 | 1.7 | 100.0 |
| Total | | 458 | 100.0 | |

*Source:* survey data

a correspondence course in book-keeping for society staff and committee members.

## *Concluding notes*

The new cooperative legislation, introduced in 1945, resulted in the registration of 790 agricultural marketing societies in African areas during the period 1946–62. Initially, the registration of societies was met by resistance from local traders and other businessmen, and then mainly because they expected their activities to be negatively affected. A typical feature of registrations before 1954 is their concentration in commercialized smallholder areas west of Rift Valley; another is that in any given year registrations were concentrated in one or two rather limited geographical areas. Explanations for the latter phenomenon are found both in the campaigns carried out by the staff of the Department of Cooperatives, and in the presence of already existing set-ups for the marketing of agricultural produce (for example poultry/eggs and ghee in Nyanza).

The period from 1954, when the Swynnerton Plan was initiated, is characterized by the administration's attempt to promote commercialized smallholder agriculture, particularly in Central province. The introduction of new crops was highly selective both in geographical and social terms. The subsequent administered expansion of coffee and pyrethrum cooperatives obviously reflected

*Table 2.6* Registrations by district and main activity, 1954–62

| | *Activity* | | | | | | | | | | | | | | |
|---|---|---|---|---|---|---|---|---|---|---|---|---|---|---|---|
| *District* | *11* | *12* | *13* | *14* | *15* | *16* | *17* | *18* | *21* | *22* | *23* | *26* | *30* | *35* | *Total* |
| Kisumu | 2 | 1 | | | | | 9 | | 1 | | | | 13 | | 26 |
| Kisii | | 13 | | | 27 | | | | 1 | | | | | 1 | 42 |
| S. Nyanza | 1 | 7 | 5 | | | | | | 5 | | | | 9 | 1 | 28 |
| Siaya | 2 | 3 | 1 | | | | | | | 1 | | | 2 | | 9 |
| Kakamega | 2 | 10 | | | | | 1 | | | | 1 | 1 | 30 | | 45 |
| Bungoma | 24 | 15 | 1 | | 1 | | | 7 | 1 | | | | 8 | 1 | 58 |
| Busia | 1 | 2 | 7 | | | | | | | | | | 2 | | 12 |
| Nakuru | | | | | | | | | | | | | 1 | | 1 |
| Baringo | 1 | | | | | | | 1 | | | | | 1 | | 3 |
| Kericho | | 1 | | | | | | | 4 | | | 1 | | | 6 |
| Uasin Gishu | | | | | 1 | | | | | | | | 1 | | 2 |
| Nandi | 1 | | | | | | | 2 | 2 | | | | 1 | | 6 |
| E/Marakwet | | | | | 3 | | | | | | | 1 | 2 | | 6 |
| W. Pokot | | | | | 1 | | | | | | | | 1 | | 2 |
| Narok | 1 | | | | 1 | | | | | | | | | | 2 |
| Kajiado | | 2 | | | | | | | 1 | | | | | | 3 |
| Nyeri | 5 | 2 | | 1 | 4 | 1 | | | 5 | | 3 | | 1 | 1 | 23 |
| Muranga | | 9 | | 2 | 2 | | | | | | 13 | | 2 | 1 | 29 |
| Kiambu | | 10 | | 3 | 3 | | | | 3 | 6 | 5 | | 3 | 2 | 35 |
| Kirinyaga | | 4 | | | | | | | | | | | | | 4 |
| Kilifi | 2 | | | | | | | | | | | | 4 | | 6 |
| Kwale | 3 | | | | | | | | | | | | 1 | | 4 |
| Tana River | | | 1 | | | | | | | | | | | | 1 |
| Taita/Taveta | | | | | | | | 1 | 1 | | | | 3 | | 5 |
| Embu | | 1 | | | 1 | | | | | | | | 3 | | 5 |
| Meru | | 19 | | | | | | 6 | 1 | | | | 20 | 1 | 47 |
| Kitui | | 2 | | | | | | | | | | | | | 2 |
| Machakos | 9 | 10 | | 2 | | | | | | 10 | | 1 | 14 | | 46 |
| Total | 54 | 111 | 15 | 8 | 44 | 1 | 10 | 17 | 25 | 17 | 22 | 4 | 122 | 8 | 458 |
| % | 11.8 | 24.2 | 3.3 | 1.7 | 9.6 | 0.2 | 2.2 | 3.7 | 5.5 | 3.7 | 4.8 | 0.9 | 26.6 | 1.7 | 100 |

*Source:* survey data
*Activity codes:* (11) cereals, (12) coffee, (13) cotton, (14) vegetables, (15) pyrethrum, (16) sisal, (17) sugar cane, (18) other crops, (21) dairy, (22) eggs/poultry, (23) pigs, (26) animals, (30) multiproduce, (35) unions.

these characteristics. This does not apply to the same extent in other types of societies.

The typical feature of the spread pattern of cooperatives is that it reflects the ability of the more commercialized, affluent and/or loyal sectors of the farming population to grasp economic opportunities offered by the administration. Given the general limits set by ecological conditions, the major force influencing the actual spread pattern was undoubtedly the colonial government. The

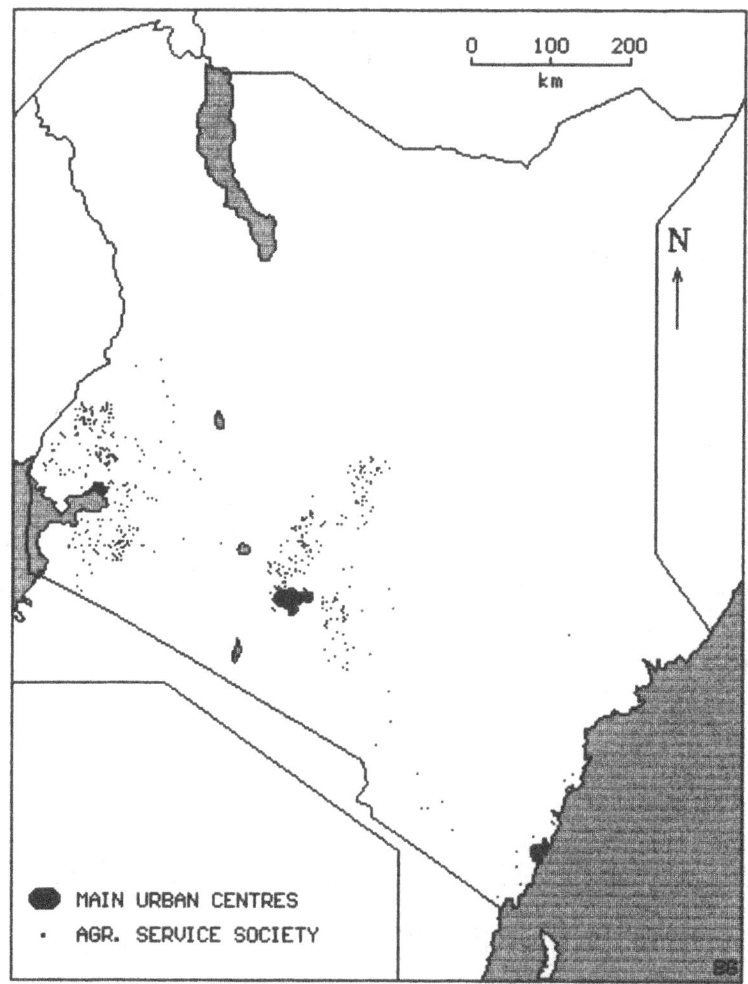


*Figure 2.2* Registrations of agricultural service societies 1954–62
*Source: survey data*

pace and pattern of introduction of the more remunerative segments of the cooperative sector were politically determined and executed by the Ministry of Agriculture with the support of the Department of Cooperative Development.

The close relationship between the implementation of the Swynnerton Plan and cooperatives is indicated by the fact that, in 1958, fifty of the Department's 110 staff members were provided under the auspices of this plan.[38] Another common feature of the expansion process seems to be, as also noted by Freeman, that cultural resistance did not negatively affect farmers' willingness to join as members of cooperative societies. The decisive consideration was instead the economic rewards linked to membership.[39]

## 2.3 Euphoria and consolidation policies (1963–72)

### *Economic development*

In addition to the Swynnerton Plan, the 'East Africa Royal Commission' in 1955 published recommendations that in many respects were more radical than those of Swynnerton. The Commission thus demanded the removal of all racial and political barriers that in any way obstructed the free movement of land, labour and capital.[40] Subsequently, the boundaries of tribal reserves and alienated areas as defined by the colonial administration were to be abolished. The Commission's recommendations had been fully accepted by 1960. The same year, the British Government had made it clear at the Lancaster House Conference that there would be an elected African majority in the next Kenyan legislature.

At independence, in 1963, over 90 per cent of Kenya's population lived in rural areas. About one-third of the male population had some kind of formal education and about 3 per cent had received a secondary education. Of a total workforce of 3 million, about 535,000 were employed in the modern sector, predominantly as unskilled wage labour in the service sector, and on large-scale farms, plantations and ranches.

The new government gave priority to achieving rapid economic growth. The political and economic strategy adopted – labelled 'African Socialism' – may be described as capitalist in nature both in domestic policy and in policy towards the world system. Although government intervention in the economy increased, private ownership was the favoured mode of production both in agriculture and industry.[41] The industrialization strategy was largely based on import substitution and, hence, dependent on both foreign capital and technology.

Expanded agricultural exports would be of vital importance to satisfy the increased foreign exchange needed for expansion of the industrial sector, including the infrastructural and complementary investment required to support the industrial technology. To achieve this, the government basically continued the same policies as those initiated through the Swynnerton Plan in 1954. The economy in African areas would be transformed through consolidation and registration of land holdings, introduction and extension of cash crops and improved livestock, and through provision of credit and supervisory services. In African areas this approach stabilized the existing distribution of land to the advantage of larger landowners and had, in terms of extension services, credit and marketing, biases built into it favouring wealthier peasants.[42]

Overall, the national development strategy had a pronounced industrial/urban orientation. Both in agriculture and industry it favoured a small part of the total economy. In agriculture, this priority rating seems to have rested on the assumption that support directed towards progressive, commercialized farmers would be sufficient to ensure trickle-down effects and rapid growth of the rural economy, even under circumstances where investments in infrastructure consistently favoured urban areas.

The rate of growth of the national economy was high during the first decade of independence: between 1964 and 1972 it averaged 6.7 per cent. Taking into account that the population increased by approximately 3.5 per cent annually during the period, this still meant a per capita growth of over 3 per cent. Manufacturing grew by well over 8 per cent and agricultural GDP by 4.9 per cent annually, with export crops outpacing domestic agriculture (6.3 and 4.4. per cent, respectively).[43] Three factors seem to have been of decisive importance for the rapid growth in agriculture: the expansion of crop areas (mainly through settlement schemes); the introduction of high-yielding varieties of maize; and the continued expansion of tree crops (coffee and tea). The high rate of aggregate economic growth was accompanied by a strong fiscal performance, low rates of inflation and manageable balance of payments current account deficits.[44]

## *Settlement schemes*

A major objective, at least during the first years of independence, was to create political stability in rural areas. In this regard the land issue was of critical importance, and particularly the land in the former White Highlands. It was clear that settler areas would have to relieve the pressure of population and the hunger for land in the traditional smallholder areas, above all among the Kikuyus.

The specific form to be given to the opening up of the White Highlands for Africans now obviously turned into a central political issue. To ensure a peaceful transition to independence and to satisfy the interests of the white settler community, the colonial authorities initiated a government-assisted programme for the transfer of land. The most important of these was the Million Acre Settlement Scheme, which largely came to be implemented after independence. The government committed itself to the purchase of about 80,000 hectares of land annually (starting in November 1961) over a period of five years. The British government provided the loans with which to purchase settler farms. These debts were to be repaid by the incoming African settlers. In addition to the cost of land, the individual settler's debt also comprised the cost of initial provisions such as seed, fertilizer, livestock, fencing and other items. A thirty-year land loan and a ten-year development loan were assumed by the smallholder when legally taking over the plot. 'High density' plots accounted for about 85 per cent of the total acreage allocated under the scheme. Most of the land purchased constituted part of the periphery of the White Highlands, close to the former 'African Reserves', and much of it consisted of low-quality land.[45] By mid-1966, almost 29,000 plots had been allocated and the bulk of the programme had been finalized.

By 1968, an estimated 32,000 families had been settled on the Million Acre Scheme and about another 14,000 on Squatter Settlement Schemes. The size of individual plots within the latter scheme was about half of that in the Million Acre Scheme, i.e. 4–6 hectares. In total, probably half a million people had been settled on smallholdings covering a total area of 430,000 hectares, i.e., at that time, less than 20 per cent of the land formerly reserved for white settlers.[46] In addition, about the same acreage had been transferred to individual Kenyans as large-scale farms. However, many of these were purchased by farm purchase societies and companies for group farming, and have since then been informally subdivided.

### *Cooperatives*

A rapid increase in the number of registered societies took place during the period 1963–66. In four years, 645 societies were formed; of these, 147 were farm purchase societies. Most of the societies registered during this particular period mirror the changes in land policies that were being implemented from 1960. Thus, as regards the Million Acre Scheme, it was divided into units, officially referred to as schemes, and comprising up to a few hundred plots. Apart from the initial provision of seeds, fertilizers, etc., the settlement administration did very little in terms of investments in physical and social infrastructure. One additional institutional measure, however, was introduced in almost all schemes: this was the establishment of an agricultural service cooperative. The intention of these societies seems to have been to serve the administration as much as to serve the farmers. Thus apart from marketing and the supply of services such as livestock dipping and artificial insemination, they had to administer members' repayment of loans to the settlement authorities. Usually they were registered as multipurpose societies. Between 1963 and 1966, 242 such societies were registered, of which 160 were located in formerly alienated areas. To this should be added another 42 cooperatives created in the former White Highlands but registered under other activity categories, mainly dairy and pyrethrum (see Table 2.7).

A second type of cooperative was the farm purchase society. They were organized with the purpose of purchasing European farms and were commonly led by African businessmen. The shareholders represented most categories of people, including poor wage-earners and smallholders. Given their objective, these societies were bound to be temporary in nature. Thus, if they managed to mobilize the funds required to buy a farm, the land would be apportioned among the shareholders. Should there at that time be a need for a service cooperative, a new registration would have to be made.

The remainder of registrations during this period (approximately 200) were concentrated in the major smallholder areas, and, in particular in parts of Central and Eastern provinces; in the latter case in the highland areas of Embu, Meru, Machakos and Kitui. Western and Nyanza provinces did not account for more than one-fifth of the total number of registered societies (Figure 2.3). Apart from multiproduce societies, a more significant number of registrations can be noted only for cotton (S. Nyanza and Busia) and for sugar (Kisumu). In the areas on the eastern side of Rift Valley, it was instead coffee, pyrethrum and dairy societies which rated high in terms of registrations.

The differences in activity orientation can of course be explained by ecological differences. However, this is not the only reason as there is certainly a potential for the more remunerative highland produce in several parts of Western and Nyanza provinces. Instead, both the much higher rate of registrations during the period (82 vs 190 societies) and dissimilarities in activity orientation reflect considerable differences in terms of conditions for continued commercialization and diversification of the smallholder sector. The implementation of the Swynnerton Plan, and related measures had, since the mid-50s, resulted in changes conducive to commercialization of agriculture primarily in Central

*Table 2.7* Registrations by district and main activity, 1963–66

| | *Activity* | | | | | | | | | | | | | |
|---|---|---|---|---|---|---|---|---|---|---|---|---|---|---|
| *District* | *11* | *12* | *13* | *14* | *15* | *16* | *17* | *18* | *21* | *22* | *26* | *30* | *35* | *Total* |
| Kisumu | | | 4 | | | | 19 | | 1 | | | 2 | 1 | 27 |
| Kisii | | | | | | | | | 4 | | 1 | 2 | | 7 |
| S. Nyanza | 1 | | 7 | | | | | | | | | 10 | 4 | 22 |
| Siaya | | | 4 | | | | | | | | | | 1 | 5 |
| Kakamega | | | | | | | 1 | | 1 | | 1 | 8 | 1 | 12 |
| Bungoma | 2 | | 1 | | | | | | 1 | | | 8 | | 12 |
| Busia | | | 11 | | | | | | | | | | 1 | 12 |
| Nakuru | | 1 | | | 4 | | | 6 | 7 | | 1 | 36 | | 55 |
| Baringo | | | | | | | | | 2 | | | 4 | | 6 |
| Kericho | | 2 | | | | | 1 | | 9 | | | 10 | 2 | 24 |
| Uasin Gishu | 1 | | | | 7 | | | | 2 | | 1 | 7 | 1 | 19 |
| Nandi | 1 | | | | | | | | 1 | | | 2 | | 4 |
| Trans Nzoia | 3 | | | | | | | 2 | 1 | | | 3 | | 9 |
| E/Marakwet | | | | | | | | | | | | 1 | | 1 |
| Laikipia | | | | | | | | | 2 | | | 5 | | 7 |
| Narok | | | | | 1 | | | | | | | 4 | | 5 |
| Kajiado | | | | | | 1 | | | 2 | 1 | 1 | 1 | | 6 |
| Nyeri | | 1 | | | | | | 2 | 4 | | | 39 | 1 | 47 |
| Muranga | | 11 | 1 | | | | | | 1 | 1 | 1 | 10 | | 25 |
| Nyandarua | | | | | 2 | | | | 2 | | | 43 | | 47 |
| Kiambu | | 4 | | 1 | 2 | | | 1 | 9 | 1 | 2 | 23 | 1 | 44 |
| Kirinyaga | 1 | 1 | | | | | | 1 | 2 | | 1 | 1 | 1 | 8 |
| Kilifi | | | | | | | | | | | | 5 | 1 | 6 |
| Kwale | 1 | | | | | | 1 | | | | | 4 | 1 | 7 |
| Lamu | | | | | | | | | | | | 1 | | 1 |
| Tana River | | | | | | | | | | | | 1 | | 1 |
| Taita/Taveta | | | | 6 | | | | | | | 1 | 1 | 1 | 9 |
| Embu | | 8 | | | | | | 1 | | | 2 | 1 | 1 | 13 |
| Meru | 3 | 2 | | | | | | 1 | 8 | | 1 | 3 | 1 | 19 |
| Isiolo | | | | | | | | | | | 1 | | | 1 |
| Kitui | 4 | | 1 | | | 2 | | 1 | | 1 | 5 | 1 | | 15 |
| Machakos | | 4 | | | | | | | 2 | | 4 | 6 | 1 | 17 |
| Marsabit | 1 | | | | | | | | | | 2 | | | 3 |
| Garissa | | | | | | | | | | | 1 | | | 1 |
| Wajir | | | | | | | | | | | 1 | | | 1 |
| Total | 18 | 34 | 29 | 7 | 16 | 3 | 22 | 15 | 61 | 4 | 27 | 242 | 20 | 498 |
| % | 3.6 | 6.8 | 5.8 | 1.4 | 3.2 | 0.6 | 4.4 | 3.0 | 12.2 | 0.8 | 5.4 | 48.6 | 4.0 | 100 |

*Source:* survey data
*Activity codes:* (11) cereals, (12) coffee, (13) cotton, (14) vegetables, (15) pyrethrum, (16) sisal, (17) sugar cane, (18) other crops, (21) dairy, (22) eggs/poultry, (23) pigs, (26) other animals, (30) multiproduce, (35) unions.

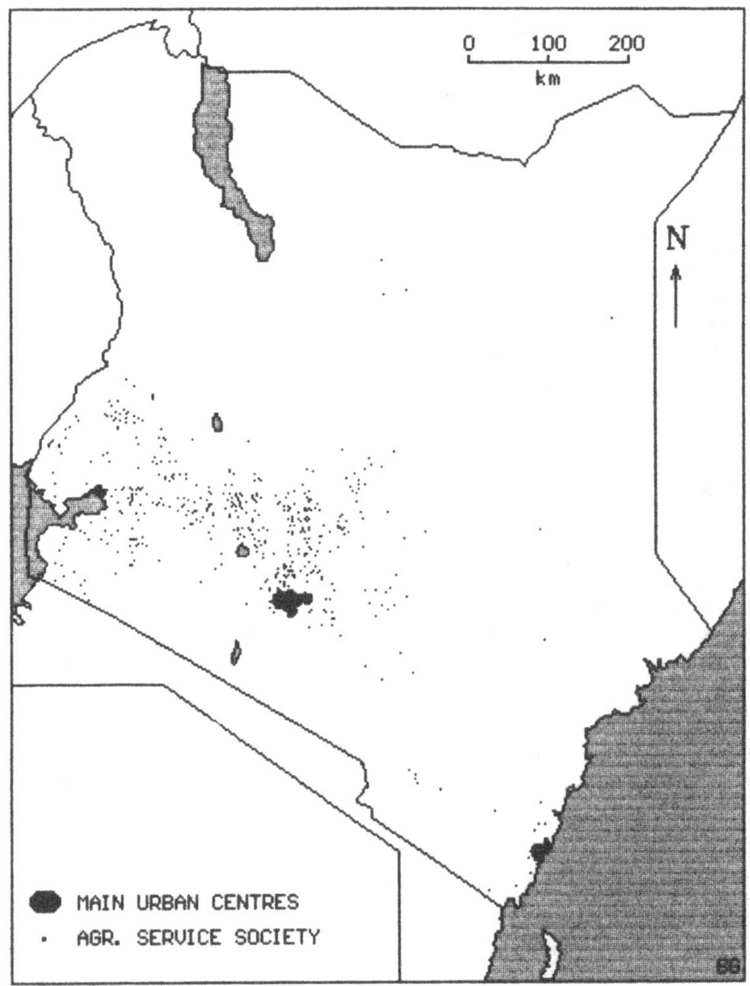


*Figure 2.3* Registrations of agricultural service societies 1963–66
*Source:* survey data

and part of Eastern provinces. These had included not only adjudication, but also land rehabilitation, extension services and improved infrastructure. The land consolidation programme had by 1963 already been finalized in Kiambu, Muranga, Kirinyaga and Nyeri; it was then extended to Embu, Meru, Nandi and Baringo. By 1965, it was in progress in most provinces but had not been finalized in Western province and Nyanza until the early 1980s (Table 2.8).

*Table 2.8* Registered land in major smallholder areas, including settlement schemes in the former White Highlands, ('000 hectares)

| *District* | *ADJ1963* | *ADJ1965* | *ADJ1971* | *ADJ1981* |
|---|---|---|---|---|
| Kisumu | 0 | 1 | 7 | 55 |
| Kisii | 0 | 3 | 156 | 218 |
| S. Nyanza | 0 | 0 | 100 | 313 |
| Siaya | 0 | 0 | 55 | 170 |
| Kakamega | 0 | 34 | 196 | 309 |
| Bungona | 0 | 30 | 167 | 228 |
| Busia | 0 | 0 | 115 | 170 |
| Nakuru | 0 | 0 | 16 | 16 |
| Baringo | 36 | 42 | 57 | 116 |
| Kericho | 0 | 0 | 105 | 247 |
| Nandi | 9 | 17 | 63 | 134 |
| Nyeri | 80 | 80 | 80 | 136 |
| Muranga | 55 | 124 | 154 | 154 |
| Nyandarua | 0 | 0 | 154 | 157 |
| Kiambu | 96 | 96 | 96 | 96 |
| Kirinyaga | 76 | 76 | 82 | 89 |
| Kilifi | 0 | 0 | 0 | 124 |
| Kwale | 0 | 0 | 6 | 171 |
| Lamu | 0 | 0 | 0 | 44 |
| Taita/Taveta | 0 | 0 | 9 | 15 |
| Embu | 51 | 61 | 61 | 100 |
| Meru | 30 | 30 | 117 | 130 |
| Kitui | 0 | 0 | 0 | 49 |
| Machakos | 0 | 0 | 52 | 156 |
| Total | 433 | 594 | 1,848 | 3,397 |

*Source:* Central Bureau of Statistics

The considerable political leverage the Kikuyus gained in independent Kenya amplified initially gained advantages. Admittedly, however, a fair share of the societies registered, particularly in Kikuyuland, was not so much a result of improved opportunities but rather a reflection of undue optimism among smallholders, often fuelled by campaigning politicians.[47] A contributory factor was that, as compared to the pre-independence period, it was now much easier to get a society registered. Large numbers of expatriate staff left the Department of Cooperative Development in 1963–64, and due to shortage of qualified staff it was not possible to appraise properly the feasibility of all applications for registration.

## *Consolidation (1967–72)*

### Institutional and organizational changes

The first government response to the turbulent development of cooperatives, particularly in the former 'African areas', was signalled in the 1964–70 and 1966–70 Development Plans. Two issues were given prominence: (i) the perceived need to strengthen the role of government to ensure a healthy future development of cooperatives and (ii) an outline of the preferred organizational structure to which the societies would have to conform. As regards the first point, the government announced that it would,

> assume a greater role in supervising cooperatives on financial and managerial matters. It is hoped that these supervisory powers will only have to be exercised for a short period, after which a viable, responsible and articulate movement, able to govern itself democratically, should emerge.
>
> (National Development Plan 1964–70:84)

Within the framework of the rural development policies, cooperatives were perceived as one, though not the only, feasible agent for providing supply and marketing services. Officially it was argued that through a rural network of primary and secondary societies, inputs and production credit could more conveniently be channelled to smallholders, particularly if these services were integrated with collection and first-stage marketing of produce. However, government regulation of agricultural output markets confined in practice the marketing activities of primary societies to specific types of produce, typically cash crops of export and non-food character. This is also clearly reflected in the activity orientation of registered societies. Very few societies registered after 1963 intended to deal either with food crops or with more than one type of produce.

As regards the formal structure of the cooperative sector, it would comprise a federation of cooperatives at national level (established in 1964) and a secondary society (union) in each district. These unions would have primary societies as members and provide them with centralized services in such fields as banking, book-keeping, staff training, transport, etc. The unions would also be given the right to appoint all graded employees of affiliated primary societies. Further, to improve the cooperatives' access to financial services, a cooperative bank was registered in 1965.

In 1966 new cooperative legislation was introduced which

constituted a major tool in configurating the structure and activities of cooperatives in line with national and agricultural development policies. Subsequently, the Cooperative Societies Act (1966) and the Cooperative Societies Rules (1969) laid the foundation for a comprehensive system of government intervention. The new legislation was justified by the expressed need for both closer government control and strengthened support, so as to transform agricultural service cooperatives into effective service organizations.

The new legislation gave the government wide powers of control. The Commissioner of Cooperative Development, i.e. the Department, was given the exclusive rights of registration, dissolution and compulsory amalgamation of societies. He was also given the power to supervise budgets and accounts; to approve remuneration, salary or other payments to officers or members of a society; to approve the hiring and dismissal of graded staff; to dictate a society's mode of organization and activity orientation by prescribing the contents of its by-laws; and to control financial transactions through counter-signature of cheques and other instruments.

There are certainly few countries whose governments do not interfere in agricultural output markets. However, this does not necessarily mean that the state is superimposing a heavy load of bureaucratic powers of direct control and intervention on what is supposed to be the farmers' own service organizations. In more than one sense it appears strange that the Kenyan government, which in its official rhetoric argued in favour of individual enterprise and achievement, introduced a control machinery of this magnitude. As a result, we can now actually talk about a cooperative sector with its primary actors, their interdependencies and power positions being subject to detailed regulation. Its outstanding feature is the symbiosis established between government institutions and cooperative organizations. The latter are able to secure recognition and continued survival, at the price of subordination, while the state can legitimize extended control of the smallholder economy.

The extensive powers assumed by the state were probably not perceived as a very controversial move; especially as officially they were warranted both by the rapid growth of cooperatives during the first half of the 1960s and by their expected future role in the economy. Even in the cooperative movement, no marked opposition can be observed. State control would increase but so would the government's direct financial and technical assistance, and most societies and unions badly needed both these forms of backing.

At a more general level, the direct subjugation of cooperatives to the state could be said to reflect a populist-oriented strategy which incorporated a central position for the state in the national economy both in relation to overall planning (regulation) and direct intervention, resulting in extended control over the sphere of circulation (marketing, banking, services) and, to some extent, production.[48] Even so, it was hardly in conflict with much of the conventional development thinking in the industrialized world. In the writings of development theorists after the Second World War, the state had, implicitly or explicitly, been identified as a central force in initiating economic growth and development.[49] In line with this, the 1950s and early 1960s saw a rapid expansion of economic development planning at national level. As observed by Gustav Ranis;

> development planning became heavily identified with extensions of Harrod-Domar models embedded in 5-year or 20-year perspective plans as required for aid recipient respectability. . . . What most of these models have in common was emphasis on an aggregative resources calculation to determine how the most development can be squeezed out of one's endowment, technology and friends abroad.
>
> (Ranis 1977:12)

Although usually undeclared, the civil service to be bestowed the responsibility not only of planning but also of intervention and implementation was supposedly Weberian in nature, i.e., 'officials appointed by merit, differentiated and stratified by function and skill, capable of achieving least-cost solutions to problems through the application of scientific knowledge' (Brett 1983:26).

Thus, the development efforts in newly independent countries, including Kenya, ought to be guided by a technocratic civil service directed by the rational economic decisions of a national planning staff. Hence, it is likely that the kind of state machinery that began to evolve in Kenya during the early 1960s was affected by this kind of external influence. This can be seen in one of the first instances of foreign assistance to agricultural service cooperatives in Kenya.

To be able to deal effectively with the problems facing the cooperative sector, and in particular agricultural service cooperatives, the government approached the Nordic countries in 1965 to discuss the possibility of technical assistance. It is interesting to note that the Nordic delegation, which later that year visited Kenya, attached certain strings to the proposed project. A first condition was that a clear priority for the development of cooperatives had to be given in the national development plan. Second, an administrative arrangement had to be worked out for co-ordination of the ministries to be involved in the programme.[50] Considering the rapid increase in foreign assistance which took place during the 1960s and 1970s, not least in the form of rural and agricultural development programmes voicing similar demands, this kind of influence was bound to have an impact on the role, size and structure of the civil service.

The negotiations between Kenya and the Nordic countries resulted in the so-called 'Nordic Project for Cooperative Assistance to Kenya'. It began in 1967 and was, by 1983, still in operation. The support provided by the project focused on technical assistance in the fields of education, management and accounting and, by and large, this profile has since been maintained. As part of the first agreement, a Cooperative College was established in Nairobi to cater for the training of staff both in societies/unions and at the Department of Cooperative Development.

In the wake of the new cooperative legislation (1966), a marked growth and diversification of institutions took place at national level. Apart from the Department of Cooperative Development, these institutions comprised the Cooperative Bank of Kenya, the Cooperative College and the Kenya National Federation of Cooperatives (KNFC). While this superstructure expanded, the rate of registrations slowed down considerably, as a result both of more limited prospects of establishing new societies and of a more restrictive attitude from the Department of Cooperative Development towards the establishment of new societies.

As a result of the new legislation, the Department started to intervene more widely in the activities of cooperative societies. But not only that; the DOCD, with the active support of the Nordic Project, started more systematically to build up a structure which established a range of interdependencies, both administrative and functional in nature, among primary societies, unions and government bodies at regional (district, province) and national level. In this new setting, the unions were given a central role. That this was an accepted policy is illustrated by the fact that the Cooperative Societies Act of 1966 conferred on the Commissioner the power to compel societies to form or join a union. The expected role of the unions is clarified by Rule 14 of the Act: 'a District Cooperative Union shall provide, organize and supervise efficient centralized services for marketing, supplies, accounting, banking, transport and such other services as may be necessary for its members, which services the members shall be bound to accept.'

Consequently, the DOCD gave high priority to the strengthening of existing active unions. Initially, this involved the strengthening of their management and position relative to primary societies. Affiliated societies' organizational structure and subordination to the unions was secured by placing the control of financial transactions and administration in the hands of the unions. Standardized book-keeping was introduced and such accounting tasks as the posting of documents, ledger postings, trial balancing and final accounts were centralized in the unions. Accounting staff at society level were employed and supervised by the unions. When standardized book-keeping had been implemented, the next step was to introduce a member transactions system. This so-called MT-system meant that the accounting system was integrated with the routines for the recording of members' produce and primary transaction with the society. It established the basis for the introduction of two major credit schemes: a seasonal store credit and the 'Cooperative Production Credit Scheme' (CPCS).

The latter scheme was expected to provide viable and stable credit services to members, and to rectify the societies' existing credit facilities, which more often than not were rather chaotic and highly personalized. The main feature of the scheme, which explains its dependence on the MT-system, was that members' credit limits were calculated as a percentage of their produce deliveries to their society, and that loan deductions were made in connection with payments.[51] Both short-term (STL) and medium-term loans (MTL) were introduced under CPCS. The STLs were granted for a period of 1.5 years and were basically to be used for the improvement of production marketed through the society. By 1972, MTLs had not yet been introduced but would be geared towards capital investments or diversification of members'/farmers' production.

Any loans needed by the societies to contribute to the financing of the credit schemes, or loans for other purposes, had to be raised and negotiated by the unions, which, in turn, had to have a written approval from the DOCD. All loans for production, through the unions, were to be handled by the newly established Cooperative Bank (CBK).

Linked to the expansion of seasonal store credit and CPCS was also the re-organization of the societies' and unions' procurement of inputs. In districts with unions, purchases were to be centralized at union level. According to this arrangement, unions would bulk orders from primary societies, organize the actual purchases of farm inputs and distribute the goods to the society stores. In addition, the unions might have their own store for sale of farm inputs. When introducing this set-up, it was expected that the unions would have to charge the societies an average commission of 3–5 per cent on the items delivered. Even so, it was believed that the new bulk purchase arrangement would ensure cheaper farm inputs, timely deliveries and the avoidance of corrupt dealings between suppliers and cooperative officials.

From 1970, the DOCD also embarked on building up credit sections in selected unions. The CPCS laid the basis for this additional activity. In a few unions they were extended into banking sections which also included a cooperative savings scheme (CSS). With CSS, members of primary societies could open their own savings account in the union's banking section. Instead of getting the proceeds from delivered produce in cash, the amount would be credited to the members' savings accounts.

The introduction of comprehensive administrative procedures, primarily in the form of standardized book-keeping and member transaction systems, resulted in considerable expansion of the volume of stationery required by societies and unions. To cater for this need, a printing press was started at KNFC. The unions were given the responsibility of procuring and keeping adequate stocks of stationery.

One obvious consequence of organizational transformation and diversification of agricultural cooperatives, initiated during a comparatively short period of time, was a rapidly increasing demand both for specialized training of staff and for committee member/member education. In 1967, a Cooperative College was started in rented premises in Nairobi. The following year it was moved to permanent premises at Langata, Nairobi. In early 1972, a second expansion phase was finalized after which the College had the capacity for 160 students per year. The college catered mainly for staff from the movement and the government, while most of the committee member/member education activities were carried out at local level. In the latter case, the unions were assigned responsibility for the actual running of the educational activities. In areas where the unions were not capable of handling these activities, they were to be carried out by the DOCD's district office.

Also the CBK's development was closely linked to the restructuring of cooperatives in rural areas. The bank was registered as a cooperative society in 1965 with cooperative societies and unions as members. In 1968, the CBK was also registered as a commercial bank (under the Banking Act). It was decided that the bank would not operate individuals' accounts. The approach used by the bank to mobilize the financial resources of the cooperative movement was instead limited to the operation of accounts for its members. In view of the short-term nature of these funds, lending was restricted to short- and medium-term finance (up to five years). From the very start, the cooperative production credit scheme constituted a major growth mechanism.[52]

Another significant consequence of restructuring the agricultural service cooperatives, was the expansion of the DOCD. The Department, in addition to the traditional role of the Registrar, now had to be involved in a wide range of supporting and controlling activities. These included the reorganization of unions; the planning, implementation and supervision of new accounting and administrative systems, credit scheme and merchandise activities; and training and educational activities. Although most of the DOCD's work focused on the stronger unions and societies in the highlands of the Central and Eastern provinces, together with Kisii and Bungoma districts west of Rift Valley, the introduction of a rather complex organizational structure in the cooperative movement and widened supporting responsibilities, certainly necessitated both a reorganization of the Department and a strengthening of its staff and financial resources.[53] The critical shortage of certain Kenyan key staff that prevailed at this decisive stage, is indicated by the fact that the accounts development and implementation function of the Department was exclusively staffed by Nordic personnel between 1968 and 1971.[54]

Following the publication of a sessional paper on 'Cooperative Development Policy for Kenya' in 1970,[55] which largely confirmed already initiated activities, the DOCD was reorganized on functional lines. At headquarters level, a number of divisions were established covering:

(i) education/training,
(ii) credit and finance,
(iii) development planning,
(iv) audit and accounts
(v) settlement.

These divisions were headed by Assistant Commissioners who directly reported to the Commissioner (CCD). A Deputy Commissioner was in charge of (i) finance and administration, (ii) legal division and (iii) field services, which included all provincial and district cooperative officers (PCOs and DCOs). The number of staff, which in 1963 was less than 200, had by 1973 more than trebled in size to 691. In addition, an average of 45–50 advisers were deployed under the Nordic project over the period 1968–72. Also the staff at the KNFC, CBK and Cooperative College increased considerably.

Taken together, the late 1960s and early 1970s meant both an

*Table 2.9* Staff establishment in the DOCD and national cooperative institutions, 1963 and 1973

| | *1963* | *1973* |
|---|---|---|
| DOCD | 163 | 619 |
| KNFC | 10 | 28 |
| CBK | – | 16 |
| Coop. College | – | 28 |
| Total | 173 | 691 |

*Sources:* Ministry of Cooperative Development; Cooperative Bank of Kenya; Kenya National Federation of Cooperatives.

organizational typecasting of agricultural service cooperatives and a considerable diversification of their activities. Central features of these changes were the centralization of essential administrative and financial functions to the unions, and the building-up or strengthening of institutions at national level, such as the CBK, DOCD and Cooperative College. By 1972, it was estimated that standardized accounting and budgeting had been implemented in about 550 societies. In about one-third of these societies, the trial balance system had also been established. The MT-system had been implemented in about forty societies. As regards the selection of societies to be given priority, it is stated in a DOCD planning document that 'the selection of geographical working areas is to be seen as a result of the priorities given and not as a criterion for giving priorities' (DOCD 1971: 7). None the less, as the major criterion used for selection was turnover per society, it obviously favoured high-value produce such as coffee, pyrethrum and dairy. Hence, it resulted in a marked geographical bias towards the commercially more developed highland areas in the Central and Eastern provinces.

While the administrative superstructure expanded at both district and central levels, the rate of registrations of primary societies now slowed down considerably. During 1967–72, 129 societies were registered, i.e. approximately one-quarter of the number of entrants during 1963–66 (see Table 2.10).

This deceleration reflected more limited prospects for newly established societies as well as a more restrictive attitude from the DOCD towards the registration of new societies, particularly in areas where agricultural service cooperatives already existed. Thus, not more than twelve societies were registered in Central province, compared to five times as many in Rift Valley. Another significant feature of the 'registration profile' for this period is the almost total absence of coffee societies. The reason for this was that the government, in accordance with the International Coffee Agreement, declared a planting ban on coffee which took effect in 1966. As the bulk of the quota was held by large farms and plantations for most of the 1960s and 1970s, the decision blocked continued diffusion of coffee production among smallholders.[56]

*Table 2.10* Registrations by district and main activity, 1967–72

| | *Activity* | | | | | | | | | | | | |
|---|---|---|---|---|---|---|---|---|---|---|---|---|---|
| *District* | *11* | *12* | *13* | *14* | *15* | *17* | *18* | *21* | *22* | *26* | *30* | *35* | *Total* |
| Kisumu | | | | | | 5 | | | | | 2 | 1 | 8 |
| Kisii | | | | | 1 | | | 1 | | | | | 2 |
| S. Nyanza | | | | | | | 3 | 1 | | | | 2 | 6 |
| Siaya | | | 1 | | | | | | | 1 | 1 | | 3 |
| Kakamega | | | | | | 3 | | | | | 5 | | 8 |
| Bungoma | | 1 | 1 | | | | | | | | | 1 | 3 |
| Nakuru | | | | | 1 | | 1 | 1 | 1 | | 8 | 1 | 13 |
| Baringo | | | | | | | | 1 | | | | | 1 |
| Kericho | | | | | | | | | | 2 | 8 | | 10 |
| Uasin Gishu | 1 | | | | | | | | | | 5 | | 6 |
| Nandi | | | | | | | | | | 1 | 7 | | 8 |
| Trans. Nzoia | 1 | | | | | | | | | | 8 | 1 | 10 |
| E/Marakwet | | | | | | | | | | | 3 | | 3 |
| Laikipia | | | | | | | | 1 | | | 2 | | 3 |
| Narok | | | | | 1 | | | | | 1 | 2 | | 4 |
| Kajiado | | | | | | | | | | | 4 | | 4 |
| Nyeri | | | | | | | | 2 | | | | | 2 |
| Muranga | | 1 | | | | | | | | | | | 1 |
| Nyandarua | | | | | | | | 1 | | | 5 | | 6 |
| Kiambu | | | | 1 | | | | | | 1 | | | 2 |
| Kirinyaga | | | 1 | | | | | | | | | | 1 |
| Kilifi | 1 | | | | | | 1 | 3 | | | 1 | 1 | 7 |
| Kwale | | | | | | | | 4 | | 2 | 1 | | 7 |
| Tana River | | | | | | | | | | 1 | 2 | | 3 |
| Embu | | | | | | | | 1 | | 1 | 2 | | 4 |
| Meru | | 1 | 1 | | | | | 2 | | | | 3 | 7 |
| Kitui | | | | | | | | | | 1 | | | 1 |
| Machakos | | | | | | | | 1 | | 3 | 2 | | 6 |
| Total | 3 | 3 | 4 | 1 | 3 | 8 | 5 | 19 | 1 | 14 | 68 | 10 | 139 |
| % | 2.2 | 2.2 | 2.9 | 0.7 | 2.2 | 5.7 | 3.6 | 13.7 | 0.7 | 10.1 | 48.9 | 7.2 | 100 |

*Source:* surveys
*Activity codes:* (11) cereals, (12) coffee, (13) cotton, (14) vegetables, (15) pyrethrum, (17) sugar cane, (18) other crops, (21) dairy, (22) eggs/poultry, (26) animals, (30) multiproduce, (35) unions.

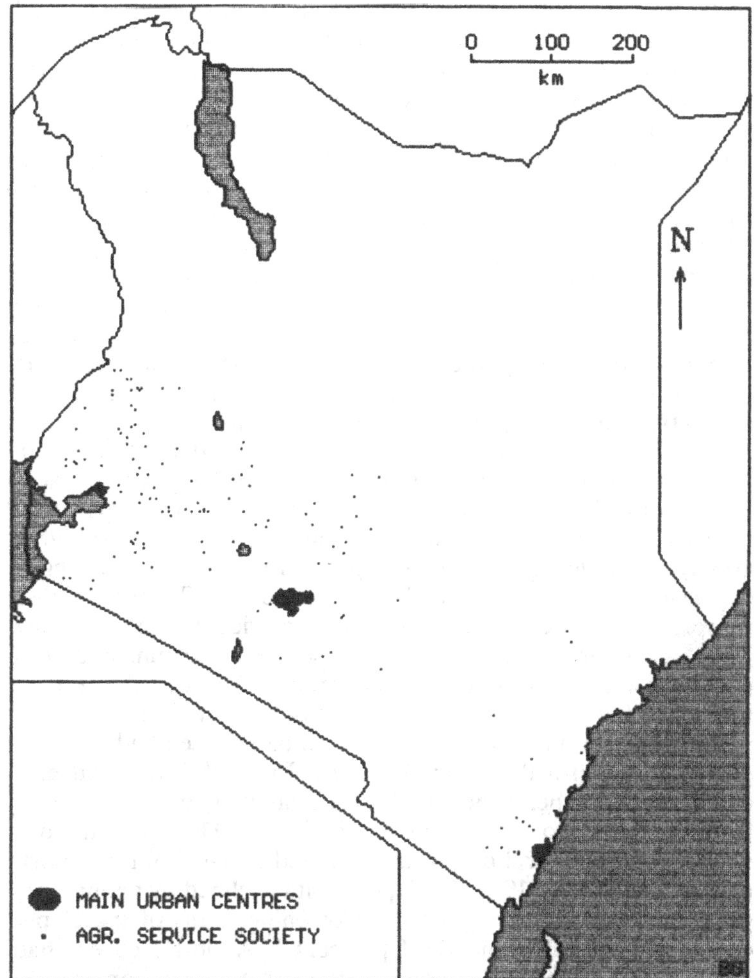


*Figure 2.4* Registrations of agricultural service societies, 1967–72

## 2.4 Supply side strategies and penetration of marginal areas (1973–83)

*National development trends*

During the first half of the 1970s, the main sources of agricultural growth neared exhaustion. The expansion of cultivated areas generated by settlement schemes had slowed down; most high-potential areas were already under cultivation, and by the early

1970s hybrid maize had been adopted by most smallholders.[57] Not only did agricultural growth lose its momentum, but in the industrial sector the import-substitution strategy made the economy increasingly dependent on imports while at the same time inhibiting growth of exports. The country also started experiencing serious fiscal and balance of payments pressures.[58] As earlier indicated, these problems were not entirely unexpected, although magnified by international events.[59] In 1974, the world oil price increases and subsequent rises in the price of other imports resulted in a loss of income, due to adverse changes in the terms of trade, equivalent to about 5 per cent of domestic income. As a consequence, GDP per capita fell. The government responded by reducing the growth of the public sector, including the development budget, and raised interest rates, income taxes, sales taxes on luxury goods and the price of petrol.

In 1976, the world coffee crop was reduced after frosts in Brazilian coffee areas, leading to rapidly increasing coffee prices and improved terms of trade. In this suddenly favourable economic climate, expansionary fiscal and monetary policies resulted in greatly expanded government expenditure. Due to the lagged expansionary effects of the high coffee prices in 1977, imports rose sharply in 1978. At the same time, coffee prices started declining while there were major price increases in petroleum and thus another reversal to deteriorating terms of trade. As a consequence, the current account balance deteriorated drastically.

The restriction of imports that had to be imposed had negative effects on the growth of manufacturing. In 1979/80, these adverse trends were further aggravated by a near doubling in crude oil prices and unfavourable climatic conditions. Drought caused a decline in agricultural output and resulted in national food shortages in 1979–81. In 1981, GDP per capita declined by about 1 per cent; however, adjusting for the worsening terms of trade, per capita income fell by nearly 4 per cent.[60] A slow recovery had begun by 1983, when GDP equalled the rate of population growth, i.e. 3.9 per cent. The world price of crude oil was again declining while higher prices were recorded for coffee and tea. In line with this, the deficit on the current account balance had fallen to the lowest level since 1977.[61]

According to national accounts estimates, agricultural GDP in constant prices rose by 3.1 per cent annually between 1972–82, i.e. considerably slower than the rate of growth for the population. However, as shown by Sharpley, actual growth has probably been higher. For the decade as a whole, it is likely that average output per capita was approximately constant, which still means a considerable deceleration compared to the period 1964–72.[62] Of total gross marketed production, smallholders accounted for a share varying from 51 to 54 per cent.[63]

Over the period 1972–82, the agricultural sector was characterized by deteriorating relative prices. This deterioration, which had started in the mid-1960s, was temporarily reversed in 1977–78 in the wake of rapidly increasing world prices for coffee and tea. However, from 1978, the index again started declining. In 1982 it was 88 per cent of its level a decade earlier. On average, real producer prices for export crops were higher than those of domestic crops.[64] Considering only the officially recorded marketing of agricultural production, Sharpley estimates that producers average per capita income declined by about 1.5 per cent annually. It should then be noted that this estimation is *not* based on farm-gate prices. Adjustments have been made for marketing board cesses and export taxes, but not for deductions by local cooperatives, council cesses and for local transport arrangements.

For the three categories comprising export crops, domestic crops and livestock/dairy products, real prices declined between 1972 and 1982. For export producers, the cash incomes grew faster than those of producers of domestic crops, and for both the expansion in marketed output was sufficient to attain cash income increases at par with the growth in total population. For livestock and dairy products, particularly adverse price trends resulted in realized cash incomes considerably below their 1972 level.[65]

Thus, while Kenya's first decade of independence was characterized by a high rate of economic growth, the trend had changed. The main sources of growth – expansion of cultivated land, continued spread of export crops and adoption of hybrid maize – had largely been exhausted, and had not been followed by any other technological developments facilitating raised productivity of land and labour. At the same time as agricultural growth slowed down, external price shocks, reinforced both by widely fluctuating prices for major export commodities and by monetary, fiscal and trade policies, produced extensive swings in the economy.[66] Continued monetization, and agricultural specialization on a few export crops, increased the vulnerability of both the rural and national economy. The overall performance of the rural economy was no doubt negatively affected by relative prices moving to the disadvantage of agriculture. Recoveries took place in 1969–70, 1972 and 1976–77 but were essentially temporary in nature. Further, large resources were siphoned off from agriculture, largely to the advantage of the urban economy.[67] Thus, while agriculture constituted the very basis for the growth of the economy, its continued expansion was impeded by a marked urban bias in the end-use of generated resources.

### *Population changes and the physical resource base*

During the 1960s and 1970s, Kenya's rate of population growth was probably among the highest in the world. Between the census years 1948 and 1962 the growth rate was 3.2 per cent; between 1962 and 1969 it was 3.4 per cent; and between 1969 and 1979, 3.9 per cent. With continued growth at the latter rate, the total size of the population in 1990 is estimated to be c. 25 million, as compared to 8.6 million in 1962. Given the physical resource endowment, dependence on agriculture and a generally low level of technological development, population growth at this remarkable rate is bound to have profound social and economic consequences.

In the 1970s, an estimated 1,600,000 people were added to the potential labour force.[68] Of this net addition, about one-quarter were employed by the modern sector.[69] The bulk of the total number of new entrants thus had to be absorbed by agriculture. This pattern will prevail during the 1980s and 1990s, during which period the economy faces the challenge of creating gainful employment for another 8–10 million people.[70]

As indicated earlier, scarcity of good agricultural land has long been a problem in Kenya. Only about 11 per cent of the land area has good potential for agriculture, and the population distribution in rural areas mirrors the physical resource endowment. An estimated 60 per cent of the rural population live in the high-potential areas, 30 per cent in medium- to low-potential areas, and 10 per cent in dry range lands.[71]

The distribution of population within the high-potential areas is,

*Table 2.11* Availability of high-potential land by province, 1979[1]

| *Province* | *Rural pop. ('000)* | *Hectares ('000)* | *Hectares per household* |
|---|---|---|---|
| Central | 2,242 | 909 | 2.2 |
| Coast | 981 | 373 | 2.0 |
| Eastern | 2,588 | 503 | 1.0 |
| Nyanza | 2,433 | 1,218 | 2.7 |
| Rift Valley | 2,962 | 3,025 | 5.5 |
| Western | 1,790 | 741 | 2.2 |
| Total | 12,996 | 6,769 | 2.8 |

*Sources:* Rep. of Kenya, Population Census 1979, Vol. I; Rep. of Kenya, Statistical Abstracts 1984, Table 73.
*Note* Excluding North Eastern and Nairobi provinces

however, far from even. In spite of the implementation of settlement programmes during the 1960s and 1970s, the zones that were set aside for large-scale agriculture in the colonial period still have a considerably lower density than that found in the traditional smallholder areas in Central province and in the lake area west of Rift Valley.

Increasingly heavy population pressure raises issues not only concerning how to absorb new entrants to the labour force productively, but also how it affects the overall productivity of land and labour. In these latter respects, the shortage of land in parts of the highland areas west and east of Rift Valley has assumed serious proportions.

*Table 2.12* Availability of high-potential land in selected, densely populated districts, 1979

| *District* | *Population ('000)* | *Hectares ('000)* | *Hectares per cap.* | *Hectares per household* |
|---|---|---|---|---|
| Kisii | 869 | 220 | 0.25 | 1.3 |
| Kakamega | 1,031 | 325 | 0.32 | 1.7 |
| Kiambu/Muranga | 1,334 | 386 | 0.29 | 1.6 |
| Machakos | 1,023 | 125 | 0.12 | 0.6 |
| Meru | 830 | 241 | 0.29 | 1.5 |
| Total | 5,087 | 1,297 | 0.26 | 1.4 |

*Sources:* Rep. of Kenya, Kenya Population Census, Vol. I; Rep. of Kenya, Statistical Abstracts 1984, Table 73.

## *Poverty and inequality*

As earlier shown, Kenya inherited an economy in which incomes and wealth were very unevenly distributed. In the 1970s, it was becoming clear that in the wake of the economic growth achieved since independence, these disparities had been widening rather than lessening both between urban and rural areas, and among rural areas.[72] It is not possible with the available data to give a more detailed picture of these changes. However, as regards urban areas, it is quite clear that Nairobi has not only maintained but strengthened its dominating position in the economy. The growth has been fuelled by the expansion of manufacturing, extensive investments in physical and social infrastructure and by a rapidly expanding public sector (Figure 2.5).

As regards the remaining provinces, the gains made by Central and Eastern provinces probably not only apply to the period covered by Bigsten's study on interregional inequalities,[73] but are likely to have characterized most of the post-independence period. As far as smallholder agriculture is concerned, it may be argued that Figures 2.5 and 2.6, due to the level of aggregation, conceal more dramatic interregional differences in economic growth. As the agricultural GDP figures include large-scale farms and plantations, they do not in all cases give a representative picture of the performance of the smallholder economy. Exclusion of large-scale enterprises would thus lower the level of GDP in all provinces, but in particular for Rift Valley, Western province and the Coast. Considering the size of the provinces, it is also evident that they within themselves cover a wide range of physical, demographic and economic conditions.

In an attempt to reflect some of this differentiation, the Integrated Rural Survey (IRS) for 1974–75 adapted the data collection to a defined agro-ecological zone covering the major smallholder areas west and east of Rift Valley. According to IRS, the income level among smallholders in the coffee and cotton zones west of the Rift, cotton east of the Rift and the Coast, were at that time significantly lower than the tea and coffee zones to the east of Rift Valley. The latter zones, which are encompassed by Central province and the northwestern fringes of Eastern province, also had a smaller proportion of households below the poverty line.[74]

In essential respects, these imbalances in the regional incidence of economic growth conform to a pattern that had already emerged during the colonial period. Since then, Central province has been drawing ahead of other areas, with high-value cash crops as the main growth generator, and with the assistance of increasingly well-developed social and physical infrastructures. A related, though more decisive, indicator of development trends is the incidence of absolute poverty. If one measures poverty in terms of insufficient household income to satisfy a minimum standard level of nutrition, then about 35 per cent of Kenya's total population belonged to the category of the absolutely poor in 1974.[75] Almost all (98 per cent) lived in rural areas. Of these, over 4 million people (more than two-thirds) were smallholders.

The rest were pastoralists, landless workers, squatters and migrants to semi-arid areas. The limited information existing about changes in the distribution of income between 1963 and 1974, seems to indicate that the number of poor increased, athough their relative share of the total number of smallholder households declined.[76] Furthermore, about 40 per cent of all smallholder households had not experienced any improvement in real income; instead the major share of the gains in real income

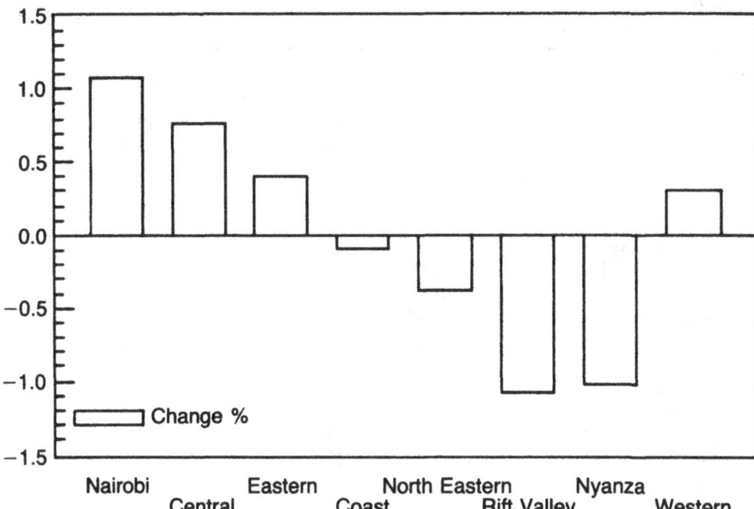


*Figure 2.5* Change in relative distribution of GDP 1967–76, by province, 1971 prices
*Source:* A. Bigsten, 1978, Table XI.17

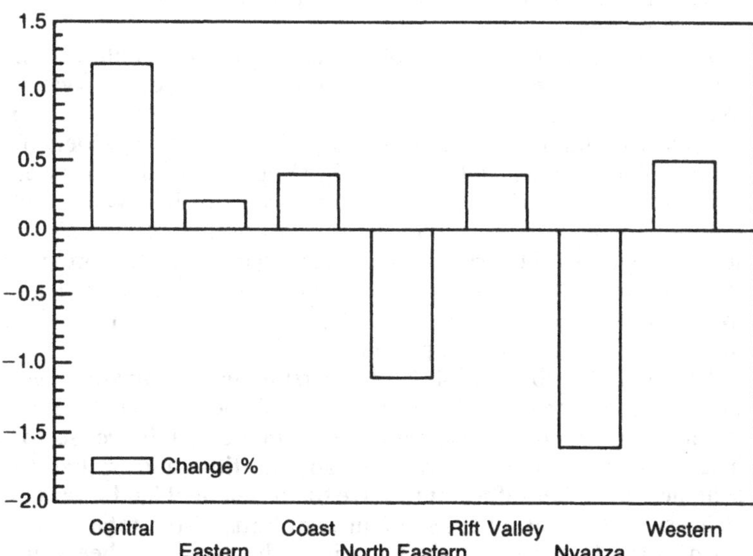


*Figure 2.6* Change in relative distribution of agricultural GDP, 1967–76 by province, 1971 prices
*Source:* A. Bigsten, 1978, Tables XI.16, XI.16.10

*Table 2.13* Distribution of households below 2,200 K.Sh. total consumption by agro-ecological zone, 1974

| *Zone* | *Number* | *% of zone total* | *% of national total* |
|---|---|---|---|
| Tea west of Rift | 76,049 | 54 | 13.3 |
| Coffee west of Rift | 98,379 | 40 | 17.2 |
| Upper Cotton west of Rift | 202,834 | 61 | 35.5 |
| | *377,262* | | *66.0* |
| Tea east of Rift | 17,882 | 11 | 3.1 |
| Coffee east of Rift | 67,086 | 20 | 11.7 |
| Upper Cotton east of Rift | 7,917 | 41 | 1.4 |
| Lower Cotton east of Rift | 67,402 | 48 | 11.8 |
| | *160,287* | | *28.0* |
| High altitude grass | 463 | 4 | 0.1 |
| Taita Hills | 7,990 | 56 | 1.4 |
| Coast, rain < 40″ | 12,062 | 54 | 2.1 |
| Coast, rain > 40″ | 10,372 | 31 | 1.8 |
| Sugar cane | 3,096 | 36 | 0.6 |
| Total | 571,532 | | 100.0 |

*Source:* Integrated Rural Survey 1974/5, Central Bureau of Statistics, Nairobi

were confined to the 30 per cent of households already having the highest incomes.

IRS I data, referring to 1974/75, also revealed a quite distinct pattern in the geographical distribution of poverty. Nyanza, Western and Eastern provinces accounted for almost 80 per cent of Kenya's total number of poor (Table 2.13). If one considers the agro-ecological zones defined by IRS, 65 per cent of the poor were living in the tea, coffee and cotton zones west of Rift Valley, and another 14 per cent in the cotton zone east of the Rift (mainly the lowland parts of Eastern province). As regards the intra-province distribution, over one-half of the smallholders in Nyanza and Western provinces belonged to this category, as compared to about one-third in Central province.[77]

Unequal distribution of landownership in combination with demographic forces is likely to be a sigificant factor behind faltering growth and widespread poverty in the smallholder sector. The land reforms, in terms of adjudication and settlement schemes, were not sufficient to solve the problem of land shortage. It is estimated that by 1978, about two-thirds of the total mixed-farm area of approximately 1.8 million hectares had been subdivided for smallholder cultivation.[78] Almost 800,000 hectares were resettled to smallholdings under the official programme. In the context of the latter, the average holding was quite large

*Table 2.14* Distribution of holdings by size, 1976/77[1]

| | Estim. no. of farms | % | Estim. area (hectares) | Estim. % total area |
|---|---|---|---|---|
| *Small farms* | *1,853,000* | (98.0) | *3,825,000* | *68.0* |
| of which: | | | | |
| <0.5 ha | 508,000 | 27.0 | | 4.0 |
| 0.5–0.9 | 405,000 | 22.0 | | 7.0 |
| 1.0–1.9 | 362,000 | 19.0 | | 12.0 |
| 2.0–2.9 | 156,000 | 8.0 | | 8.0 |
| 3.0–3.9 | 88,000 | 5.0 | | 5.0 |
| 4.0–4.9 | 59,000 | 3.0 | | 5.0 |
| 5.0–7.9 | 67,000 | 4.0 | | 8.0 |
| >7.9 ha | 59,000 | 3.0 | | 15.0 |
| Irrig. schemes | 4,724 | 0.3 | 8,728 | 0.2 |
| Unofficial sub-divisions of mixed farms[2] | 144,000 | 8.0 | 315,000 | 6.0 |
| *Gap farms*[3] | *40,000* | 2.1 | *1,000,000* | *18.0* |
| *Large farms* | *1,675* | 0.1 | *770,000* | *14.0* |
| of which: | | | | |
| – mixed farms | 1,200 | | 585,000 | 10.0 |
| – plantations[4] | 475 | | 185,000 | 4.0 |
| Total | c.1,895,000 | | c.5,595,000 | 100.0 |

*Sources:* World Bank, 1983, Vol. II, p. 337–39; I. Livingstone, 1981, p. 12.3–12.5.

*Notes:*

1 Excluding ranches.

2 At least one-third of the total area of mixed farms has been unofficially subdivided.

3 Number and area are estimates. Information on gap farms, most of which are in the size range of 20–50 ha, is not covered by either IRS or CBS' Large Farm Survey.

4 Cropped area only.

(above 10 hectares), and the programme has subsequently been of direct benefit to comparatively few households (c. 71,000).[79]

In the major smallholder areas both east and west of Rift Valley, available, though very limited, evidence suggests that the concentration of landholdings has continued to increase. Apparently, this process has been accompanied by growing fragmentation among the smallest holdings. Thus, considering the overall distribution of land, it seems evident that towards the end of the 1970s at least one third of the population in smallholder areas were either landless or critically short of good agricultural land (Table 2.14).

A disproportionately high share of income generation was confined to a few districts dominated by plantations and commercialized smallholders, with tea and coffee as their major cash crops. Even in these favoured areas – particularly the highlands of Central and Eastern provinces – mounting population pressure resulted in deepening social and economic stratification. According to estimates by Collier and Lal, the poorest two-fifths of the population saw their share of total income decrease from about 24 to 18 per cent between 1963 and 1974, i.e. by approximately 25 per cent. Similar trends have been observed for Nyanza, in spite of a considerably lower overall income level of this province.[80]

The major concentrations of very small holdings (below 0.5 ha.) are to be found west of Rift Valley.[81] On the other hand, landlessness seems more common in Central province, from where most of the 200,000 or so landless people who have migrated to dry, agriculturally marginal land seem to originate, bringing with them techniques of cultivation which now seriously threaten the ecological balance of these areas.

## Summary

In the 1970s, rural areas were characterized by continued rapid population increase, faltering economic growth and increasing social and economic disparities. The net capital outflow from agriculture increased, to the benefit of other sectors of the economy, mainly in urban areas. Also the number of landless and poor households increased, with parts of Nyanza and Western provinces having the highest concentrations of poor smallholders. The settlement of households in Rift Valley continued but was grossly inadequate as a means of easing the growing pressure on land west and east of Rift Valley. Instead a growing number of landless households were migrating to agriculturally marginal land.

## *The creation of cooperative delivery systems*

In spite of the weak performance of smallholder agriculture in the 1970s and early 1980s, as reflected in a low growth rate as well as in decreasing shares of GDP and of total marketed production, the number of registered agricultural service societies continued to increase and so did the directly controlling and supporting government machinery. As almost 50 per cent of the total number of registered societies were located in the former White Highlands, it may be assumed that most of these registrations reflect continued commercialization and the spread of smallholder agriculture in these areas. They also reflect the spill-over of sedentary agriculture into areas with medium or low agro-ecological potential. As indicated above, both these areas generally performed poorly in terms of growth of marketed smallholder production. In the traditional smallholder areas, a significant increase in registrations can be noted for both Western and Nyanza provinces (Tables 2.15 and 2.16). This feature may also seem contradictory, considering their character of being 'lagging regions'. In the 1970s, however, the registration of new societies could be linked to the extended roles rural and agricultural development policies assigned cooperatives.

Ever since cooperatives were introduced three decades earlier, the state had continuously attempted to use them as an organizational means of influencing and controlling strategic strata of the smallholder community. Between 1954 and 1975, cooperatives were important tools for a controlled linking-up of specific, often privileged smallholder strata to the market economy. This was clearly the case both under the Swynnerton Plan and in the contexts of the settlement programmes and the organizational renovation initiated in the latter half of the 1960s.

After the introduction of a new legislation in 1966, there could no longer be any doubt about the subordination of cooperatives to the state; they were turned into an administrative tool for implementing agricultural policies. The approach certainly was top-down in character. It must have been assumed that the government, supported by a technocratic superstructure engineering the design and activities of cooperatives, would be able effectively to promote agricultural and rural development. By the early 1970s, this strategy had seemingly been successful, at least among smallholders growing coffee and pyrethrum. Restructuring of the administration of these cooperatives, combined with introduction of production credit and other supporting services, had contributed to improved economic performance and stability with positive consequences for production and income generation.

The experience of the kind of support given coffee societies seemed to confirm that improved supplies of production credit and inputs through cooperatives would be instrumental in realizing increased agricultural production. Although technical information and credit for the purchase of inputs had been an ingredient of small-farm development programmes ever since the 1950s, the CPCS was the first to be judged as an unequivocal success.

However, in the early 1970s, the government still had a rather cautious attitude towards the expansion of credit and input supply services through cooperatives. The idea of promoting more input-intensive technologies was certainly supported, but it was emphasized that cooperatives first had to prove their managerial capability before taking on these additional activities. At the same time, though, increasing concern was being expressed regarding deepened social and regional stratification in rural areas. Following the ILO mission's report in 1972 on 'Employment, Income and Equality',[82] the incidence of poverty in rural areas was being paid considerable attention. Discussing the employment problem of school leavers, the report emphasized the prevalence of other serious imbalances in the economy. Thus,

> These other problem groups include the landless, the women who are heads of rural households and the pastoralists in rural areas. . . . Moreover, there are strong and continuing inequities within rural areas, within urban areas, and between regions of the country. Disparities of income and wealth are all-pervasive, persons at the lower end of the spectrum being generally among the working poor.
>
> (ILO 1972:47)

Influences of the political debate following the ILO report can be noted in Sessional Paper No. 14 of 1975 on 'Cooperative Development Policy for Kenya', in which it is noted that,

> cooperatives will increasingly continue to be powerful tools in mobilizing the natural, human and financial resources for national development. Their vital role as agents for opening up development in less developed areas has been duly recognized and will be enhanced.
>
> (Republic of Kenya 1975:5)

In these 'less developed areas', seasonal credit and improved input supplies were identified as important instruments for promoting raised production and income levels. This is clearly expressed in the last paragraph of Sessional Paper No. 14 of 1975:

> In agriculture, in particular, the government wishes to see a greater number of the small-scale farmers so that it can efficiently supply agricultural inputs and be an effective channel for seasonal credit to the small-scale farming sector.
>
> (Republic of Kenya 1975:26)

This approach obviously was acceptable to those in control of the socio-economic system. The most obvious alternative means of providing employment and income opportunities, i.e. land redistribution, was not explicitly considered. Neither was the need for heavy, and geographically redistributed, investment in physical and social infrastructure.

It all boiled down to stimulating production and economic growth in lagging areas by providing a selective supply of credit and inputs. In this setting, the cooperative structure was again perceived as a feasible organizational device. At the time, it was apparently in line with the kind of 'conventional development wisdom' many external donor agencies were representing. Lack of credit and inputs were usually perceived as binding constraints on agricultural growth. In financial terms it was also cheap, certainly so compared to alternative approaches. Thus, from the mid-1970s, a number of integrated, largely donor-financed, rural development programmes were implemented. One of their common features has been the objective of increasing the supply of farm inputs through the medium of cooperatives (Figures 2.7–2.13).[83] Their estimated costs and scheduling were as follows:[84]

| *Project/programme* | *Period* | *Estim. project cost, K. Sh. million* |
|---|---|---|
| SPSCP | 1976–80 | 101 |
| FISS (I and II) | 1976–84 | 38 |
| IADP I | 1977–82 | 288 |
| MIDP | 1978–82 | 200 |
| SCIP | 1979–83 | 498 |
| IADP II | 1979–84 | 688 |
| ASAL (KITUI) | 1980–84 | 140 |
| Total | | 1,953 |

*Source:* Min. of Coop. Development
*Notes*
FISS: Farm Input Supply Scheme
SPSCP: Smallholder Production Services and Credit Programme
IADP: Integrated Agricultural Development Programme
MIDP: Machakos Integrated Development Programme
SCIP: Smallholders' Coffee Improvement Programme
ASAL: Arid and Semi-Arid Lands Development Programme

Of the total provisions made, about K.Sh. 780 million were to be utilized by cooperative institutions for storage facilities, vehicles, farm inputs, credit and management support.

The geographical profile of most of these programmes was to the advantage of rural areas characterized by low-income levels and widespread poverty, i.e. Western and Nyanza provinces together with those parts of Eastern province having less favourable agro-ecological conditions. One major deviation from this pattern was the support given to smallholders in the highlands of Rift Valley. In spite of comparatively favourable physical conditions, marketed production had developed unfavourably. Another exception was SCIP, which provided support for farm rehabilitation and renovation of pulping units in all coffee-growing areas. By 1983, almost 300 primary societies were linked to the implementation

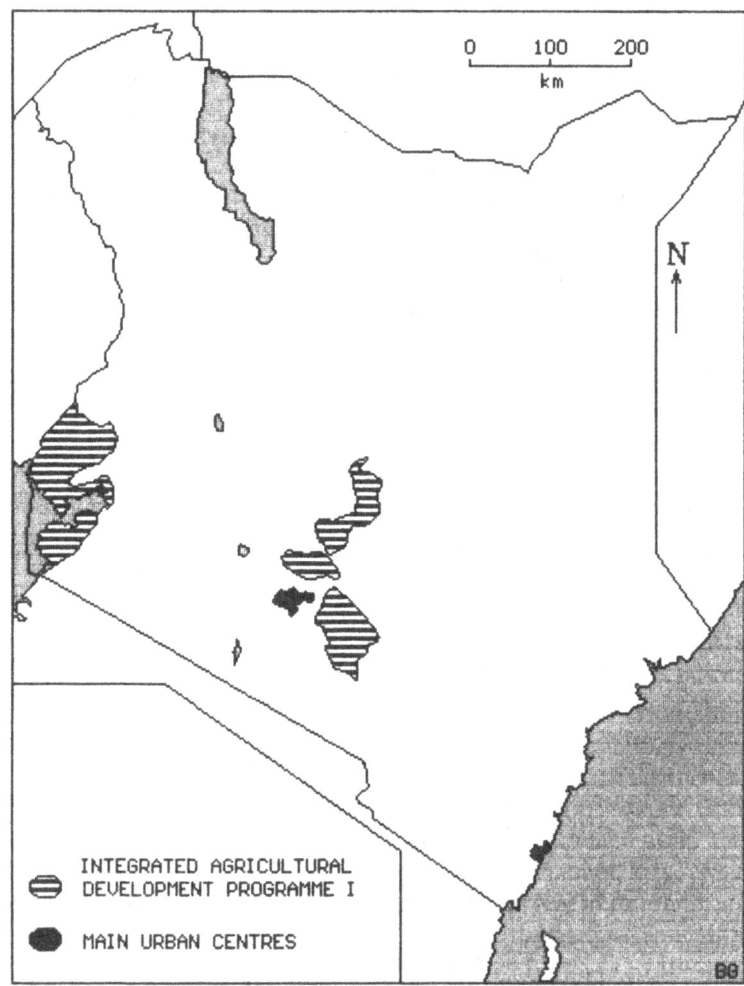


*Figure 2.7* Integrated Agricultural Development Project I
*Source:* Research and Evaluation Unit, MOCD, 1981.

of programmes through which credit and inputs would be made accessible to smallholders (excluding CPCS).

Although the intention was to use only already established and functioning societies, it is interesting to note that about 20 per cent of the societies participating in the programmes seem to have been registered in direct response to the inflow of resources. Further, excluding coffee, the registration of societies over the period 1973–83

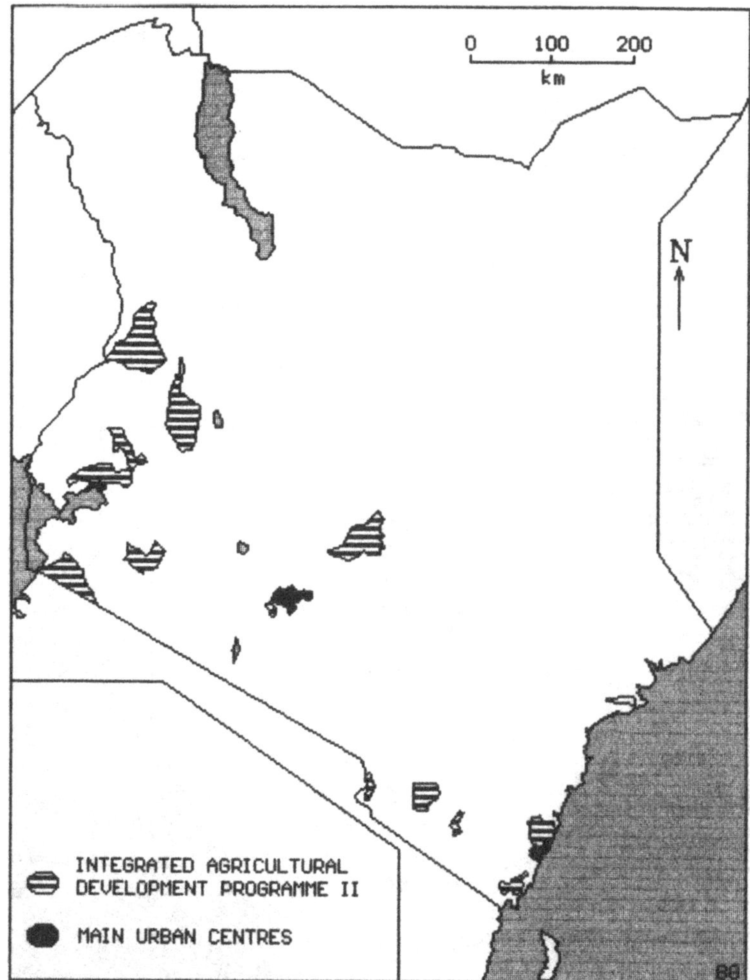


*Figure 2.8* Integrated Agricultural Development Project II
*Source:* Research and Evaluation Unit, MOCD, 1981.

largely reflects the various supporting measures introduced by the government (Figs 2.7–2.8, Tables 2.15–16). Thus, over 90 per cent of the societies registered over this period were located in areas where one or several of the mentioned rural development programmes were being implemented. In addition, it may be assumed that the membership increased of already registered societies in cases where they were affected by the programme

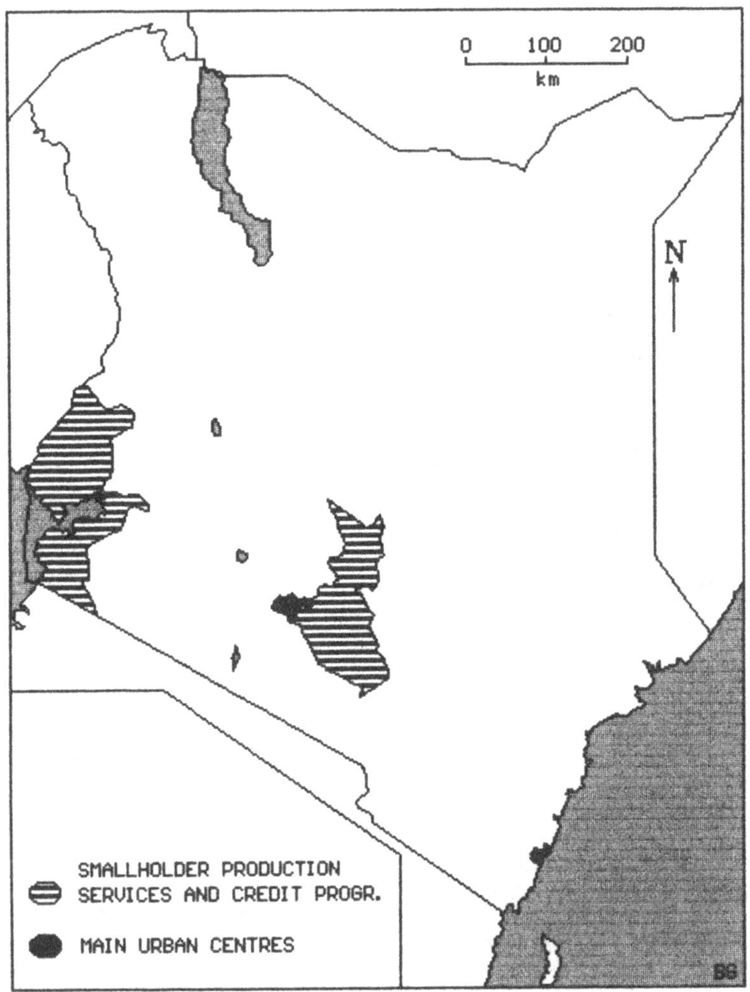


*Figure 2.9* Smallholder Production Services and Credit Programme
*Source:* Research and Evaluation Unit, MOCD, 1981

activities. This is hardly surprising; it is rather a perfectly rational response in a rural economy critically short of resources. It also supports, however, our earlier argument that smallholders effectively are taught that membership of cooperatives is primarily a means of securing benefits provided by the state. This rationale obviously offers an explanation for the fact that registrations of primary marketing societies continued in spite of a stagnating rural

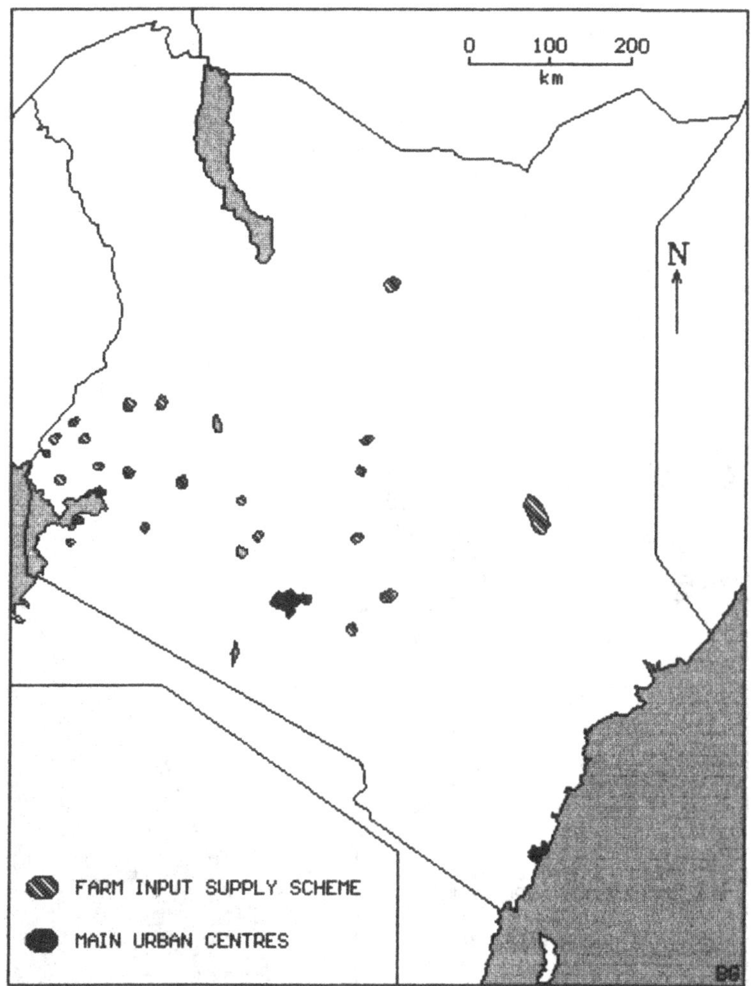


*Figure 2.10* Farm Input Supply Scheme
*Source:* Research and Evaluation Unit, MOCD, 1981

economy. They merely reflect attempts by local communities to take advantage of the resources provided (Figures 2.14–2.15).

## Unions

As mentioned earlier, the 1966 Cooperative Societies Act stipulated that a range of vital activities would be carried out by district

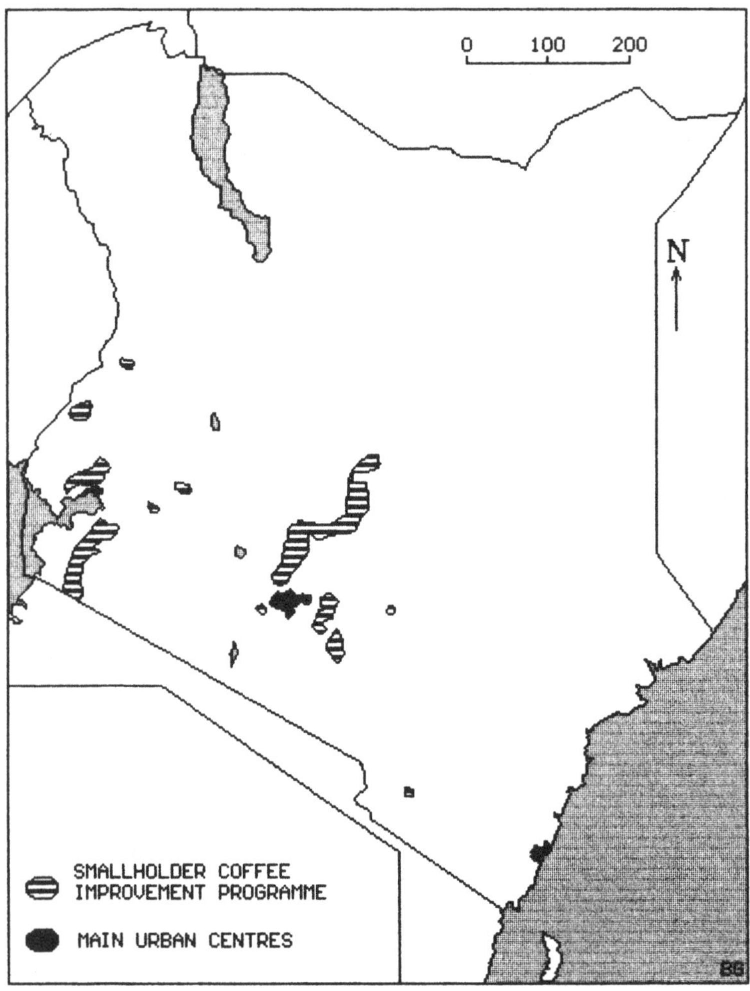


*Figure 2.11* Smallholder Coffee Improvement Project
*Source:* Research and Evaluation Unit, MOCD, 1981

cooperative unions, i.e. accounting, credit, banking, and input supply services. By the early 1970s, unions had been registered in most smallholder areas. The additional registrations that took place between 1973 and 1983 were, as in the case of primary societies, geographically biased towards regions receiving support under various input supply/credit programmes.

At national level, increasing attention was being paid, particularly

*Figure 2.12* Machakos Integrated Development Programme
*Source:* Research and Evaluation Unit, MOCD, 1981

by donor agencies, to the role the Kenya National Federation of Cooperatives (KNFC) could play in the cooperative sector. When the KNFC was established in 1964, its declared main functions were to represent the movement and to carry out publicity and information activities about cooperatives. Annual fees from its members together with a printing press supplying the movement with stationery constituted the economic basis for the

*Figure 2.13* Kitui Arid and Semi-Arid Lands Project
*Source:* Research and Evaluation Unit, MOCD, 1981

federation. As a consequence of the new administrative systems introduced in societies and unions in the late 1960s, the KNFC's printing activities expanded substantially.

The KNFC also started operating an insurance agency and in the early 1970s, support was given by various donor agencies, including the Nordic Project (NP) and the World Bank, to further diversify the activities of the KNFC. The NP supported the

*Table 2.15* Registrations by district and main activity, 1973–77

| | *Activity* | | | | | | | | | | | | | |
|---|---|---|---|---|---|---|---|---|---|---|---|---|---|---|
| *District* | *11* | *12* | *13* | *14* | *15* | *17* | *18* | *21* | *22* | *23* | *26* | *30* | *35* | *Total* |
| Kisumu | 1 | | | | | 8 | | | | | 1 | 1 | 1 | 12 |
| Kisii | | | | | | | 1 | 1 | | | | 1 | | 3 |
| S. Nyanza | | | | | | | 1 | | | | | 4 | 1 | 6 |
| Siaya | | | | | | | | | | | | 3 | | 3 |
| Kakamega | 1 | | | | | | | | 1 | | | 14 | | 16 |
| Bungoma | | 1 | | | | | | | | | | 3 | | 4 |
| Busia | | | 1 | | | 1 | | 1 | | | | | | 3 |
| Nakuru | | | | | 3 | | 2 | | | | | 7 | | 12 |
| Baringo | | | 1 | | | | | 1 | | | 1 | | 1 | 4 |
| Kericho | | 4 | | | | | 5 | | | | | 3 | | 12 |
| Uasin Gishu | | | | | | | 1 | | | | | 2 | | 3 |
| Nandi | | 1 | | | | | 2 | 2 | | | | | 1 | 6 |
| Trans-Nzoia | 4 | | | | | | | 2 | | | | 1 | 1 | 8 |
| E/Marakwet | | | | | | | 1 | | | | | 2 | | 3 |
| W. Pokot | | | | | | | | | | | 1 | 4 | | 5 |
| Laikipia | | | | | | | | | | | | 1 | 1 | 2 |
| Narok | | | | | 1 | | | 1 | | | 1 | 1 | | 4 |
| Kajiado | | | | | | | | | | | 1 | | | 1 |
| Turkana | | | | | | | | | | | 1 | 1 | | 2 |
| Nyeri | | | | | | | | 1 | | | | 1 | | 2 |
| Muranga | | 2 | | 1 | | | | 2 | | 1 | | 1 | | 7 |
| Nyandarua | | | | | | | | | | | | 8 | 2 | 10 |
| Kiambu | | 2 | | | | | 1 | 2 | | 2 | | 2 | 1 | 10 |
| Kirinyaga | | | | 1 | | | | | | | | | | 1 |
| Kilifi | | | | | | | | | | | | 1 | | 1 |
| Kwale | | | | | | | 1 | | | | 1 | 1 | | 3 |
| Lamu | | | | | | | | | | | 1 | 1 | | 2 |
| Tana river | | | | | | | | | | | | 1 | | 1 |
| Taita/Taveta | | | | | | | | | | | | 1 | | 1 |
| Embu | | 1 | | | | | 1 | | | | | 2 | | 4 |
| Meru | | | | | | | | 1 | | | | 3 | | 4 |
| Kitui | | | | | | | | | | | | 3 | 1 | 7 |
| Machakos | | | | | | | 4 | | | | 3 | 9 | | 13 |
| Marsabit | | | | | | | | | | | 1 | | | 1 |
| Garissa | | | | | | | | | | | 1 | | | 1 |
| Mandera | | | | | | | | | | | | 1 | | 1 |
| Total | 6 | 11 | 2 | 2 | 4 | 9 | 20 | 14 | 1 | 3 | 13 | 83 | 10 | 178 |
| % | 3.4 | 6.2 | 1.1 | 1.1 | 2.2 | 5.1 | 11.2 | 7.9 | 0.6 | 1.7 | 7.3 | 46.6 | 5.6 | 100 |

*Source:* survey data
*Activity codes:* (11) cereals, (12) coffee, (13) cotton, (14) vegetables, (15) pyrethrum, (17) sugar cane, (18) other crops, (21) dairy, (22) eggs/poultry, (23) pigs, (26) animals, (30) multiproduce.

*Table 2.16* Registrations by district and main activity, 1978–83

| *Activity* | | | | | | | | | | | | | | |
|---|---|---|---|---|---|---|---|---|---|---|---|---|---|---|
| *District* | *11* | *12* | *13* | *14* | *15* | *17* | *18* | *21* | *22* | *23* | *26* | *30* | *35* | *Total* |
| Kisumu | | | 1 | | | 14 | 1 | | | | | 8 | 2 | 26 |
| Kisii | | | | | 2 | | 1 | | | | | 1 | 1 | 5 |
| S. Nyanza | 1 | 2 | | | | | 4 | | | | | 6 | 2 | 15 |
| Siaya | | | | | | 1 | 3 | | | | | 1 | 1 | 6 |
| Kakamega | | 1 | | 1 | | 2 | | | | | 1 | 5 | | 10 |
| Bungoma | | 2 | | 1 | | 1 | 1 | | | | | 4 | 1 | 10 |
| Busia | | 1 | | | | | 1 | | | | | 1 | 1 | 4 |
| Nakuru | | 1 | | | 2 | | 9 | 4 | 1 | | | 3 | | 20 |
| Baringo | | | | | 1 | | 3 | | | | | 1 | | 5 |
| Kericho | | | | | | 4 | 15 | 2 | | | 1 | 6 | | 27 |
| Uasin Gishu | | | | | | | 17 | | | | | 2 | 1 | 20 |
| Nandi | | 1 | | | | | 5 | 2 | | | | 7 | | 15 |
| Trans Nzoia | 1 | | | 1 | | | 17 | | | | | 4 | | 23 |
| E/Marakwet | | | | | | | 4 | | | | | 2 | | 6 |
| W. Pokot | | | | | | | 2 | 1 | | | | 1 | 1 | 5 |
| Laikipia | | | | | | | 5 | 3 | | | 1 | 5 | | 14 |
| Narok | | | | | | | 3 | | | | 1 | 1 | | 5 |
| Kajiado | 1 | 1 | | 2 | | | | | | | 1 | 1 | | 6 |
| Turkana | | | | | | | 1 | | | | | | | 1 |
| Nyeri | | | | | | | 3 | 3 | 1 | | | 2 | | 9 |
| Muranga | | 2 | | | | | | 3 | | 1 | | | | 6 |
| Nyandarua | | | | 1 | | | 2 | 1 | | | | 5 | | 9 |
| Kiambu | | 2 | | 1 | | | 1 | | 1 | | | 1 | | 6 |
| Kirinyaga | | 1 | | 1 | | | 1 | | | | | 2 | | 5 |
| Kilifi | | | | | | | 1 | | | | 1 | 2 | | 4 |
| Kwale | 1 | | | | | | | | | | | | | 1 |
| Lamu | | | | | | | | | | | | 1 | | 1 |
| Taita/Taveta | | | | | | | | | | | | 3 | | 3 |
| Embu | | 5 | | 1 | | | | 1 | | | 2 | 1 | | 10 |
| Meru | | | 7 | | | | 1 | 3 | | | | 6 | | 17 |
| Isiolo | | | | | | | 1 | | | | 1 | 4 | | 6 |
| Kitui | 1 | | | 1 | | | 3 | | 1 | | 1 | | | 7 |
| Machakos | | 1 | | 1 | | | 3 | 1 | | | 1 | 2 | | 9 |
| Marsabit | | | | | | | | | | | | 1 | | 1 |
| Garissa | | | | | | | 1 | | | | 1 | | | 2 |
| Wajir | | | | | | | 1 | | | | 2 | | | 3 |
| Mandera | | | | | | | 2 | | | | | | | 2 |
| Total | 5 | 20 | 8 | 11 | 5 | 22 | 112 | 24 | 4 | 1 | 14 | 89 | 10 | 325 |
| % | 1.5 | 6.1 | 2.5 | 3.4 | 1.5 | 6.8 | 34.5 | 7.4 | 1.2 | 0.3 | 4.3 | 27.4 | 3.1 | 100 |

*Source:* survey data
*Activity codes:* (11) cereals, (12) coffee, (13) cotton, (14) vegetables, (15) pyrethrum, (17) sugar cane, (18) other crops, (21) dairy, (22) eggs/poultry, (23) pigs, (26) animals, (30) multiproduce, (35) unions.

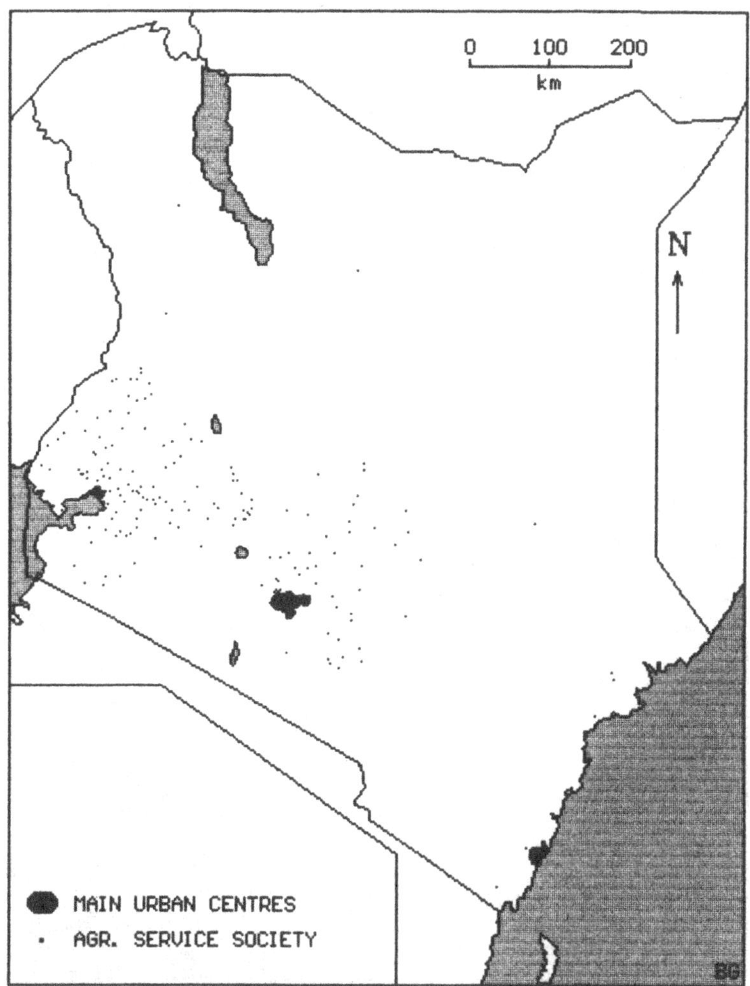


*Figure 2.14* Registrations of agricultural service societies, 1973–77
*Source:* survey data

expansion of education and information activities, the establishment of an audit section and the start-up of a merchandise activity. The latter, supported also by the World Bank, aimed at giving the KNFC the responsibility for centralized procurement and supply of agricultural inputs and processing materials for agricultural cooperatives. The results of these efforts were quite discouraging. In terms of staff, however, the support received

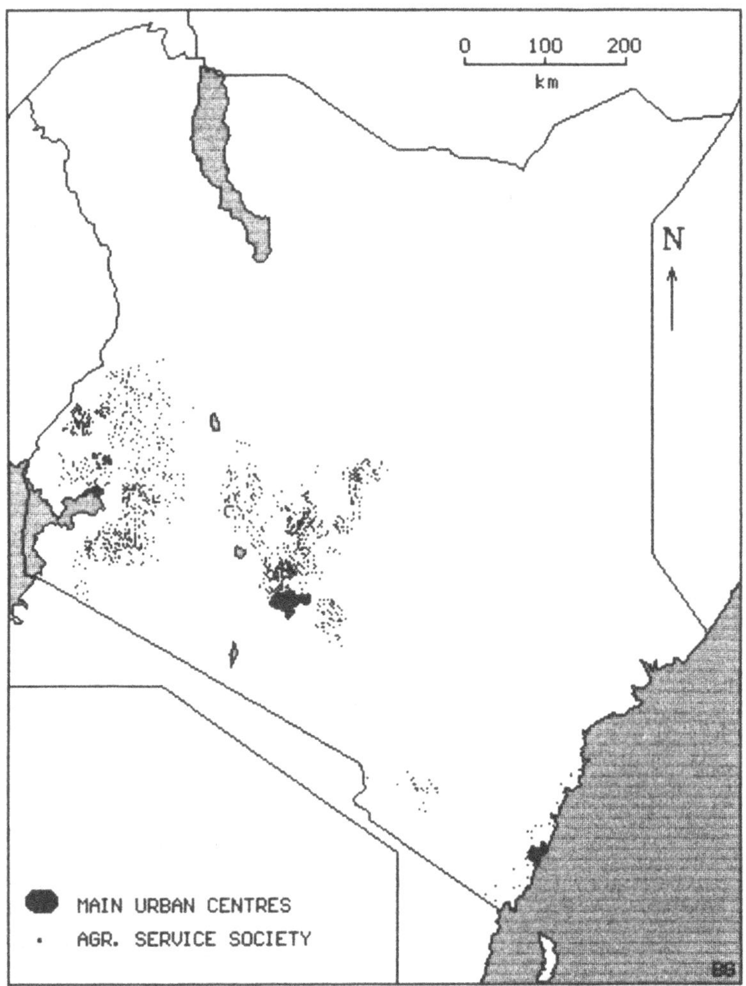


*Figure 2.15* Registrations of agricultural service societies, 1978–83
*Source:* survey data

resulted in a considerable expansion of the organization (Table 2.19).

Also the Cooperative Bank of Kenya grew rapidly and like the KNFC, donor-assisted activities constituted a major growth impetus. The Bank's expansion path thus was closely related to the widening range of donor-backed credit programmes and funds for channelling through the cooperative network. While the Bank's operations were confined mainly to CPCS lending in the early 1970s, well over twenty different donor-supported schemes were handled in 1983.

As most of the individual schemes have their own set-up of strings attached – in terms of target groups, utilization and general loan conditions – they are administratively demanding and thus had direct consequences for the CBK's organization and staff development. In order to handle its widening responsibilities satisfactorily, the CBK found it necessary to build up a field organization. By 1983, branch/field offices had been established in Kisumu, Mombasa, Meru, Nakuru, Eldoret and Nyeri. The total staff of the Bank increased from 16 in 1973 to over 200 in 1983 (Table 2.19).

### Cooperative Insurance Society (CIS)

In the late 1970s, the KNFC's insurance activities were taken over by the CIS, which in 1978 was registered and licensed under the Insurance Companies Act to transact non-life insurance business. The CIS' membership is composed of primary and secondary cooperative societies, and its main purpose is to provide the movement with relevant insurance services.

### Ministry of Cooperative Development (MOCD)

The development and implementation of standardized accounting systems, initiated in the late Sixties, continued and one or several such systems had been introduced in practically all active societies by 1983. Revision of the accounts systems, and related administrative routines, involved a range of organizational and administrative changes in both unions and primary societies. A first basic step was the introduction of a standardized accounts plan, followed by routines for budgets, trial balances, cash control, final accounts and for the use of loose-leaf ledgers. The implementation schedule was largely based on the turnover of societies, which meant that coffee societies were given first priority, followed by dairy and pyrethrum.

A decisive step in the renovation of the accounts systems was the introduction of an 'MT-system', facilitating control of all transactions between members and their societies, and the centralization of book-keeping to the unions. By 1977, the MT-system was used by most coffee, dairy and pyrethrum societies while MT for multiproduce, cotton and sugar were either at the stage of design/testing or under implementation.

To cater for implementation of the accounting systems in the societies/unions, accounts implementation teams (AITs) were established at district level. After completion of the work in a particular district, one government officer remained to supervize the maintenance of the systems. Obviously, the transformation of the administrative structure of all agricultural service cooperatives imposed a considerable work burden on the MOCD's staff. For the period 1974–77 alone, it was estimated that about 180 man-years would be required for implementation, excluding development, testing and supervision.

A closely related activity was the continued implementation of the Cooperative Production Credit Scheme (CPCS). Only societies meeting specified accounting and management standards were permitted to join the scheme. In addition to the implementation task, expansion of the number of CPCS-loanees required considerable staff resources. The scheme was governed by detailed rules, specifying qualification criteria for loans, clearance, approval and supervision routines. For the actual operation of the scheme, the unions had to open 'credit sections' so as to act as the local distribution channel for loans. To get loans, primary societies had to be affiliated to such unions. By 1983, 280 societies were linked to the CPCS, among which coffee and dairy societies predominated. The total number of loan accounts then stood at *c.* 82,000. Assuming one loan account/member, it would mean that the scheme in that year reached about 12–15 per cent of the members.

To facilitate increased self-financing of the CPCS and improved services to individual members, a savings scheme (CSS) was established in the early 1970s. Unions judged as having the capacity to participate in the CSS had their credit sections upgraded to 'banking sections'. Members of affiliated primary societies were given individual savings accounts which administratively were designed as an integrated part of the MT-system. Thus, when the society prepared to pay its members for delivered produce, deductions were first made for any credit/loans and other service charges, whereafter the balance was credited to the member's savings account in the union's banking section.

In 1974, the CSS had been implemented in parts of Eastern and Central provinces. By 1983, the CSS covered sixteen unions and affiliated societies. The total number of savings accounts amounted to about 450,000.

In addition to these development activities, aimed at improving the management performance and diversifying the services of unions and societies, the MOCD also involved itself in a range of other control- and development-oriented activities. These included improved auditing routines and the introduction of merchandise activities and improved transport services at union level.

After 1967, the MOCD (DOCD) no doubt used its legally sanctioned powers to carry out a profound structural and organizational transformation of cooperatives in the agricultural sector. Until the mid-1970s, the entire operation focused on the economically most important societies and unions. Geographically this meant a systematic bias to the advantage of the highland areas in Central and Eastern provinces, and to a few districts west of Rift Valley, primarily Kisii and Bungoma. With the reorganization and diversification of a considerable portion of the cooperative sector, there followed a drastically increased demand for managerial professionalism, and thus for training of staff employed by societies, unions and the MOCD. Consequently, machinery had to be built to cater for these needs.

Before 1971, education and training activities had been directed mainly towards government and movement staff. Educational efforts in support of members were few and sporadic. One obvious result was that members were unable to exercise any effective control over their societies, thus creating opportunities for favouritism and intentional mismanagement among leaders and staff. The gravity of this problem obviously magnified with the introduction of more sophisticated administrative routines.

In 1974, the MOCD introduced a comprehensive programme for member and committee member education. The activities were intended to involve the ministry, the KNFC and the Cooperative College, and to be monitored by a 'Co-ordination Group for Cooperative Education'. The member education activities of the MOCD, which were planned and implemented in the provinces by 'education teams', aimed at improving members' knowledge on issues, thereby enabling them to control the operation of their societies. This encompassed not only members' rights and obligations in the context of 'the cooperative mode of organization', but also more technical elements regarding payment routines and the internal administrative system of the societies. As regards committee members, the programme sought to give them the skills required to determine and solve management problems effectively.

The education activities for both committee members and ordinary members were operationalized into a seven-step instructional programme, with each step assigned measurable objectives and quantitative targets. The organization that was built up was dimensioned to reach about 140,000 members and 4,000 committee members annually. The MOCD carried the main responsibility for the education activities at local level. Due to financial constraints, most unions had limited opportunities to make any significant contribution in this field. The Cooperative College was linked to these activities by conducting education broadcasts over the radio in English and Kiswahili. The college also produced education material.

The college's main role, however, has been to provide movement and ministry staff with more advanced managerial skills. A variety of courses were offered, ranging from a two-year diploma course to one-week courses for committee members. The college expanded considerably during the 1970s, in terms of both courses offered and student enrolment.

*Table 2.17* Courses and students at the Cooperative College, 1967–70 and 1980–82

| *Average no. of courses* | | *Average no. of particip. days* | |
|---|---|---|---|
| *1967–70* | *1980–82* | *1967–70* | *1980–82* |
| 27 | 45 | 11,355 | 57,754 |

*Source:* Coop. College, annual reports

Since the late 1970s, the college has operated at maximum capacity but this has not been sufficient to meet the training needs. According to a feasibility study conducted by an external consultant a few years ago, the college would need to expand to three times its present capacity.

The cooperative legislation, tabled in 1967, established close interdependencies between supervisory and supporting government bodies and cooperative organizations. It thereby constituted the foundation for the organizational and administrative transformation designed and implemented over the following fifteen-year period. The introduction of these changes had far-reaching repercussions not only on the cooperative organizations at local and regional levels but also, as indicated above, on government institutions and other organizations at central level. The implementation in itself obviously generated a staff expansion. With implementation finalized, it was gradually also realized that the organizationally more complex cooperatives put additional demands on the MOCD. To meet its supervisory and controlling obligations, the ministry had to expand its capacity considerably, both in terms of staff and other resources.

Thus the restructuring of existing agricultural cooperatives put considerable pressure on the MOCD and the Cooperative College in particular. To this has to be added the consequences of the various rural development programmes introduced from the mid-1970s onwards. As observed earlier, these programmes generally favoured less developed rural areas and could be seen as a response to growing criticism of the unequal growth which characterized the economy during the first decade of independence. These donor initiated/supported programmes all regarded improved access to production inputs among smallholders as vital for raised production and income levels.

As was earlier observed, the introduction of these credit/input supply programmes had a considerable impact on the CBK's organizational and staff requirements. To a large extent, the same was true of the MOCD, whence most of the administrative capacity required for implementing and supervising the programmes derived. In this respect the programmes were quite demanding as each of them (i) consisted of several components, (ii) was geographically spread, and (iii) had its own specific 'strings attached' in terms of target group definitions, procurement procedures, approval and processing of loans, reporting routines, etc. This is also reflected in the MOCD's deployment of district staff, which, by 1983, clearly was biased to the advantage of the regions targeted by the rural development programmes. During the late 1970s, a number of projects were also introduced, under a 'diversification and expansion programme', which supported the development of cooperatives in fisheries, handicrafts and small-scale rural industries. Basically, these shared the 'administration-intensive' characteristics of the earlier mentioned rural development programmes.

Generally, non-agricultural societies grew considerably in importance during the 1970s. This applied in particular to urban savings and credit societies (Table 2.18). These societies are concentrated in Nairobi and Mombasa. The 'common bond' of members is regular employment in the modern sector; in terms of education and income they are considerably better off than most smallholders. Further, the savings and credit societies are organizationally simple constructs. For both social and organizational reasons, members are thus in a better position to control their societies. For the same reasons, this category of societies puts modest supervisory demands on the MOCD as compared to the agricultural service societies.

As can be seen from Table 2.19, the size of the organizations at the top of the cooperative hierarchy increased quite dramatically

*Table 2.18* Growth indicators, savings and credit societies

| | *1972* | *1982* |
|---|---|---|
| Number of active societies | 101 | 716 |
| Membership, '000 | 36 | 403 |
| Borrowers, '000 | 15 | 181 |
| Total savings, K. Sh. million | 16 | 1,500 |
| Total loans, K. Sh. million | 10 | 940 |

*Source:* Copac, 1984, Table 13

*Table 2.19* Total no. of staff in the MOCD, Coop. College, CBK, KNFC and CIS, 1973–83

| | *1963* | *1973* | *1978* | *1983* |
|---|---|---|---|---|
| Ministry of Cooperative Development | 163 | 619 | 1,197 | 1,869 |
| Cooperative College | 10 | 28 | 122 | 148 |
| Cooperative Bank | – | 16 | 71 | 219 |
| KNFC | – | 28 | 57 | 130 |
| Coop. Insurance Soc. | – | N/A | N/A | 43 |
| Total | 173 | 691 | 1,447 | 2,409 |

*Sources:* Internal documentation at the MOCD, Coop. College, CBK, KNFC and CIS.

over the period 1973–83. With the possible exception of the KNFC, this expansion cannot be seen simply as a case of bureaucratic proliferation. Although the MOCD, in terms of staff deployment, has increased considerably above the norm for central government institutions (Figure 2.16), this has not taken place without reason.

## *Concluding comments*

Since their inception in the mid-1940s, agricultural cooperatives have been subject to a considerable degree of state promotion, control and intervention.

In the 1950s and 1960s, they were used as an organizational means of influencing and controlling the politically and economically strategic strata of the smalholder community. This was clearly the case both under the Swynnerton Plan and in the context of the settlement programmes. Further, in the 1960s, changes in land tenure and the introduction of cash crops formerly monopolized by white settlers, were institutionally tied to agricultural service cooperatives. It was no doubt hoped that, taken together, these

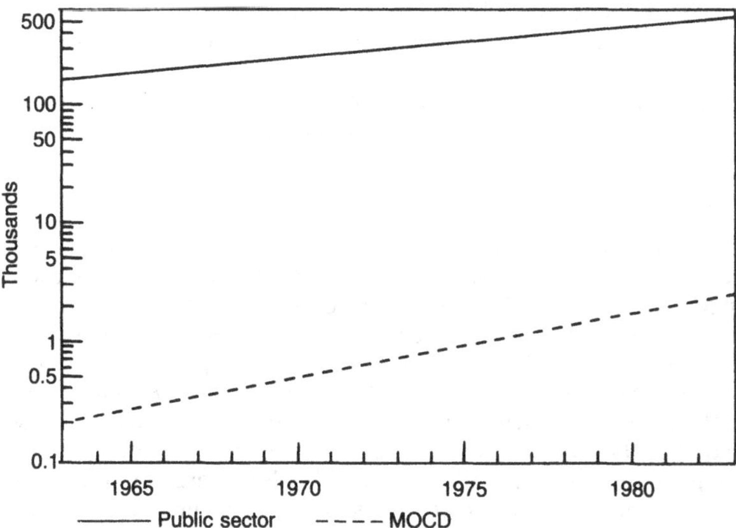


*Figure 2.16* Employment: MOCD and total for the public sector, 1963–83 (sem. log. scale)
*Source:* MOCD

measures would stimulate economic growth, stem opposition among influential strata of the farming community, and facilitate improved control of events in the countryside.[85]

In the 1970s, in response to decelerating economic growth and increasing social and regional inequalities, economic and rural development policies were adjusted. Within this context, the role of cooperatives was redefined and widened. Increasing emphasis was now laid on their role as a delivery system for channelling production credit and inputs to smallholder agriculture, with the intention of disseminating more productive, input-intensive technologies and revitalizing the agricultural economy. This reorientation was combined with increased financial and technical development support to cooperatives in lagging or agriculturally less favoured regions.

Basically, the approach seems to have been used as a substitute for, rather than a supplement to, more basic measures that could improve employment and income opportunities, such as land redistribution, expanded investment in rural infrastructure and liberalization of the economy. It therefore just added to a wide range of earlier state initiatives aimed at 'capturing the peasantry'[86] but which, in reality, seem to have resulted in little more than bureaucratic proliferation, increased repressive tendencies and social segmentation. To those in control of the socio-political system, however, the strategy apparently was acceptable, at least in the medium term.

As regards the expansion pattern characterizing the cooperative sector, available data support the following general observations.

## Activity orientation

A decisive factor conditioning the registration of societies has been government regulations stipulating that smallholders – below a specified size of the holding – had to be members of cooperative societies in order to have access to market channels for certain types of produce. This has applied to coffee, pyrethrum, sugar, cotton (this condition was abolished in the early 1980s) and, to a certain extent, dairy produce. The adoption of any of these activities thus had to be anteceded by the registration of a primary cooperative society. Although smallholders were not forced to become members of a society, the material incentives obviously were strong.

A second type of state-instigated registration has been the settlement society. In this case, however, the main concern behind the ordinance was not so much promotion of commercialized agriculture as orderly repayment of settler loans. In addition to the regulation-induced registration of societies, there have also been the more genuine cases. Judging from available data, though, these constitute a small share of the total number of registrations.

## Phasing (Figures 2.17–18)

Four periods with high frequencies of registration can be observed, which are characterized by specific government initiatives. These were the late 1940s and 1950s, the mid-1960s and the late 1970s. The first peak was largely a result of campaigns carried out by the Registrar of Cooperatives in areas west of Rift Valley. The second wave of registrations resulted from the implementation of the Swynnerton Plan, the third from the government's settlement programme, and the latest from the introduction of input-intensive technologies and a reorientation of development support towards smallholder areas with low income levels and/or stagnating agriculture. In this context, it is interesting to note that the registration frequency does not in any systematic manner follow the growth performance of the agricultural economy.

A variety of means have been used for inducing or persuading smallholders to join societies, including campaigns, crop-specific

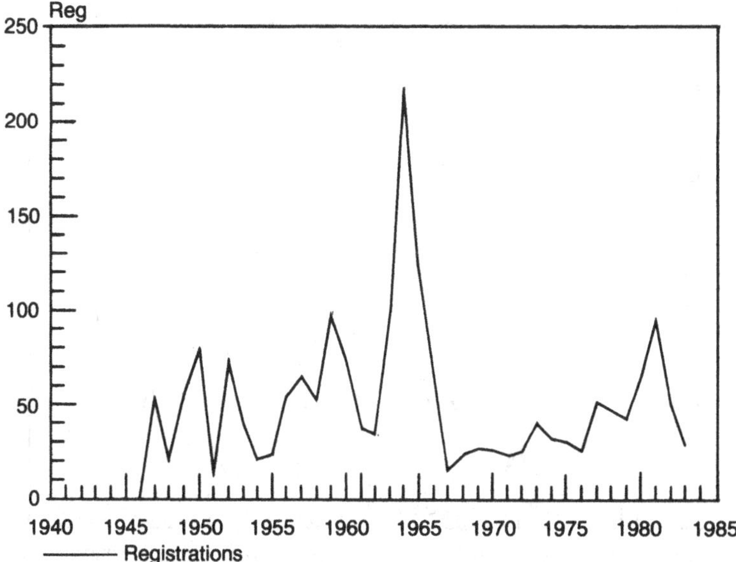


*Figure 2.17* Registrations of agricultural service societies, 1946–83
*Source:* Survey data

conditions, loan regulations (settlement) and access to credit and farm inputs. The considerable effectiveness of these measures, as indicated by subsequent registrations, imply strong and rational responses among smallholders to opportunities to improve their material conditions. From this it follows, that the way in which cooperatives have been promoted fosters the view among smallholders that the major quality of cooperatives has been their access to resources provided/controlled by the state. In the circumstances, the perception of the vertical relation state–cooperative–member as the critical one is fully understandable. This kind of rationale, however, obviously runs counter to the kind of logic conventionally expected to govern the formation of cooperatives.

## Geographical distribution

The ecological limits for produce channelled through cooperative marketing societies have determined the basic geographical pattern of registrations. Changes in spread profile over time thus is a function

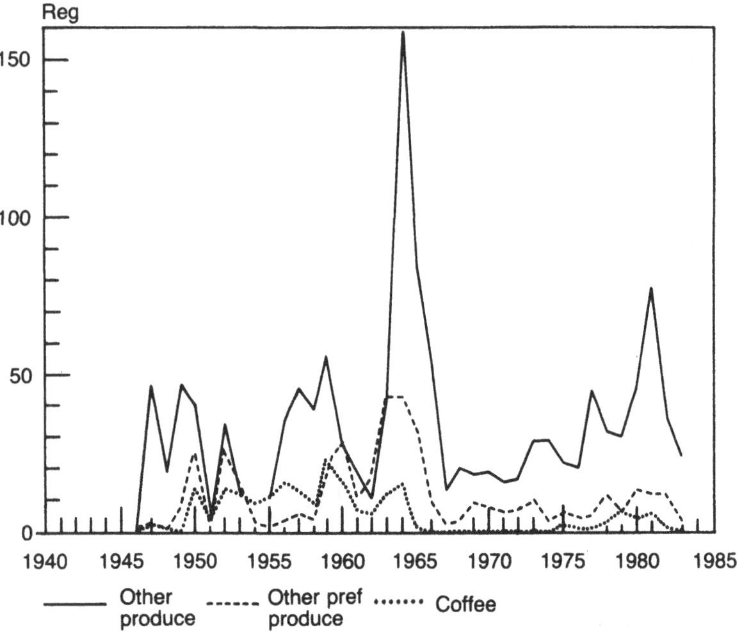


*Figure 2.18* Registrations of agricultural service societies by main marketing activity, 1946–83
*Source:* Survey data

of this factor in combination with specific government initiatives. Before independence, registrations were concentrated in campaign areas and in the major coffee zones east and west of Rift Valley. In the 1960s, the pattern became more dispersed, reflecting both the implementation of settlement programmes and the 'cooperativization' of the cotton industry in the Lake Victoria region. At the time, registration densities were increasing in all major smallholder areas. After the mid-1970s, the pattern becomes even more dispersed, now reflecting active state support directed towards economically lagging smallholder areas, including ecologically marginal lands (Figure 2.19).

## Organizational structure

The imprint of state powers is not confined to the registration of societies. It is clearly visible also in the organizational structure

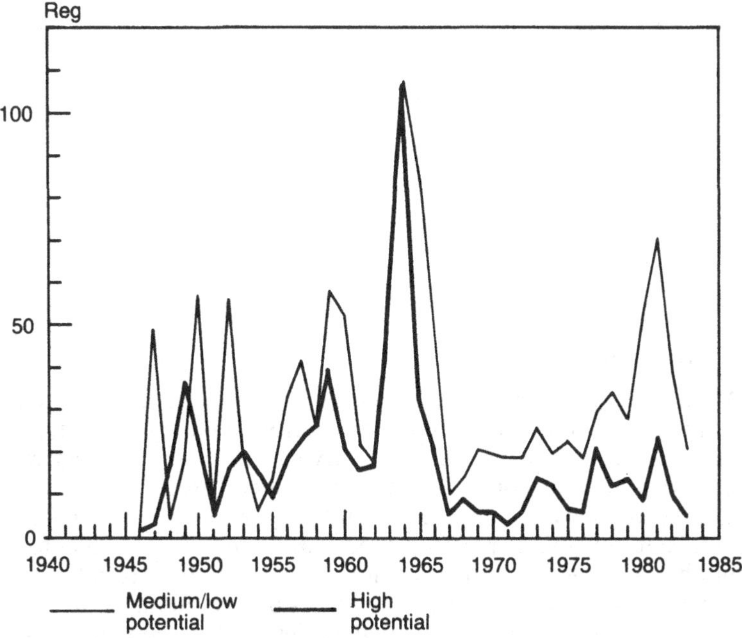


*Figure 2.19* Registrations of agricultural service societies, by agro-ecological potential, 1946–83
*Source:* Survey data

which has emerged, particularly after 1966 when a new Cooperative Societies Act was promulgated. By means of direct government intervention, societies and unions have had their activities, administrative structures and interrelationships prescribed in quite some detail. To improve the effectiveness of development support and control, their operations have been increasingly closely integrated with a national superstructure of organizations which, apart from the MOCD, comprise the Cooperative Bank, the KNFC, the Cooperative College and the CIS. It has had considerable reverberations for the central bodies themselves in terms of staff size, administrative complexity and costs. Finally, it should be noted that the institution-building process both at local and central levels has actively involved a range of donor agencies. A pertinent feature of these involvements is their substantial inflating impact on the size of the MOCD and other central bodies.

Chapter three

# Survival

## 3.1 Introduction

A first step towards the identification of conditions that, in important respects, affect the performance and impact of cooperatives is to examine basic 'survival' and 'mortality' characteristics. The concept 'mortality rate' is here used to denote the portion of societies that have either gone dormant or been liquidated during a particular period, in relation to the total number of societies in register during that period.[1] Mortality and survival may be seen as simple measures but, when linked to other information about the individual societies and their respective environments, they can in some basic respects shed light on conditions that are of importance for their serviceability.

To establish the actual status of societies has in itself been a rather tedious exercise. Official records are reliable as far as liquidations are concerned. However, the MOCD's follow-up of dormancies and changes caused by amalgamations and split-ups leaves much to be desired. Hence, as part of the survey, the classification of all registered societies was examined, and in many instances revisions had to be made. In this work, staff at the district cooperative offices and at unions and societies gave invaluable assistance. According to our data, the total number of active societies is about 20 per cent lower than the official figure.

According to official terminology, a society is classified as 'dormant' if it has ceased to operate for more than two years. As 1983 is the reference year of the study, societies registered after 1980 have not officially existed for more than a period of one to three years. This is here seen as too short a period to ascertain whether an apparent dormancy is permanent or due to initial difficulties in establishing regular service activities. Societies registered after 1980 are therefore not considered at the present stage of the analysis.

In most of the following analyses, we will relate dormancies to periods rather than to individual years; these periods are 1946–62, 1963–70 and 1971–83.

When relating mortality frequencies to the earlier mentioned time periods, it can be noted that they have been subject to a rather steady decrease. This also applies to the mortality rate (Table 3.1). Moreover, the geographical distribution of liquidations and dormancies differs quite distinctly between the three periods.

*Table 3.1* Societies in register[1] and mortality frequency[2] for the periods 1946–62, 1963–70 and 1971–83 (by province)

| | *1946–62* | | | *1963–70* | | | *1971–83* | | |
|---|---|---|---|---|---|---|---|---|---|
| *Province* | *In rg.*[3] | *LD (%)*[4] | | *In rg.* | *LD(%)* | | *In rg.* | *LD(%)* | |
| Nyanza | 213 | 121 | 57 | 170 | 35 | 21 | 195 | 47 | 24 |
| Western | 170 | 97 | 57 | 132 | 40 | 30 | 135 | 78 | 58 |
| Rift | 29 | 15 | 52 | 175 | 72 | 41 | 262 | 68 | 26 |
| Central | 171 | 112 | 65 | 250 | 91 | 36 | 214 | 43 | 20 |
| Coast | 28 | 15 | 54 | 45 | 19 | 42 | 42 | 8 | 19 |
| Eastern | 107 | 72 | 67 | 120 | 37 | 31 | 148 | 32 | 22 |
| N. Eastern | – | – | – | 2 | 2 | 100 | 7 | 4 | 57 |
| Total | 718 | 432 | 60 | 894 | 296 | 33 | 1,003 | 280 | 28 |

*Source:* Survey data

*Notes*

1 Number of societies active at the beginning of each of the periods + registrations during 1946–60, 1961–68 and 1969–80.

2 Number of societies liquidated or having gone dormant during each of the periods 1946–62, 1963–70 and 1971–83.

3 In rg.: 'societies in register'.

4 LD: number of liquidated and dormant societies.

In the 1946–62 period, they were approximately equally divided among the major smallholder areas west and east of Rift Valley. During the 1960s, a more dispersed pattern can be observed with the main point having shifted towards Central and Eastern provinces with concentrations to Nyeri and Kiambu districts. After 1971, the pattern has again changed, now with Nyanza and Western provinces accounting for almost half of the total number of liquidations/dormancies. As distinct from other parts of the country, the mortality rate increased in the regions west of Rift Valley during 1971–83. The mortality rates are now particularly high in Kakamega, Bungoma and S. Nyanza (see also Figures 3.3, 3.6 and 3.9).

In line with our earlier arguments, it may be hypothesized that the survival performance of societies is conditioned by two sets of circumstances, namely (i) the local environment and (ii) the society's activity orientation, including its organizational structure and interdependencies.

Activity orientation is of significance because it both raises different demands on the local environment, and results in varied institutional linkages for marketing operations. The organizational interdependencies, as defined here, also include relations to other cooperative organizations at district and central levels, and to the government administration (MOCD).

## 3.2 A conceptual note

### *Local environment*

The concept 'local environment' here covers a number of specific aspects which we judge as being of direct consequence for the performance of the societies and their members. These are agro-ecological conditions, access to arable land, level of development of physical and social infrastructure, and degree of differentiation of the local economy.

#### Agro-ecology

Under circumstances where prevailing technologies give little room for controlling or improving existing production potentials, smallholder agriculture is critically dependent on a secure physical resource base. In Kenya, good agricultural land covers only slightly more than one-tenth of the total land area. It is, however, supporting about 60 per cent of the population. In the medium-potential areas, covering another 10 per cent of the land area, production based on conventional smallholder technology is subject to considerable risk-taking. Thus, intermittently, drought and other environmental hazards seriously strain both smallholder households and the operations of supporting service organizations such as cooperatives. The resistance to such fluctuations is certainly higher among households than among organizations. Also, in the absence of a market demand for their services, cooperatives obviously have to cover financially the cost of maintaining the organization. Their ability in this respect is indicated in the data on liquidations and dormancies. Thus, while every second society registered in high-potential areas had ceased operating by 1983, two-thirds of the societies in medium- and low-potential areas had closed down.

## Population

As noted in Chapter 2, Kenya is experiencing a high rate of population growth. In agro-ecologically favoured areas such as Kakamega, Kisii Kiambu and Machakos, the shortage of good agricultural land has already assumed serious proportions.[2] However, it cannot be generally stated that a high rate of population growth necessarily is negative in nature. A certain size and density of population may be a prerequisite for sizeable investments in physical, social and commercial infrastructure – these, in turn, are essential for effective dissemination of improved technologies, and, hence, for raised productivity of land and labour, and for economic differentiation. On the other hand, in the absence of the kind of qualitative changes made possible by adequate transport and communication networks, by education and health facilities and by commercial services, the process may look very different. Ecological changes are part of the picture. Although soil degradation is difficult to measure and diffuse in its effects, its consequences are felt in most of the densely populated areas, and then particularly by already poor households with small holdings. Deforestation, for instance along the Mau Escarpment and the slopes of the Aberdares, can be seen as side effects of this development. The same process is reflected in the spill-over of sedentary argiculture, by the medium of landless smallholders, into ecologically fragile areas of lower potential, as for example in Kitui and Machakos.

Land fragmentation in already densely populated farming areas manifests itself in a growing number of very small holdings. Assuming that most of the households give priority to meet their subsistence requirements, the average marketable surplus per household is likely to decrease or remain stagnant, although total output increases. As will be further discussed in Chapter four, this process may then also undermine the rationale of the mode of organization characterizing cooperatives in Kenya. Households may of course try the alternative of maintaining a commercially oriented production while buying their subsistence requirements. A prerequisite for these 'sell-to-subsist' households,[3] observed for example in Kiambu and Muranga as early as the 1940s,[4] is however the existence of employment opportunities outside the family holding. Even then, it means that the cooperative society has to deal with the collection of an increasing number of small entities of surplus produce with distinct consequences for collection/marketing costs and financial viability and, ultimately, for members' net proceeds. Although it is unlikely that smallholdings with sufficient land to produce both for the market and, if

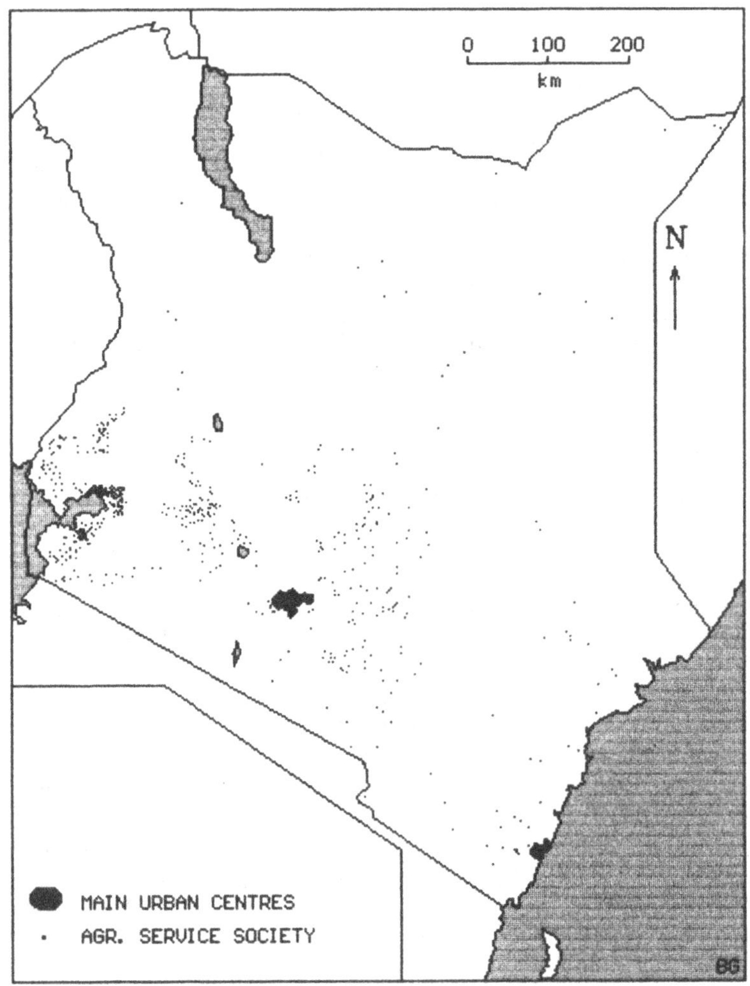


*Figure 3.1* Agricultural service societies registered 1946–83, located in areas with high agro-ecological potential
*Source:* Survey data

needed, for subsistence, will disappear, already a reduction of the stock of such holdings is likely to have repercussions on the viability and impact of the kind of service cooperatives now operating in rural areas.

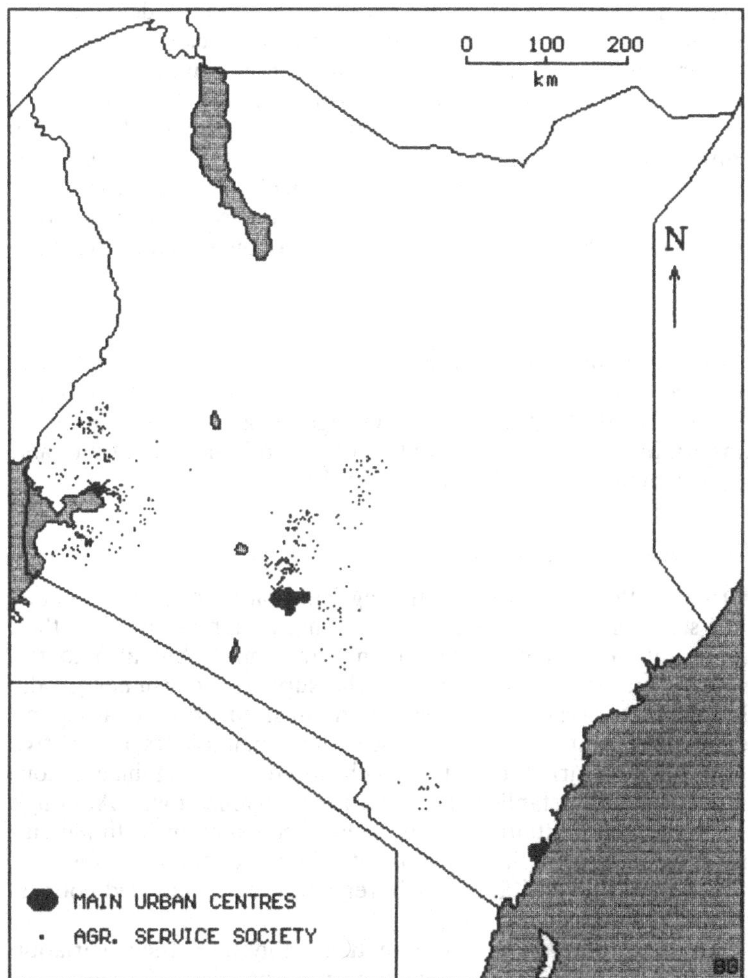


*Figure 3.2* Agricultural service societies registered 1946–83, located in areas with medium or low agro-ecological potential
*Source:* Survey data

## Infrastructure

As regards roads, a dense and reliable network is obviously important both for farmers and societies by reducing costs of interaction. For political and economic reasons, areas with advantageous agro-ecological conditions in combination with a sizeable population generally tend to be given priority in the development of both roads and other types of physical and social infrastructure in rural areas. Apart from the distortions characterizing the colonial period, this has largely also been the case in Kenya. None the less, even among high-potential smallholder areas considerable differences can be observed. In the following it will be assumed that the position of any particular area in terms of the size and density of the road network, can be used as an indication of its rating with regard to other categories of physical infrastructure.

### Education

It may be assumed that raising the level of education in rural areas positively affects the capacity to realize increased production and income levels.[5] This kind of change is also likely to be of importance for members' ability to control the operations and management of societies and unions.[6]

### Economic differentiation

Urban settlements in the major agricultural areas provide goods and services necessary for more productive agriculture. We then refer not only to farm implements and inputs but also to the production-incentives created by the supply of consumer goods. Intensified interaction between medium-sized urban centres and their rural hinterlands may also offer smallholders alternative markets or market outlets, which could have significant consequences for established cooperative organizations. Although economic differentiation can be seen as concomitant with agricultural development, it may also introduce a competitive element which may prove difficult for bureaucratically controlled cooperatives to handle.

To determine these basic features and how their variation affects the operations of cooperative societies, a number of variables have been selected as environmental indicators (see p. 112, 'Survival 1963–70'). In line with the arguments put forward above, environments characterized by high combined ratings in these respects are likely to be of positive consequence for the survival performance of agricultural service cooperatives. The data used for these analyses refer to 1963–70 and to 1971–83. Due to lack of data, the conditions pertaining to the pre-independence period (1946–62) will be considered only in broad terms.

### *Activity orientation and institutional arrangements*

First it should be noted that quite a number of societies are officially registered as multiproduce, although they deal with only one specific type of produce. As part of the compilation of the empirical data base, the activity orientation of such societies has as far as possible been re-classified so as to reflect better their actual marketing operations.

The relationship between survival rate and activity orientation partly follows from the fact that different types of produce have different requirements in terms of timing and physical handling at the stages of collection, transportation, storage and processing. However, it also has to do with their differing requirements in terms of market knowledge, flexibility and efficiency, with the latter being conditioned by government regulations and the operations of public market organizations. The major types of produce marketed through cooperatives are coffee, pyrethrum, cotton, sugar cane, cashew and dairy. Other marketing activities include eggs/poultry, cereals, vegetables and animals.

#### Coffee

Coffee is a high-value crop in terms of returns per hectare. As cherry is heavy and bulky in relation to clean coffee, local first-stage processing is necessary. In smallholder agriculture, it makes sense to organize this kind of activity collectively. Each such 'coffee factory' or hulling unit covers a very limited geographical area. Thus, some of the big coffee societies may each run a considerable number of factories. After hulling and drying, the coffee is delivered to the Kenya Planters' Cooperative Union in Nairobi for grading and final marketing. To get a licence to grow coffee, a smallholder has to be a member of a primary coffee society through which the produce has to be delivered.

#### Pyrethrum

Smallholders deliver their crop through cooperative societies. Only societies and large-scale producers are recognized as suppliers to the Pyrethrum Board's processing plant in Nakuru.

#### Cotton

In Kenya, cotton is also a smallholder crop and cultivation is concentrated in the Lake Victoria region and Eastern province.

Cotton cultivation has consistently given low yields/ha. Due to the bulkiness of the crop, it is dependent on local processing (ginning). Several ginneries were taken over by cooperative unions from private owners in the early 1970s. Primary societies have been granted the right of being exclusive buying agents on behalf of the Cotton Marketing Board within their respective areas of operation.

### Sugar cane

Due to the weight and bulkiness of the crop, cultivation of cane assumes access to local, large-processing capacity (an alternative, though second-best, is the jaggery). In the 1960s, sugar factories were operating only in the so-called Sugar Belt (Kisumu district) and around the coast. Among the cooperatives started in the Sugar Belt in the early 1960s, two categories can be defined. One type is a combined production and marketing society. In 1965, members vested about one acre of land in such primary cooperatives. In return they got parcels at different stages of production cycle, an arrangement which was intended to ensure a steady income. These societies also market their members' privately grown cane. Another type of society is purely marketing-orientated and dominant in the Muhoroni settlement area. For individual members of both categories, there are no obvious alternatives to deliveries through cooperative channels.

### Cashew

In Kilifi and Lamu districts, which are the main production areas, cooperative societies have been granted a marketing monopoly for this crop.

What these types of crops have in common is that they are fairly standard and not very perishable. Furthermore, the individual societies enjoy a marketing monopoly within their geographical areas of operation, and the collected/processed crops are linked to pre-established market channels. This category of produce, to which dairy also belongs, we will term 'preferential'.

### Dairy

Milk collection is demanding both from the time and transport point of view, and thus requires both a developed transport network and access to vehicles. For milk production to be viable, processing plants have to be within a reasonable distance from the production area. Large-scale plants are run by the Kenya Cooperative Creameries and are found mainly in the former White

Highlands. Only large-scale producers and cooperative societies can deliver directly to these plants. For small-scale producers there is of course the option of selling fresh milk on the local market. However, production that cannot be absorbed locally has to be channelled through a cooperative society.

Other activities (produce)

For food crops, eggs/poultry and animals, there are no regulations of the character mentioned above. Although there is a licensing arrangement for maize, this also involves private traders. With reference to the activity classification, these conditions apply to societies classified under cereals (11), vegetables (14), sisal (16), other crops (18), eggs/poultry (22), animals (26) and multiproduce (30). Thus, almost all societies falling under 'other activities' are operating in more competitive environments and often also with types of produce that, in terms of handling, are more demanding.

Summary

In summary, it can be observed that the 'marketing activity' for major types of produce involves collection, first-stage processing, transport of produce, and payment to producers/members. With the exception of food produce, only limited market knowledge is required as parastatals are expected to be able to absorb/pay for delivered produce.

Second, in the cases of coffee, dairy, cotton, sugar, pyrethrum and cashew, cooperatives have been given either preferential treatment or an outright monopsonistic position in relation to primary producers. Or the other way around: in most cases smallholders involved in either of these types of produce have no or very insignificant marketing options. It may be expected that this preferential treatment also has contributed to a superior survival ability of these categories of societies.

### 3.3 Survival 1946–62

*Local environment*

The geographical distribution of registrations and liquidations/dormancies is illustrated in Figures 3.3 and 3.4, while more specific information referring to agro-ecology, districts and activities is given in Tables 3.2–3.5. As regards the role of agro-ecological conditions, our earlier argument that they constitute a basic determinant of the societies' survival prospects seems largely endorsed (Table 3.2).

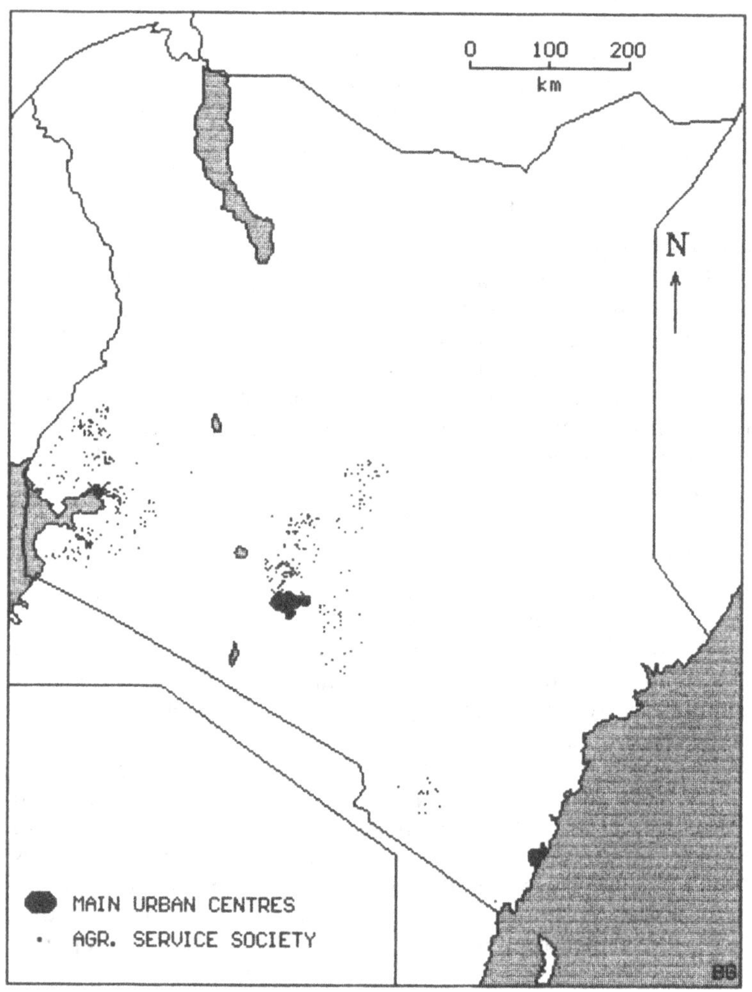


*Figure 3.3* Agricultural service societies liquidated/dormant during 1946–62
*Source:* survey data

However, the 'infrastructural hypothesis' is seemingly not supported as high mortality rates are also found in smallholder districts which, in this respect, offered a more favourable environment (Table 3.3).

This contradiction is more apparent than real. In this initial phase of cooperative development, it was in the districts with,

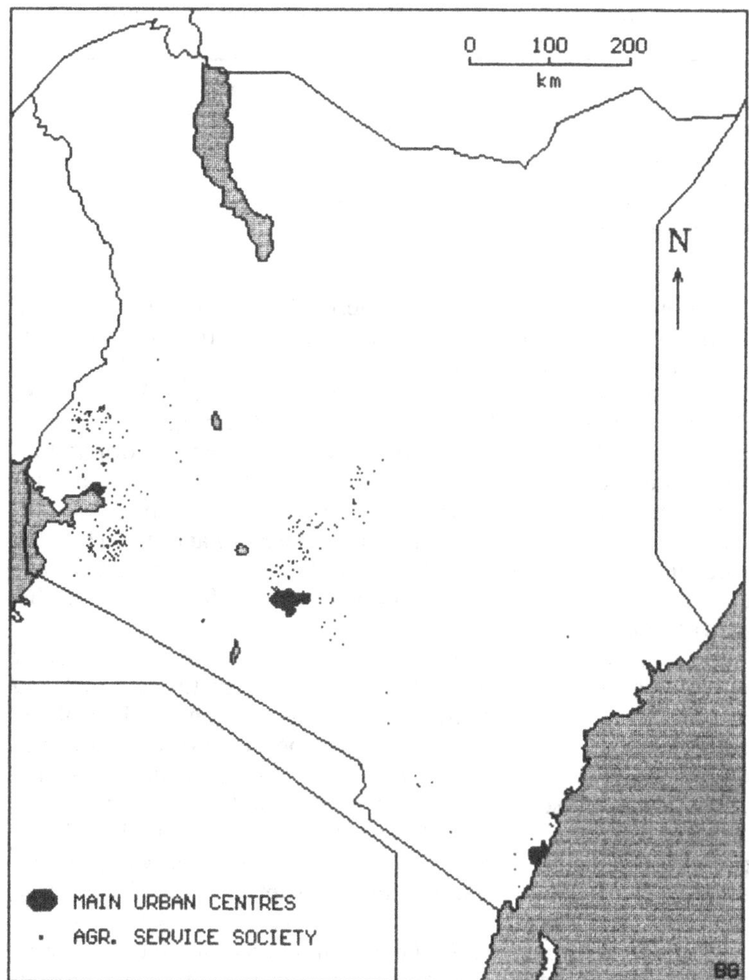


*Figure 3.4* Active agricultural service societies, 1962
*Source:* survey data

relatively speaking, the most differentiated rural economy that cooperatives were first tried. Given the social conditions at the time, though, it has to be assumed that knowledge about how to organize and run cooperatives was thinly spread in rural areas, and it was difficult to get the necessary training. To this should be added the fact that although the early adoptions were concentrated in districts which, in relative terms, were enjoying favourable

*Table 3.2* Societies in register and mortality frequency 1946–62 in relation to agro-ecological conditions

| | *In reg.* | *LD* | *LD %* |
|---|---|---|---|
| High potential | 524 | 293 | 56 |
| Medium/low potential | 194 | 139 | 72 |
| Total | 718 | 432 | 60 |

*Source:* survey data

environmental conditions, they were often probably not, in an absolute sense, sufficiently developed to constitute a stable basis for commercial operations.

The mortality frequencies and rates in Tables 3.3–3.5 illustrate the interdependencies between, on the one hand, activity orientation and local environment and, on the other, activity orientation and institutional linkages to the market. Vegetables and fruit belong to a category of produce which, due to its perishability, require close links to the markets and efficient handling. The high mortality rate for this type of society clearly indicates that neither local conditions nor market knowledge were sufficient to enter this activity successfully.

To a certain extent, the same can be said to apply to dairy operations, which, additionally, require access to transport and to processing facilities within a reasonable distance. Most of the dairy societies established during this period, however, did not market fresh milk but ghee. The main reason behind the close-down of around seventy such societies in the Nyanza and Kisumu districts was that the marketing board which purchased the produce was closed down. In open competition with private traders, the societies did not manage to capture a sufficiently large share of the market.

A similar reason lay behind the liquidation of a large number of egg/poultry marketing societies in western Kenya. During and immediately after the Second World War, the government was a main buyer of this kind of produce. After this arrangement was abolished in the late 1940s, the societies were not able to establish alternative market outlets. In Central province, a substantial number of pig marketing societies were established in the 1950s following a campaign by the Uplands Bacon Factory and the colonial aministration. However, prices and demand did not develop as anticipated, which obviously had adverse repercussions on producers and societies. The majority of societies listed under the categories 'cereals' and 'multiproduce' were most probably

*Table 3.3* Societies in register and frequencies of liquidations/dormancies by district, 1946–62

| *District* | *In reg.* | *LD* | *LD(%)* |
|---|---|---|---|
| Kisumu | 62 | 48 | 75 |
| Kisii | 58 | 4 | 7 |
| S. Nyanza | 73 | 58 | 75 |
| Siaya | 16 | 11 | 69 |
| Kakamega | 71 | 43 | 61 |
| Bungoma | 88 | 50 | 54 |
| Busia | 12 | 4 | 33 |
| Nakuru | 1 | 0 | 0 |
| Baringo | 2 | 1 | 50 |
| Kericho | 15 | 12 | 80 |
| Uasin Gishu | 2 | 1 | 50 |
| Nandi | 3 | 1 | 33 |
| Trans-Nzoia | – | – | – |
| Elgeyo Marakwet | 5 | 0 | 0 |
| West Pokot | 1 | 0 | 0 |
| Laikipia | – | – | – |
| Narok | – | – | – |
| Kajiado | – | – | – |
| Turkana | – | – | – |
| Samburu | – | – | – |
| Nyeri | 49 | 36 | 73 |
| Muranga | 35 | 17 | 49 |
| Nyandarua | – | – | – |
| Kiambu | 83 | 59 | 71 |
| Kirinyaga | 7 | 0 | 0 |
| Kilifi | 4 | 0 | 0 |
| Kwale | 4 | 1 | 25 |
| Lamu | – | – | – |
| Tana River | 1 | 0 | 0 |
| Taita/Taveta | 19 | 14 | 74 |
| Embu | 8 | 6 | 75 |
| Meru | 54 | 35 | 65 |
| Isiolo | – | – | – |
| Kitui | – | – | – |
| Machakos | 45 | 31 | 69 |
| Marsabit | – | – | – |
| Garissa | – | – | – |
| Wajir | – | – | – |
| Mandera | – | – | – |
| Total | 718 | 432 | 60 |

*Source:* survey data

*Table 3.4* Societies in register and frequencies of liquidations/dormancies by activity, 1946–62

| *Activity* | *In reg.* | *LD* | *LD %* |
|---|---|---|---|
| Cereals | 70 | 39 | 56 |
| Coffee | 143 | 28 | 20** |
| Cotton | 5 | 1 | 20** |
| Vegetables, fruits | 32 | 29 | 91 |
| Pyrethrum | 42 | 7 | 17** |
| Other crops | 7 | 7 | 100 |
| Dairy | 92 | 70 | 76 |
| Eggs/poultry | 105 | 99 | 94 |
| Pigs | 31 | 27 | 74 |
| Other animal marketing | 4 | 8 | 50 |
| Multiproduce | 171 | 112 | 69 |
| Unions | 16 | 10 | 63 |
| Total | 718 | 432 | 60 |

*Source:* survey data
*Note*
** Preferential crops

involved in maize marketing, an activity which involved a large number of private traders and thus stiff competition.

Considering the activities with notably high survival rates, primarily coffee and pyrethrum, these societies were breeding under the protection of the marketing monopolies they had been granted. Further, both types of produce were 'robust' in the sense that they did not have to meet very strictly set time constraints during handling and processing. The investments in coffee pulperies were financially supported by the government, and for the farmers the returns were attractive by comparison with those attainable for conventional staple crops. In the case of pyrethrum, required investments in fixed structures and equipment were modest and the whole handling chain, including transport, was clearly compatible with local conditions in the areas meeting necessary agro-ecological conditions.

## 3.4 Survival 1963–70

### *Local environment*

The district is the lowest common level of aggregation for the variables used to depict basic features of the smallholder economy at local level. Although it admittedly introduces an element of over-simplification, the data collected at this level have been used to outline a profile of the local environment of each individual society.

*Table 3.5* Mortality frequency by district and main activity, 1946–62

| | | *Activity* | | | | | | | | | | | | | |
|---|---|---|---|---|---|---|---|---|---|---|---|---|---|---|---|
| *District* | *D. No.* | *11* | *12* | *13* | *14* | *15* | *17* | *18* | *21* | *22* | *23* | *26* | *30* | *35* | *Total* |
| Kisumu | 2 | | | | | | | | 12 | 24 | | | 12 | | 48 |
| Kisii | 3 | | 2 | | | 2 | | | | | | | | | 4 |
| S. Nyanza | 4 | 1 | 1 | | | | | | 47 | | | | 9 | | 58 |
| Siaya | 6 | | 1 | 1 | | | | | | 6 | | | 3 | | 11 |
| Kakamega | 10 | 2 | 3 | | | | 1 | | 2 | 18 | 1 | | 16 | | 43 |
| Bungoma | 11 | 23 | 3 | | | | | | | 10 | | | 11 | 3 | 50 |
| Busia | 12 | 1 | 1 | | | | | | | | | | 2 | | 4 |
| Baringo | 21 | | | | | | | | | | | | 1 | | 1 |
| Kericho | 22 | | | | | | | | 2 | 9 | | 1 | | | 12 |
| Uasin Gishu | 23 | | | | | 1 | | | | | | | | | 1 |
| Nandi | 24 | | | | | | | | 1 | | | | | | 1 |
| Nyeri | 50 | 4 | | | 5 | 2 | | | 5 | | 11 | | 5 | 4 | 36 |
| Muranga | 51 | | 2 | | 3 | 1 | | | | | 10 | | 1 | | 17 |
| Kiambu | 54 | | 4 | | 17 | 1 | | | | 13 | 5 | | 18 | 1 | 59 |
| Kwale | 67 | 1 | | | | | | | | | | | | | 1 |
| Taita/Taveta | 70 | | | 3 | | | | 1 | 1 | 5 | | | 4 | | 14 |
| Embu | 80 | | 3 | | | | | | | | | | 3 | | 6 |
| Meru | 81 | | 6 | | | | | 6 | | 4 | | | 17 | 2 | 35 |
| Machakos | 84 | 7 | 2 | | 1 | | | | | 10 | | 1 | 10 | | 31 |
| Total | | 39 | 28 | 1 | 29 | 7 | 1 | 7 | 70 | 99 | 27 | 2 | 112 | 10 | 432 |
| | | 9.0 | 6.5 | 0.2 | 6.7 | 1.6 | 0.2 | 1.6 | 16.2 | 22.9 | 6.3 | 0.5 | 25.9 | 2.3 | 100.0 |

*Source:* survey data
*Activity codes:* (11) cereals, (12) coffee, (13) cotton, (14) vegetables, (15) pyrethrum, (17) sugar cane, (18) other crops, (21) dairy, (22) eggs/poultry, (23) pigs, (26) animals, (30) multiproduce, (35) unions.

Two sets of district data, which exclude Nairobi and Mombasa, have been compiled. One refers to 1969–71 and is used to analyse the survival performance of societies during 1963–70. The second relates to 1979–83 and is linked to the period 1971–83.

The intra-district differentiation is particularly pronounced in terms of agro-ecological conditions. As regards this specific type of information, however, it was collected for each individual society as part of the survey carried out during 1984–85 (Figures 3.1 and 3.2). To establish broadly the reliability of this classification, it was subsequently checked against the ecological zones defined by IRS 1974–75 and by IADP. Moreover, it is expected that the other indicators used are acceptably representative.

The following indicators have been selected in order to broadly taxonomize the local environments in which service cooperatives operate.[7]

(a) Agro-ecological conditions (HIGH6370, HIGH7183)[8]
*Assumption*: Directly affect stability and level of surplus production.

(b) Population density (DENS70, DENS83)[9]
*Assumption*: In combination with well-developed infrastructure and favourable agro-ecological conditions, high population density contributes to low interaction costs and, hence, to economic integration and differentiation.

(c) Road density (RDCOV70, RDCOV83)[10]
*Assumption*: High densities generally favour interaction, and thus commercialized production, although the magnitude of these effects is conditioned by (a) and (b).

(d) Wage employment (EMPLOY69, EMPLOY79)[11]
*Assumption*: Indicates degree of differentiation of the local economy which here is assumed to positively influence commercialization and productivity in agriculture.

(e) Educational infrastructure (ENROLM69, ENROLM79)[12]
*Assumption*: A generally positive influence on technological and economic development.

(f) Land adjudication (ADJ71, ADJ81)[13]
*Assumption*: Contributes to commercialization of smallholder agriculture.

It would be useful to represent variations in these conditions in more general terms. From Table 3.6 can be observed that the variables are quite closely related, indicating the expediency of such an approach.

Evidently, and in line with the arguments presented earlier, high population density is closely correlated with the coverage of the road network. It is moderately associated with agro-ecological potential and school enrolment ($r>0.5$), while less clearly so with land adjudication and wage employment. An explanation for the low and negative association with wage employment is that the most differentiated economic structure, outside the two main urban centres, developed in the white settler areas. The importance of these districts is accentuated by the fact that the figures on wage employment also include agriculture. Both plantations and large-scale farms have continued to play a significant role in Rift Valley.

Generally high bivariate correlation coefficients can be observed between population density, road density, school enrolment and favourable agro-ecological conditions, while the bivariate association between each of these variables and land adjudication and employment, respectively, are weaker. To capture these multivariate features and 'summarize' them into basic dimensions

*Table 3.6* Correlation matrix, 1963–70

| *Correlations:* | *DENS70* | *RDCOV70* | *ENROLM69* | *HIGH6070* | *ADJ71* | *EMPLOY69* |
|---|---|---|---|---|---|---|
| DENS70 | 1.0000 | 0.8648 | 0.5075 | 0.5559 | 0.3877 | −0.0416 |
| RDCOV70 | 0.8648 | 1.0000 | 0.5617 | 0.5476 | 0.3138 | 0.0982 |
| ENROLM69 | 0.5075 | 0.5617 | 1.0000 | 0.5891 | 0.3242 | 0.4001 |
| HIGH6070 | 0.5559 | 0.5476 | 0.5891 | 1.0000 | 0.1970 | 0.3306 |
| ADJ71 | 0.3877 | 0.3138 | 0.3242 | 0.1970 | 1.0000 | −.1894 |
| EMPLOY69 | −0.0416 | 0.0982 | 0.4001 | 0.3306 | −.1894 | 1.0000 |

*Source:* see text
*Note*
No. of cases: 39

would facilitate further exploration of the relation between variations in local environment and the survival performance of agricultural service cooperatives. The kind of 'dimensions' we are interested in are, of course, those representing clusters of interrelated variables that delineate general patterns of covariation in the data.

The principal components technique produces a solution to this by successively extracting the maximum amount of variance for each such dimension in the data set. Each extracted component will be independent of the others. If there is a major underlying dimension, the first component will account for a large amount of the total variance. Further, if the set of variables is highly interrelated, just a few components may suffice to capture the patterns of covariation in the original data. In this case, two factors, or dimensions, seem sufficient to represent the data. Factor 1 (F1) represents the linear combination of the observed values accounting for the largest amount of variance (50.9 per cent). Another 22.3 per cent of the total variance is attributable to Factor 2 (F2) (see Table 3.7).

The communality specified in Table 3.9 shows how much of the variance of each variable that is accounted for by the two factors. In the factor pattern matrix (Table 3.8) is listed the weights given each variable in defining F1 and F2. These factor loadings offer a basis for interpreting the nature of the underlying dimensions. This is more clearly illustrated by the rotated factor matrix (Table 3.10). The varimax rotation maximizes the number of high and low loadings, and therefore reduces the number of intermediate loadings.

The dimension captured by F1 could be depicted as an agro-ecologically favoured but undifferentiated, agricultural economy dominated by smallholders and with, relatively speaking, a favourable position in terms of transport and education. In its Kenyan context, as earlier argued, this dimension could be termed 'pro-cooperative'. It thus should constitute an environment better suited for the development of agricultural service cooperatives than F2.

The latter dimension portrays a scattered population with a generally lower level of education. Outside a large-scale farm sector, the productivity of both land and labour is lower and the prospects for intensification are impeded by unfavourable agro-ecological conditions and rudimentary physical infrastructure. In its 'pure' form, this dimension would depict a 'pre-cooperative' environment.

*Table 3.7* Principal component analysis, reference period 1963–70

| *Variable* | *Communality* | *Factor* | *Eigenvalue* | *% of var* | *Cum. %* |
|---|---|---|---|---|---|
| DENS70 | 1.00000 | 1 | 3.05607 | 50.9 | 50.9 |
| RDCOV70 | 1.00000 | 2 | 1.33939 | 22.3 | 73.2 |
| ENROLM69 | 1.00000 | 3 | 0.73173 | 12.2 | 85.4 |
| HIGH6070 | 1.00000 | 4 | 0.42674 | 7.1 | 92.5 |
| ADJ71 | 1.00000 | 5 | 0.32743 | 5.5 | 98.0 |
| EMPLOY69 | 1.00000 | 6 | 0.11865 | 2.0 | 100.0 |

*Table 3.8* Factor pattern matrix, reference period 1963–70

| | *Factor 1* | *Factor 2* |
|---|---|---|
| DENS70 | 0.86143 | −0.29735 |
| RDCOV70 | 0.87469 | −0.15070 |
| ENROLM69 | 0.80167 | 0.26749 |
| HIGH6070 | 0.78314 | 0.26516 |
| ADJ71 | 0.47319 | −0.56013 |
| EMPLOY69 | 0.26270 | 0.87901 |

Interpretation of the factor loadings in relation to the individual districts, here representing the societies' local environment, can be taken further by calculating factor scores. The regression factor scores listed in Table 3.12 have been obtained by summing the products of the observed values for the original variables by district and the factor score coefficients in Table 3.11.

Considering the relative position of each district as indicated by F1 and F2, four broad categories of districts (environments) can be identified, of which two are more closely related to the 'pure' dimensions (Figure 3.5).

*Table 3.9* Communality, reference period 1963–70

| *Variable* | *Communality* | *Factor* | *Eigenvalue* | *% of var.* | *Cum. %* |
|---|---|---|---|---|---|
| DENS70 | 0.83048 | 1 | 3.05607 | 50.9 | 50.9 |
| RDCOV70 | 0.78779 | 2 | 1.33939 | 22.3 | 73.2 |
| ENROLM69 | 0.71423 | | | | |
| HIGH6070 | 0.68362 | | | | |
| ADJ71 | 0.53766 | | | | |
| EMPLOY69 | 0.84167 | | | | |

*Table 3.10* Rotated factor matrix (varimax) and factor transformation matrix, reference period 1963–70

| *Variable* | *Factor 1* | *Factor 2* |
|---|---|---|
| DENS70 | 0.90375 | −0.11712 |
| RDCOV70 | 0.88710 | 0.02918 |
| ENROLM69 | 0.73107 | 0.42398 |
| HIGH6070 | 0.71340 | 0.41795 |
| ADJ71 | 0.57663 | −0.45295 |
| EMPLOY69 | 0.07964 | 0.91396 |
| *Factor transformation matrix* | *Factor 1* | *Factor 2* |
| Factor 1 | 0.97937 | 0.20209 |
| Factor 2 | −0.20209 | 0.97937 |

*Table 3.11* Factor score coefficient matrix, reference period 1963–70

| *Variable* | *Factor 1* | *Factor 2* |
|---|---|---|
| DENS70 | 0.32093 | −0.16045 |
| RDCOV70 | 0.30305 | −0.05235 |
| ENROLM69 | 0.21655 | 0.24860 |
| HIGH6070 | 0.21096 | 0.24567 |
| ADJ71 | 0.23616 | −0.37828 |
| EMPLOY69 | −0.04844 | 0.66011 |

Category 1 (C1 63–70)

F1 scores high (>0.9 and F1>F2). Relatively speaking, these districts are those most resembling the 'pro-cooperative' environment. As might be expected, this category covers the major smallholder districts east and west of Rift Valey, i.e.:

| | | |
|---|---|---|
| Kisumu | Bungoma | Nyandarua |
| Kisii | Nyeri | Kiambu |
| Kakamega | Muranga | Kirinyaga |

*Table 3.12* Factor scores by district, reference period 1963–70

| *District* | *Factor 1* | *Factor 2* |
|---|---|---|
| 2 Kisumu | 1.23529 | 0.44722 |
| 3 Kisii | 2.09808 | −1.04615 |
| 4 S. Nyanza | 0.45251 | −0.85610 |
| 6 Siaya | 0.78580 | −0.66934 |
| 10 Kakamega | 1.61879 | −1.01086 |
| 11 Bungoma | 1.10549 | −0.55719 |
| 12 Busia | 0.70780 | −0.69447 |
| 20 Nakuru | −0.30098 | 2.02054 |
| 21 Baringo | −0.62916 | −0.44341 |
| 22 Kericho | 0.29721 | 0.55248 |
| 23 U. Gishu | −0.16031 | −2.13167 |
| 24 Nandi | 0.45065 | 0.55577 |
| 25 T. Nzoia | −0.21759 | 2.23287 |
| 26 Jarakwet | 0.02439 | −0.32596 |
| 27 W. Pokot | −0.43107 | 0.21545 |
| 28 Laikipia | −0.19902 | 2.90364 |
| 29 Narok | −0.41771 | −1.26911 |
| 30 Kajiado | −0.13833 | −1.80814 |
| 31 Turkana | −1.22103 | −0.65504 |
| 32 Samburu | −1.26587 | −0.39185 |
| 50 Nyeri | 1.05767 | 0.53398 |
| 51 Muranga | 1.80582 | −0.33799 |
| 52 Nyandarua | 0.88849 | 0.54453 |
| 54 Kiambu | 1.71219 | 0.67690 |
| 55 Kirnyaga | 1.09871 | −0.30453 |
| 66 Kilifi | −0.60421 | 0.01125 |
| 67 Kwale | −0.74098 | −0.09430 |
| 68 Lamu | −1.22384 | −0.22597 |
| 69 T. River | −1.27223 | −0.46444 |
| 70 Taita | −0.32976 | 1.35986 |
| 80 Embu | 0.48133 | −0.01946 |
| 81 Meru | 0.30251 | −0.24282 |
| 82 Isiolo | −1.18275 | 0.11418 |
| 83 Kitui | −0.93034 | −0.42853 |
| 84 Machakos | −0.04087 | 0.06433 |
| 85 Marsabit | −1.24595 | −0.51833 |
| 95 Garissa | −1.17075 | −0.60553 |
| 96 Wajir | −1.31709 | −0.70160 |
| 97 Mandera | −1.35954 | −0.69356 |

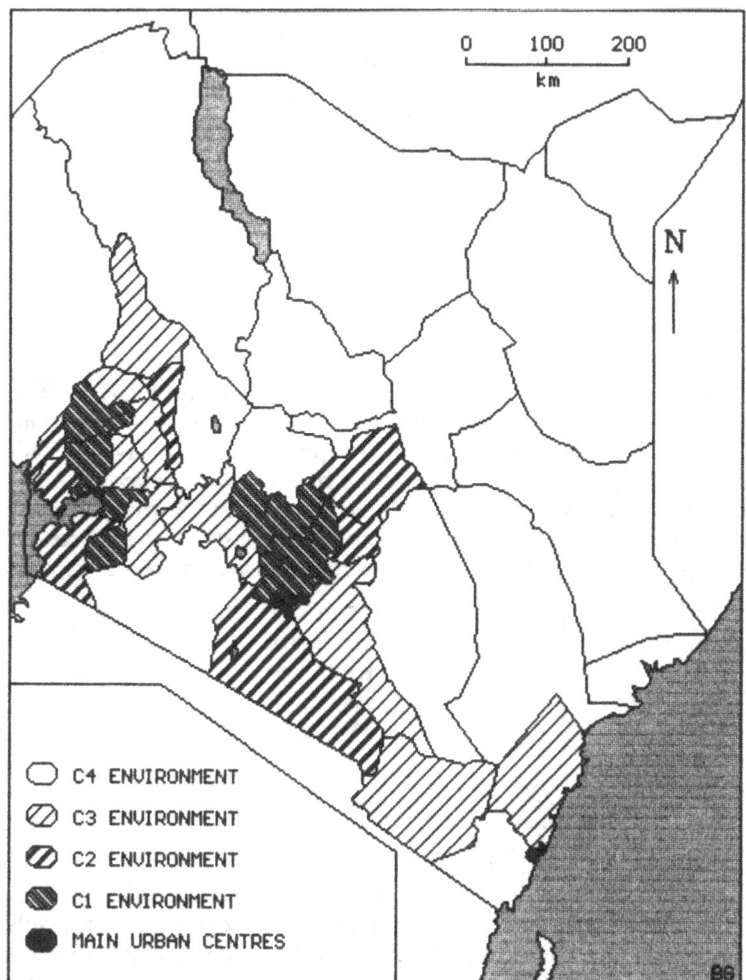


*Figure 3.5* Categories of environments, 1963–70
*Source:* survey data

Within this group, Kisii and Kakamega have slightly deviating profiles caused by high negative scores on F2, indicating that they were lagging behind in terms of land adjudication and economic differentiation.

Category 2 (C2 63–70)

Moderate or low F1 scores (F1>0 and F1>F2). Population density is lower, the road network less developed and agro-ecological conditions more 'mixed', though predominantly favourable. Kajiado is a rather unrepresentative member of this group. The main reason for entrance is its high rating in terms of land adjudication. Districts falling in this category are:

| | |
|---|---|
| S. Nyanza | Kajiado |
| Siaya | Embu |
| Busia | Meru |
| Marakwet | |

Category 3 (C3 63–70)

Low or negative F1 scores (F1>−1.2 and, mostly, F2>F1). The main portion of districts constitutes part of the former White Highlands. Main features are low population density, 'mixed' agro-ecological conditions – with a bias towards unfavourable – and a road network favouring those parts of the districts covered by plantations and large-scale farming. The districts, which can be said to capture features of the 'pre-cooperative' environment, are:

| | |
|---|---|
| Nakuru | Taita |
| Kericho | W. Pokot |
| Nandi | Kilifi |
| U. Gishu | Isiolo |
| T. Nzoia | Machakos |
| Laikipia | |

Category 4 (C4 63–70)

Very low F1 and F2 scores. Semi-arid or arid conditions predominate. Small and scattered population. Low education levels and poor infrastructure. The districts, which can be seen as accentuated 'pre-cooperative', are:

| | |
|---|---|
| Narok | Tana River |
| Baringo | Kitui |
| Turkana | Marsabit |
| Samburu | Garissa |
| Kwale | Wajir |
| Lamu | Mandera |

Calculating the survival rate of societies by each of these four categories of environments, for the period 1963–70, gives the following results;

| *Environment* | *Survival rate* |
|---|---|
| C1 63–70 | 71% |
| C2 63–70 | 68% |
| C3 63–70 | 66% |
| C4 63–70 | 38% |

The findings largely support the argument that the operational environment of agricultural service cooperatives is of direct consequence for their survival performance (Figures 3.6 and 3.7).

To explore further the survival characteristics of societies in relation to the rating of their respective local environments (districts), the factor scores have been included as independent variables in a linear regression model. The presence of a linear relationship (MR=0.61, R2=0.37) again seems to suggest that the local environment, as here defined, exerts a conditioning influence (Table 3.13).

*Table 3.13* Multiple regression; relationship between environmental characteristics at district level (F1 and F2) and survival rates of agricultural societies

| | | | |
|---|---|---|---|
| Multiple R. | | .61186 | |
| R. square | | .37438 | |
| Adjusted R. square | | .33527 | |
| Standard error | | 26.13607 | |
| *Variables in the equation* | | | |
| *Variable* | *B* | *SE B* | *BETA* |
| Factor 2 | 7.23963 | 4.32471 | 0.23488 |
| Factor 1 | 19.69012 | 4.72387 | 0.58484 |
| (Constant) | 52.62662 | 4.48017 | |

The regression model also offers an opportunity to consider more directly survival profiles at district level. Thus, comparison of observed survival performance with that predicted by the regression model facilitates the identification of deviations from expected performance as given by environmental characteristics.

### *Activity orientation and institutional arrangements*

Referring to Table 3.14, some districts display high negative or positive residuals. In the first category, five districts can be singled out: Laikipia (28), Narok (29), Kajiado (30), Nyeri (50) and Kiambu (54), while large positive residuals can be noted for Baringo (21) and Kilifi (66).

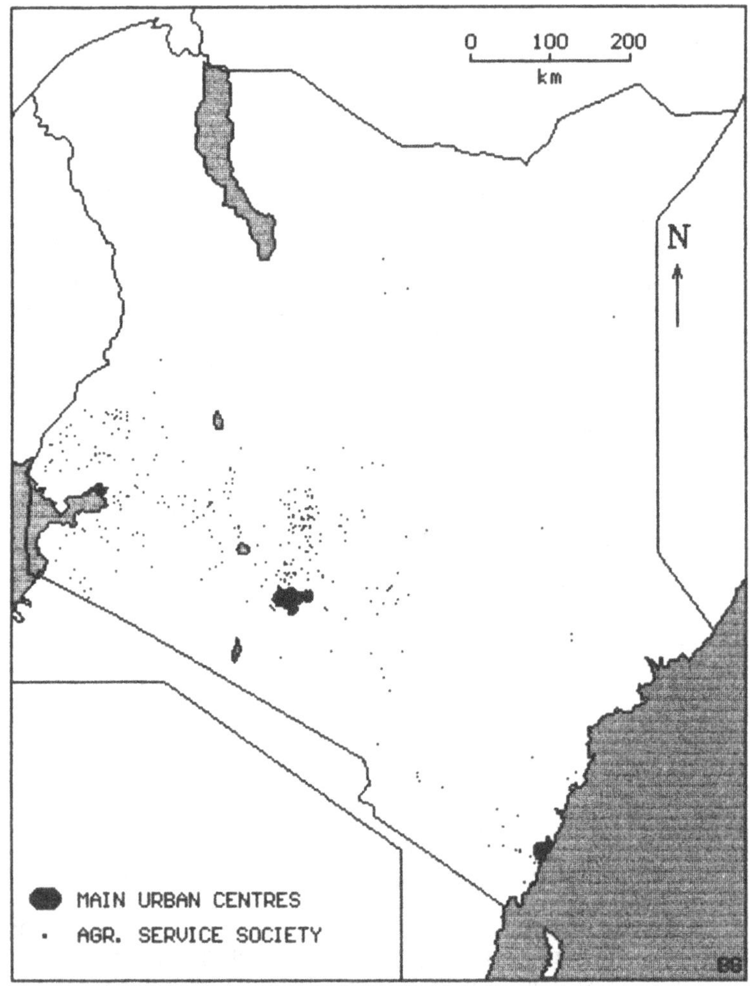


*Figure 3.6* Agricultural service societies liquidated/dormant, 1963–70
*Source:* survey data

It has earlier been argued that activity orientation and institutional characteristics exert a conditioning influence on the survival ability of societies. Hence, there is reason to examine to what extent these aspects may have contributed to observed deviations in predicted survival performance.

Considering activity orientation, the districts representing high negative residuals in the environmental model are specified in

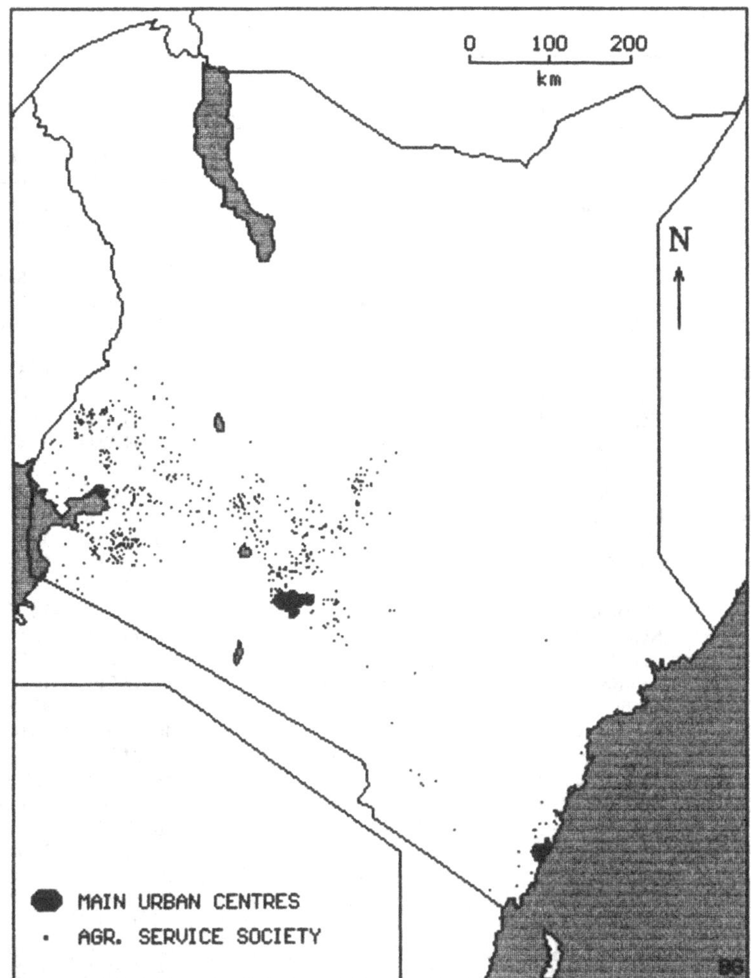


*Figure 3.7* Active agricultural service societies, 1970
*Source:* survey data

Table 3.15. The number of societies in register by activity is listed as well as liquidation/dormancy frequencies. In one respect it appears evident that activity orientation is of consequence. Thus, if one excludes coffee, pyrethrum and dairy, the survival rate of societies in the two districts is 33 per cent (as compared to 75 per cent in other C1 districts). If one considers only the three types of preferential produce, the survival rate is 70 per cent (other C1

*Table 3.14* Casewise plot of standardized residual, reference period 1963–70

| *Case no.* | *District* | *Environm.* | *–3.0 0.0 3.0*<br>*0: . . . . . . . : . . . . . . . :0* | *Surv6370* | **Pred* | **Resid* |
|---|---|---|---|---|---|---|
| 1 | Kisumu | 1 | . *. . | 74 | 80.1881 | –6.1881 |
| 2 | Kisii | 1 | . .* . | 94 | 86.3552 | 7.6448 |
| 3 | Homa Bay | 2 | . .* . | 67 | 55.3308 | 11.6692 |
| 4 | Siaya | 2 | . .* . | 75 | 63.2500 | 11.7500 |
| 5 | Kakamega | 1 | . *. . | 67 | 77.1721 | –10.1721 |
| 6 | Bungoma | 1 | . .* . | 80 | 70.3519 | 9.6481 |
| 7 | Busia | 2 | . * . . | 40 | 61.5294 | –21.5294 |
| 8 | Nakuru | 3 | . * . . | 44 | 61.3412 | –17.3412 |
| 9 | Baringo | 4 | . . * . | 100 | 37.0266 | 62.9734 |
| 10 | Kericho | 3 | . . * . | 76 | 62.4797 | 13.5203 |
| 11 | Uasin G. | 3 | . * . | 68 | 64.9164 | 3.0836 |
| 12 | Nandi | 3 | . . * . | 90 | 65.5248 | 24.4752 |
| 13 | T. Nzoia | 3 | . . * . | 89 | 64.5223 | 24.4777 |
| 14 | Elgeyo M. | 2 | . . * . | 86 | 50.7474 | 35.2526 |
| 15 | W. Pokot | 3 | . * . | 50 | 45.6989 | 4.3011 |
| 16 | Laikipia | 3 | . * . . | 38 | 69.7496 | –31.7496 |
| 17 | Narok | 4 | . * . . | 0 | 35.2049 | –35.2049 |
| 18 | Kajiado | 2 | . * . . | 11 | 42.2452 | –31.2452 |
| 19 | Nyeri | 1 | . * . . | 38 | 77.3182 | –39.3182 |
| 20 | Muranga | 1 | . * . . | 63 | 85.7308 | –22.7308 |
| 21 | Nyandarua | 1 | . . * . | 98 | 74.0638 | 23.9362 |
| 22 | Kiambu | 1 | . * . . | 59 | 91.2407 | –32.2407 |
| 23 | Kirinyaga | 1 | . . * . | 87 | 72.0499 | 14.9501 |
| 24 | Kilifi | 3 | . . * . | 86 | 40.8151 | 45.1849 |
| 25 | Kwale | 4 | . .* . | 46 | 37.3544 | 8.6456 |
| 26 | Tana River | 4 | . .* . | 33 | 24.2121 | 8.7879 |
| 27 | Taita T. | 3 | . *. . | 43 | 55.9907 | –12.9907 |
| 28 | Embu | 2 | . .* . | 71 | 61.9611 | 9.0389 |
| 29 | Meru | 2 | . . * . | 86 | 56.8220 | 29.1780 |
| 30 | Isiolo | 3 | . * . . | 0 | 30.1697 | –30.1697 |
| 31 | Kitui | 4 | . * . . | 18 | 31.2044 | –13.2044 |
| 32 | Machakos | 3 | . . * . | 79 | 52.2886 | 26.7114 |
| 33 | Marsabit | 4 | . * . . | 0 | 24.3416 | –24.3416 |
| 34 | Garissa | 4 | . * . . | 0 | 25.1889 | –25.1889 |
| 35 | Wajir | 4 | . * . . | 0 | 21.6135 | –21.6135 |
| *Case no.* | *District* | *Environm.* | *0: . . . . . . . : . . . . . . . :0*<br>*–3.0 0.0 3.0* | *Surv6370* | **Pred* | **Resid* |

Residual statistics

| | *Min* | *Max* | *Mean* | *STD Dev* | *N* |
|---|---|---|---|---|---|
| *Pred | 21.6135 | 91.2407 | 55.8857 | 19.6143 | 35 |
| *Resid | –39.3182 | 62.9734 | –.0000 | 25.3557 | 35 |
| *ZPred | –1.7473 | 1.8025 | .0000 | 1.0000 | 35 |
| *ZResid | –1.5044 | 2.4094 | –.0000 | .9701 | 35 |

*Table 3.15* Societies in register and liquidations/dormancies by activity in Kiambu and Nyeri districts, 1963–70

| *Activity* | *Act. No.* | *Nyeri* | | *Kiambu* | |
|---|---|---|---|---|---|
| | | *IR* | *LD* | *IR* | *LD* |
| Cereals | 11 | 1 | 1 | – | – |
| Coffee | 12** | 6 | 2 | 16 | 3 |
| Vegetables | 14** | 3 | 3 | 1 | 1 |
| Pyrethrum | 15** | 4 | 4 | 8 | 0 |
| Sisal | 16 | 1 | 1 | – | – |
| Other crop mark | 18 | 2 | 1 | 1 | 1 |
| Dairy | 21** | 9 | 4 | 12 | 2 |
| Eggs/poultry | 22 | – | – | 6 | 2 |
| Pigs | 23 | 1 | – | – | – |
| Other animals | 26 | – | – | 3 | 3 |
| Multiproduce | 30 | 40 | 26 | 25 | 17 |
| Unions | 35 | 1 | – | 2 | 1 |
| Total | | 68 | 42 | 74 | 30 |

*Note*
** Preferential produce

districts 90 per cent). Thus, although there are distinct differences between societies dealing with competitive and protected produce, respectively, these do not explain the *generally* low survival rates. Evidently, one reason has been the political characteristics of Central province during the 1960s. As has been observed by Hydén and Karanja, many politicians saw the creation of cooperatives as a way of furthering both their own interests and those of their respective constituencies.[14] Frequently, these creations were commercially ill-conceived and many of the societies actually registered probably never started any activity.

*Table 3.16* Liquidations/dormancies by activity and Baringo and Kilifi districts, reference period 1963–70

| | | *Baringo* | | *Kilifi* | |
|---|---|---|---|---|---|
| *Activity* | *Act. No.* | *IR* | *LD* | *IR* | *LD* |
| Cereals | 11 | 1 | – | 3 | 2 |
| Pyrethrum | 15 | – | – | – | – |
| Other crops | 18 | 1 | – | 1 | – |
| Dairy | 21 | 3 | 1 | – | – |
| Animals | 26 | – | – | – | – |
| Multiproduce | 30 | 4 | – | 9 | – |
| Unions | 35 | – | – | 1 | – |
| Total | | 9 | 1 | 14 | 2 |

Remaining districts with high negative residuals, i.e. Laikipia (28), Narok (29) and Kajiado (30) all belong to the rural periphery and it can be assumed that, apart from the disadvantageous relative location, lack of knowledge among members about co-operative and managerial issues has played a decisive role.

The high positive residuals noted for Baringo (21) and Kilifi (66) appear rather perplexing. This applies in particular to Baringo. In this case, however, a closer examination of the circumstances under which societies in the district were established, reveals that their registration coincided with the introduction of smallholder settlement programmes. As earlier mentioned, these societies normally constitute part of a 'settlement package' delivered by the state. In that capacity they are assigned the task of administering the repayment of settlement loans. Being as much part of the public sector as cooperative organizations, the societies are likely to be kept alive even in the absence of commercial justification.

Most of the societies in Kilifi are located close to the coast, which also is reflected in their activity orientation. Thus, of the societies classified under 'multipurpose' or 'other crops', six market cashew nuts and the rest copra. The cashew nuts are easy to handle and require a minimum of equipment at the level of the primary society. Moreover, the local market is limited and the societies have been granted a marketing monopoly. In conclusion, it is evident that most of the larger residuals observed at district level can be explained by specific circumstances dependent mainly on activity orientation or institutional arrangements.

There is reason also to more generally consider the importance of the societies' activity orientation and the institutional arrangements to which they are linked. A distinction then has to be made between societies involved in 'protected' marketing activities and those operating under competition from other actors performing a similar function. Generally, it may be expected that these differences are reflected in the survival of the two categories of societies: as shown in Tables 3.17–18, this also seems to be the case.

Societies which operate under more competitive conditions generally have lower survival rates. This can partly be explained by the fact that a much higher proportion of this category of cooperative is found in less favourable environments (C3/C4). Their consistently higher mortality rates may of course also be due to singularly disadvangeous changes in prices and volumes of marketed produce. Using current prices and volumes recorded by

*Table 3.17* Mortality frequency by activity in C1–C4 districts, reference period 1963–70

| | | *Survival rates (%)* | | | |
|---|---|---|---|---|---|
| *Activity* | *Act. No.* | *C1* | *C2* | *C3* | *C4* |
| Cereals | 11 | 74 | 33 | 75 | 40 |
| Coffee | 12** | 88 | 88 | 100 | 50 |
| Cotton | 13** | 75 | 63 | – | 0 |
| Vegetables | 14 | 20 | – | 14 | – |
| Pyrethrum | 15** | 85 | 100 | 92 | 0 |
| Sisal | 16 | 0 | 0 | – | 0 |
| Sugar | 17** | 77 | – | 100 | 100 |
| Other crops | 18 | 82 | 0 | 64 | 100 |
| Dairy | 21** | 73 | 79 | 76 | 100 |
| Eggs/poultry | 22 | 57 | 0 | 50 | 0 |
| Pigs | 23 | 100 | – | – | – |
| Other animals | 26 | 37 | 57 | 55 | 0 |
| Multiproduce | 30 | 58 | 50 | 55 | 53 |
| Unions | 35 | 91 | 60 | 50 | 0 |
| | Average | 71 | 68 | 66 | 38 |

*Note*
** Preferential produce

the marketing boards 1963–70 we can draw up the following information:

| | *Price change (%)* | *Change in output (%)* |
|---|---|---|
| Sugar ** | 17 | 280 |
| Coffee ** | 35 | 41 |
| Cotton ** | –10 | 59 |
| Pyrethrum ** | 0 | 0 |
| Dairy ** | –22 | 0 |
| Maize | –16 | 0 |
| Meat products | 5–50 | N/A |
| Cashew ** | 45 | N/A |

*Note*
** Preferential produce

In the case of sugar cane, coffee and cotton, most of the growth was achieved through expansion of the cultivated area, i.e. by new farmers adopting the crops. As regards cotton, pyrethrum, dairy and maize, prices fell and, with the exception of cotton, marketed volumes stagnated. Generally, it can be observed that the relative position of protected produce was not significantly better than that of the competitive ones, in terms of changes in price and volume.

*Table 3.18* Survival rates by categories of activity and local environment, reference period 1963–70 (excluding unions)

| | *Coffee* | | *Other pref. produce* | | *Other produce* | | *Total* | |
|---|---|---|---|---|---|---|---|---|
| *Environment* | *No. IR* | *Surv (%)* | *No. IR* | *Surv (%)* | *No. IR* | *Surv (%)* | *No. IR* | *Surv (%)* |
| C1 63–70 | 101 | 88 | 117 | 78 | 243 | 60 | 461 | 71 |
| C2 63–70 | 42 | 88 | 63 | 70 | 44 | 35 | 149 | 64 |
| C3 63–70 | 17 | 100 | 41 | 75 | 132 | 51 | 190 | 61 |
| C4 63–70 | 2 | 50 | 9 | 12 | 58 | 31 | 69 | 29 |
| Total/aver. | 162 | 89 | 230 | 73 | 477 | 51 | 869 | 64 |

Consequently, environmental influences and prices are not enough to explain their superior survival rates. Implicitly, this supports our earlier argument that high survival rates are linked to the lower efficiency requirements that follow from marketing protection and which, in turn, implies a more costly intermediary level.

*Conclusions*

During the period 1963–70, marketing was the predominant activity of practically all agricultural service cooperatives. The effects of the new cooperative legislation were still limited. Using survival/mortality rates as a basic performance indicator, it can be concluded that the environment, as here defined, exerted a considerable influence on the survival ability of agricultural service cooperatives. Furthermore, this ability is not determined simply by a specific 'environment threshold'. Rather, survival prospects, conditioned by activity orientation and various institutional arrangements societies may be subjected to, can be arranged along a scale of positions parsimoniously determined by agro-ecology, access to arable land, density of transportation network, education levels, land tenure and degree of economic differentiation.

## 3.5 Survival 1971–83

*Local environment*

To illuminate possible changes in the influence exerted by the local environment, the same basic approach will be followed as in previous sections. If one first considers the overall survival rate of societies during the period (see Table 3.1), it evidently is higher than in the 1960s. This in itself is notable, in view of the considerably lower growth rates experienced both for agriculture and the national economy (see Chapter two). The value of gross marketed production (at constant 1976 prices) developed as follows for major 'cooperative' activities between 1975 and 1983:[15]

| | *Average rate of annual growth (%)* |
|---|---|
| Maize | 3.5 |
| Coffee | 5.5 |
| Pyrethrum | –7.0 |
| Sugar cane | 10.0 |
| Seed cotton | –0.5 |
| Dairy | 0.7 |
| Cashew | –7.0 |
| Livestock prod. (excl. dairy) | 6.6 |

The above figures are based on total values, i.e. including the large-scale sector. However, from this does not necessarily follow that the growth rate for the cooperatively organized smallholder sector would be higher. Thus, the high growth rate recorded for sugar cane has principally been due to the expansion of outgrower schemes and not to increased production among members of cooperatives. Another supporting indication is that the smallholder sector's share of gross marketed production went down from 52.5 per cent in 1972 to 51.2 per cent in 1983.

When examining conditioning influences of the local environment on the survival of societies, highly aggregated indicators are of limited use. Hence, it is again necessary to focus on relations between local conditions (as measured by earlier defined indicators) and on survival rates. Within this context it is apparent that the rural economy underwent changes. By the early 1980s, the land registration programme had been more or less finalized, school enrolment rates had risen substantially, the road network had expanded and, not least, population had grown by over 45 per cent. As regards the level of wage employment in the formal sector, it had fallen slightly and so had the share of societies located in area with favourable agro-ecological conditions.

Compared to 1963–70, raised levels of bivariate correlations can be noted for most of the indicators. Population density is now more closely related to road coverage, school enrolment, high agro-ecological potential and wage employment. As the wage employment ratio, on average, has changed only marginally, the pattern of correlations indicates a shift in favour of the main smallholder areas. The weaker relation between DENS83 and ADJ81 simply illustrates that most of the land adjudication activities have expanded into more sparsely populated areas. Not surprisingly, RDCOV83 shows a stronger association with wage employment and so does school enrolment, as well as agro-ecological conditions. EMPLOY79, on the other hand, is negatively correlated with land adjudication, which supports our earlier observation that a spatial shift of such employment has taken place.

As shown in Table 3.21, principal components analysis results in two factors (dimensions). Of total explained variance (74.6 per cent), 56.1 per cent is attributable to F1 and 18.5 per cent to F2. Compared to 1963–70, the current data set differs both in the sense that covariation generally is higher and that less of the variation now is explained by F2. Basically, however, the two dimensions still retain their basic underlying properties as reflections of what here is perceived as 'pro-cooperative' and 'pre-cooperative' environments (see rotated factor matrix, and score coefficients).

*Table 3.19* Correlation matrix, 1971–83

| *Correlations:* | *SURV7183* | *DENS83* | *RDCOV83* | *ENROLM79* | *HIGH7183* | *ADJ81* | *EMPLOY79* |
|---|---|---|---|---|---|---|---|
| SURV7183 | 1.0000 | .2670 | .3291 | 5152 | .4523 | .0718 | .2298 |
| DENS83 | .2670 | 1.0000 | .9469 | .6656 | .5826 | .0217 | .2250 |
| RDCOV83 | .3291 | .9469 | 1.0000 | .7137 | .6419 | .0131 | .3277 |
| ENROLM79 | .5152 | 6656 | .7137 | 1.0000 | .6985 | –.0094 | .4716 |
| HIGH7183 | .4523 | .5826 | .6419 | .6985 | 1.0000 | –.0529 | .4723 |
| ADJ81 | .0718 | .0217 | .0131 | –.0094 | –.0529 | 1.0000 | –.1554 |
| EMPLOY79 | .2298 | .2250 | .3277 | .4716 | .4723 | –.1554 | 1.0000 |

*Note*
No. of cases:39

*Table 3.20* Principal component analysis; initial statistics, reference period 1971–83

| *Variable* | *Communality* | * | *Factor* | *Eigenvalue* | *% of var.* | *Cum. %* |
|---|---|---|---|---|---|---|
| DENS83 | 1.00000 | * | 1 | 3.36638 | 56.1 | 56.1 |
| RDCOV83 | 1.00000 | * | 2 | 1.11092 | 18.5 | 74.6 |
| ENROLM79 | 1.00000 | * | 3 | .79478 | 13.2 | 87.9 |
| HIGH7183 | 1.00000 | * | 4 | .39911 | 6.7 | 94.5 |
| ADJ81 | 1.00000 | * | 5 | .28261 | 4.7 | 99.2 |
| EMPLOY79 | 1.00000 | * | 6 | .04620 | .8 | 100.0 |

*Table 3.21* Factor pattern matrix, reference period 1971–83

| | *Factor 1* | *Factor 2* |
|---|---|---|
| DENS83 | .87022 | .26535 |
| RDCOV83 | .91514 | .20224 |
| ENROLM79 | .87716 | –.00876 |
| HIGH7183 | .83292 | –.09996 |
| ADJ81 | –.04543 | .84953 |
| EMPLOY79 | .55352 | –.51752 |

*Table 3.22* Communality, reference period 1971–83

| *Variable* | *Communality* | * | *Factor* | *Eigenvalue* | *% of var.* | *Cum. %* |
|---|---|---|---|---|---|---|
| | | * | | | | |
| DENS83 | .82770 | * | 1 | 3.36638 | 56.1 | 56.1 |
| RDCOV83 | .87839 | * | 2 | 1.11092 | 18.5 | 74.6 |
| ENROLM79 | .76948 | * | | | | |
| HIGH7183 | .70374 | * | | | | |
| ADJ81 | .72377 | * | | | | |
| EMPLOY79 | .57422 | * | | | | |

*Table 3.23* Rotated factor matrix (varimax) and factor transformation matrix, reference period 1971–83

| | *Factor 1* | *Factor 2* |
|---|---|---|
| DENS83 | .90521 | –.09107 |
| RDCOV83 | .93700 | –.02043 |
| ENROLM79 | .85871 | .17916 |
| HIGH7183 | .79758 | .26002 |
| ADJ81 | .12063 | –.84215 |
| EMPLOY79 | .44232 | .61528 |
| | *Factor 1* | *Factor 2* |
| Factor 1 | .98091 | .19446 |
| Factor 2 | .19446 | –.98091 |

*Table 3.24* Factor score coefficient matrix, period 1971–83

| | *Factor 1* | *Factor 2* |
|---|---|---|
| DENS83 | .30002 | −.18403 |
| RDCOV83 | .30205 | −.12569 |
| ENROLM79 | .25406 | .05837 |
| HIGH7183 | .22520 | .13638 |
| ADJ81 | .13546 | −.75275 |
| EMPLOY79 | .07070 | .48893 |

*Table 3.25* Factor scores by district

| *Distr. Name* | *Factor 1* | *Factor 2* |
|---|---|---|
| 2 Kisumu | 1.37822 | .28727 |
| 3 Kisii | 2.11377 | −1.07244 |
| 4 S. Nyanza | .40508 | −1.05044 |
| 6 Siaya | .75673 | −.89723 |
| 10 Kakamega | 1.37875 | −.88499 |
| 11 Bungoma | .77249 | −.42182 |
| 12 Busia | .49725 | −.63532 |
| 20 Nakuru | .09524 | 1.67122 |
| 21 Baringo | −.43951 | .01435 |
| 22 Kericho | .84192 | .67279 |
| 23 U. Gishu | .47697 | 1.34956 |
| 24 Nandi | .75442 | 1.00579 |
| 25 T. Nzoia | .42224 | 1.33982 |
| 26 Marakwet | −.04396 | .15323 |
| 27 W. Pokot | −.24691 | −.42091 |
| 28 Laikipia | −.16093 | 1.02246 |
| 29 Narok | −.78068 | −1.88145 |
| 30 Kajiado | −.25964 | −4.16794 |
| 31 Turkana | −1.47670 | −.06804 |
| 32 Samburu | −1.31890 | .15525 |
| 50 Nyeri | 1.03722 | .28268 |
| 51 Muranga | 1.50241 | −.31798 |
| 52 Nyandarua | .52630 | .41685 |
| 54 Kiambu | 1.70573 | .92281 |
| 55 Kirinyaga | .94134 | −.15712 |
| 66 Kilifi | −.59652 | .06914 |
| 67 Kwale | −.47575 | −.08722 |
| 68 Lamu | −.93704 | .39894 |
| 69 T. River | −1.26197 | .20694 |
| 70 Taita | −.34610 | 1.29646 |
| 80 Embu | .36049 | .12478 |
| 81 Meru | .19594 | .08236 |
| 82 Isiolo | −1.10812 | .49446 |
| 83 Kitui | −.82399 | .00527 |
| 84 Machakos | .08620 | .00890 |
| 85 Marsabit | −1.48608 | .09211 |
| 95 Garissa | −1.47309 | .14276 |
| 96 Wajir | −1.53003 | −.06814 |
| 97 Mandera | −1.48277 | −.08517 |

Four groups of district-related environmental profiles can be identified which reflect the same basic properties as the categories having 1963–70 as reference period. As noted below, however, the relative position of some districts has changed.

Category 1

High F1 scores (>0.9) and F1>F2. As earlier argued, this category typifies an environment that, relatively speaking, offers the most favourable conditions for agricultural service cooperatives. Of the districts belonging to this category 1963–70, Bungoma and Nyandarua have shifted to category 2; in both cases the change in position can be linked to, relatively speaking, less favourable road coverage.
Districts:

Kisumu
Kisii
Kakamega
Nyeri
Muranga
Kiambu
Kirinyaga

Category 2

Moderate or low F1 scores (F1>0) and F1>F2. As before, this category of districts is characterized by lower population density, less developed road networks and 'mixed', though in most cases mainly favourable, agro-ecological conditions and high enrolment ratios. To this group has been added, apart from Bungoma and Nyandarua, also Kericho and Machakos. Parts of these districts support large, commercially oriented smallholder populations. Kericho's high F2 scores reflect the importance of the district's tea plantations in terms of wage employment. As regards Machakos, the scores mirror the fact that a major portion of the district has low agricultural potential.
Districts:

S. Nyanza
Siaya
Busia
Embu
Meru
Kericho
Bungoma
Nyandarua
Machakos

Category 3

Low or negative F1 scores and, mostly, F2>F1. As before, most districts formerly part of the White Highlands now belong to this

category. Districts having upgraded their positions and which now belong to this category include Lamu and Kwale at the coast and Kitui (Eastern province). In these cases, the higher F1-scores recorded seem mainly to be due to drastically improved school enrolment ratios.
Districts:

| | |
|---|---|
| Nakuru | Baringo |
| U. Gishu | Kitui |
| Nandi | Taita |
| Marakwet | Kilifi |
| Trans Nzoia | Kwale |
| Laikipia | Lamu |

Category 4

Very low F1 scores and low F2 scores. The scores largely replicate the profile linked to 1963–70, i.e. adverse agro-ecological conditions, low population density, low school enrolment ratio and poor road coverage.
Districts:

| | |
|---|---|
| Narok | Isiolo |
| Kajiado | Marsabit |
| W. Pokot | Garissa |
| Samburu | Wajir |
| Turkana | Mandera |
| Tana River | |

No drastic changes have taken place in the relative position of individual districts. Very generally it can be said that districts at the coast and parts of Central and Eastern provinces have gained while the opposite is true for districts on the fringes of Rift Valley and in the Lake Victoria region (Figure 3.8).

An aspect of interest at this stage of the analysis is the changes that have taken place in the four categories of environments. Considering first the total picture, substantially raised levels can be observed primarily for population density, school enrolment and land adjudication. Road coverage has improved, but not markedly, while the overall level of wage employment is unchanged and the proportion of societies located in areas with favourable agro-ecology has decreased (Table 3.26).

As regards changes in the relative position of the four categories of environments between the reference periods, it can, for the 1971–83 period be noted, that the differences between C1 and C2 are less pronounced (Table 3.27).

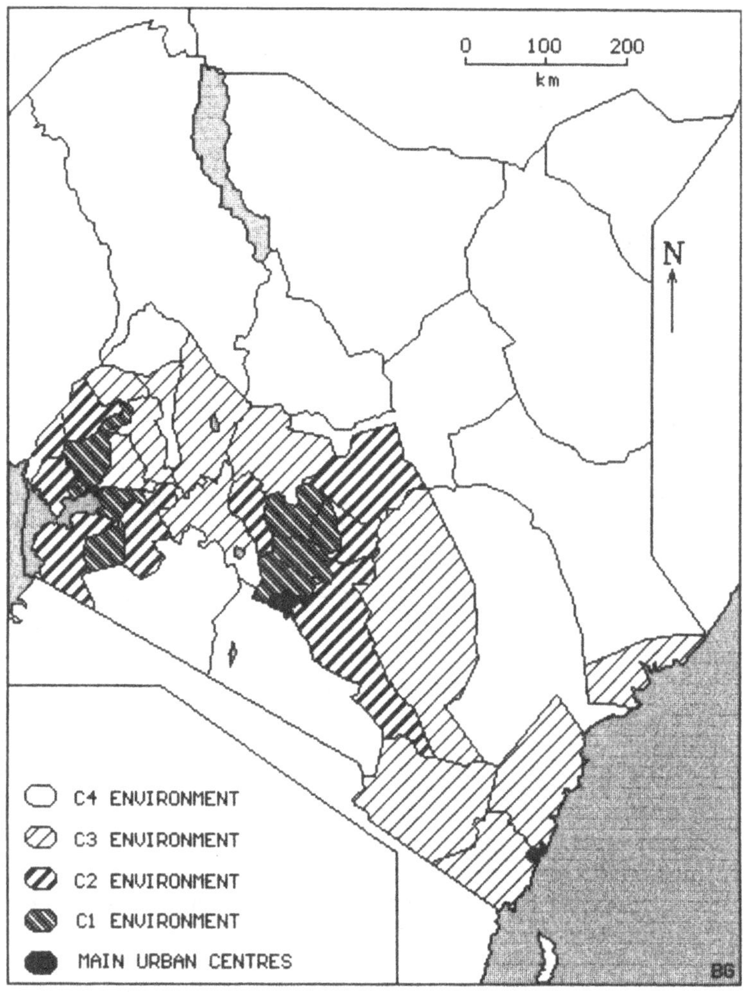


*Figure 3.8* Categories of environments, 1971–83
*Source:* survey data

At the same time, it can be observed that the 'distance' between C1/C2 and C3/C4 has increased. Shifts having contributed to this are particularly evident in the cases of population density, road coverage and wage employment. It may thus be argued that C1/C2, compared to C3/C4, now more distinctly reflect environmental conditions that could be assumed to favour cooperative development. In line with our earlier reasoning, this would also be

*Table 3.26* Changes in environmental indicators between 1969–71 and 1979–83 (1969–71=100)

| | *1969–71* | *1979–83* |
|---|---|---|
| Population density | 100 | 145 |
| Road coverage | 100 | 114 |
| School enrolment | 100 | 221 |
| High agro-eco. potential | 100 | 98 |
| Land adjudication | 100 | 242 |
| Wage employment | 100 | 100 |

*Table 3.27* Environmental profiles, 1963–70 and 1971–83 (Index A) 63–70=100 (B) 71–83=100)

| *Ref. period* | *Envir. categ.* | *Pop. density* | *Road coverage* | *School enrolment* | *High pot. land* | *Adjud. land* | *Wage employm.* |
|---|---|---|---|---|---|---|---|
| 1963–70 | C1 | 100 | 100 | 100 | 100 | 100 | 100 |
| | C2 | 49 | 58 | 74 | 55 | 104 | 44 |
| | C3 | 22 | 29 | 71 | 82 | 18 | 211 |
| | C4 | 5 | 13 | 26 | 16 | 27 | 33 |
| 1971–83 | C1 | 100 | 100 | 100 | 100 | 100 | 100 |
| | C2 | 58 | 60 | 97 | 79 | 118 | 75 |
| | C3 | 18 | 28 | 79 | 66 | 42 | 108 |
| | C4 | 2 | 12 | 26 | 12 | 153 | 33 |

reflected in survival rates. This, however, is not the case (Figures 3.9–10). There is actually a negligible difference in survival rates between environments of type C1–C3, and even for C4 the rate has risen considerably. As illustrated below, the differences are small also between C1/C2 and C3/C4.

| *Environmental category* | *Survival rate* |
|---|---|
| C1 71–83 | 70 |
| C2 71–83 | 75 |
| C3 71–83 | 73 |
| C4 71–83 | 53 |
| C1/C2 71–83 | 74 |
| C3/C4 71–83 | 70 |

In contradistinction to the periods 1946–62 and 1963–70, the local enrvironment apparently has lost much of its influence on the survival rate of agricultural societies. The weakened relation between environmental differentiation and variations in survival

*Table 3.28* Multiple regression; relationship between environmental characteristics at district level (F1 and F2) and survival rates of agricultural societies (reference period 1971–83)

| | | | |
|---|---|---|---|
| Multiple R. | | .40044 | |
| R. square | | .16035 | |
| Adjusted R. square | | .11237 | |
| Standard error | | 24.67006 | |
| *Variables in the equation* | | | |
| *Variable* | *B* | *SE B* | *BETA* |
| Fact2 | 1.88703 | 4.00338 | .07301 |
| Fact1 | 10.40997 | 4.09954 | .39331 |
| (Constant) | 67.09377 | 4.00458 | |

*Table 3.29* Casewise plot of standardized residual, reference period 1971–83

| *Case no.* | *District* | *Environm.* | *–3.0 0.0 3.0*<br>*0: . . . . . . . : . . . . . . . :0* | *Surv7183* | **Pred* | **Resid* |
|---|---|---|---|---|---|---|
| 1 | Kisumu | 1 | . *. . | 77 | 81.9831 | –4.9831 |
| 2 | Kisii | 1 | . .* . | 95 | 87.0743 | 7.9257 |
| 3 | S. Nyanza | 2 | . * . . | 53 | 69.3284 | –16.3284 |
| 4 | Siaya | 2 | . *. . | 67 | 73.2782 | –6.2782 |
| 5 | Kakamega | 1 | . * . . | 48 | 79.7765 | –31.7765 |
| 6 | Bungoma | 2 | . * . . | 45 | 74.3394 | –29.3394 |
| 7 | Busia | 3 | . .* . | 83 | 71.0713 | 11.9287 |
| 8 | Nakuru | 3 | . * . | 69 | 71.2389 | –2.2389 |
| 9 | Baringo | 3 | . . * . | 87 | 62.5456 | 24.4544 |
| 10 | Kericho | 2 | . .* . | 87 | 77.1277 | 9.8723 |
| 11 | Uasin G. | 3 | . .* . | 83 | 74.6057 | 8.3943 |
| 12 | Nandi | 3 | . * . | 74 | 76.8452 | –2.8452 |
| 13 | T. Nzoia | 3 | . *. . | 62 | 74.0175 | –12.0175 |
| 14 | Elegeyo M. | 3 | . . * . | 82 | 66.9253 | 15.0747 |
| 15 | W. Pokot | 4 | . .* . | 71 | 63.7291 | 7.2709 |
| 16 | Laikipia | 3 | . *. . | 56 | 67.3479 | –11.3479 |
| 17 | Narok | 4 | . . * . | 70 | 55.4165 | 14.5835 |
| 18 | Kajiado | 4 | . * . | 60 | 56.5260 | 3.4740 |
| 19 | Turkana | 4 | . * . . | 33 | 51.5930 | –18.5930 |
| 20 | Nyeri | 1 | . *. . | 73 | 78.4246 | –5.4246 |
| 21 | Muranga | 1 | . *. . | 71 | 82.1338 | –11.1338 |
| 22 | Nyandarua | 2 | . . * . | 99 | 73.3592 | 25.6408 |
| 23 | Kiambu | 1 | . * . . | 64 | 86.5917 | –22.5917 |
| 24 | Kirinyaga | 1 | . . * . | 94 | 76.5966 | 17.4034 |
| 25 | Kilifi | 3 | . . * . | 94 | 61.0145 | 32.9855 |
| 26 | Kwale | 3 | . *. . | 56 | 61.9766 | –5.9766 |
| 27 | Lamu | 3 | . . * . | 100 | 58.0920 | 41.9080 |
| 28 | Tana River | 4 | . *. . | 50 | 54.3472 | –4.3472 |
| 29 | Taita T. | 3 | . . * . | 90 | 65.9373 | 24.0627 |
| 30 | Embu | 2 | . . * . | 91 | 71.0819 | 19.9181 |
| 31 | Meru | 2 | . .* . | 76 | 69.2889 | 6.7111 |

| | | | –3.0 0.0 3.0 | | | |
|---|---|---|---|---|---|---|
| *Case no.* | *District* | *Environm.* | *0: . . . . . . . : . . . . . . . :0* | *Surv7183* | **Pred* | **Resid* |
| 32 | Isiolo | 4 | . * . . | 0 | 56.4913 | –56.4913 |
| 33 | Kitui | 3 | . *. . | 54 | 58.5261 | –4.5261 |
| 34 | Machakos | 2 | . . * . | 89 | 68.0079 | 20.9921 |
| 35 | Marsabit | 4 | . * . . | 0 | 51.7976 | –51.7976 |
| 36 | Garissa | 4 | . .* . | 60 | 52.0283 | 7.9717 |
| 37 | Mandera | 4 | . . * . | 100 | 51.0376 | 48.9624 |
| 38 | Wajir | 4 | . * . . | 0 | 51.4974 | –51.4974 |
| *Case no.* | *District* | | *0: . . . . . . . : . . . . . . . :0* | *SURV7183* | **Pred* | **Resid* |
| | | | *–3.0 0.0 3.0* | | | |

Residuals statistics

| | *Min* | *Max* | *Mean* | *STD Dev* | *N* |
|---|---|---|---|---|---|
| *Pred | 51.0376 | 87.0743 | 67.4474 | 10.4855 | 38 |
| *Resid | –56.4913 | 48.9624 | .0000 | 23.9940 | 38 |
| *ZPred | –1.5650 | 1.8718 | –.0000 | 1.0000 | 38 |
| *ZResid | –2.2899 | 1.9847 | .0000 | .9726 | 38 |

rates is supported by regression analysis (Table 3.28). As expected, observed survival rates frequently are below those predicted by the regression model in C1 environments while they tend to exceed predicted values in the less favourable environments (Table 3.29).

### *Activity orientation and institutional arrangements*

Examination of the major categories of activities further supports the observation that environmental conditions explain little of the survival characteristics of primary societies in the period 1971–83 (Table 3.30).

The survival rates have risen for the three major activity types, *including* societies operating under more competitive conditions. For the latter category, however, can also be noted a rather odd distribution of rates among the main categories of local environments. Thus, C1, which according to our taxonomy offers more favourable conditions, displays a survival rate which is below even that of marginal areas. Some of the reasons will be dealt with in the following chapter in connection with the analysis of societies' managerial performance. Already here though, there is ground to consider some aspects of the relationship between state and cooperatives.

The reduced importance of the local environment seems to be

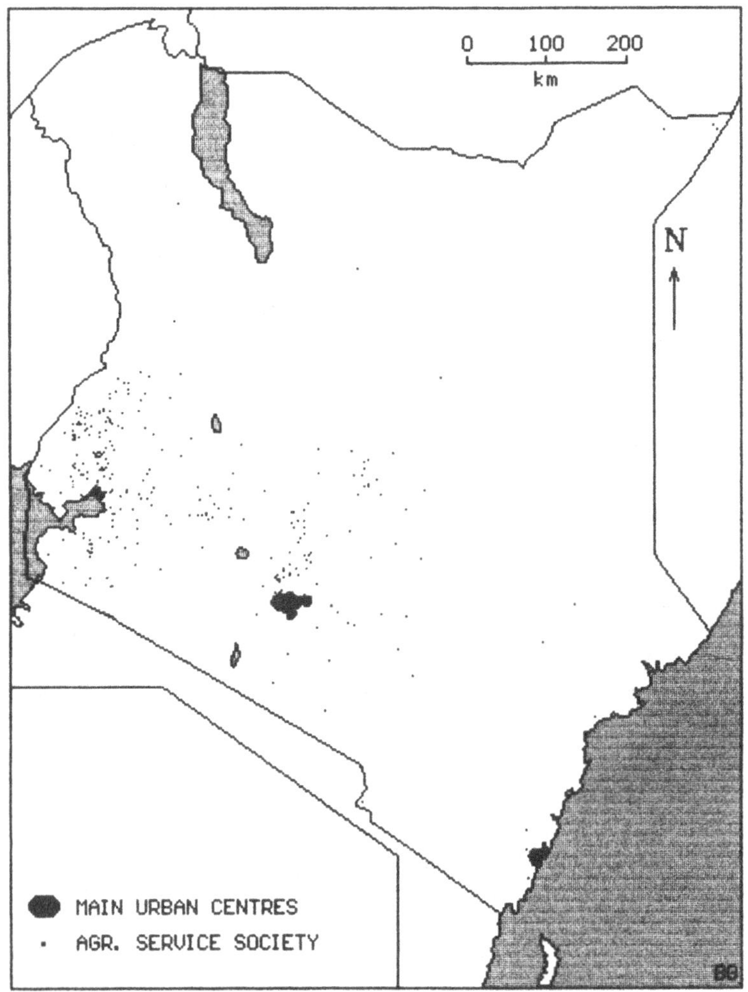


*Figure 3.9* Agricultural services societies, liquidated/dormant, 1971–83
*Source:* survey data

closely linked to two consecutive, and related, changes in institutional relations between the state and cooperatives, namely strengthened state control and expanded development support. As earlier mentioned, there was the introduction of new cooperative legislation in the late 1960s (the Act 1967, the Ordinance 1969). The new law established the foundation for a second innovation,

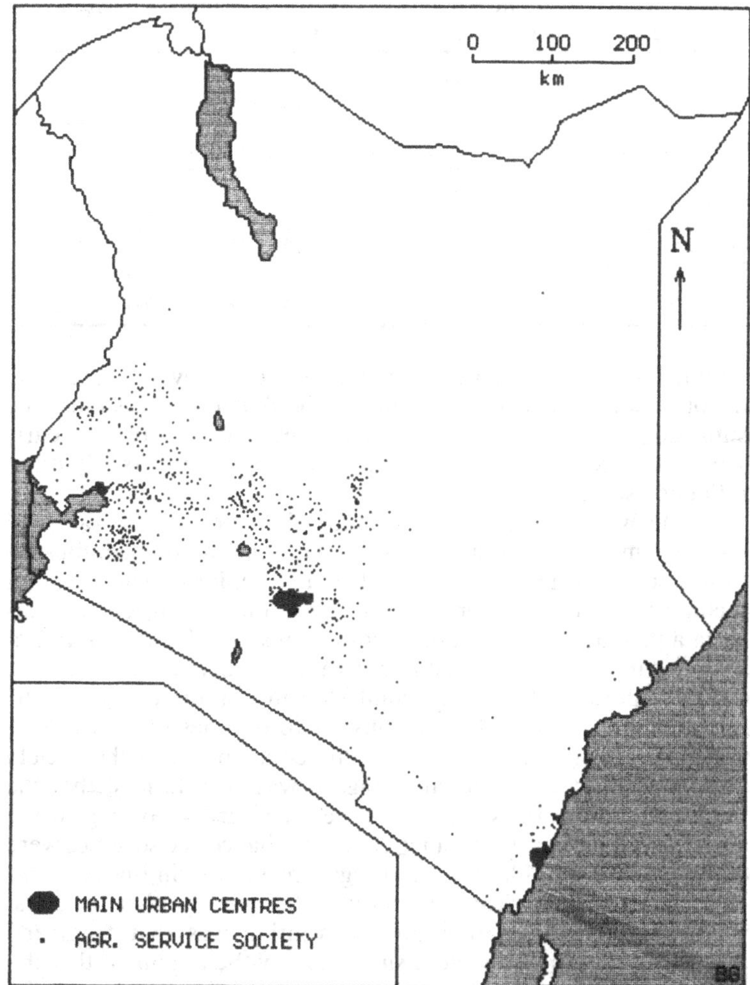


*Figure 3.10* Active agricultural service societies, 1983, excluding societies registered 1981–83
*Source:* survey data

namely the integration of cooperatives with the government's rural and agricultural development activities.

It is clear that the legislation made cooperative organizations subordinate to government to such an extent that members in most respects lost their right to manage their societies independently. The Commissioner was empowered to regulate, in quite some

*Table 3.30* Survival rates by category of activity and local environment, 1971–83 excluding secondary societies (unions)

| | *Coffee* | | *Other pref. produce* | | *Other produce* | | *Total* | |
|---|---|---|---|---|---|---|---|---|
| *Environment* | *No. IR* | *Surv. (%)* | *No. IR* | *Surv. (%)* | *No. IR* | *Surv. (%)* | *No. IR* | *Surv. (%)* |
| C1 71–83 | 78 | 94 | 124 | 88 | 120 | 35 | 322 | 69 |
| C2 71–83 | 87 | 95 | 81 | 77 | 203 | 66 | 371 | 75 |
| C3 71–83 | 4 | 75 | 48 | 94 | 179 | 68 | 231 | 73 |
| C4 71–83 | 1 | 100 | 3 | 66 | 41 | 52 | 45 | 53 |
| Total/aver. | 170 | 94 | 256 | 85 | 543 | 58 | 969 | 72 |

detail, the organization of individual societies, even at the level of providing exhaustive designs of book-keeping systems and supporting administrative routines. During the 1970s and early 1980s, additional regulations further reduced members' ability to influence society operations.

In the wake of the new legislation there followed a range of concrete measures intended to streamline the internal administration and management of societies and unions. These rather technocratic, donor-supported and centrally designed systems were a product of the ambition both to ensure effective control of societies/unions and to facilitate diversified services to members. As then perceived, an important step in this direction was the introduction of integrated administrative routines to record marketing, credit and input supply transactions between the society and its members. At an early stage it was also decided that the implementation of systems would be scheduled according to the societies' economic importance. It meant that coffee societies were given priority, and the system designs introduced in this category of societies were basically to be replicated also in other societies.

The official justification for intervention was that members' interests had to be protected, supported by the argument that the measures were temporary in nature. According to the official view, the necessary steps would be taken to ensure cooperatives a more independent position, but not until they were judged as sufficiently mature. In the early 1970s, the possible long-term consequences of this socialization drive seems to have been overshadowed by perceived short-term gains in the form of improved stability and diversified services to members. In this respect the achievements in the coffee sector largely set the pace for subsequent interventions in other societies.

The increasing number of societies that were reorganized and subjected to strengthened government control, was possibly the major reason behind the higher survival rates. Gross mismanagement of societies could no longer go on unnoticed by the authorities. The fact that cooperatives gradually were being officialized may also have contributed to increasing reluctance among government officers at provincial and district levels to allow societies to cease existing, i.e. to have them liquidated. Considerations of this nature certainly are applicable to the large number of service societies that had been established in settlement schemes in Rift Valley and Central province. As these societies conventionally were assigned the responsibility of collecting members' repayment of settlement loans, by deducting amortization from proceeds on delivered produce, dormancies and liquidations had to be avoided even in the absence of member support.

As has been noted earlier, the officialization of agricultural service cooperatives had considerable consequences for the size and complexity of government administration at central level. The staff changes at the MOCD, in particular, could be used to substantiate further the possible relation between strengthened government control and raised survival rates among agricultural service societies. To adjust for the impact of the expansion of non-agricultural societies on the MOCD during the period 1971–83, the figures used in the following (Table 3.31) are based on the *exclusion* of *all* staff deployed at headquarters and provincial levels.

Generally, the information in Table 3.31 seems to confirm that the MOCD's rather spectacular expansion has been of consequence for the survival of cooperatives. With reference to 1983, though, no apparent variations can be noted as regards staff/society ratios for C1–C3 environments. On the other hand, a clear differentiation can be observed if instead staff deployment in relation to total number of members of agricultural service societies is considered. This may be partly due to the fact that environments of types C3/C4 cover large geographical areas and therefore are more demanding in terms of staff. When considering changes over the period, however, it becomes evident that this is not the only explanation. As the differences have become more accentuated, it can be concluded that the MOCD has intensified its supervisory and supporting activities outside the major smallholder areas. This would also be a major reason behind the unexpectedly high survival rates of societies operating in these less favourable environments. An additional, closely related reason can be identified for both the generally raised survival rates and the positive deviations notable for societies operating under inimical environmental conditions.

*Table 3.31* MOCD-staff and MOCD-staff ratios by type of local environment, 1973 and 1983

| Environm. category | Survival rate (%) 1963–70 | Survival rate (%) 1971–83 | District staff[1,3] 1973 | District staff[1,3] 1983 | Ratio staff/ IR71–83[2] | Ratio[3] staff time[4]/ members[5] 1970 | Ratio[3] staff time[4]/ members[5] 1983 |
|---|---|---|---|---|---|---|---|
| 1 | 71 | 70 | 126 | 347 | 1.04 | 0.9 | 1.3 |
| 2 | 68 | 75 | 74 | 433 | 1.12 | 1.6 | 2.1 |
| 3 | 66 | 73 | 126 | 243 | 1.02 | 4.2 | 6.5 |
| 4 | 38 | 53 | 38 | 142 | 3.15 | 10.9 | 32.6 |
| Total/aver. | 67 | 72 | 364 | 1,165 | 1.16 | 1.4 | 2.3 |

*Source:* Min. of Coop. Development, survey data

*Notes*

1 See Appendix 2 for listing by district.
2 See Table 3.1 for definition and Appendix 2 for listing by district.
3 To facilitate comparison of the ratios for 1973 and 1983, respectively, data on staff 1973 and members 1970 refer to 'B-environments' and 1983 data to 'C-environments'.
4 Assuming 1,900 working hrs per year and staff member.
5 See Appendix 1 for listing by district.

In the early 1970s, as noted in Chapter two, donor agencies voiced increasing concern over deepening social and regional inequalities both within a national context and with reference specifically to rural areas.[16] It had become clear that agricultural growth was losing momentum and this trend was further aggravated by changes in the international economy, principally the direct and indirect effects of the first so-called oil crisis. To be able to raise the productivity and growth of agriculture, an 'integrated approach' to smallholder development was seen as necessary. Strengthening of conventional types of infrastructure was seen as less important than investment into 'directly productive sectors'.[17] Essential components of this strategy included strengthened research and extension services, and, not least, improved access to credit and farm inputs. Increased efforts to spread input intensive technologies, in turn, made it necessary to strengthen existing delivery systems for smallholders.[18] Geographically, areas of medium potential and relatively sparsely populated were to be paid particular attention as they were seen as offering good prospects for realizing raised production and income levels (i.e. areas largely equivalent to the C3-environment).

For the cooperative sector, constituting part of the so-called delivery system, these particular adjustments of the rural and agricultural development strategies had obvious repercussions. In a sessional paper of 1975, is thus confirmed a shift in cooperative development policy which, at that time, already had significantly affected the activity profile of societies and unions in high potential areas. Thus,

> In agriculture, in particular, the government wishes to see the cooperative movement being strengthened and able to reach a greater number of the small-scale farmers so that it can efficiently supply agricultural inputs and be an effective channel for seasonal credit to the small-scale farming sector.
>
> (Rep. of Kenya 1975: 26)

Subsequent to the introduction of reformed administrative systems, primarily in coffee societies, a Cooperative Production Credit Scheme had been implemented. In the early 1970s, it was generally considered as a success. However, in line with the control philosophy characterizing the new organizational structure, the CPCS was confined mainly to societies with proven financial viability and which marketed produce for which they enjoyed a monopsonistic position relative to their members.

According to these criteria, most societies did not qualify for the CPCS. Outside the coffee zones, the majority of societies were either financially weak or could not base their credit activities on sufficiently secure types of 'anchor produce'.

*Table 3.32* Number of loan disbursements channelled through Cooperative Bank, 1977–83 and estimated number of primary societies reached 1971–83

| *Environment* | *No. of loans disbursed to unions/societies* | *No. of societies reached* |
|---|---|---|
| C1 71–83 | 319 | 165 |
| C2 71–83 | 427 | 203 |
| C3 71–83 | 150 | 87 |
| C4 71–83 | 25 | 12 |
| Total | 921 | 467 |

*Source and notes:* see Table 3.33

With changing strategies, now emphasizing the role of input-intensive technologies and the delivery systems on which they would depend, development support to these categories of societies increased markedly. From 1974, a growing number of schemes, usually financed or supported by donor agencies, were introduced to improve smallholders' access to credit and inputs. In almost all cases, agricultural service cooperatives were utilized as part of the delivery system. Hence, apart from providing financial and technical assistance required for credit and input supply services, these

*Table 3.33* Loan disbursements* from Cooperative Bank by 'activity produce' profile and category of local environment** (K.Sh. '000)

| *Category* | *Coffee* | *Other pref. produce* | *Non-protected produce* | *Unions**** | *Total* |
|---|---|---|---|---|---|
| C1 71–83 | 71,992 | 13,084 | 3,503 | 50,506 | 139,085 |
| C2 71–83 | 102,909 | 3,409 | 18,449 | 181,934 | 306,701 |
| C3 71–83 | 466 | 3,728 | 18,422 | 30,036 | 52,652 |
| C4 71–83 | – | – | 5,340 | – | 5,340 |
| | *175,367* | *20,221* | *45,714* | *262,476* | *503,778* |
| Unions' loans according to 'produce profile' of affiliated societies | 50,593 | 180,221 | 31,662 | (262,476) | |
| Total | 225,960 | 200,442 | 77,376 | 503,778 | |

*Sources:* Cooperative Bank, Intern. Records, survey data

*Notes*

* Original loan disbursements by CBK for loans with balances outstanding by the end of 1983. Most of these loans were disbursed during the period 1977–83.

** Loan/credit schemes included are NSCS, CPCS, FISS, IADP, SCIP, SPSCP, MIDP, NPDP, FGM, Coop. Dev. Fund, KFW, Cotton advances, vehicle loans, loans for buildings, and for working capital. As regards CPCS, only funds provided by CBK have been considered; most of CPCS's financial requirements are covered internally by participating cooperatives.

*** Usually, funds for smallholder credit are lent to unions, which in turn on-lend to affiliated primary societies. Due to the time and resources required for data collection, it has not been possible to determine exactly how much of the disbursements have actually reached individual primary societies and their members either as production credit or for other uses.

*Table 3.34* Average size of loan disbursements per member by type of local environment and produce profile (K.Sh.)

| *Category* | *Coffee* | *Other pref. produce* | *Other produce* | *Total excl. unions* | *Total incl. unions* |
|---|---|---|---|---|---|
| C1 71–83 | 277 | 84 | 165 | 203 | 319 |
| C2 71–83 | 432 | 67 | 283 | 352 | 867 |
| C3 71–83 | 677 | 476 | 479 | 482 | 1,122 |
| C4 71–83 | – | – | 915 | 915 | 915 |
| Average | 352 | 95 | 350 | | |
| Average, incl. unions | 454 | 940 | 590 | | 523 |

*Source:* See Table 3.33

projects or schemes usually also included measures to strengthen the operational capacity of societies through construction of stores, procurement of vehicles and other equipment, training, and through subsidies to cover the cost of hiring additional staff.

Tables 3.32–34 indicate the importance of schemes/projects

with credit/loan components channelled through the Cooperative Bank. A note should be made regarding the low survival rates that can be observed for some districts west of Rift Valley, in particular Kakamega and Bungoma. Although the MOCD's staff deployment ratios are high in both districts, this factor alone apparently has not been enough to compensate for the fact that (i) a high proportion of societies dealt with 'competitive' produce, and (ii) that the support in the form of credit and loans has been rather low, particularly in Kakamega. More generally, however, shifts in agricultural policies in favour of delivery systems, and subsequent changes in support of agricultural service cooperatives, have contributed significantly to both raised overall survival rates characterizing the 1971–83 period and to unexpectedly high survival rates in less favourable environments.

### *Summary and conclusion*

Over the period 1946–83, the survival rate of agricultural service cooperatives rose steadily, i.e. from 40 per cent in 1946–62 to 67 per cent in 1963–70, and 72 per cent in 1971–83. Additionally, during the first two periods, the rates of survival were clearly influenced by environmental conditions. Thus, environments being favoured in terms of agro-ecology and basic infrastructure normally also displayed lower mortality rates. Survival was also influenced by the kind of produce societies were handling. Produce for which cooperatives enjoyed a monopsony status *vis-à-vis* smallholders, generally displayed higher survival rates.

In the period 1971–83, however, the relation between environment and survival became insignificant, and also the association between produce orientation and survival seemed less clear. According to our analysis, two principal causes can be identified. The first one has its origins in the new cooperative law promulgated in the late 1960s, which resulted in intensified state supervision and control of societies. Major subsequent changes included organizational and administrative transformation of societies and unions, and strengthening of the ministry's field staff.

Second, while in the 1960s agricultural development in the smallholder sector largely focused on markets and produce, i.e. the introduction and spread of 'new' types of produce such as coffee, tea, pyrethrum, sugar, dairy and hybrid maize, the policies in the 1970s began to centre on the input side and on production. It was perceived as essential that rural delivery systems were strengthened so as to ensure effective channelling of the types of resources required for upgrading prevailing production technologies. Essential components of these more productive technologies included extension services, credit and inputs.

As cooperatives were seen as one type of delivery system, cooperative policies shifted in favour of supply functions, and the resources devoted to strengthen societies and unions increased rapidly. In terms of technical support, this change has been demanding and resulted in a further expansion of the MOCD and related bodies at central level.

As regards deployment of staff, it tended to be consistently biased towards less favourable environments. This feature was further accentuated when increasing attention started being paid to cooperatives as rural delivery systems for credit and input supplies.

Evidently, the state has been quite successful in building up a rather complex organizational infrastructure in rural areas. The mere existence of these cooperatives does not, however, necessarily mean that they as marketing and supply organizations effectively contribute to agricultural and rural development. It is to this issue that we now turn our attention.

Chapter four

# Performance

## 4.1 Introduction

As argued in Chapter one, prices are decisive determinants of the pattern and rate of growth of agricultural output in Africa as elsewhere. At the same time, it is clear that their actual effectiveness as a production incentive is influenced by a multitude of other factors. Geographically, such factors vary in significance and texture and, hence, also in terms of their combined, place-bound, consequences. The taxonomy of environments arrived at in Chapter three, expresses a few facets of spatial differentiation. As seen here, this classification takes cognizance of physical, social and economic circumstances that in vital respects affect smallholder production.

A significant aspect regarding prices of farm produce and inputs is that their influence is conditioned by the cost of maintaining links to the market. To the smallholder, it is obviously the farm-gate prices on produce and inputs rather than those announced by marketing boards and central supply agencies that are of relevance.

For the sake of simplicity we may here term the difference between official prices and the farm-gate price 'transaction costs'. These costs may be direct or indirect in nature. In our context, the former category refers to the costs incurred by cooperatives when carrying out collection, marketing and distribution activities. Principal elements are costs generated by the operation of collection-delivery points, stores and vehicles, by the documentation-recording and subsequent administrative tasks caused by transactions (deliveries, loans, payments) between members and the primary society. They also comprise 'costs of integration and decision-making' which emanate from the transport and communication activities that are generated by the functional and institutional integration of societies, unions and government offices (see p. 150). To these have to be added overhead costs in the form of buildings, machinery, equipment and the administrative superstructure at society and union levels.

Indirect transaction costs here refer to the quality of services offered to members. A cooperative may be able to cut its direct transaction costs in collection, marketing and distribution and thereby apparently improve its cost efficiency. However, in reality it will then often mean a transfer of part of the total transaction costs to the members, who then will have to spend more time, energy and money to link up with the market, i.e. the service quality deteriorates. It follows that it is important not only to carry out marketing and supply functions at a reasonable cost, but the right inputs should be available in the appropriate places at the time they are needed by the farmers, produce collection has to be reliable and the handling adequate, and payments have to be correct and timely.

The contribution of cooperatives to agricultural and rural development thus can be expected to be basically determined by their ability to offer smallholders incentives for market integration, i.e. by their performance in terms of efficiency and quality of service. Hence, factors of central concern to smallholders/members include their society's ability to realize advantageous producer prices and low marketing costs, to offer competitive input prices, to provide credit/loans on reasonable terms and, generally, to ensure accessibility, timeliness and reliability of services.

The importance of these elements will be influenced by environmental conditions. Thus, a setting characterized by adverse agro-ecological conditions and/or with less developed physical and social infrastructure, and with less diversified and reliable access to material inputs and commercial services, is bound to result in more costly operations of the service cooperative. Further, compared to more favoured environments, the volume of surplus produce, in total and per member, is likely to be lower – which in itself will add to the cost per marketed unit of produce.

However, it would be an oversimplification to argue that direct transaction costs and service quality are singularly determined by the environment. They are also functions of the particular modes of organization which shape the service activities. It is obviously essential to allow for the development of organizations that facilitate reasonable levels of both efficiency and service quality in different types of environments.

In Chapter three it was noted that since the early 1970s, the government, with the support of donor agencies, has been successful in building and maintaining a network of primary and secondary societies in rural areas. A generally high survival rate has been achieved, i.e. also under varying environmental conditions. This apparent success, however, is not very solid. The basic reason for this is that their mode of organization is mostly incompatible with local conditions. It embodies a basic inability to adapt to the kind of capacity constraints that, in various configurations, often constitute part of the rural economic landscape. Consequently, the mode of organization is usually unable to realize acceptable levels of cost efficiency and service quality.

The intention behind the cooperative policy has been to offer a network of service nodes in rural areas which combine first-stage processing and marketing with supply of credit and inputs. In order to achieve this, a rational and orderly development of the cooperative sector has been seen as a prerequisite. Given the perceived lack of adequate knowledge and organizational capacity in rural areas, it was then also seen as axiomatic that the government would have to be the *modus operandi* in designing and directing this process.

The outline of a basic organizational architecture was not seen as enough. The real challenge was to ensure a technically rational structure of unions and societies. Hence, the institution-building process involved prescriptions of the organization and administration of cooperative activities, and, as a consequence, in basic respects also of their management behaviour. Intervention of this magnitude was perceived as essential for effectively realizing both *functional* and *institutional* integration of the cooperative sector.

### *Installed scale and functional integration*

As regards functional integration, it was made clear that the government had to define the basic activity pattern. A first step in this direction was to stipulate that cooperatives had to agree to operate within a prescribed range of marketing activities. The kind of produce given priority was typically of high-value, export and non-food character.[1] As they have different ecological requirements (except dairy vs. coffee and pyrethrum), it geared the marketing activities of each individual society towards only one of these types of produce. This mono-marketing structure has been petrified by the administrative blueprint the government imposed on societies. It focused on devising administrative systems for linking of the primary societies' marketing activities with credit and input supply services. A decisive step in the reformation of the accounts systems was thus the introduction of produce-specific 'member transaction systems' (MT-system), facilitating administratively integrated recording and control of all transactions,

*Table 4.1* Standard forms required for the administration of a primary society (in this example a dairy society)

| | | |
|---|---|---|
| *Budget forms* | | |
| Income/expenditure | Expenditure (cont.) | Surplus and loss account |
| Cash budget | Statistics | Income, farming |
| Expenditure, farming | | |
| *Trial balance forms* | | |
| Income/expenditure | Expenditure | Surplus and loss account |
| Assets | Liabilities | Income, farming |
| Expenditure, farming | TB; work sheet | TB; list of adjustments |
| *General ledger* | | |
| Cash journal (small) | Cash journal (large) | Ledger card |
| Ledger journal | Guide card | Index card |
| Official receipt | Payment voucher | Bank reconciliation |
| Credit advice | Debit advice | Pay-out order |
| *General MT-forms* | | |
| Index card | Member's personal a/c | Debtors' members journal |
| Reconciliation | Calculation tables | Analysis of salaries |
| *MT-Dairy* | | |
| Members' produce record | Milk journal – AM | Milk journal – PM |
| Milk delivery note | Cash sales statement | Quantity control card/ CC-route |
| Quantity control card/ dairy | Summary of milk intake | Net payment journal |
| Summary of net payment journ. | Payment calculation/ request | Sales tickets |
| *Stores* | | |
| Stock card | Invoices | Credit sales journal |
| Cash sales receipts | Cash sales journal | Credit notes |
| Credit note journal | Purchase journal | Stocktaking journal |
| Goods receipt | Internal delivery notes | Order |
| *Credit and savings* | | |
| Loan application | Loan agreement | List of loan applications |
| Funds available for lending | Report about credit act. | Loan withdrawal vouchers |
| Loan withdrawal journals | Loan invoices/ Loan sales j. | Loans in kind notification |
| Loan deduction list | Monthly report (society) | Monthly report (union) |
| Union register, loan agreem. | Loan ledger card | Loan journal |
| | Member's envelope | Deposit slip |
| Savings passbook | Passbook register | Savings journal |
| Interest slip | Liquidity calculation form | Physical cash report |
| Withdrawal voucher | | |
| *Transport* | | |
| Transport invoice | Transport cash receipt | Vehicle card |
| Cash sales journal/ transport | Credit sales journal/ transp. | Service log-book |
| Vehicles business record | | |

*Source:* Min. of Coop. Development, Audit and Accounts Division

related to marketing, input supplies and payments, between a member and his society. Their implementation was preceded by revisions of the accounting systems; a standardized accounts plan had been introduced, followed by routines for budgets, trial balances, cash control, final accounts and the use of loose-leaf ledgers.

The administrative system devised for the integration of payments for produce deliveries with the provision of credit and inputs is both demanding and costly. First, independent of the actual scale of operation, there is the cost of maintaining the system, i.e. to pay for offices, qualified staff, equipment and stationery. Second, practically every transaction between a member and his society results in a number of records. Hence, the share of farmers' gross payments deducted to cover the society's operations will be dependent not only on total turnover but also on the number and average value of transactions between members and the society.

The local agricultural economy, as defined by a cooperative's membership, has to be able to support both the society's overhead costs and part of those incurred by the union. The ability to support should, in this context, be interpreted as the capacity of smallholders to market volumes sufficient to keep transaction costs, and thus their 'farm-gate returns', at a level where commercial production is perceived as worthwhile. In this respect, the size of the administrative superstructure in combination with the construct 'single produce-multipurpose' has negative effects. As frequently only a portion of the smallholder community constitutes the membership of these produce specific societies, and productivity levels are low, a relatively large umland is needed to achieve a reasonable scale of operation. However, the scale economies accruing from improved utilization of a bulky, in-built organizational and administrative infrastructure may then be more than offset by poor infrastructure, which escalates transport and communication costs and results in low service quality (in terms of accessibility, timeliness and reliability).

In the Kenyan context, there is this kind of basic incompatibility between service cooperatives with sizeable, in-built scale requirements and rural environments with unstable production, low agricultural productivity and high costs of interaction. The latter types of deterrents, in turn, are the singular or combined result of factors such as unfavourable agro-ecological conditions, land fragmentation, inadequate transport networks and poorly developed social and commercial infrastructure.

## Institutional interdependencies

The institutional aspect concerns two principal issues: (i) the integration of primary societies with unions at district level and (ii) regulations and procedures facilitating effective government supervision and development support.

As earlier noted, the government laid down a basic three-tiered federative structure of the cooperative sector. It consists of a national federation (KNFC), secondary societies (unions) and primary societies. Geographically, the typical union covers a district with existing primary societies as members. The union, as well as affiliated societies, may operate various establishments such as stores for input sales, consumer shops, hotels, etc. To this structure is linked supervisory and supporting functions executed by the Ministry of Cooperative Development, which has the headquarters, province and district as the main administrative levels.

As regards the first aspect mentioned above, i.e. the integration of primary societies and unions, the accounting system has constituted a principal tool. Thus, primary societies are assigned only the physical operations and the recording of members' transactions. Such accounting tasks as posting of documents, ledger postings, payment calculations, trial balancing and final accounts have been centralized and given to the unions. This move was justified by the fact that the skills required to run the systems were in short supply in rural areas. However, this form or vertical integration also coincided with the state's interest in establishing firm control of the cooperative sector (see Chapter two).

Furthermore, in order to 'achieve greater efficiency faster' (Rep. of Kenya 1970:8)[2], primary societies would have to accept all services offered by the unions. The range of such services varies among unions depending on their size and differentiation but usually includes (apart from centralized accounting) the procurement of inputs and credit and transport services. As regards the input supplies, unions bulk orders from primary societies, organize the actual purchases of farm inputs and distribute the goods to the society stores. In addition, the unions may have their own stores for resale. The credit sections established in the unions for the administration of production credit have in some cases been extended into banking sections.

Integration by means of transferring vital functions to the union level, largely enables the primary societies to influence their own management and operational performance. Staff and committees at primary level are made dependent on higher echelons in the administrative hierarchy both for management information about their local organization and for decisions pertaining to collection, marketing, procurement and distribution activities. Apart from the demands this construct puts on stable and reliable transport and communication linkages between the primary and secondary levels, it confirms the merely symbolic influence of members and committees of primary societies.

The administrative systems also have provided a device for close institutional integration of cooperatives with the government bureaucracy. Through built-in 'stops-and-checks', management and decision-making have been divided between government officers, and staff/officials at the union and society levels, with the former having the last say in most matters of any significance. Thus hardly any decision of significance can be taken without being subjected either to direct approval or control by government officers. As examples of this kind of prescribed institutional interdependencies, it can be mentioned that government officers have to:

- attend budget meetings of all cooperative societies to ensure compliance with regulations and policies;[3]
- control and approve budgets and trial balances (which societies and unions have to submit to the MOCD);[4]
- approve unions' appointments of graded staff;
- attend committee meetings and annual general meetings of all societies;
- approve/countersign societies' and unions' cheques;
- approve/countersign societies' and unions' orders for goods and merchandise;
- examine, recommend or reject applications for loans, borrowing power and distribution of surplus;
- approve conditions for loans to members;
- approve procedures for purchases;[5]
- approve investments by societies;[6]
- approve dismissal of cooperative employees.[7]

The execution of these and a range of other supervisory obligations is facilitated by means of a 'systems approach'. The administrative mode of carrying out each line of service activity is defined and formalized (documented) in quite some detail, thereby prescribing the 'standard behaviour' of the staff of societies and unions. Thus, the construct relies on a 'command style', rather than on more independent modes of management. As a result, we can talk about a cooperative sector with practically all actors being subjected to detailed regulation. At local, regional and national levels, the division of activities creates a cobweb of prescribed interdependencies among societies, unions, central bodies and the administrative hierarchy of the ministry.

One of the outstanding features of this structure is the separation of essential management functions and decision-making from the local establishments interacting with the members. This managerially top-heavy, federative structure combined with meticulous government control, has resulted in prolific detailing of actions and procedures, and, hence, in a bulky and geographically scattered administration. Primary societies can be perceived as the bottom plane in a pyramid defined by vertically oriented and prescribed institutional relations. Along these vertical linkages is elevated information from the primary societies to the higher administrative echelons (union, national bodies and government offices). This information is transferred by means of personal visits, telephone calls and written documentation. It may comprise recorded business activities or documentation referring to 'intended decisions' (applications for approval of decisions). In response are downloaded approvals, goods, centralized services and financial resources.

It is obviously a rather complex machinery. Already the seemingly trivial fact that the structure is kept together by flows in geographical space has important implications. In the kind of environment in which most cooperative societies operate, transport is expensive, unreliable and time-consuming. Telephone networks are usually overloaded, if they at all exist, and postal services are poor. Apart from the cost aspect, it follows that the rural economy is frequently unable to meet very moderate logistical requirements.

Additionally, excessive documentation and manual techniques of administration create bottlenecks in the processing of information, and this not only effectively undermines much of the basic intention of providing control and management information, but also delays decision-making. Spatially overstretched management systems also have 'qualitative' implications. One is that decisions are made by staff with limited knowledge about local conditions. This knowledge tends to be replaced either by a set of simplistic criteria or is based on policies which usually leave ample room for subjective interpretation. In this interrelated structure, both delays and uninformed decision-making, particularly in strategic nodes (union and government ofices), will have obvious repercussions on the performance of subordinate nodes (mainly the primary societies).

The volatility of the environments in which service cooperatives operative is also due to the vagaries of weather, world market prices and the performance of external institutions, principally marketing boards, each of which may seriously disturb performance. In the case of such events, the petrified organizational structure and prescribed institutional dependencies that characterize the societies, largely exclude the possibility of flexible adaptation. The same problem applies if a society committee wishes to adopt a new strategy, for example by extending its marketing services to a wider range of produce. A constraint which then is likely to be prohibitive is that the administrative systems of individual societies are designed for marketing one principal type of produce, e.g., coffee *or* dairy *or* pyrethrum. A changed activity orientation necessitates revised administrative routines which, in turn, have to be approved, designed and implemented by the MOCD.

In conclusion, the organizational structure devised for agricultural service cooperatives in Kenya displays fundamental weaknesses when exposed to the vagaries of the environment on which it essentially depends, i.e. the smallholder economy. It then becomes evident that the design rests on a number of implicit assumptions that may be met only in industrially organized environments, such as ease of interaction in geographical space, a certain scale of operation, management skills and stability. These in-built threshold requirements, imparted on societies and unions, can in most cases be met only partially, if at all. Hence, in fundamental respects they will condition the expected rationality and benefits of cooperatives. If accepting that the symbiosis with government institutions has favourably influnced their survival capacity, it is at the same time negatively affecting their performance and contributions to agricultural and rural development.

In view of the arguments presented above, it is here hypothesized that the mode of cooperative organization established in Kenya is viable only under rather specific, and favourable, environmental conditions. These include fairly high and stable (or increasing) transaction values per member, large total turnover and well-developed physical, social and commercial infrastructures.

To probe into this issue, a first step will be to consider changes in prices and aggregate output levels for each major type of produce. Next, attempts will be made to establish to what extent performance, in terms of produce sales, marketing costs and service quality, has been affected by the cooperative mode of organization and its interplay with the local environment and external institutions (primarily marketing boards).

## 4.2 Some basic features

Between 1971 and 1983, during which period government supervision and support increased significantly, cooperatives lost ground as marketing organizations (Table 4.2). The fact that this contraction has taken place in a context where the agricultural sector as a whole suffered from decelerating growth, accentuates their generally poor performance. In the case of societies that market types of produce other than coffee, the position has deteriorated quite dramatically.

This trend is reflected in changes in total turnover. In real terms, total turnover increased at an average of about 4 per cent per annum between 1976 and 1983, while the value of smallholders' gross marketed production grew to 4.5 per cent. During the same period, the total registered membership increased at twice this rate, resulting in a decrease in average sales per member from *c.* 1,900 K.Sh. to 1,440 K.Sh.

In Chapter three, it was observed that in the 1960s the survival performance of agricultural service societies was influenced by basic features of the local environment. Between 1971–83, on the other hand, the survival rate was higher in environments which, according to our taxonomy, offered less conducive conditions both for agricultural production and for commercial activities. It was concluded that this unexpected 'over-achievement' primarily was due to strengthened government supervision and to the introduction of a range of supporting measures, not least credit and input supply programmes.

If one considers basic aspects of the operational performance of primary societies, rather than merely survival, a different picture emerges (Table 4.4). Using produce sales as a performance indicator, it seems evident that the local environment, as defined in Chapter three, plays a decisive role. As illustrated by Table 4.5, coffee societies dominate both in terms of turnover and membership. Their geographical distribution, governed largely by agro-ecological conditions, is therefore a main factor behind the combined rating of each type of environment. However, both when considering coffee societies in isolation and when excluding them, it is clear that the performance of societies is affected by the type of environment in which they operate (Table 4.6).

Also in the case of secondary societies, i.e. unions, the local environment is of importance (Table 4.7). This is evident particularly with reference to their role as suppliers of inputs. As will be dealt with later, considerable differences exist among unions, not only in terms of sales and commercial viability but also as regards the range of services they render affiliated societies and individual members.

*Table 4.2* Share of gross marketed production of smallholders and agricultural service societies (selected years)

| *Year* | *Smallholders' share of value of gross marketed production (%)* | *Cooperatives' share of value of smallholders' gross marketed production (%)* | *Coops, excl. coffee (%)* |
|---|---|---|---|
| 1971 | 51 | 48 | 25 |
| 1978 | 55 | 46 | N/A |
| 1983 | 51 | 43 | 10 |

*Sources: Economic Survey*, MOCD and survey data

*Table 4.3* Turnover of agricultural marketing societies, 1976–83 (million K.Sh. at constant 1976 prices)

| *Year* | *Turnover* |
|---|---|
| 1976 | 1,045 |
| 1977 | 1,294 |
| 1978 | 1,432 |
| 1979 | 1,474 |
| 1980 | 1,289 |
| 1981 | 1,352 |
| 1982 | 1,177 |
| 1983 | 1,330 |

*Sources:* MOCD and survey data

*Table 4.4* Vale of marketed produce by type of environment, 1982–83 (K.Sh. '000)

| *Environm.* | *Number of societies*[1] | *Value of marketed produce (sales)* | *Average sales/soc.* | *Total no. of members* |
|---|---|---|---|---|
| C1 71–83 | 244 | 1,433,347 | 5,874 | 490,536 |
| C2 71–83 | 307 | 825,311 | 2,688 | 374,431 |
| C3 71–83 | 209 | 160,223 | 767 | 71,151 |
| C4 71–83 | 28 | 12,081 | 431 | 8,270 |
| Total | 788 | 2,430,962 | 3,085 | 944,388 |

*Source:* survey data

*Note*

1 Number of primary societies with recorded produce sales among societies on register 1980 plus those regisered 1981–83.

To facilitate both a more detailed examination of the role of the local environment and of other conditioning forces, we have chosen the activity orientation of societies as our point of departure. Thus, in the following, societies sharing a common activity

*Table 4.5* Value of marketed produce 1982–83, by activity orientation (primary societies) (K.Sh. '000)

| *Activity* | *Act. no.* | *No. of societies* | *Value of marketed prod.* | *Total no. of members* |
|---|---|---|---|---|
| Cereals | 11 | 38 | 53,372 | 10,988 |
| Coffee | 12 | 171 | 1,839,528 | 506,533 |
| Cotton | 13 | 54 | 42,449 | 92,492 |
| Pyrethrum | 15 | 79 | 28,504 | 82,981 |
| Sugar cane | 17 | 54 | 84,654 | 27,670 |
| Dairy | 21 | 253 | 291,735 | 146,560 |
| Misc. | | 139 | 90,720 | 77,224 |
| Total | | 788 | 2,430,962 | 944,448 |

*Source:* survey data

*Table 4.6* Value of marketed produce by type of environment, excl. coffee societies, 1982–83 (K.Sh. '000)

| *Environm.* | *No. of societies* | *Value of marketed produce* | *Average sales/soc.* | *Total no. of members* |
|---|---|---|---|---|
| C1 71–83 | 164 | 222,441 | 1,356 | 210,502 |
| C2 71–83 | 223 | 201,404 | 903 | 155,891 |
| C3 71–83 | 205 | 155,642 | 759 | 65,170 |
| C4 71–83 | 26 | 11,947 | 460 | 7,743 |
| Total | 618 | 591,434 | 957 | 439,306 |

*Source:* survey data

*Table 4.7* Selected performance features of unions, by type of local environment, 1982/83 (K. Sh. millions)

| *Environm.* | *No. of unions* | *Sales of inputs* | *Total turnover* | *Financial result* |
|---|---|---|---|---|
| C1 71–83 | 12 | 123.2 | 205.4 | 10.4 |
| C2 71–83 | 17 | 45.1 | 176.9 | –6.7 |
| C3 71–83 | 5 | 8.8 | 17.3 | 1.0 |
| C4 71–83 | 1 | 0 | 0.2 | 0.1 |
| Total | 35 | 177.1 | 399.8 | 4.8 |

*Sources:* survey data and union accounts

orientation will provide the foundation for successive analyses of the mode of cooperative organization and how its interplay with varying local and institutional environments affects performance.

The analyses will be confined to the major activity orientations only (i.e. coffee, pyrethrum, cotton, dairy, sugar, cashew) and to the unions to which these primary societies are affiliated.

## 4.3 Coffee

Coffee is economically the dominating produce marketed by agricultural service societies. Its importance has also steadily increased during the period 1970–83. Thus, while this crop accounted for 58 per cent of the gross value of the total smallholder production marketed by cooperatives in 1970, its share had risen to 75 per cent in 1983.

Kenyan coffee is solely Arabica. Cultivation is concentrated along the eastern slopes of the Aberdare range and around the south and east sides of Mount Kenya. There are also considerable smallholder acreages west of Rift Valley, in Kisii, Bungoma and Kakamega districts. The areas eligible for coffee planting are defined in detail in the Coffee Ordinance; planting elsewhere is considered illegal. The Ordinance also stipulates that coffee grown by smallholders has to be marketed by cooperatives. Hence, the geographical distribution of primary societies largely mirrors the areas of cultivation (Figure 4.1).

*Table 4.8* Major smallholder coffee areas classified according to ecological characteristics

| *Zone* | *Coffee area (%)*[1] | | | | *Proportion shaded(%)* |
|---|---|---|---|---|---|
| | *UM1* | *UM2* | *UM3* | *Total* | |
| Central province and Embu district | 22 | 25 | 6 | 53 | 3 |
| Meru | 8 | 14 | 7 | 29 | 50 |
| Machakos | – | – | 9 | 9 | 2 |
| Kisii | 9 | – | – | 9 | 32 |
| Total | 39 | 39 | 22 | 100 | 19 |

*Source:* J. de Graaf, 1986, op. cit., Table 6.7

*Note*

1 UM1: coffee-tea zone, UM2: main coffee zone, UM3: marginal coffee zone.

Altitude, through its close relation with rainfall, and temperature, largely defines the limits for cultivation of coffee. In the areas east of Rift Valley, rain-fed coffee can be grown at altitudes between 1,400 and 2,000 m. West of the Rift, coffee can be grown at an altitude of *c.* 2,100 m (Mt Elgon). Cultivation close to the upper and lower altitude limits usually has negative consequences on yields or quality. An average annual rainfall of *c.* 1,800 mm is considered ideal for coffee.[8]

The main coffee-growing areas east of Rift Valley generally receive considerably less rainfall, or in the range of 900–1,300 mm. To compensate for the limited precipitation, soils require a considerable depth to ensure adequate water storage. The predominant soil type in Central province – 'Kikuyu red loam' – is derived from recent volcanic deposits and is rich and well drained. Comparable soil qualities are found also in Eastern province, south and east of Mount Kenya, and in Kisii district in Nyanza province. In western province (Kakamega and Bungoma) as well as in Rift Valley, the soil types are less fertile.[9]

The major smallholder coffee zones can be further differentiated with regard to their ecological characteristics into what is termed UM1, UM2 and UM3 zones (Table 4.8). UM1 represents high altitude/high rainfall and UM3 low rainfall areas. In the former zone, weeding is important whereas mulching is a major activity in UM3 areas. The latter method contributes not only to the preservation of soil moisture but also to weed control. When coffee is shaded, e.g. by bananas, weeding is less important. The practice of shading is usually accompanied by limited use of fertilizers, and by modest yields.[10]

During the period 1955–65, the cultivated area and total production increased rapidly (Figure 4.2, Table 4.11). When the area under coffee had reached about 50,000 ha (125,000 acres) in 1964, a planting ban was declared by the government. This decision was in adherence with the International Coffee Agreement which took effect in 1966.[11] Consequently, the cultivated area changed only marginally between 1965 and 1976. As a result of improved productivity per hectare, total production still more than doubled during the period. When coffee prices escalated in the mid-1970s, the government lifted the planting ban. Between 1976 and 1984 total production doubled, but so did the cultivated area (Figure 4.2). Geographically, most of the expansion has taken the form of extending the original core areas, primarily in the Eastern and Central provinces. Further, much of the expansion has been confined to already existing primary societies. Thus, by 1983, 134 societies registered before independence accounted for over 90 per cent of both membership and total sales.

## Marketing structure and prices

Practically all societies operate at least one coffee 'factory' to which the individual members bring their cherry for procesing into 'clean coffee' or parchment coffee (Table 4.9).

*Table 4.9* Basic features of primary coffee societies, 1983

| District | Number of societies | Number of factories | Value[1] of marketed production | Members |
|---|---|---|---|---|
| Kisumu | 1 | 2 | 314 | 784 |
| Kisii | 27 | 71 | 99,990 | 89,778 |
| S. Nyanza | 8 | 13 | 7,902 | 10,626 |
| Siaya | 1 | – | 91 | 800 |
| *Nyanza prov.* | *7* | *86* | *108,297* | *101,988* |
| Kakamega | 9 | 11 | 10,253 | 8,910 |
| Bungoma | 22 | 25 | 45,384 | 21,011 |
| *Western prov.* | *31* | *36* | *55,637* | *29,921* |
| Baringo | 1 | 5 | 1,128 | 1,425 |
| Kericho | 1 | 3 | 450 | 360 |
| Nandi | 2 | 4 | 918 | 702 |
| West Pokot | 1 | 1 | 111 | 403 |
| Kajiado | 1 | 2 | 23 | 124 |
| *Rift valley* | *6* | *15* | *2,630* | *3,014* |
| Nyeri | 4 | 63 | 282,643 | 54,246 |
| Muranga | 19 | 99 | 399,081 | 64,642 |
| Kiambu | 13 | 67 | 187,541 | 30,354 |
| Kirinyaga | 8 | 54 | 224,810 | 29,345 |
| *Central* | *44* | *283* | *1,094,075* | *178,587* |
| Taita/Taveta | 1 | 5 | 3,075 | 4,169 |
| *Coast prov.* | *1* | *5* | *3,075* | *4,169* |
| Embu | 14 | 39 | 127,855 | 27,211 |
| Meru | 23 | 145 | 352,296 | 112,306 |
| Kitui | 1 | – | 19 | 305 |
| Machakos | 14 | 65 | 95,644 | 49,032 |
| *Eastern prov.* | *52* | *249* | *575,814* | *188,854* |
| Total | 171 | 674 | 1,839,528 | 506,533 |

*Sources:* Survey data; Kenya Planters' Cooperative Union; Coffee Board of Kenya.
*Note*
1 Based on price paid by the Coffee Board (parchment price)

The number of registered members of these coffee societies was about 506,000. Of these, an estimated 450,000 could be considered as active. In the 1982/83 season, they produced 52,000 tonnes of clean coffee with an export value of K.Sh. 1,982 million. In addition, 31,000 tonnes of coffee was produced by about 700 estates, of which most are found in the southern parts of Central province.

Processing involves pulping, fermentation, washing and drying. The largest societies may each run more than twenty factories. A total of 674 factories were owned and operated by primary

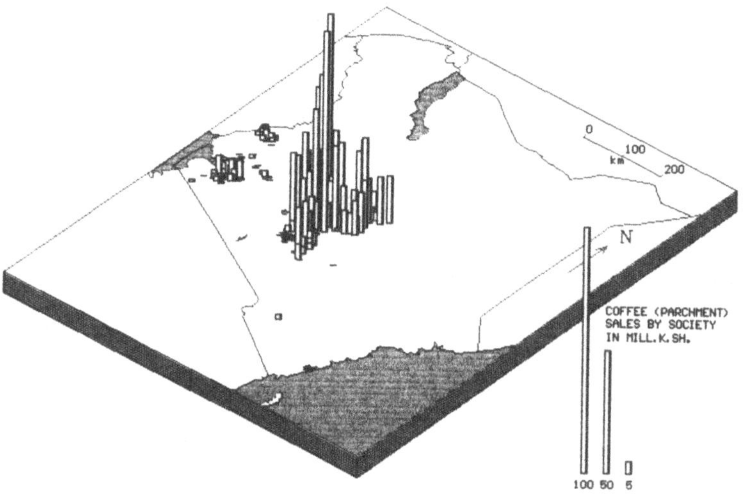


*Figure 4.1* Active coffee societies, 1983
*Source:* survey data

societies in 1983 (Table 4.9). After drying, the coffee is graded and packed in 50 kg bags. Usually the union arranges for transport of the crop to a regional KPCU-store or directly to the KPCU's factory in Nairobi. On behalf of the Coffee Board, the KPCU takes care of the hulling, grading and classification of the parchment coffee.

About 20 per cent of the coffee delivered through cooperatives is of top quality. In this respect Kirinyaga and Nyeri are the leading districts. For estates, this share is much lower. On the other hand, the proportion of low-quality coffee delivered by cooperatives is higher than that for estates. In 1983, 15 per cent of total smallholder production was so-called *mbuni*, or sun-dried coffee berries (as compared to 5 per cent for estates), and over the period 1978–83 this share has been increasing (Table 4.10). After classification, the coffee is bought by the Coffee Board. The lots are bagged and stored for sale on a weekly auction.

In the 1960s, the government introduced an export tax on coffee which in 1977 was replaced by a progressive *ad valorem* tax. In 1982/83, the tax amounted to 5.15 per cent of the export value. The Coffee Board also charges a statutory levy on sales of coffee and this is used to finance the activities of the Coffee Research Foundation. Also a County Council cess is levied which is 3 per cent of the gross payment to farmers. In the 1982/83 crop year, the export tax and various levies amounted to slightly more than 10 per cent of the export value. Adding charges to cover direct operational expenses of the Coffee Board and the KPCU, the total deductions at central level rise to 13.7 per cent. Cooperatives at district and local level cost the smallholders another 11.3 per cent, resulting in a payment rate averaging 75 per cent of the export value (Table 4.10).

The price of coffee no doubt has an impact on the total output levels in the smallholder sector. For the period 1965–84, it can be observed that more significant price changes are covarying with output levels, i.e. yields per hectare (Table 4.11 and Figure 4.3).

*Table 4.10* Estimated handling, processing and marketing costs for coffee produced by smallholders, 1982–83 crop season

| | | % |
|---|---|---|
| Export value, K.Sh. million | 1,982.0 | 100.00 |
| (Average auction price, K. Sh. 37.70) | | |
| Coffee Board: | | |
| – direct marketing expenses | 19.0 | 0.96 |
| – Intern. Coffee Organization | 3.2 | 0.16 |
| – Statutory levy | 18.4 | 0.93 |
| – Export tax | 102.1 | 5.15 |
| | *142.7* | *7.20* |
| (Average parchment price, K. Sh. 35.06)[1] | | |
| KPCU: | | |
| – commission, levy | 31.3 | 1.58 |
| – milling charges, outturn fees | 43.8 | 2.21 |
| – county council cess | 52.9 | 2.67 |
| | *128.0* | *6.46* |
| (Aver. local producer price, K. Sh. 32.61) | | |
| District coop. unions | 17.1 | 0.86 |
| Primary coop. societies | 212.5 | 10.72 |
| | *229.6* | *11.58* |
| Paid to growers | 1,481.7 | 74.76 |
| (Aver. farm-gate price, K.Sh. 28.19) | | |

*Sources:* Coffee Board, Annual Report 1983; KPCU, internal records; survey data.
*Note*
[1] This figure, based on KPCU data, is slightly higher than that given by Coffee Board (cf. Table 4.11).

*Table 4.11* Smallholder production of coffee 1955–84

| Year | Production tons[1] | Share mbuni(%)[2] | Cultivated area (ha)[3] | Yield Kg/ ha | Price[4] Sh./Kg Current | Real[5] |
|---|---|---|---|---|---|---|
| 1955 | 1,133 | – | 3,044 | 372 | 8.54 | – |
| 1960 | 6,476 | – | 13,410 | 483 | 7.96 | – |
| 1965 | 16,200 | – | 52,649 | 307 | 7.54 | – |
| 1970 | 30,400 | – | 54,800 | 555 | 7.47 | – |
| 1975 | 35,000 | – | 56,600 | 618 | 10.00 | – |
| 1976 | 36,135 | 10.2 | 56,600 | 638 | 21.24 | 21.24 |
| 1977 | 47,660 | 6.7 | 56,600 | 842 | 44.28 | 37.52 |
| 1978 | 47,744 | 8.2 | 56,600 | 843 | 31.06 | 25.76 |
| 1979 | 46,079 | 9.3 | 62,574 | 736 | 26.34 | 20.52 |
| 1980 | 51,900 | 10.0 | 71,172 | 729 | 30.52 | 21.70 |
| 1981 | 64,007 | 14.8 | 84,710 | 755 | 25.58 | 16.52 |
| 1982 | 52,531 | 16.3 | 94,473 | 556 | 28.52 | 16.75 |
| 1983 | 52,469 | 15.2 | 103,063 | 509 | 34.88 | 18.73 |
| 1984 | 74,683 | – | 114,235 | 653 | 36.29 | 18.57 |

*Sources:* Coffee Board of Kenya; *Economic Survey* (1976–85); J. de Graaf, 1986, op. cit., Table 6.3; *Economic Survey*, various issues, 1972–85; Min. of Cooperative Development; J. K. Maitha, *Coffee in the Kenyan Economy. An Econometric Analysis*, Appendix V., 1974.

*Notes*

1 Refers to 'clean coffee' (parchment coffee). The ratio clean coffee/cherry is usually around 1:6.7.

2 Unripe or overripe cherry which is dried and sold as low quality '*mbuni* coffee'.

3 Area with mature coffee.

4 Price paid by the marketing board, i.e. before deduction of KPCU's costs, county council cess, union commissions and deductions by primary societies.

5 Calculation of real price is based on price index in Statistical Abstract (1976=100).

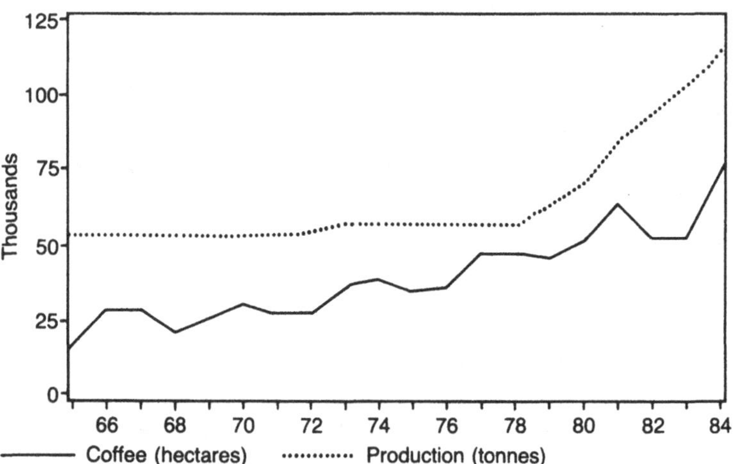


*Figure 4.2* Production (clean coffee) and planted (mature) area of coffee, 1965–84

*Source:* Coffee Board

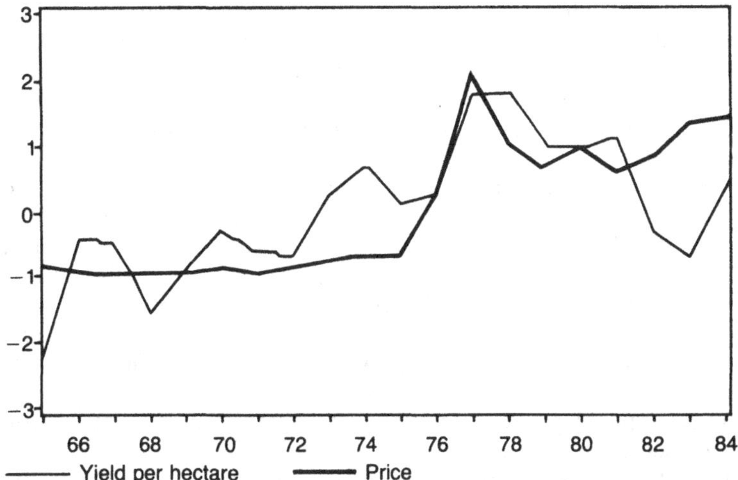


*Figure 4.3* Fluctuations in coffee yields/ha and parchment price/kg, 1965–84. Normalized scale. Current prices
*Sources:* Coffee Board; *Economic Survey*, various issues 1968–85.

As coffee is a perennial crop, a fall in prices obviously does not result in the uprooting of the trees, at least not in the short term. Instead smallholders seem to respond to price changes by varying the intensity of husbandry and picking. When prices develop unfavourably, less attention is paid to the crop and the yields fall, while the opposite applies in a situation with rising prices. As can be seen from Table 4.11 and Figure 4.3, the price boom in 1976–78 clearly influenced yields. Another feature seemingly contradicts this kind of response pattern. Thus, seen over the period 1968–75, coffee yields/ha increased while the producer price[12] in real terms deteriorated. In the period 1979–83, on the other hand, more attractive, though falling, real prices were coupled with stagnating productivity of land.

One reason for this phenomenon is that the prices used here are gross, i.e. they refer to the price paid by the Coffee Board, before deductions for handling, processing and marketing at local and central level. Thus, assuming that the efficiency and service quality improve significantly at one level of the marketing chain, for example among cooperatives, this may result in favourable changes in the actual payout in spite of stagnating gross prices. In the period 1968–75, this actually seems to have been the case. As described earlier in this study, many coffee societies were grossly mismanaged in the mid-1960s. In reaction to this, government control and intervention increased which, apart from revision of their administration, resulted in extended training and education activities and strengthened credit and input supply services. These changes affected practically all coffee societies and had positive consequences at least in the large societies in Central and Eastern provinces.

However, as regards both the positive trend in yields that can be observed for the period 1968–75 and the negative one discernible for 1976–84, other factors also seem to have been of importance. At this stage there is thus reason to consider very briefly the fact that changes in the price of coffee cannot be treated in isolation from other such price changes in the economy that are of direct consequence for the coffee growers' total farm income. In this context, we will confine ourselves to the output side and then only to one type of produce, namely tea. After 1960, tea cultivation increased rapidly in the smallholder sector. The expansion of tea production was planned, organized and implemented by the Kenya Tea Development Authority (KTDA). In 1959, the total area under the crop was 636 ha.[13] By 1984, the total crop area had reached 56,000 ha and the number of growers 150,000. The same year, the total export value of tea almost equalled that of coffee (Figure 4.4).

In terms of agro-ecology, tea cultivation partly overlaps with coffee. The expansion of tea cultivation that has taken place since independence therefore has competed for land with coffee, not least in the Central and Eastern provinces in areas at altitudes between 1,500 m and 1,800 m. Many smallholders at this altitude range grow both tea and coffee. Further, they do so under favourable conditions and account for a sizeable share of total coffee and tea production in the smallholder sector. Apparently, their response to changing relative prices for coffee and tea has an impact on coffee yields. In periods when relative prices move to the advantage of coffee, these farmers tend to give priority to coffee; tea is given priority when prices move in the other direction.

As indicated by Figure 4.5, which shows the variations in the price ratio (coffee/tea) and coffee yields per hectare, this kind of response pattern offers one explanation for observed fluctuations in coffee yields in the periods 1968–75 and 1979–83. It also illustrates the fact that fluctuations in producer prices will have varying geographical impacts depending on the ability of smallholders to respond to changing relative prices. In the cases of coffee and tea, farmers in high altitude areas obviously have this option while growers in, say, the southern and eastern parts of

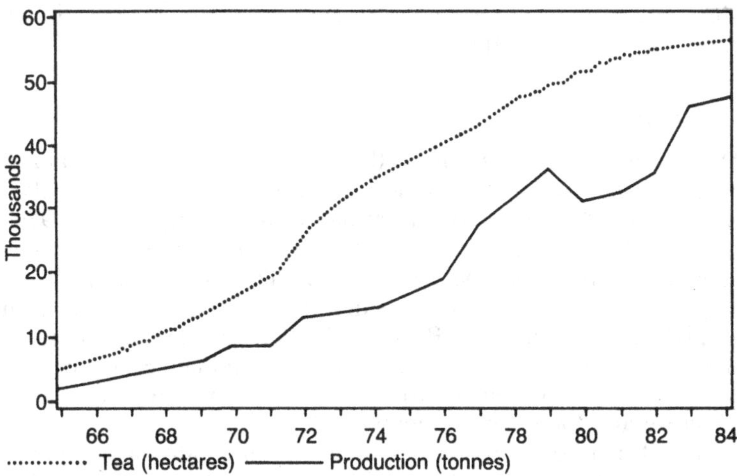


*Figure 4.4* Tea production (made tea equiv.) and planted (mature) area of tea, 1965–84
*Sources: Economic Survey*, various issues 1977–85; B. Gyllström, op. cit. 1977.

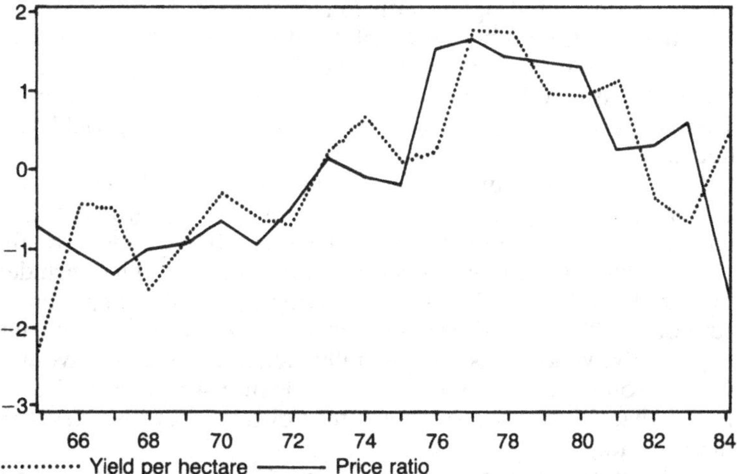


*Figure 4.5* Fluctuations in coffee yields/ha and price ratio coffee/tea (Board prices) 1965–84. Normalized scale
*Sources: Economic Survey*, various issues 1977–85; B. Gyllström, op. cit. 1977.

Meru and Embu will respond differently as coffee here constitutes part of a different output mix.

### *Performance and environment*

The overall picture in terms of the average payment rate realized by the marketing system in general, and cooperatives in particular, is better in 1983 than in the latter half of the 1970s[14] and in 1980–82.[15] Raised export prices rather than improved cost efficiency seem to be the basic determinant of this development. Disaggregated information also shows that the improvement is far from a universal phenomenon. Prices and payments vary considerably among districts and societies. In order to illuminate causes behind these variations we now turn our attention to the cooperative structure and the environmental context.

First it can be noted that agro-ecological conditions obviously influence coffee yields. The latter also constitute a basic determinant of the level of coffee yields. As indicated in Table 4.8, the potential for coffee production varies considerably among coffee-growing areas and no doubt contributes to the differences in actual yield levels observable at district level (Table 4.12). Two cases in point are Machakos and Meru. In both districts the planted area of coffee has increased significantly in recent years. As the expansion of coffee at altitudes between 1,500 and 1,800 m had been blocked to some extent by the tea industry, it is likely that part of the planting was diverted towards lower and less favourable altitudes. This has probably contributed to the fall in average yields per hectare.

It is, however, unlikely that observed variations in yield levels can be explained solely by reference to agro-ecological conditions. The productivity of land is affected also by the demographic, economic and social conditions of the kind included in our classification of different environments. This argument is supported by the information given in Table 4.12. Not unexpectedly, yield levels are generally higher in the more favoured C1-environments. With reference to Figure 4.6, it can also be noted that C2-yields display a rather distinct, negative development trend.

The differences between the C1 and C2 environments are not confined to on-farm performance but, as indicated in Figures 4.8–9 and Table 4.14, they also apply to the performance rating of cooperatives in terms of average coffee deliveries per member, sales and marketing costs. The highest yield levels and average size of deliveries can be observed for the districts which most closely

*Table 4.12* Yields of clean coffee/ha by district, 1982–83

| *District* | *Environm.* | *Kg/ha* |
|---|---|---|
| Nyeri | C1 71–83 | 921 |
| Muranga | C1 71–83 | 889 |
| Kirinyaga | C1 71–83 | 839 |
| Kiambu | C1 71–83 | 530 |
| Kisii | C1 71–83 | 446 |
| Kakamega | C1 71–83 | 173 |
| Embu | C2 71–83 | 565 |
| Bungoma | C2 71–83 | 380 |
| Machakos | C2 71–83 | 302 |
| Meru | C2 71–83 | 292 |
| South Nyanza | C2 71–83 | 223 |
| Other districts | | 185 |

*Sources:* Min. of Coop. Development; Coffee Board of Kenya.

resemble the 'ideal' C1-type of environment (Nyeri, Muranga and Kirinyaga), and it is also here we find the leading societies in terms of sales and payment rates. Their performance is basically a function of the districts' superior infrastructure and higher level of economic differentiation. The importance of these factors stands out clearly when examining in more detail the degree of 'internal' differentiation of C1 (Table 4.14). It shows that yield levels are significantly lower in districts with low scores on levels of economic differentiation as, in particular, Kakamega and Kisii. Kisii's agro-ecological yield potential differs only marginally from that of the districts in Central province. As the hectarage per member is less than half that for Central province, and the pressure on land is generally very high, comparatively high yields per hectare might be expected. This, however, is not the case. Not only is Kisii inferior in this respect, but also the general trend in productivity of coffee land is quite alarming (Figure 4.7).

The achievements recorded in the 'core region' (Nyeri, Muranga, Kirinyaga) are likely to have been accentuated by the ability of cooperatives to reap scale economies (Figure 4.10). Processing costs are sensitive to variations in volume (Figure 4.11). This also applies to the administration of the societies, though only providing that the average value of members' transactions (which largely reflects yield levels) can be kept at a reasonably high level. Both yield levels and the average size of transactions decisively affect marketing costs. As they are closely related, their respective influence is difficult to isolate (Figure 4.14). A comparison of societies with approximately similar levels of total

*Table 4.13* Basic performance characteristics of primary coffee societies by type of environment and size category (coffee sales), 1982–83

| *Environm. category* | *Size category, parchment sales (mill. Sh.)* | *Number of societies* | *Parchment sales (mill. Sh.)* | *Member-ship ('000)* | *Average sales/ member (Sh.)* | *Pay ratio %* |
|---|---|---|---|---|---|---|
| C1 71–83 | < 2.0 | 23 | 16.5 | 24.4 | 680 | 68.1 |
| | 2.0– 3.9 | 15 | 44.9 | 40.5 | 1,110 | 73.0 |
| | 4.0– 5.9 | 8 | 38.4 | 26.4 | 1,450 | 74.3 |
| | 6.0– 9.9 | 7 | 58.0 | 23.7 | 2,450 | 74.9 |
| | 10.0–19.9 | 5 | 77.4 | 13.5 | 5,730 | 83.8 |
| | 20.0–29.9 | 8 | 188.5 | 32.3 | 5,840 | 84.8 |
| | 30.0–49.9 | 8 | 299.8 | 40.7 | 5,370 | 83.2 |
| | >49.9 | 7 | 481.1 | 76.5 | 6,290 | 84.3 |
| Subtotal | | *81* | *1,204.6* | *278.0* | *4,330* | *82.7* |
| C2 71–83 | < 2.0 | 27 | 25.5 | 26.8 | 950 | 71.7 |
| | 2.0– 3.9 | 11 | 34.5 | 21.2 | 1,630 | 71.3 |
| | 4.0– 5.9 | 7 | 33.0 | 22.1 | 1,490 | 71.3 |
| | 6.0– 9.9 | 21 | 165.5 | 63.1 | 2,620 | 73.6 |
| | 10.0–19.9 | 9 | 131.6 | 36.3 | 3,615 | 78.9 |
| | 20.0–29.9 | 6 | 136.0 | 44.1 | 3,085 | 77.5 |
| | 30.0–49.9 | 3 | 104.1 | 8.1 | 12,870 | 80.6 |
| Subtotal | | *84* | *630.2* | *221.7* | *2,840* | *76.4* |
| C3 71–83 | < 2.0 | 3 | 1.4 | 1.8 | 775 | 85.4 |
| | 2.0– 3.9 | 1 | 3.1 | 4.2 | 740 | 80.6 |
| C4 71–83 | < 2.0 | 2 | 0.1 | 0.5 | 250 | 67.2 |
| Total | | *171* | *1,834.8* | *499.7* | *3,670* | *80.5* |

*Sources:* survey data, MOCD

sales shows a high negative correlation (r=−0.8) between the average value of deliveries per member and marketing cost per tonne.

Generally speaking, the superior performance of cooperatives in the three districts mentioned above is basically determined by the fact that the environment allows the societies to exploit the scale economies built into their mode of organization without these being superseded by rapidly increasing direct transaction costs. Under these circumstances, produce sales of K.Sh. 10 million seem to represent a critical level above which the societies are able to realize high payment rates for their members (Table 4.13).

*Table 4.14* Basic performance characteristics of primary coffee societies by type of environment and district, 1982–83

| *Environm. category* | *District* | *Number of societies* | *Parchment sales (mill. Sh.)* | *Membership ('000)* | *Average sales/ member (Sh.)* | *Pay ratio %* |
|---|---|---|---|---|---|---|
| C1 71–83 | Kisumu | 1 | 0.3 | N/A | N/A | N/A |
| | Kisii | 27 | 100.0 | 89.7 | 1,110 | 69.9 |
| | Kakamega | 9 | 10.3 | 7.9 | 1,300 | 77.5 |
| | Nyeri | 4 | 282.6 | 54.2 | 5,210 | 85.6 |
| | Muranga | 19 | 399.1 | 64.6 | 6,180 | 84.8 |
| | Kiambu | 13 | 187.5 | 30.4 | 6,170 | 80.0 |
| | Kirinyaga | 8 | 224.8 | 29.3 | 7,670 | 83.3 |
| Subtotal/C1 | | *81* | *1,204.6* | *276.1* | *4,360* | *82.7* |
| C2 71–83 | S. Nyanza | 8 | 7.9 | 10.6 | 750 | 63.7 |
| | Siaya | 1 | 0.1 | 0.8 | 130 | 59.3 |
| | Bungoma | 22 | 45.4 | 21.0 | 2,160 | 76.9 |
| | Kericho | 1 | 0.5 | 0.4 | 1,250 | 74.9 |
| | Nandi | 1 | 0.6 | 0.6 | 1,050 | 59.9 |
| | Embu | 14 | 127.9 | 27.2 | 4,700 | 73.8 |
| | Meru | 23 | 352.3 | 112.3 | 3,140 | 79.0 |
| | Machakos | 14 | 95.6 | 49.0 | 1,950 | 71.7 |
| Subtotal/C2 | | *84* | *630.3* | *221.9* | *2,840* | *76.4* |
| C3 71–83 | Baringo | 1 | 1.1 | 1.4 | 790 | 83.8 |
| | Nandi | 1 | 0.3 | 0.1 | 3,280 | 80.1 |
| | Taita/Taveta | 1 | 3.1 | 4.2 | 740 | 80.6 |
| | Kitui | 1 | 0.02 | 0.3 | 70 | 57.8 |
| C4 71–83 | West Pokot | 1 | 0.1 | 0.4 | 250 | 69.3 |
| | Kajiado | 1 | 0.02 | 0.1 | 200 | 56.5 |
| Total | | *171* | *1,839.5* | *504.5* | *3,650* | *80.5* |

*Source:* survey data, MOCD

This is reflected in the performance profile of coffee cooperatives. In the 1982/83 season, 46 of the 171 coffee societies had sales of parchment coffee exceeding K.Sh. 10 million. They accounted for 77 per cent of total coffee sales and for almost 80 per cent of the total payments to coffee farmers. Most of them are located within a limited area of Central province (Figure 4.12). These twenty-eight cooperatives, which generally record the lowest marketing costs, are far above the average size of coffee societies in terms of sales (K.Sh. 37 million) and account for 60 per cent of total coffee payments to farmers.

About three-fifths of the remaining 125 coffee societies, with

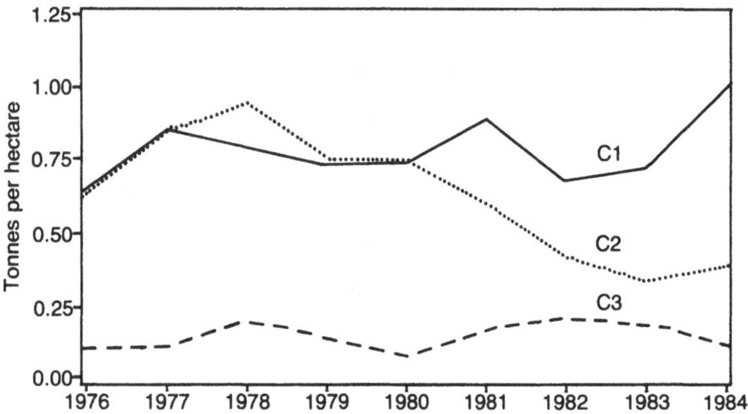


*Figure 4.6* Coffee yields/ha in C1–C3 environments, 1976–84
*Source:* Coffee Board

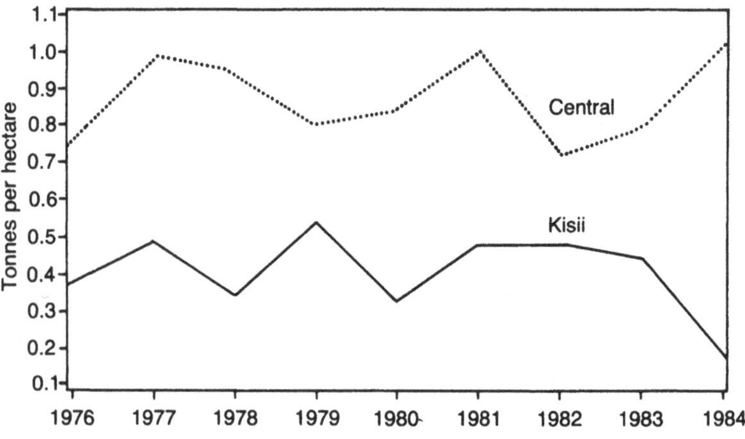


*Figure 4.7* Coffee yields/ha in Central province and Kisii district, 1976–84
*Source:* Coffee Board

sales below K.Sh. 10 million, operate in C2/C3 environments and about half of them in areas west of Rift Valley (Figure 4.14). Not surprisingly, their average marketing cost is more than twice as high, that is, *c.* 20 per cent of parchment sales.

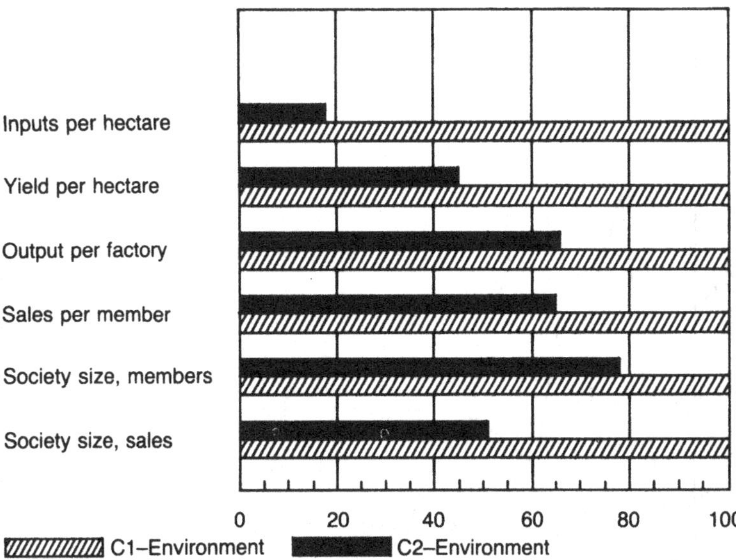


*Figure 4.8* Coffee. Performance levels of farmers and societies in C2-environments in relation to C1, 1982–83 (index C1 = 100)
*Source:* survey data

## *Credit and input supplies*

As earlier argued, yield levels are not only due to agro-ecological conditions but also to the general level of social and economic development within a society's area of operation. These environmental characteristics will be of consequence also for activities that may directly contribute to improved yield performance such as extension services, production credit and input supplies. As cooperatives are major suppliers of credit and inputs to coffee smallholders, it may be argued that these factors will also affect their ability to influence agricultural production and, hence, their own cost efficiency.

As regards production credit, practically all societies are linked to the CPCS. Unfortunately, available data do not permit us to give any detailed picture of the distribution of this production credit by society. However, in basic respects input sales by unions can be assumed to covary with variations in the volume of credit channelled through their affiliated primary societies.

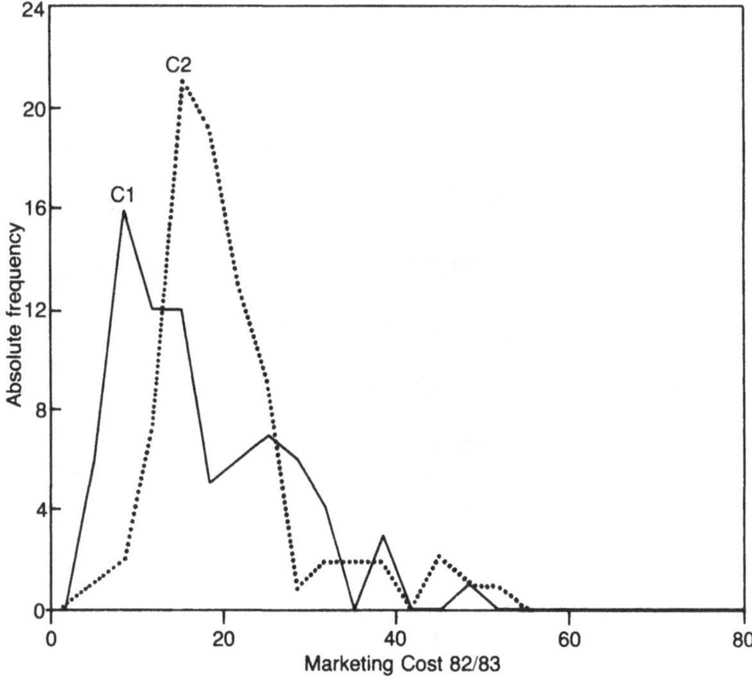


*Figure 4.9* Coffee. Frequency distribution of coffee societies in C1/C2-environments by marketing cost (% of parchment price)
*Source:* survey data

According to our survey data, based on the adjusted accounts of unions, sales of farm inputs amounted to K.Sh. 177 million in 1982/83. In a study by Whitaker,[16] also referring to the 1982/83 season, it is estimated that total sales would be in the region of K.Sh. 200 million. If it is assumed that unaffiliated primary societies account for part of this difference, the figures may be accepted as largely compatible. In the following we will use our data as supplements to those of Whitaker.

First it can be noted that the use of fertilizers, and most other chemicals, is not only far below the average level for estates, but the variations among the major coffee zones are also large. It seems as if the mark-up on inputs sold by cooperatives usually is in the range of 8–10 per cent. Only in Muranga are the prices charged markedly below the average. This is probably due both to a better procurement performance and to lower distribution costs. A

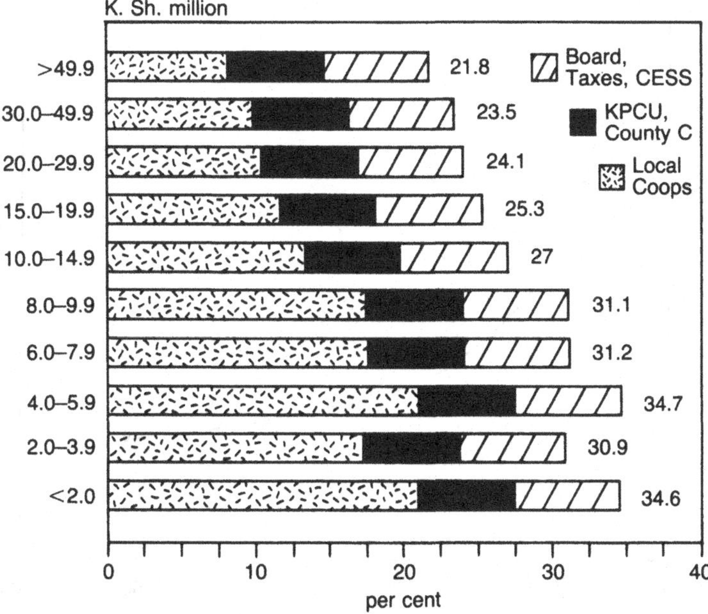


*Figure 4.10* Marketing costs in relation to parchment sales of coffee societies, 1982–83
*Source:* survey data

generally more important influence on the prices paid by farmers is that of geographical location in relation to main suppliers. Thus, for the most common types of fertilizers, differences in transport costs seem to result in 10–20 per cent higher prices in peripheral coffee zones as compared to districts close to Nairobi, particularly those in Central province.

Although the above estimations of input usage levels have to be interpreted with caution, it is evident that Muranga plays a leading role. As illustrated in Figure 4.15, there is also more generally a quite clear relation between cooperative sales of farm inputs and yield levels. However, the relation input–yield also contains reciprocal influences. Thus, most of the input sales of cooperatives are linked to the provision of production credit to the members. The amount of production credit for which a member is eligible is calculated as a percentage of the average value of coffee deliveries over the previous three years. Hence, the sales of inputs are largely determined by realized yields and coffee prices.

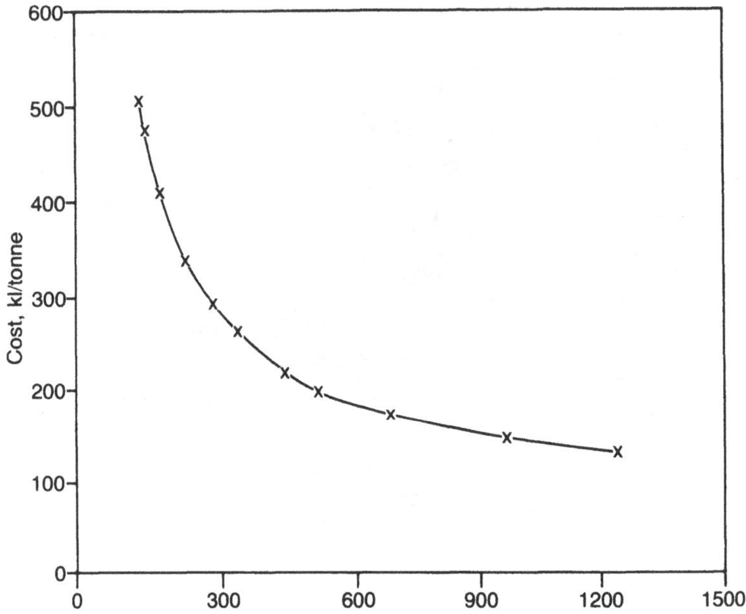


*Figure 4.11* Coffee factories. Processing costs (K£ per tonne) vs. intake of cherry (cwt)
*Source:* M. J. Whitaker, J. D. Roe, 'Coffee processing costs in the co-operative sector pp. 431–40 in *Kenya Coffee*, September 1985

*Figure 4.12* Coffee societies with parchment sales ⩾ K.Sh. 10 million
*Source:* survey data

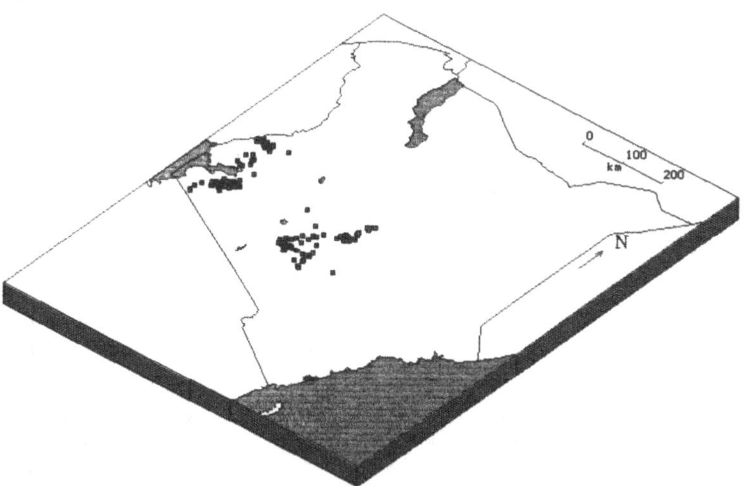


*Figure 4.13* Coffee societies with parchment sales < K.Sh. 10 million
*Source:* survey data

The interdependency between yield levels and input sales also means that cooperatives will tend to amplify both negative and positive changes in productivity. Thus, farmers whose yields have decreased will be able to buy less inputs on credit and, consequently, may encounter difficulties in improving their crop husbandry sufficiently to reverse the trend. This kind of problem may be particularly pronounced when population pressure or/and land fragmentation results in smaller coffee plots per member. Under these circumstances, the cost of maintaining the delivery system (credit and inputs) will also increase. Owing to the small volumes of produce delivered, farmers/members will gradually be less inclined to implement crop husbandry practices that, in terms of yields per hectare, may be significant but which are less interesting if the coffee *shamba* (smallholding) covers, for example, oneetenth of a hectare. Processes of this nature obviously cannot be curbed by service cooperatives: rather they may be perpetuated.

## *Kisii vs. the Central Highlands*

A comparison of Kisii with the districts in Central province may illustrate some of the points put forward above regarding decisive

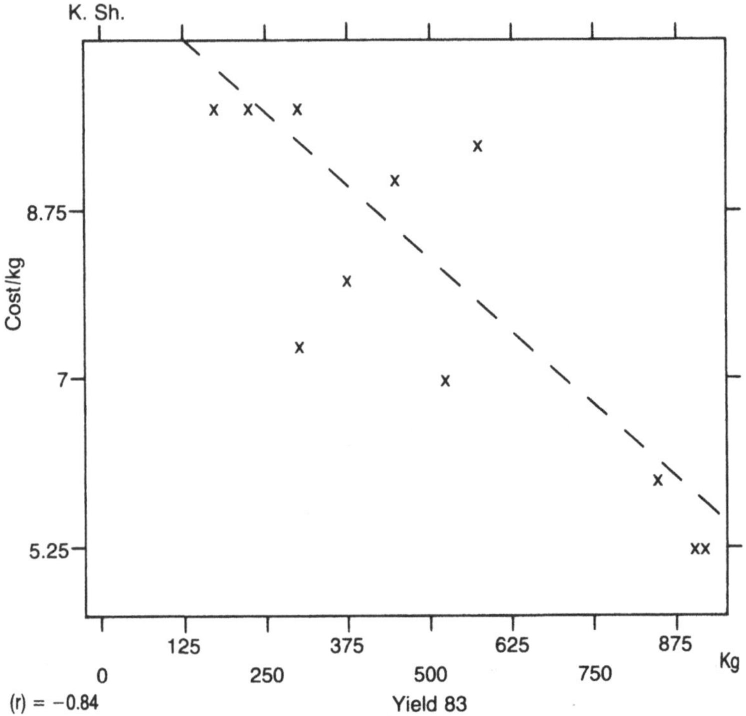


*Figure 4.14* Plot of cooperative marketing cost/kg clean coffee with yields in all major coffee districts, 1982–83
*Source:* survey data

*Table 4.15* Estimated sales of inputs to coffee smallholders by cooperatives, 1982/83 season

| *District* | *Ground fertilizers (tonnes)* | *Fungicides (tonnes)* | *Insecticides Herbicides ('000 L)* |
|---|---|---|---|
| Kisii | – | – | 5 |
| Kiambu | 3,272 | 330 | 31 |
| Muranga | 15,333 | 963 | 104 |
| Kirinyaga | 1,439 | 149 | 118 |
| Embu | 836 | 105 | 15 |
| Nyeri | 498 | 499 | 38 |
| Meru | 1,489 | 163 | 88 |
| Machakos | 596 | 69 | 11 |
| Total | 23,436 | 2,278 | 410 |

*Sources:* M. J. Whitaker, op. cit., p. 283; survey data

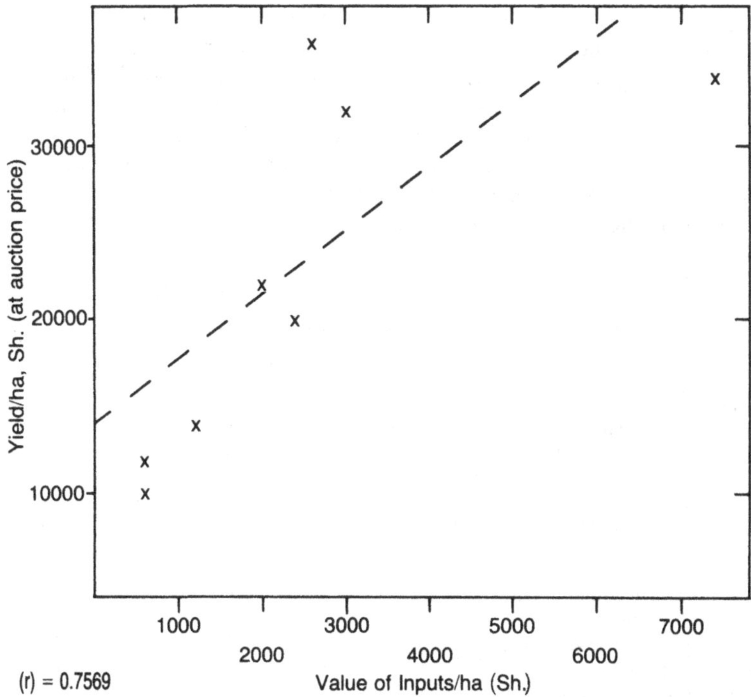


*Figure 4.15* Value of cooperative input sales/ha in relation to yields/ha, by district
*Sources:* J. M. Whitaker, 1985, op. cit; survey data

factors for the marketing and supply performance of service cooperatives. As earlier noted, Kisii displays a rather dismal trend in terms of yields/ha compared to the area covered by Central province (Figure 4.7). In the taxonomy of districts arrived at in Chapter 3, both areas were found to belong to the C1-type of environment, i.e. an environment which could be expected to offer comparatively favourable conditions for agricultural production. However, it was also observed that this classification was quite broad, and that major differences characterized districts even when they belonged to the same basic category.

In the case of Kisii, it is evident that its lower intra-category scores are due primarily to a lower level of differentiation of the economy, which among other things is reflected in a generally very low level of non-agricultural employment. To this could be added Kisii's rather unfavourable geographical location in relation to major urban and industrial centres. Although the size of the population has been increasing rapidly both in Kisii and Central province, its consequences for the development of agriculture have been quite different. In Kisii, agriculture has absorbed more or less the entire growth. This has not, however, generated significantly raised levels of productivity of land, at least not in terms of non-food production, through a gradual improvement of production technologies. The result has been increased pressure on land rather than intensified land use.

*Table 4.16* Profiles of environments of primary coffee societies in Kisii district and Central province

| | *1975/76* | *1983/84* |
|---|---|---|
| **Kisii** | | |
| – number of members ('000) | 36 | 89 |
| – area of mature coffee (ha) | 6,745 | 7,019 |
| – average deliveries/member (clean coffee) | 63 | 14 |
| – average yield/ha (clean coffee) | 334 | 182 |
| – area of mature coffee/member (ha) | 0.19 | 0.08 |
| **Central** | | |
| – number of members ('000) | 112 | 179 |
| – area of mature coffee (ha) | 26,404 | 43,507 |
| – average deliveries/member | 177 | 280 |
| – average yield/ha | 714 | 1,152 |
| – area of mature coffee/member (ha) | 0.24 | 0.24 |

*Sources:* survey data; Coffee Board

The economic-technical environment of Central province is markedly different. Most of the area is within Nairobi's sphere of influence. Physical infrastructure as well as public and commercial services are well developed, and non-agricultural employment is significant. The employment aspect is important not only because it is easing the absorption requirements of agriculture, but also because a considerable portion of the earnings go back as expenditure or investments in agriculture. The impact on agricultural, and hence cooperative development, of these contrasting environments is indicated by changes in coffee yields per hectare and member over the period 1975/76–1983/84.

As seen from the table above, membership has increased in both areas but apparently for different reasons. In Kisii, the planted area has remained more or less intact, and the growth of membership would thus be due mainly to fragmentation of coffee holdings. Production per hectare has stagnated and as the average area of coffee per member for 1984 was less than half that for 1976, average deliveries per member have fallen drastically. These trends are bound to have cost-inflating effects on coffee societies in the area, both in marketing and supply activities. Considering the magnitude of change in agriculture, it is conceivable that the cost increases 'forced' upon the individual societies have been so big that they have amplified the negative effects generated in the local environment.

As argued earlier, the economically and technically more advanced environment of Central province has facilitated continued improvements in the productivity of land. At the same time, the area under coffee has expanded by about 65 per cent. In spite of a considerable growth of membership, these developments have resulted in a rise in average deliveries per member. For the societies, the combined effects of areal expansion and raised yield levels have meant a quite dramatic growth of marketed volume, which has facilitated improved cost efficiency in processing and handling, and thus higher payment rates to members.

The impact of each of these trends is clearly visible in the performance profiles of the coffee societies in 1982/83. From (6) in Table 4.17 it can be seen that the quality of the coffee sold is considerably lower in Kisii. The lower price reflects poor husbandry practices which are partly the result of deficiencies in the quality of services provided by cooperatives. Further, there are obvious defects in management and equipment, and, generally, the societies are unable to meet in-built scale requirements. The societies' marketing costs/kg of parchment coffee are more than twice as high as the average level in Central province.

It also seems evident that without changes in the local environment to facilitate improved quality and significantly raised yields, measures to improve the cost efficiency of societies are likely to be of very limited consequence.

Thus, if we assume that the marketing costs in Kisii district are reduced to the same level as in Central province, i.e. K.Sh. 3.23 per kg parchment coffee, the coffee societies would have to cut their marketing costs by over 55 per cent. A cost reduction of that magnitude is totally unrealistic, considering both the constrained production capacity of the local environment and the cost-inflating elements inherent in the marketing structure.

In conclusion, the performance of coffee cooperatives indicates that under conditions where the productivity of land increases sufficiently to maintain a stable or rising value of deliveries per member (household), they seem to play a constructive role. The

*Table 4.17* Performance profiles of primary coffee societies in Kisii district and Central province

| | *Kisii* | *Central* |
|---|---|---|
| (1) Number of societies | 27 | 44 |
| (2) Number of members | 89,778 | 178,587 |
| (3) Sales, parchment, '000 Sh. | 99,990 | 1,094,100 |
| (4) Average sales/society, '000 Sh. | 3,703 | 24,866 |
| (5) Average factory output, tonnes | 45 | 109 |
| (6) Aver. price/kg, parchment coffee | 31.15 | 35.35 |
| (7) Aver. price/kg, paid to members | 21.50 | 29.65 |
| (8) Aver. coop. marketing cost/kg | 7.47 | 3.23 |
| (9) Payment rate, i.e. (6) ./. (8) ./. milling charges and county council cess in % of parchm. price | 69.97 | 83.87 |

*Sources:* survey data, Coffee Board and KPCU

creation of these kinds of condition, however, requires a differentiated rural economy with low transaction (interaction) costs, access to information and improved technologies, and employment and income-earning opportunities outside smallholder agriculture.

Less favourable environments are either unable to support the scale requirements of cooperatives or, alternatively, realized economies of scale will be superseded by escalating direct transaction costs. In both instances it will negatively affect efficiency and service quality. These adverse effects may of course coincide, in which cases the cost-inflating impact will be further accentuated (Table 4.13).

When also combined with the lower yield levels usually characterizing these types of environment, the organizational construct will be trapped in a 'high-cost/inflexibility' pocket which obstructs its ability to realize acceptable levels of efficiency and service quality. It may rather amplify the cost multiplier inherent in already disadvantaged environments. The performance rating of cooperatives thus is very sensitive to the kind of environment in which operations take place.

One decisive aspect of this is that they tend to perpetuate prevailing spatial stratification processes by generating cumulatively positive influences in favoured and expanding environments, while the opposite kind of influence is propagated simultaneously in regressing or disadvantaged and stagnant environments. Even in the case of a high-value crop such as coffee, it seems as if the former category of influences appears only in fairly unique types of environment.

Hence, contrary to what may seem self-evident, the observed behaviour of coffee cooperatives supports the conclusion that the mode of organization, as applied in Kenya, does not have the capacity autonomously to influence basic determinants of its own success and members' well-being.

## 4.4 Cotton

Cotton is grown in areas with a warm and fairly dry climate. Most of Kenya's cotton is produced in the Lake Victoria region, in the low altitude areas of Eastern and Central provinces, and at the coast. Cotton is also grown under irrigation in Tana River district and on a more limited scale in the northern part of Rift Valley. The crop is entirely grown by smallholders who often have cotton as the only or major cash crop. Intercropping with maize and beans is common in some areas. As noted in Chapter two, cotton was cultivated in Nyanza and Western provinces as early as the 1920s and was also introduced at an early stage along the coast. In other areas production started up after independence and most of the expansion has taken place since the early 1970s.

Available information about total hectarage under cotton and, hence yield levels, is very unreliable. As regards the Lake Victoria area and Machakos district (Eastern province), it is commonly held that yields are in the range of 200–300 kg per ha. In Meru, Embu (both in Eastern province) and Kirinyaga (Central province) yields are probably at least twice as high and on the irrigation scheme in Tana River district they stand at over 2,000 kg per ha. Most of the growth of output recorded between 1964–84 (Figure 4.16), however, seems to have been due to areal expansion rather than raised yield levels per hectare.

The total area planted in 1983 is likely to have been in the range of 75,000–80,000 ha. Information about the total number of growers is not available. One indication is the total membership of primary cotton societies which amounted to *c.* 101,000 in 1983. In the same year, cooperatives accounted for about two-thirds of total deliveries.

The seed cotton delivered by growers is processed into lint at ginneries. A residual output of ginning is cotton seed, which contains about 20 per cent oil and is therefore a valuable by-product for use in the manufacture of soap, cooking oil, etc. Fourteen ginneries were in operation in 1983: seven in the Lake Victoria area, four in Central/Eastern provinces and three in the Coast province. The output of lint expanded during the latter half of the 70s and reached a record level of *c.* 68,000 bales (38,000

*Table 4.18* Primary cotton societies, estimated membership and production of seed cotton by district, 1982–83

| *Environm.* | *District* | *No. of Societies* | *No. of Members* | *Seed cotton tonnes* | *No. of ginneries* |
|---|---|---|---|---|---|
| C1 71–83 | Kisumu | 4 | 9,620 | 1,190 | 1 |
| C2 71–83 | S. Nyanza | 12 | 17,473 | 2,676 | 2(U) |
| C2 71–83 | Siaya | 7 | 17,942 | 1,334 | 1(U) |
| C1 71–83 | Kakamega | 4 | 5,085 | 667 | – |
| C2 71–83 | Bungoma | 3 | 700 | 398 | 1(U) |
| C2 71–83 | Busia | 6 | 10,975 | 2,296 | 2(U) |
| C3 71–83 | Baringo | 1 | 1,007 | 361 | 1 |
| C4 71–83 | Turkana | 1 | 0 | 111 | – |
| C1 71–83 | Kirinyaga | 1 | 6,647 | 2,275 | 1 |
| C3 71–83 | Kilifi | 0 | 0 | 2,216 | 1 |
| C3 71–83 | Lamu | 0 | 0 | 177 | 1 |
| C4 71–83 | Tana River | 1 | 607 | 1,433 | 1 |
| C2 71–83 | Meru | 1 | 337 | 4,231 | 1(U) |
| C3 71–83 | Kitui | 0 | 0 | 2,018 | 1 |
| C2 71–83 | Machakos | 19 | 30,212 | 3,338 | 1 |
| Total | | 60 | 100,605 | 24,721 | 15 |

*Sources:* MOCD and CLSMB
*Note* U=ginnery owned by union; in Meru jointly with CLSMB

tonnes seed cotton) in 1980. Production has since then decreased and was *c.* 40,000 bales in 1984. Domestic consumption is estimated at about 45,000 bales (*c.* 25,000 tonnes seed cotton).[17]

## *Marketing structure and prices*

The main activities at the first stages of the marketing process comprise (i) growers delivering seed cotton to buying centres, where each lot is (ii) graded, weighed, bagged and recorded before being (iii) transported to a field store or to a main ginnery store, from where it is taken for (iv) ginning after which (v) the lint and seed are transported to a godown of the Cotton Lint and Seed Marketing Board (CLSMB). Although these operations involve a variety of actors and arrangements, it is the CLSMB which controls all marketing stages of the industry. The duties assigned to the Board include the purchase of seed cotton from growers and of all lint and seed from ginners, at prices set by the Ministry of Agriculture (at the recommendation of the Board). Buying, transportation and ginning can be carried out either by the Board itself or by the agency of any other organization or person. In addition, the CLSMB has the duty and authority to carry out extension services, and to purchase and operate ginneries. The

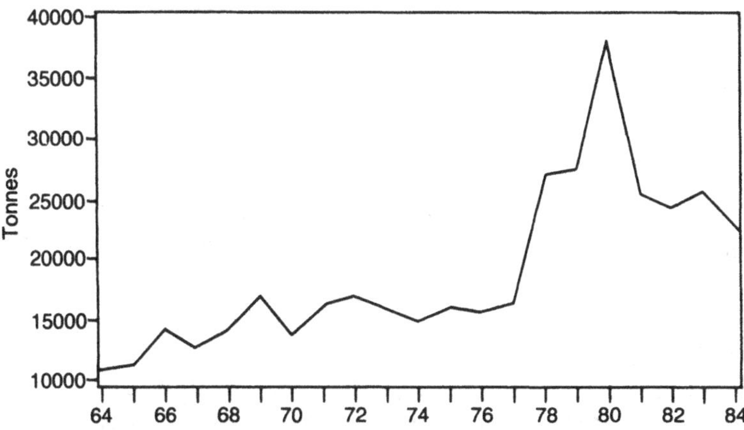


*Figure 4.16* Production of seed cotton, 1964–84 (tonnes)
*Source:* survey data

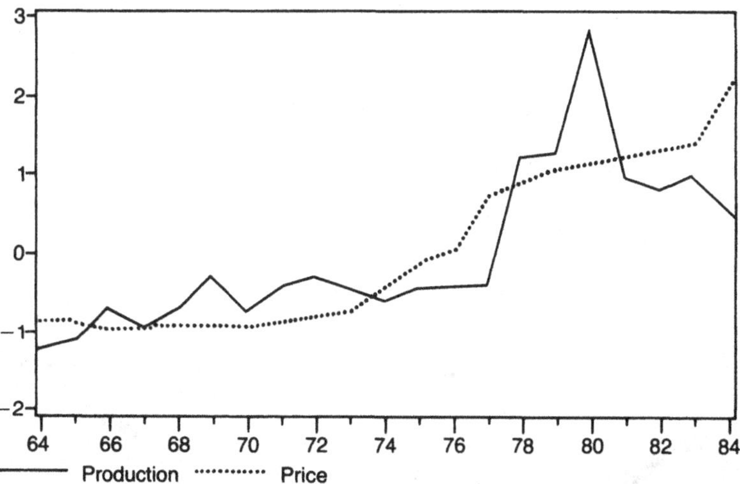


*Figure 4.17* Variations of production of seed cotton and average current producer prices 1964–84. Normalized scale
*Sources:* Ministry of Cooperative Development; Cotton Lint and Seed Marketing Board; Central Bureau of Statistics

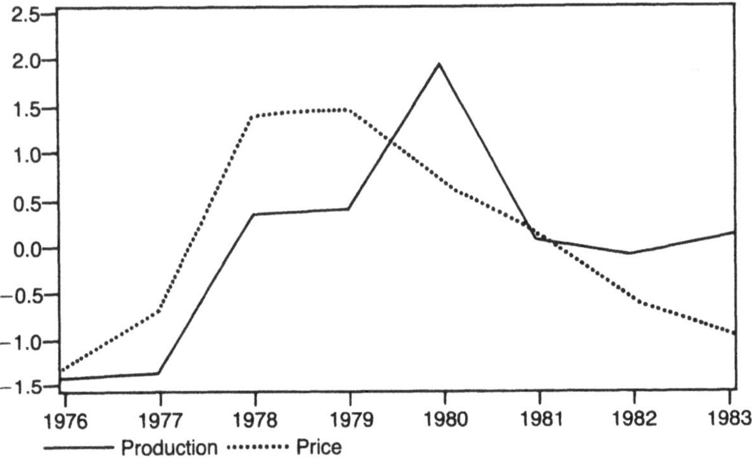


*Figure 4.18* Changes in seed cotton production and average producer prices (at 1976 prices) 1976–83. Normalized scale
*Sources:* Ministry of Cooperative Development; Cotton Lint and Seed Marketing Board; Central Bureau of Statistics

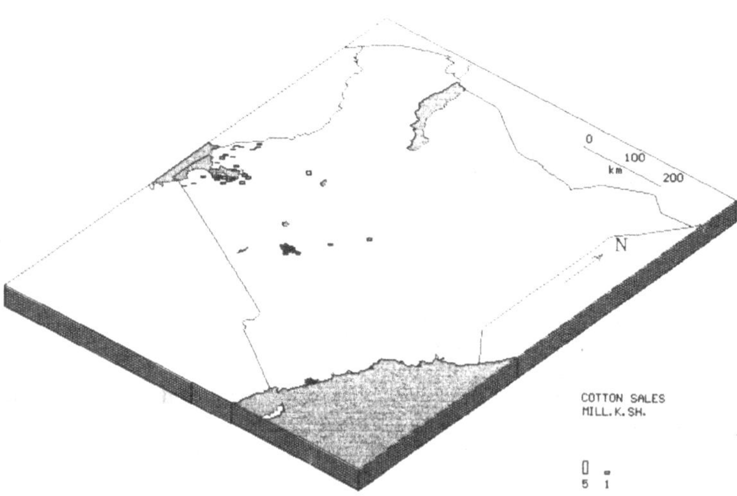


*Figure 4.19* Active cotton societies, 1983
*Source:* survey data

Board is also responsible for the final sale of lint and cotton seed. While these latter activities are carried out by the Board itself, buying and ginning often involve cooperative societies and unions as agents. As buying agents, they thus handled an estimated two-thirds of the crop in 1983.

In Nyanza and Western provinces, cooperatives were established in the 1960s. In the 1970s, existing privately owned ginneries were taken over by cooperative unions. The main activity of the primary cotton societies has been to run buying centres to which growers could deliver their crops. Buying teams, permanently stationed at one such centre during the season, also cover one or two adjacent centres. In the early 1980s primary societies in these two provinces were operating about 230 buying centres.

In Eastern and Central provinces, the buying activities are more centralized. In Kirinyaga and Meru districts the operations are restricted to two societies which use four or five mobile teams to cover about 110 buying centres. In Machakos district, it is instead the union which does all the buying using mobile teams, while the activities of primary societies are confined to credit and input supplies. About 200 buying centres are covered by the union. In other areas, buying is done either by the CLSMB or by private agents.

The price paid to farmers refers to seed cotton delivered at the buying centres. The price received depends on the quality of grade – AR usually being paid at twice the rate of BR. The society, union or private agent receives a fixed commission from the CLSMB for the seed cotton buying. This does not include the cost of storage of seed cotton in the field, before transport to a ginnery, which is covered by the Board. In most cases, storage cannot be arranged at the buying centre, and the crop therefore has to be taken to either a field store or to the ginnery on the same day it is bought. The cost of transport is paid by the Board.

In 1983, fifteen ginneries were in operation, of which six were owned by cooperatives, five by the Board, three by private firms, and one jointly by the Board and a primary cotton society (Meru) with the latter as the majority shareholder. With the exception of the Meru ginnery, all cooperatively controlled plants are located in Nyanza and Western provinces. According to the CLSMB, the technical capacity of the ginneries was *c.* 110,000 bales in 1983, and a further expansion to *c.* 133,000 bales was planned. About 45 per cent of the capacity was controlled by cooperatives (Table 4.18). The Board pays the ginners a commission which is expected to cover the processing cost of lint from the time seed cotton has been delivered until the bales of lint can be collected. Separate commissions are paid for bagging of cotton seed for milling and for dressing/packing of seed for planting.

As noted earlier, the production performance of the cotton industry deteriorated during the 1980s. Between 1980 and 1984, total output fell by over 40 per cent. Further, seen over the period 1964–84, the high output levels between 1977–80 could be seen as a temporary deviation from a generally poor record (Figure 4.16). As could be expected however, there is no single easily observable reason for the dismal performance of the cotton industry, although the producer price apparently has accounted for changes in total output (Figures 4.17 and 4.18).

A second serious problem has been that the commissions set by the Board neglect the differences in production costs that exist among the major cotton areas. The buying commission is paid by the CLSMB to appointed agents and is expected to cover the cost of staff, internal transport, general administration, bags, scales and other equipment. In the West Rift as well as in Meru and Kirinyaga, practically all buying was done by primary cotton societies in 1982/83. In Machakos this operation was run by the union. The buying commission then was 20 cts/kg and had developed as follows;

| | |
|---|---|
| 1974/75 | 0.07 Sh./kg |
| 1975/76 | 0.18 Sh./kg |
| 1979/80 | 0.15 Sh./kg |
| 1982/83 | 0.20 Sh./kg |
| 1983/84 | 0.25 Sh./kg |

According to a detailed assessment carried out by the Kenya National Federation of Cooperatives (KNFC) in 1981, the commission was grossly inadequate and the same year the CLSMB therefore was requested to raise it from 15 cts/kg to at least 25 cts/kg, including the cost of bags.[18]

As regards the ginning commission (per kg lint), the following rates were paid between 1975/76 and 1982/83;

| | *AR* | *BR* |
|---|---|---|
| 1975/76 | 1.50 | 1.50 |
| 1977/78 | 1.50 | 1.50 |
| 1979/80 | 1.50 | 1.50 |
| 1980/81 | 1.50 | 1.50 |
| 1981/82 | 2.50 | 2.80 |
| 1982/83 | 3.25 | 3.50 |
| 1983/84 | 3.25 | 3.50 |

According to the KNFC's analysis, which refers to 1981, the

commission should then have been Sh. 2.35 per kg. In 1983, a committee with representatives from the Board concluded that the commission would need to be raised to Sh. 3.25 per kg of AR lint and Sh. 3.50 per kg of BR lint. It should also be mentioned that the KNFC study arrived at the conclusion that at 50 per cent utilization of installed ginning capacity, the cost would exceed Sh. 5 per kg lint. As can be seen from Table 4.19, the average utilization rate in the 1982/83 season was about 40 per cent. Further, the commission for the handling of seed for planting had been fixed at Sh. 27.50 per ton for over ten years. After a recommendation from the KNFC, it was raised to Sh. 60 per ton in 1981/82.

The way in which the marketing board (CLSMB) has determined both producer prices and the various commissions seems to have contributed to the serious problems facing the cotton industry, particularly in the areas West of the Rift. As a result, the financial position of CLSMB had gradually and seriously deteriorated, which has had negative consequences for the Board's operational performance. These problems escalated into a crisis when production started falling during the first half of the 1980s.

It is worth noting that although the price management may have contributed to this development, producer prices and commissions have increased more rapidly than the market prices of lint and seed. The basic problem, generating many of the other difficulties that characterize the cotton industry, is apparently the smallholders' low production and yield levels. These can also be expected to reflect local conditions and the performance of the organizational infrastructure devised for marketing and supply services. Hence, have cooperatives managed to encourage increased production among their members and to what extent have they been successful?

## *Performance and environment*

One set of explanations can be related to the environmental characteristics of the main cotton-producing areas. In the following, we will therefore confine ourselves to the *major smallholder areas* which also cover practically all farmers who are members of primary cotton societies (Figure 4.19). These areas are found in Nyanza/Western provinces ('West Rift') and Central/Eastern ('East Rift'). In the former area, which used to be predominant not only in terms of cooperative membership but also as regards production, a considerable deterioration evidently has taken place. Over the period 1971–83, its share of national output of cotton has decreased from about two-thirds to one-third, while over the same period Central and Eastern provinces ('East Rift') increased theirs from 14 to 48 per cent. This development is also illustrated by regional differences in the utilization of existing ginning capacity (Table 4.19).

*Table 4.19* Production of lint (number of bales), ginning capacity and utilization, 1982–83 season

| *Area* | *Members* | *Bales* | *Technical capacity* | *% Utilization* |
|---|---|---|---|---|
| West Rift | 61,795 | 15,400 | 41,475 | 37 |
| Rift | 1,007 | 850 | 5,250 | 16 |
| East Rift | 37,196 | 21,350 | 39,900 | 54 |
| Coast | 607 | 6,890 | 23,700 | 29 |
| Total | 100,605 | 44,490 | 110,325 | 40 |

*Sources:* MOCD and CLSMB, internal documentation

As noted in Chapter three, the cotton belt in western Kenya is characterized by a significantly higher incidence of poverty than other smallholder areas. Based on IRS data, it has been estimated that the zone 'Upper Cotton West of Rift' comprises one-quarter of all 'very poor', and that Nyanza and Western provinces cater for over half of all 'poor'.[19] Generally, the physical infrastructure is grossly inadequate, very few urban centres of any importance exist and, even less, a developed network of viable, rural service centres.

Most of the cotton zone 'West Rift' actually constitutes a rural economy at a rudimentary level of development, which has been lacking both the ability and the support required to improve prevailing conditions of agricultural production and economic enhancement to any significant degree. An indication of the low income level of households growing cotton is that the deliveries per member (1982/83 season) averaged 100–150 kg seed cotton, resulting in a gross revenue of Sh. 400–600. This also means that the average household plants about one acre of cotton, which then is usually their only or major cash crop. The low productivity is of course part and parcel of an unfavourable socio-economic environment, ultimately reflected in 'poor husbandry'. Additionally, owing to unreliable rainfall, the cotton zone has a lower agricultural potential than most other smallholder areas.

Given these conditions, the prospects for ensuring efficient production, collection and processing of cotton seed are far from good, and they do not seem to have improved as a result of the involvement of cooperatives, the MOCD and the CLSMB.

Although most of the cotton production in East Rift is also found in drought-prone areas with generally poorer infrastructure than that of neighbouring highlands, the environment offers some advantages compared to that of 'West Rift'. One is the area's relative location. As the area constitutes a fringe to the dynamic rural economy of the highlands, and is also within Nairobi's zone of influence, it has easier access both to public and private services and to non-farm employment. As earlier argued in this study, all these factors are of consequence for crop husbandry and yield performance. Also, the production structure differs in important respects from that of West Rift. First, cultivation is geographically more concentrated, which has obvious effects on transport costs both at the level farm–buying centre and between buying centres and ginnery. Second, two out of the three ginneries in the East Rift zone were built in the 1970s and none of the three has less than sixteen gins. In West Rift, on the other hand, old ginneries with an average of twelve gins per establishment were bought by the unions between 1972 and 1978. In terms of cost efficiency, the latter clearly are inferior to those in East Rift.

The problems facing the cotton industry seem in part to be a consequence of the management performance of CLSMB. It was earlier mentioned that the Board, among other things is responsible for the purchase, transport and processing of seed cotton. Through a complex and often inconsistent agency system, activities have been handed over to agents. Thus, although the CLSMB has appointed buying agents, the Board itself is at the same time involved in field storage and transport of seed cotton to ginneries and from the ginneries to its godowns. This has resulted in an unclear division of responsibilities between the Board and its agents, which has negatively affected both agents and the farmers. In West Rift, problems with the CLSMB's transports from the field and from the ginneries have often meant either that the ginneries do not get enough seed cotton to maintain regular operations or that the ginnery stores get so congested that ginning has to be halted. In both cases, payments to both farmers and agents are delayed.

Given the extensive powers of the government bureaucracy over cooperative societies and unions, it would, as earlier argued, be a mistake to expect members' ideological commitments to carry much weight. We will instead pay attention to managerial aspects that, in our view, can be expected to be of decisive importance for their ability to contribute to increased production and improved material well-being among members. One main contribution in this direction would be to ensure efficiency in the marketing and processing activities, and another would be to provide farmers with support and services that enhance their production performance.

As regards the first aspect, we will now consider the buying of seed cotton, payment routines, ginning and, with reference to the second, credit and input supply services, and union management.

## Buying and payments

In Machakos, which is the main producer area in the East Rift zone, all buying and payment activities have traditionally been carried out by the union. As noted earlier, mobile buying teams are used. The same applies in Kirinyaga and Meru. Payments to farmers are scheduled and made at the buying centres by mobile teams. In Machakos, the teams are assisted by staff from the primary societies who prepare the payments, i.e. recorded production credit or advances from the societies are deducted from each farmer's gross proceeds. The actual cost for seed cotton buying seems to have been lowest in Kirinyaga and Meru (*c.* 15 cts/kg) as compared to about 20–33 cts/kg in Machakos. The lower cost in Kirinyaga and Embu is due both to shorter transport distances and generally higher yields of seed cotton per hectare. The payment system seems to have worked satisfactorily.

In the West Rift zone, the societies have been in charge of the buying, using teams covering a few buying centres each. In most cases, primary societies have paid part of their buying commission (3–5 cts) to the unions. As the commission constitutes the main income source of the societies, it also has to cover the cost of their general administration. Since the late 1970s, it seems highly unlikely that the buying commission has been sufficient to cover actual costs. A peculiar feature is that the CLSMB provided bags free of charge in East Rift but not in this area. In practice, this means that the West Rift zone received a commission that was 3–4 cts/kg lower. It has not been possible to establish the justification for this regional differentiation of subsidies.

From the smallholders' point of view, the decentralized system has certain advantages. Thus, during the harvesting period, the crop can be taken more or less daily to a buying centre. Deliveries are recorded and aggregated monthly, when arrangements for payment are made. Hence, it has probably not been so much the collection activity as deficiencies in the payment routines that have contributed to the fall in production experienced after 1980. The critical shortcoming then was that the transfer of payments due to farmers from the CLSMB through the CBK, the unions and primary societies were consistently very late. According to our sources,[20] delays of six months have been common. The main reasons for this have been a combination of liquidity problems, red tape and inefficiency both at unions and the CLSMB. The last-mentioned aspect then includes the effects of serious deficiencies in the transport organization both as regards deliveries from field stores to ginnery and from ginnery to godown which have disturbed the ginning operations and, ultimately, the timing of payments.

According to an agreement reached between the CLSMB and the MOCD in December 1983,[21] the Board was to take over the buying and then use mobile teams. It was specified that a certain minimum number of staff would continue to be employed in each society, in addition to the staff deployed by the CLSMB for 'lorry-buying', and that the MT-system would be maintained.

Apparently, however, very few activities remain at society level. In 1985, the only role of primary societies in South Nyanza seemed to be the recording of the total quantity bought by the CLSMB, so that the commission due to the society could be calculated. For this purpose, copies of 'cotton-buying receipts' were received from the Board. In addition, the societies were required to provide the Board with information about member's outstanding loans, so that these could be deducted before payments were made.

With the revised organization, the individual smallholder seems to be worse off than before. In accordance with the system with 'lorry-buying', seed cotton is collected at specified times at each buying centre. The CLSMB makes payments based on each such collection round. Due to lack of transport and long distances, farmers cannot at any single time carry much seed cotton to the buying centres (collection points). If the buying team is delayed, there is nobody to take care of the crop and, according to our sources, these delays are a matter not of hours but of days. Finally, as a result of the reorganization, the CLSMB claimed that it would be possible to pay farmers at the sites of the Board's field stores every fortnight. Apparently, however, the payment performance has remained poor.

## Ginning

The ginneries in East Rift, most of which have been established during the last twenty years, are either private (one plant) or owned by the CLSMB (in Meru jointly with a cooperative society). Although we have not had access to accounts and detailed production statistics of Board-owned ginneries, it may be assumed that they are generally more efficient than the five cooperative ginneries in West Rift. The latter were acquired between 1972 and 1978. For the financing of this investment, the unions fell back on their members for contributions and on the CBK for loans. The prices paid, ranging between Sh. 0.5–7 million per ginnery, seem far too high considering that all plants were built during the 1930s or earlier.

As the machinery is run-down, breakdowns are common and the costs for spare parts, repairs and fuel are high. Thus, while the installed processing capacity would allow for a ginning period of 6 months/year, most plants operate 10 to 12 months. These problems have been further perpetuated by miserable performance in seed cotton collection and transports, and by poor management of unions/ginneries. One reflection of the status of ginnery management is the staff establishment. A committee[22] studying the labour utilization at the cooperative ginneries in 1981/82 arrived at the following results as regards actual and recommended staff deployment:

| | *No. of casuals* | *No. permanent* | *Total* |
|---|---|---|---|
| Actual | 666 | 171 | 837 |
| Required | 346 | 122 | 468 |

Taking together the various deficiencies characterizing the ginning operations, they have resulted in heavy losses for the unions. This, in turn, has led to the unions at times appropriating part or most of the buying commission intended for affiliated primary societies.

In 1983/84, the Lake Victoria Union financially collapsed, and most of the other unions were heading in the same direction. In Lake Victoria, measures were taken to restructure the union and a new (interim) management was appointed. The union's activities resumed in 1984/85. By 1985, however, little had changed: the 1983/84 crop had been a disappointment and, seemingly, ginneries operated at very low levels of capacity utilization both at Lake Victoria and Rachuonyo (at Kendu Bay). In spite of that, both unions continued with an inflated staff establishment. Considering the level of operations in 1985, the number of staff deployed could probably have been reduced by 50 per cent.

## Credit and input supplies

In East Rift, the Machakos union runs the buying operations. The activities of primary cotton societies are largely confined to the provision of production credit and inputs. The latter activities have been made possible through financial and technical assistance from Machakos Integrated Development Programme (MIDP).[23] Thus, the introduction of credit services and input supplies has been linked to the establishment of produce and input stores at primary level and to improved management information services to the societies. As important as these measures may be, they have constituted only part of a wider range of investments and development activities aimed at strengthening the production capacity and preserving the physical environment of semi-arid and arid areas in the district.

As regards the credit programme, it was expected to reach about 24,000 smallholders. In the period 1979–82, the credit services seem to have been quite successful at least compared to the achievements of other programmes. The repayment level in 1981/82 was about 60 per cent, and it was expected that it could be raised to at least 80 per cent. However, cotton production decreased in 1982/83, and apparently the repayment performance deteriorated.[24] It also seems clear that the diversification of the MDCU's operations, not least the extension of its operations to cotton production in semi-arid and arid areas, had by 1983 weakened the union's commercial viability (Table 4.20). Given the prescribed structure of the cooperative sector, however, an improvement in this respect largely falls outside the union's sphere of control, i.e. in basic respects it is not a management issue. A positive development will instead be dependent on whether investments in improved crop husbandry, rural infrastructure and economic differentiation will raise productivity and levels of surplus production sufficiently to enable agriculture to support the cooperative set-up.

Also in West Rift, production credit was seen as a major device for stimulating agricultural growth and rural development. The necessary support, however, was conceived more narrowly than by the MIDP. Apart from the necessary financial component, it apparently was judged sufficient to create a machinery for procurement, storage, transport and sales of inputs. Very little attention was generally paid to the type of environment in which these activities were expected to constitute a self-sustained and growth-inducing force. Thus, under the main credit programmes introduced in West Rift,[25] the credit component convention was integrated with supporting measures such as (i) stores for farm inputs and produce, (ii) vehicles, (iii) extension services, demonstrations and (iv) management training. Furthermore, all these programmes simply added to the activities of existing cooperative unions and societies.

Initially, that is between 1977–80, the programmes seem to have contributed to increased production of cotton. Soon, however, their shortcomings both in terms of design and implementation became quite evident. Frequently, loans were too large in relation to what could be practicably achieved in terms of increased farm production. Also, owing to red tape and logistical constraints, loans and/or inputs were too often available at the wrong time. As a result, repayment failures soon became rampant; a further contributory factor was the poor recording of loanees. From having had an initial positive effect on production, the impact of the credit programmes turned mainly negative. This applies not only to on-farm production but also to the performance of cooperatives. Farmers owing their society money, and being unable to repay the loans, obviously tried to avoid dealing with it. The stores for sales of inputs had to close down, and in some cases vehicles and buildings were auctioned to meet debts incurred by the unions.

Moreover, the funds for credit were channelled through the unions to affiliated societies and their members. These administratively aggrandized and poorly managed unions, already having incurred heavy losses both on their ginning operations and other activities, evidently started using part of their funds as working capital. Considering their continuous losses, it was actually a question not merely of using but of consuming the funds. This happened not only to money transferred from the CBK through the unions, but evidently also to loan repayments by members of affiliated primary societies. Consequently, a situation developed where it was close to impossible to establish where disbursed funds or repaid loans had disappeared. The general confusion was furthered augmented by the limited and very sporadic attempts made by the MOCD staff to sort out the matter. Audits were generally several years in arrears, and follow-up and corrective actions on budgets and trial balances did not seem to exist.

In the 1984/85, however, various arrangements seemed to have been agreed upon between the CLSMB, the MOCD and the CBK to clear some of the debts incurred by the Lake Victoria Union and its affiliated societies. Thus, although the primary societies were practically dormant, they were officially paid the buying commission of 25 cts/kg. From this commission, it was directed, 10 cts were to be deducted for repayment of CBK-loans and another 5 cts for the union. Thereby the problem with loan recovery could be left to the individual societies. As the produce is no longer marketed through the societies, this is probably an impossible task. In reality it means that the farmers collectively will have to pay back individual members' loan defaults.

*Table 4.20* Selected performance indicators for Machakos DCU and cotton unions in West Rift (K.Sh)

| *Union* | *No. of staff* | *Turn-over ('000)* | *Input sales ('000)* | *Profit/ loss ('000)* | *Total liabts ('000)* | *Debt to CBK ('000)* | *Loans to members ('000)* | *Member sales ('000)* |
|---|---|---|---|---|---|---|---|---|
| (1) Machakos | 419 | 9,631 | 5,246 | –1,254 | 19,700 | 20,642 | 4,077 | 112,000 |
| (2) Siaya | 36 | 11,717 | 400 | –374 | 17,200 | 8,894 | 8,087 | |
| (3) Rachuonyo | 51 | 7,205 | 149 | –263 | 13,335 | 21,055 | 7,807 | |
| (4) Victoria | 70 | 8,343 | 211 | –490 | 15,786 | 12,660 | 6,429 | |
| (5) Luanda | 217 | 4,385 | 602 | –342 | 25,151 | 12,539 | 7,185 | |
| (6) Nambale | 111 | 3,243 | 505 | –883 | 7,944 | N/A | 2,556 | |
| (7) Malaba | 188 | 13,974 | 146 | –1,724 | 24,616 | 29,196 | 4,200 | |
| (2) through (7); SUM | 673 | 48,867 | 2,013 | –4,076 | 104,032 | 84,344 | 36,264 | 25,000 |

*Source:* Union accounts and Cooperative Bank (CBK)

Even by 1983, it seemed clear that the cooperative infrastructure, with the assistance of credit programmes, was contributing towards an eventual collapse of the cotton industry in West Rift. They were all making losses and their assets included K.Sh. 36 million owed by members (crop production loans). Loans to the CBK amounted to more than double the size of their total turnover.

## *Conclusions*

The dismal performance of the cotton industry in the first half of the 1980s can be ascribed to a range of factors, though predominantly to prices, the structure of the industry (including state intervention) and the types of environments the main producer areas represent. In the cotton areas west of Rift Valley, where most of the first-stage marketing is carried out by cooperatives, the deterioration in performance has been particularly pronounced. State intervention, largely made possible by the support of donor agencies and usually taking the form of 'supply-side' incentives and organizational manipulation, has not eased the problems facing the smallholder economy in this region. Neither the credit programmes, nor the cooperative organizations, nor the two combined, can in themselves make any decisive, positive contribution towards a transformation of the rural economy. Instead they may actually retard development when generating bureaucratic, authoritarian and largely unproductive modes of effecting social change.

The reasons behind low agricultural productivity and widespread poverty are more basic in nature: physically, technically and economically the environment facing cotton-producing smallholders is too rudimentary to support increased and diversified production. To cite an example, in the appraisal preceding IADP, it was estimated that 0.56 Sh. would have to be spent on infrastructural development for every shilling spent on smallholder credit. This figure was later revised to 9 shillings! Seen in relation to the conditions prevailing in the West Rift region, even the latter figure is grossly underestimated. The only programme that seems to have taken these aspects seriously is that of MIDP in Machakos.

## 4.5 Pyrethrum

Pyrethrum is an annual herb with daisy-like flowers, from which an insecticide is extracted. It is grown at altitudes of 2,000 m or more and requires a well-distributed average rainfall of at least 1,000 mm annually. The pyrethrin extracted from the dried flowers has some major advantages over most synthetics. It has a superior safety record when used for humans, a rapid effect and no residues accumulate in flora or fauna.[26] Pyrethrum's major disadvantage, which has so far limited the market, is its price.

Pyrethrum was first introduced into Kenya in 1931 and during most of the colonial period it was grown on a large scale by the settlers. In the wake of the Swynnerton Plan in the 1950s, pyrethrum was also introduced among smallholders in Kiambu and Kisii. Production was closely controlled and smallholders who were given permission to grow the crop had to market the dried flowers through cooperative societies. After independence, the cultivated area expanded, particularly in the former White Highlands (Figures 4.20 and 4.21). Already in the early 1970s, smallholders accounted for 90 per cent of the crop. On the world market, Kenya then held a dominant position with a market share of about 70 per cent.[27]

In 1960, the average annual yield was about 440 kg/ha. When production shifted from large-scale farms to smallholdings, yields fell to about 280 kg/ha. During the latter half of the 1970s and early 1980s, the average annual yield levels were in the range of 300–350 kg/ha. A pyrethrin content of 2 per cent or above is considered very good. In the 1973–83 period, the average rate was in the range of 1.3–1.5 per cent. The pyrethrin content is affected by the planting material, crop husbandry, ecological conditions – mainly altitude – and by drying techniques.

### *Marketing structure and prices*

After picking, the flowers are dried either by the smallholders themselves or by a cooperative society. In the former case, sun drying is predominant. Particularly in areas with prolonged misty conditions, such as Central province and part of Rift Valley, primary societies may operate kerosene- or charcoal-fired driers. As the drying results in a weight loss of about 75 per cent, the latter arrangement obviously means that the farm-society transports will be more demanding. If professionally done, on the other hand, artificial drying is likely to result in a higher pyrethrin content. The dried flowers are packed into 30-kg bags and either the primary society or the union to which it is affiliated arranges for transport to the factory. Processing is done at a factory located at Nakuru and owned by the Pyrethrum Board of Kenya. The PBK is also responsible for the final sales (exports) of pyrethrin. Realized prices, combined with forecasts of how export markets develop, constitute the basis for determining the producer price. The price paid to farmers is directly dependent on the pyrethrin content. Unfortunately it has not been possible to elicit information about the PBK's processing and marketing costs. In published statistics, the price paid by the Board is based on 'extract equivalents', while the export price refers to 'extract'. As long as the conversion rate between extract and extract equivalent is not made available, we are unable to establish a complete price chain.

Recapitulating some basic price and output features characterizing the industry after independence, it can first be noted that total output fell in the latter half of the 1960s and then probably mainly as a result of unfavourable prices. In 1970–75, the trend changed and total output more than doubled (Figure 4.22). Production expanded considerably on the newly established settlement schemes in Rift Valley and then, in particular, in Nyandarua district (Figures 4.20 and 4.21). This period of growth also coincided with the government's restructuring of societies and unions in Kiambu, Nyandarua and Kisii. A major innovation,

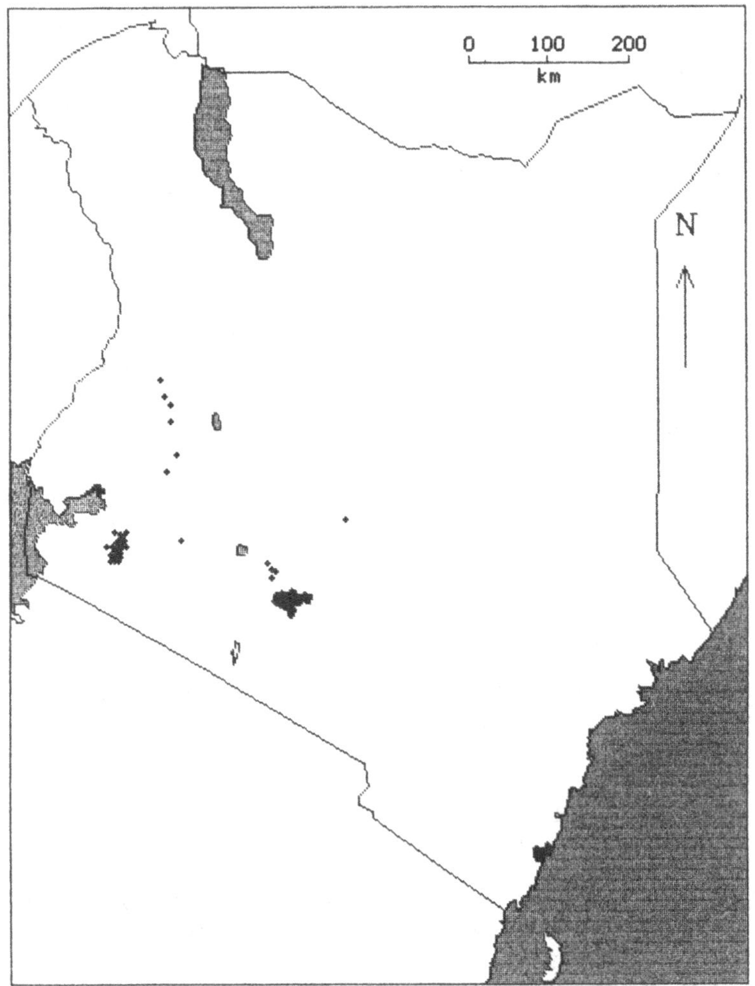


*Figure 4.20* Pyrethrum societies registered before independence
*Source:* survey data

apart from a new administrative system, was the introduction of production credit (CPCS). After 1975, however, the trend again took a down-turn. One reason for this is indicated in Figure 4.26, which illustrates that the price ratio pyrethrum/tea switched to the advantage of the latter. In areas with a potential for tea cultivation and where the necessary organizational infrastructure (KTDA) existed, primarily in Kisii Kiambu (env. C1), this resulted in

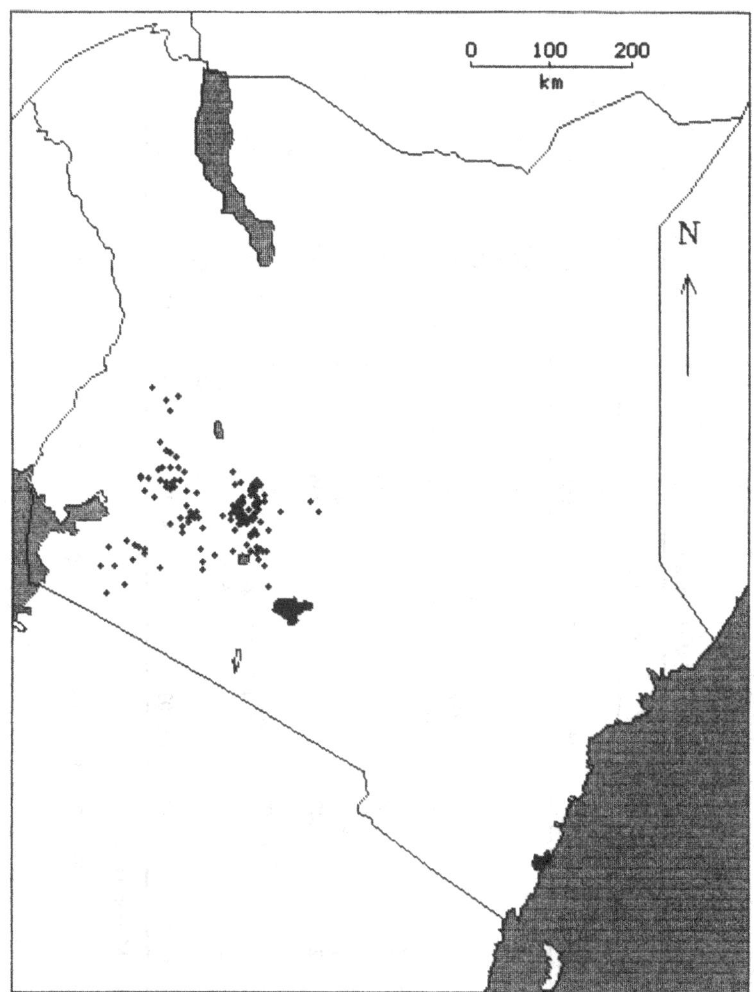


*Figure 4.21* Pyrethrum societies registered after independence
*Source:* survey data

changes in output mix and land use. Not until the nominal price on pyrethrum had more than doubled compared to 1975 did production revive. Record outputs were achieved both in 1981 and 1982, after which production again fell but now more dramatically than on any earlier occasion. In Kisii, with twenty-nine primary societies marketing pyrethrum and having over 58,000 registered members, cultivation had practically ceased by 1985. A seemingly puzzling

*Table 4.21* Value of pyrethrum sales (at board prices) by district and category of primary society, 1982–83.[1]

| | *No. of societies* | | *Sales (Sh. '000)* | | *Members* | | *Total* | | |
|---|---|---|---|---|---|---|---|---|---|
| *District* | *Mono* | *Mixed* | *Mono* | *Mixed* | *Mono* | *Mixed* | *Sales* | *Members* | *Sales per member, Sh.* |
| Kisii (3) | 23 | 4 | 19,638 | 3,231 | 51,618 | 7,120 | 22,869 | 58,738 | 389 |
| Nakuru (20) | 19 | 5 | 5,261 | 384 | 3,948 | 583 | 5,645 | 4,531 | 1,246 |
| Baringo (21) | 1 | 2 | 0 | 359 | 217 | 657 | 359 | 874 | 411 |
| Kericho (22) | 1 | 7 | 4,471 | 332 | 2,610 | 1,982 | 4,803 | 4,592 | 1,046 |
| U. Gishu (23) | 9 | 4 | 4,879 | 856 | 2,498 | 828 | 5,735 | 3,326 | 1,724 |
| Nandi (24) | – | 6 | – | 1,888 | – | 1,154 | 1,888 | 1,154 | 1,636 |
| Elgoy-M (26) | 5 | 7 | 818 | 695 | 2,541 | 3,644 | 1,513 | 6,185 | 245 |
| West Pokot (27) | – | 1 | – | 180 | – | 570 | 180 | 570 | 316 |
| Laikipia (28) | 1 | 1 | 725 | 50 | 50 | 400 | 775 | 450 | 1,722 |
| Narok (29) | 3 | 2 | 342 | 262 | 1,578 | 234 | 604 | 1,812 | 333 |
| Nyeri (50) | – | 3 | – | 319 | – | 777 | 319 | 777 | 410 |
| Nyandarua (52) | 7 | 44 | 7,129 | 11,028 | 3,605 | 12,322 | 18,157 | 15,927 | 1,140 |
| Kiambu (54) | 8 | – | 2,233 | 319 | 13,630 | – | 2,233 | 13,630 | 187 |
| Taita (70) | 1 | – | 157 | – | 96 | – | 157 | 96 | 1,635 |
| Embu (80) | 1 | – | 487 | – | 590 | – | 487 | 590 | 825 |
| Total | 79 | 86 | 46,140 | 19,903 | 82,981 | 30,271 | 65,724 | 113,252 | 583 |

*Sources:* survey data; annual accounts (Masaba union).

*Note*

1 In the category 'mixed', 83 societies have dairy as the main marketing activity, two societies have animals and one has wheat.

feature is of course how this could happen in the absence of seriously deteriorating prices and *before* a major deterioration of the price ratio pyrethrum/tea had taken place (Figures 4.23–24 and Table 4.21).

In our opinion, the main reason for the fall in production is to be found in the price and marketing strategies of the PBK. As mentioned earlier, Kenya had developed into a major supplier of pyrethrin on the world market. In 1978–80, it was apparently felt by the PBK that major price increases, justified by the need to turn around the negative trend in production, would be accepted and absorbed by the market. In retrospect, it is evident that this was a serious mistake. Main consumer countries responded by switching to synthetic substitutes and, as a consequence, the PBK found it increasingly difficult to pay farmers for their deliveries. Smallholders, in turn, responded by switching to other crops with disastrous effects for total output. Thus, by 1984, production was hardly more than one-tenth that of the 1982-level.

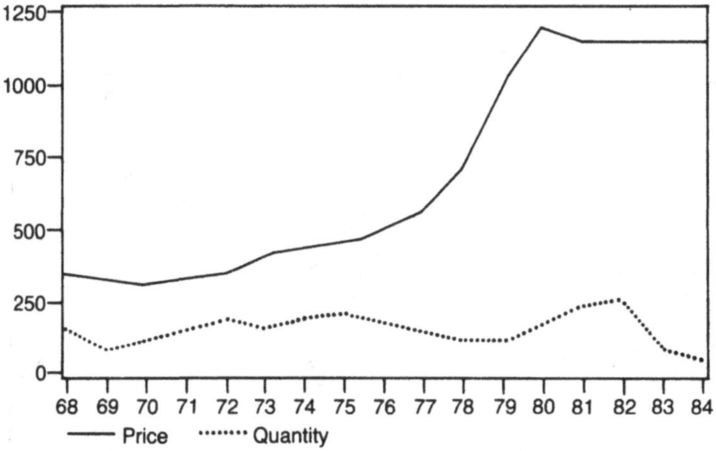


*Figure 4.22* Production of pyrethrum, 1968–84 (tonnes and K.Sh./tonne)
*Source:* survey data

## *Performance and environment*

As indicated above, the functions of cooperatives are fairly simple. In the case of individual drying, the society is responsible for the recording of delivered produce, for transport and, with the assis-

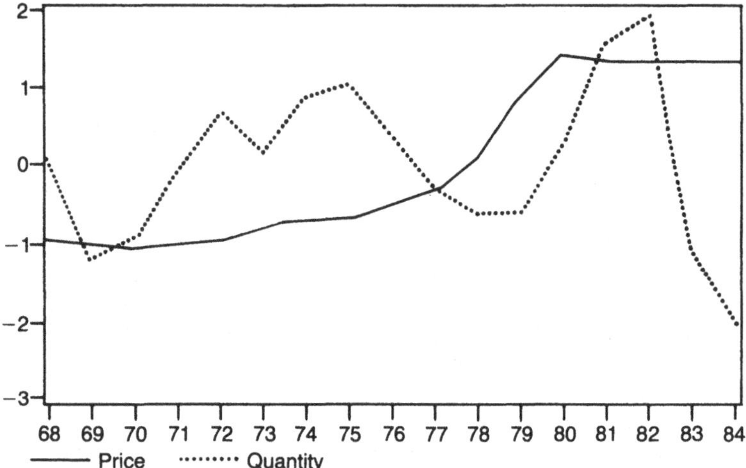


*Figure 4.23* Variations in production of pyrethrum and current producer prices, 1968–84. (Normalized scale)
*Source:* survey data

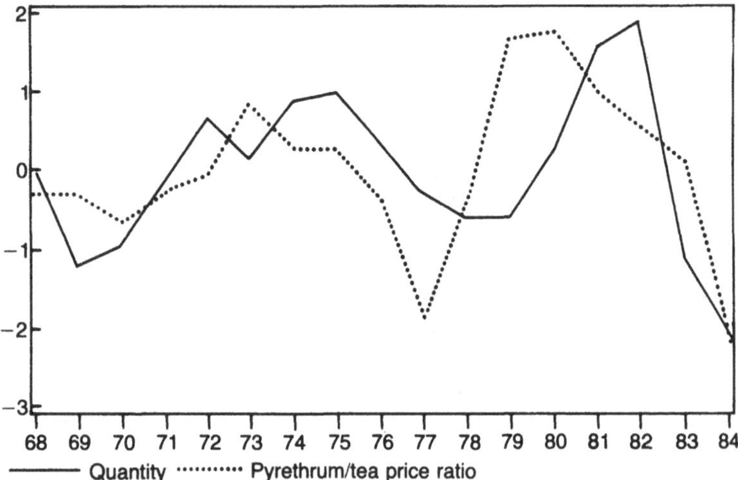


*Figure 4.24* Variations in production of pyrethrum and price ratio pyrethrum/tea, 1968–84. (Normalized scale)
*Source:* survey data

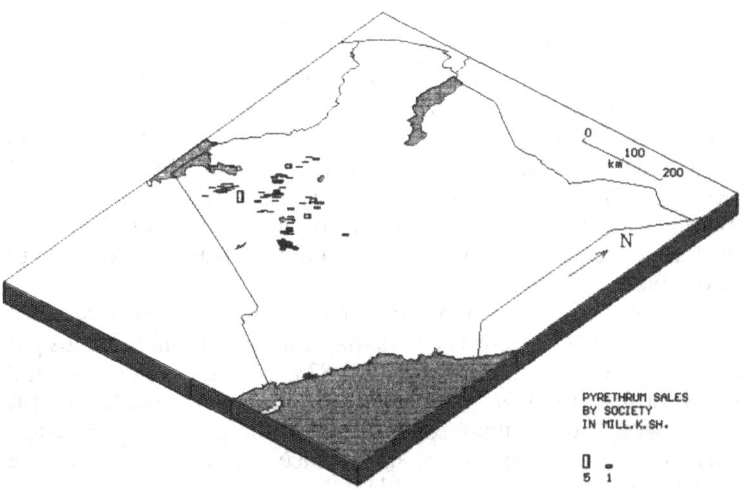


*Figure 4.25* Societies marketing pyrethrum only, 1983
*Source:* survey data

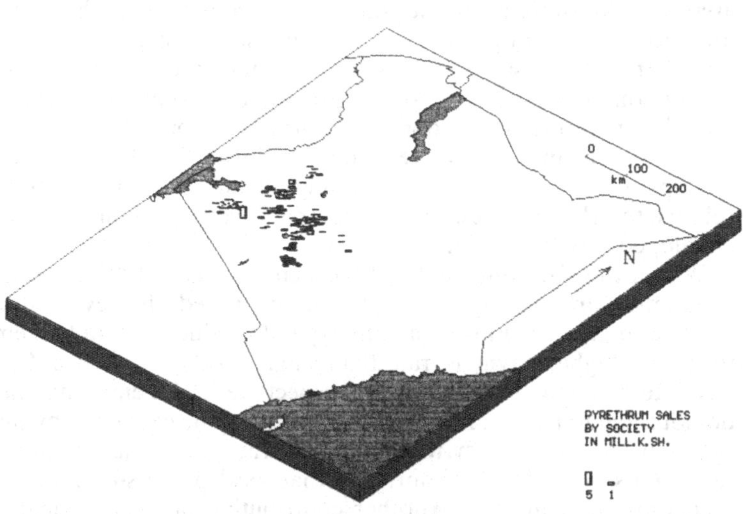


*Figure 4.26* All societies marketing pyrethrum, 1983
*Source:* survey data

tance of the union, for channelling the payments from the PBK to the individual farmers. To this can at most be added the activity of artificial drying. While practically all coffee societies are mono-produce in character, societies marketing pyrethrum often also deal with other types of produce, mainly dairy (Table 4.21). Actually, in terms of the value of marketed production, pyrethrum is the least important type of produce among the majority of societies. That the combination of pyrethrum-dairy is common is obviously a result of agro-ecological conditions. At altitudes above 2,000 m these activities, together with tea cultivation, are likely to be the most feasible.

Although the membership of societies that market pyrethrum exceeds 110,000, the crop is not a major income-earner. Yields per hectare have remained low – in 1982/83 *c.* 300 kg dry flowers – and only in a few districts, mainly on the settlement schemes in Rift Valley with their comparatively large holdings, are the average deliveries per member of any significance. Generally, the average sales per society are small (Table 4.22).

The C1-type of environment used to dominate pyrethrum production. In 1982/83, however, production fell drastically in the traditionally important producer districts such as Kisii, Nyeri and Kiambu and by 1984 it had practically ceased. The regional output profile of the pyrethrum industry in 1982/83 and 1983/84 thus is atypical. An interesting question is of course why the most dramatic falls in output are recorded in the C1-environment. As seen here, the basic reason is that in these areas farmers had the option of responding to the price and marketing problems affecting pyrethrum by adopting alternative crops. In the short term, these include maize, vegetables and fruit, in which case the C1-type of environment is generally favoured by its location relative to urban markets and by, comparatively speaking, a better developed infrastructure.

Within the size range defined by society sales in 1982/83, scale economies are not apparent. It can be noted, however, that societies marketing more than one type of produce generally seem to have a higher payment rate than single-produce societies. It is also interesting to note that in this respect the C1/C2 environments do not seem to be superior to C3/C4. This may be explained by the fact that the crop is easy to handle and transport, that it requires few inputs apart from labour, and that local processing requirements are very limited. Another contributing factor is probably that the PBK's factory is located at approximately the same distance from the major producer centres.

How then did the cooperative infrastructure react to mitigate

*Table 4.22* Value of pyrethrum sales (at board prices) and payment rates by category of environment, 1982–83

| | *Number of societies* | | *Sales (Sh. '000)* | | *Average sales per society* | | | *Payment rate (%)* | | *Average sales per member (Sh.)* |
|---|---|---|---|---|---|---|---|---|---|---|
| *Environment* | *Mono* | *Mixed* | *Mono* | *Mixed* | *Mono* | *Mixed* | | *Mono* | *Mixed* | |
| C1 71–83 | 31 | 7 | 21,871 | 3,550[1] | 705 | 507 | (832)[2] | 83.0 | 84.7 | 351 |
| C2 71–83 | 9 | 51 | 12,087 | 11,360 | 1,343 | 223 | (1,484) | 80.2 | 89.2 | 1,110 |
| C3 71–83 | 36 | 25 | 11,840 | 4,232 | 329 | 169 | (1,271) | 87.7 | 83.8 | 967 |
| C4 71–83 | 3 | 3 | 342 | 442 | 114 | 147 | (662) | 86.5 | 91.9 | 329 |
| Total | 79 | 86 | 46,140 | 19,584 | 584 | 228 | (1,340)[2] | 83.5 | 87.2 | 580 |

*Sources:* survey data; annual accounts (Masaba union).

*Notes*

1 Value of pyrethrum sales.

2 Average of total value of marketed produce.

the negative impact of turbulence hitting the industry in the early 1980s? To shed some light on this point, the largest pyrethrum union and its affiliated societies, located in Kisii district, may serve as a rather representative case.[28]

In 1983, Masaba Union had twenty-nine affiliated societies, of which twenty-two dealt exclusively with pyrethrum. The total registered membership of these societies amounted to *c.* 58,000. The main union activities were:

1 Transport services; collection of pyrethrum (dried flowers) at the societies for delivery to the PBK in Nakuru and collection of milk for delivery to Kisii (7 societies);
2 Sales of inputs;
3 Credit and savings services provided by a banking section with about 29,000 accounts. Less than half of the affiliated societies were linked to these services as the income increase expected from including all individual members would be too small to cover incremental costs;
4 Production credit (CPCS); in 1982/83 about 5 per cent of the members had outstanding loans.

The crisis that hit pyrethrum production had not been entirely unpredictable but rather developed over several years. Thus, members of the primary societies began to face serious problems with prices and payments as early as 1981/82. Apart from a decrease in the gross payment from Sh. 11.50 to 10.50, due to low pyrethrin contents, payments were delayed. According to union staff, the lowered price actually did reflect quality deficiencies. They were seen as being the result of picking at the wrong time and of inferior drying and storage by individual members.

The payment problem escalated further in 1982/83. The PBK now found itself unable to pay for delivered produce. For smallholders who were dependent on pyrethrum for their cash earnings, this obviously had serious consequences. In 1984, it was thus very common in pyrethrum-growing areas for families to remove their children from school as they could not pay the necessary fees. At this time, the PBK owed growers linked to Masaba some K.Sh. 24 million.

In response to these developments, many farmers in the northern part of the division started planting tea or turned to dairy, while in the southern parts maize seems to have been the major substitute. The following figures on the volume of dried flowers delivered by growers, clearly illustrate their reaction:

| | *Deliveries of dried flowers* |
|---|---|
| 1980/81 | 7.6 million kg |
| 1981/82 | 6.1 million kg |
| 1982/83 | 2.4 million kg |
| 1983/84 | 0.6 million kg |

It is of course interesting to see how the main organizational actors with a stake in the industry acted in order to moderate the negative impact of a drastically contracted market for pyrethrum. Those of principal interest in this context would be the PBK, the MOCD and, evidently, the union and primary societies in their role as the producers' own organizations. As regards the PBK, the Board never bothered to provide the farmers or the cooperatives with information about changes taking place in the export markets and their implications for production. Not even when payments could no longer be made did the PBK make the effort to go to the major producer area to clarify the position to local authorities and the cooperative organizations.

Even worse, however, is the fact that the union and its affiliated societies seem to have been managerially paralysed. By 1984 few, if any, initiatives had been taken to get a financial settlement with the PBK or, at least, a proper explanation from the Board for the reasons behind the payment failures. Even less had been done to pass on to the growers the little information that *was* available, which is quite remarkable considering that the market collapse was of direct consequence for the growers'/members' welfare and also posed a serious threat to the very survival of both the union and its affiliated societies. In the absence of these basic abilities, it is not surprising that nobody seemed to bother about widening the economic base of the cooperatives by actively promoting the marketing of additional types of produce.

As the union also was very slow in adapting its staff establishment and scope of service activities intended to support pyrethrum production, it faced an insolvency situation in 1984. The net debt then corresponded to *c.* 80 per cent of members' savings in the banking section. Further, the liquidity of the union was such that it was practically impossible for members to make withdrawals from their savings accounts. One indication of how this situation developed, and how slowly the management responded, is the relation between the number of staff and gross income. In 1981/82 the latter amounted to Sh. 3.2 million and in 1983/84 to 0.4 million; in spite of that, 75 per cent of the 81/82 staff establishment remained intact in 83/84. It is no exaggeration to conclude that the management of the union had gone astray and that the committee was unable to represent basic producer interests. In our view, the grounds for this are found in the mode of organization characterizing cooperatives in Kenya. Thus, according to their 'terms of reference', which by implication follow from legislation and regulations, staff and committee members are in practice directed to deal with repetitive tasks within a bureaucratic framework. This organizational context assumes stable and habitual operations. For anything falling outside the everyday routine, they have – also in Masaba union – to rely on decisions made by the MOCD and other government bodies. This kind of dependency creates a passive 'management culture' void of ability to adapt to external influences and their local repercussions. Hence, it also involves a loss of creativity, flexibility and close contact with the membership. Thus, although both the staff and the committee were aware of the seriousness of the situation, no specific action was taken. The exchange of information was very poor within the organization and practically non-existent in relation to affiliated primary societies and their members.

How then did the Ministry of Cooperative Development react to the crisis of the pyrethrum industry in the district? By and large, the MOCD's behaviour conformed with that of the PBK and the cooperative organizations. In spite of a district office with fifty-two staff members, the problem apparently was not seen as serious enough to warrant any major initiative. With the exception of the technical assistance provided by a donor agency, the MOCD's staff continued to concentrate on the formal aspects of the society/union activities, such as the number of budgets and trial balances submitted to the office, and the union's/societies' recording and book-keeping procedures.

## *Conclusions*

The misfortunes characterizing the pyrethrum industry and its cooperative organizations bear the imprint of various forms of state intervention. The immediate cause behind the collapse of production in the first half of the 1980s can be found in the price and marketing strategies of the PBK. Another contributory factor was that the PBK preferred not to provide information about market conditions and their implications for future production.

As pyrethrum is a type of produce which is simple to handle, process and transport, and which requires few inputs except labour, the local environment does not seem to be of much importance as a determinant of marketing costs. However, the response of members to deteriorating prices and service quality is closely linked to the local environment and the options it offers in terms of alternative lines of production. These varying reactions have obvious consequences for the future of pyrethrum cooperatives.

The problems facing the industry have been further exacerbated by a cooperative infrastructure that is unable to articulate and, even less, promote their members' interests in their role as producers. The negative financial repercussions on the cooperative organizations themselves have been inflated by government supervision, single-produce orientation and poor management. Even in the middle of the crisis, the MOCD concerned itself mainly with procedural matters and its contribution to finding ways of improving the situation left much to be desired.

## 4.6 Dairy

### *Marketing structure and prices*

The introduction of grade cattle, the enclosure of smallholdings and, not least, the establishment of settlement schemes that began in the early 1960s, resulted in an increase in the production and sale of milk and dairy produce. From a very low level in 1960, smallholder sales amounted to about 80 million litres in 1968, equivalent to about one-third of total marketed production.[29] Although we lack information about total production in the 1970s, the rate of growth seems to have been lower than during the preceding decade. In 1981, the national herd of dairy cows numbered an estimated 1.5 million heads and produced about 1,300 million litres of milk. Of this output, about 500 million litres were marketed, of which about 45 per cent was delivered to the Kenya Cooperative Creameries (KCC). The KCC has an effecitve monopoly over the urban market and virtually a complete monopoly in processed dairy products.[30] Cooperative societies then accounted for about 25 per cent of the total marketed volume. Thus,

| | |
|---|---|
| Total milk production 1981, million litres | 1,300 |
| Marketed volume: | 500 |
| official marketing channels (KCC) | 220 |
| by cooperative societies | 120 |
| to KCC | 90 |

Our survey data indicate that total sales of cooperative societies in 1982/83 remained at approximately the same level as in 1981. As total marketed production then reached 260 million litres, it would mean that the cooperative share of the officially marketed volume had fallen from 55 to about 45 per cent. It has to be recognized, however, that figures on the dairy industry in general and on smallholder production in particular are extremely unreliable. This also applies to the cooperative sector. There will be reason to return to this issue later.

As illustrated by Figure 4.27, the total officially recorded volume of marketed milk (equivalents) has not increased over the period 1970–84. It can also be seen that the annual fluctuations have been substantial. Partly these reflect variations in weather conditions (not least during the period 1979–81). Based on Figure 4.28, it can additionally be argued that the development of official producer prices has been of consequence for smallholders' propensity to use the KCC for their surplus production, particularly in areas where alternative market outlets exist. Thus, in 1985, society managers in Kiambu district told us that only milk left after local sales was delivered to the KCC. The reason for this priority rating was simply that the local price was more favourable.

The main activity of most primary dairy societies is to collect milk delivered by members to collection centres. In addition, they may sell animal feeds and some veterinary products. Societies affiliated to larger unions may also offer their members savings and credit services.

Depending on the societies' access to vehicles, the area of operation may be defined by a number of routes. Usually the primary societies are equipped with cooling facilities. Milk is

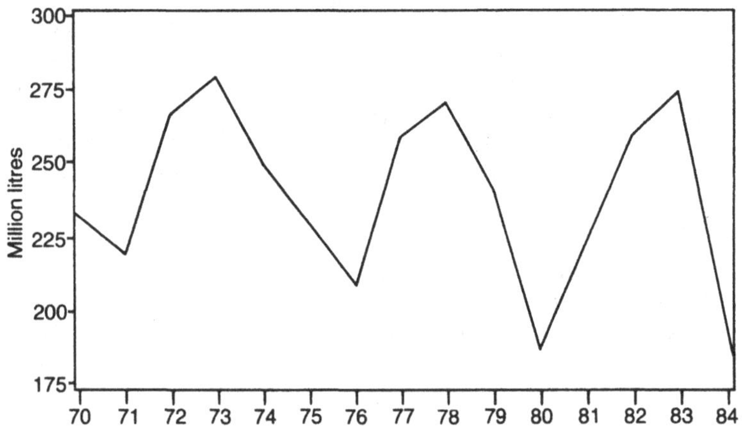


*Figure 4.27* Officially recorded volume of marketed milk (million litres) 1970–84
*Source:* survey data

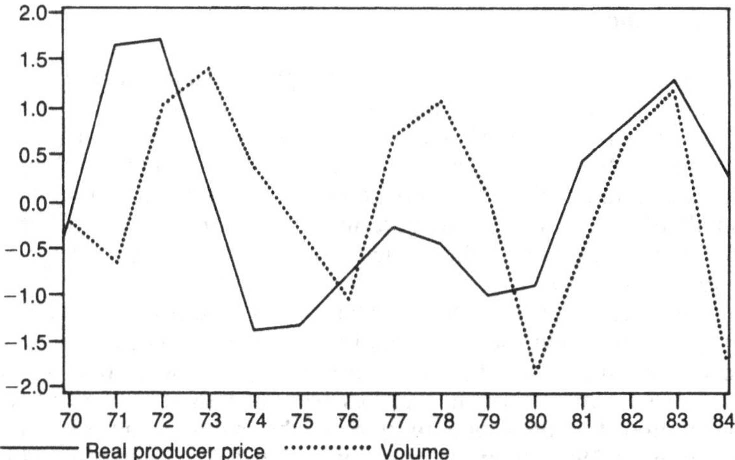


*Figure 4.28* Variations in marketed milk production and real producer price, 1970–84
*Source:* survey data

collected in the morning and kept at the society for subsequent delivery to the KCC or to local customers. Some societies also collect evening milk, but as the quantity is smaller, such collection seems to be confined to nearby collection centres and is also dependent on season.

Unfortunately, the MOCD's taxonomy for primary societies, makes it practically impossible to use available statistics to indicate the development of dairy societies in the 1970s and early 1980s. Although 'dairy' is used as an activity, most societies in operation actually sort under the category 'multipurpose' together with many other types of societies. As earlier mentioned, we have revised the taxonomy so that it reflects the actual activity orientation of societies. This, however, was only possible for 1982/83. According to the MOCD's classification, 74 dairy societies were then active, as compared to an actual number of 293.

There is little reason to expect that the volume marketed by cooperatives during the period 1970–84 deviated positively from the trend that can be observed in Figure 4.27. Judging from the figures available for 1981 and 1982/83, the market share of cooperatives then was decreasing, and seen for the period as a whole it is unlikely that the picture would be drastically different.

## Performance and environment

As shown in Figure 4.29, most of the primary dairy societies are located in formerly alienated areas (environments C2 and C3). Also in terms of marketed production, these settlement areas dominate. In 1982/83 they accounted for almost two-thirds of total sales by dairy societies. Although densely populated, 'traditional' smallholder areas dominate in terms of membership and, with this definition, also have the largest societies – average sales per member are low.

Table 4.24 shows that the membership of most primary societies is quite small. On the other hand it seems clear that, in terms of sales per member, they compare favourably with the larger societies. Thus although societies with less than 500 members accounted for only one-quarter of the membership of dairy societies in 1983, their share of milk sales was 45 per cent. This reflects the superior access to grazing land in the settlement areas in Rift Valley. It also implies that the introduction of zero-grazing in the major smallholder areas still has not made much of an impact, at least not on the cooperative sector outside Kiambu district.

*Table 4.23* Basic performance characteristics of primary dairy societies by category of environment, 1982–83

| *Environm. category* | *Number of societies with dairy as 1st prod.* | *2nd prod.* | *Milk sales (mill. Sh.)* | *Member-ship ('000)* | *Average sales/ member* | *Pay rate %* |
|---|---|---|---|---|---|---|
| C1 71–83 | 58 | 5 | 103.3 | 79.8 | 1,300 | 80 |
| C2 71–83 | 116 | 10 | 116.7 | 54.0 | 2,200 | 80 |
| C3 71–83 | 75 | 25 | 65.6 | 28.3 | 2,300 | 81 |
| C4 71–83 | 4 | – | 2.2 | 1.2 | 1,800 | 78 |
| Total | 253 | 40 | 287.8 | 163.3 | 1,800 | 80 |

*Source:* survey data and MOCD

The location of societies relative to KCC's factories[31] apparently influences their cost of operation and thus payment ratios. Favoured districts in this respect – primarily Kericho, Nandi, Uasin Gishu, Nyandarua, Nyeri and Kiambu – account for three-quarters of total sales and reach an average payment ratio of 82 per cent as compared to 75 per cent for societies in other districts (Table 4.25). The only major milk-producing area not covered by the KCC was Meru district, where a 'mini-dairy' is operated by

*Table 4.24* Basic performance characteristics of primary dairy societies by size category (membership), 1982–83

| *Size catg (members)* | *Aver. no. of memb.* | *Number of societies with dairy as 1st prod.* | *2nd prod.* | *Milk sales (mill. Sh.)* | *Members ('000)* | *Average sales/ member* | *Pay rate %* |
|---|---|---|---|---|---|---|---|
| N/A | N/A | 7 | – | 12.7 | – | – | 83 |
| ≤–499 | 195 | 171 | 33 | 130.2 | 40.1 | 3,200 | 81 |
| 500–999 | 695 | 38 | 5 | 57.4 | 29.9 | 1,900 | 81 |
| 1,000–1,999 | 1,405 | 23 | 2 | 41.8 | 35.1 | 1,200 | 78 |
| 2,000–4,999 | 3,175 | 12 | – | 33.3 | 38.1 | 900 | 83 |
| >4,999 | 10,050 | 2 | – | 12.4 | 20.1 | 600 | 77 |
| | 570 | 253 | 40 | 287.8 | 163.3 | 1,800 | 80 |

*Source:* survey data and MOCD

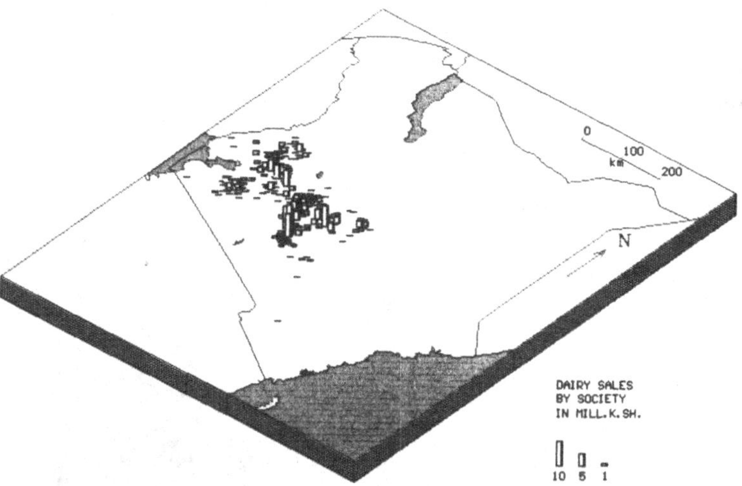


*Figure 4.29* Societies marketing dairy, 1983
*Source:* survey data

Meru Central Farmers' Union. Various operational problems have been encountered which have negatively affected the payment ratio.[32]

Also within the core itself, however, differentiation can be noted. The highest payment ratios are attained by societies in Nandi, Nyandarua and Kiambu districts. The latter case, and to a certain degree also Nandi, can be explained by high shares of local sales. This factor certainly plays a significant role in Kiambu,

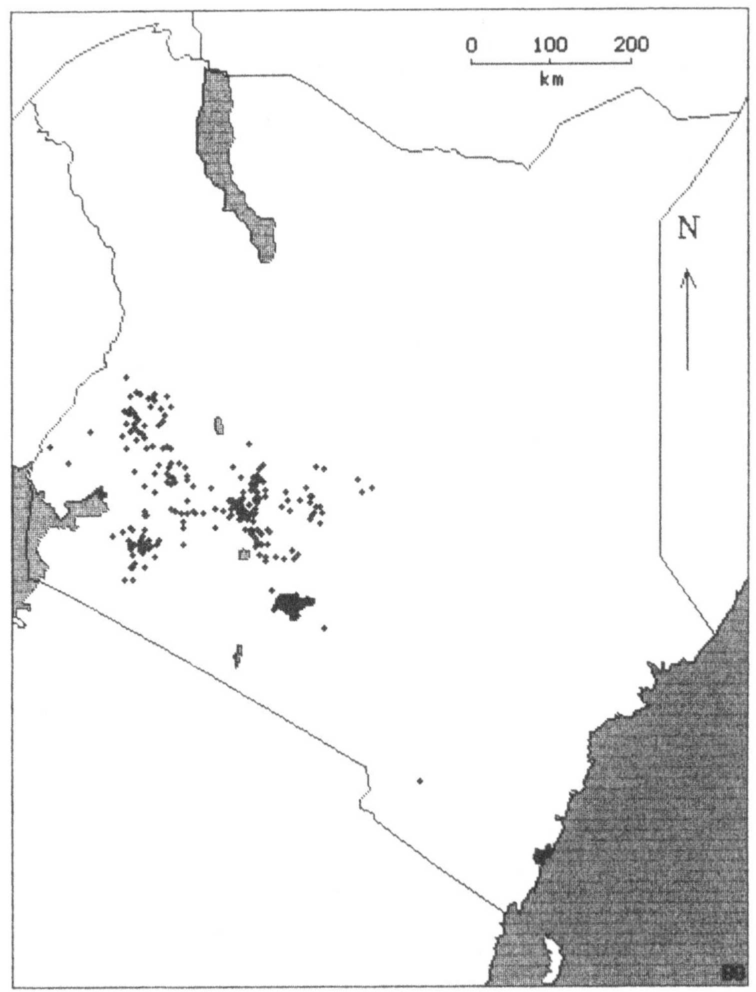


*Figure 4.30* Dairy societies < 500 members, 1983
*Source:* survey data

where favourable local prices have resulted in a consistent attempt by the societies to limit their milk deliveries to the KCC.

In Nyandarua, the generally small areas of operation in combination with high deliveries per member seem to facilitate efficient utilization of vehicles (mostly Land Rovers) and other infrastructure, and thus lead to comparatively high-payment ratios. Considering the low standard of the road network in the

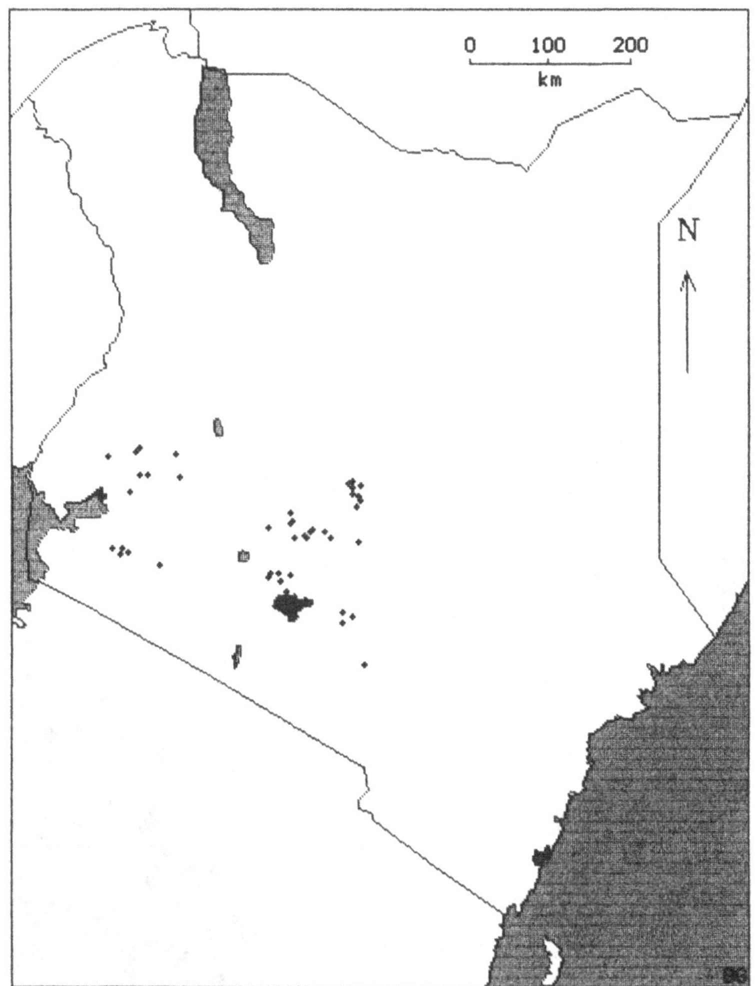


*Figure 4.31* Dairy societies ≥ 1,000 members, 1983
*Source:* survey data

district, it represents, together with other settlement areas, a sizeable untapped production potential.

As regards environmental conditions, it may be concluded that payment ratios are influenced primarily by,

1 the societies' geographical location in relation to the KCC's dairy plants;
2 local market demand;

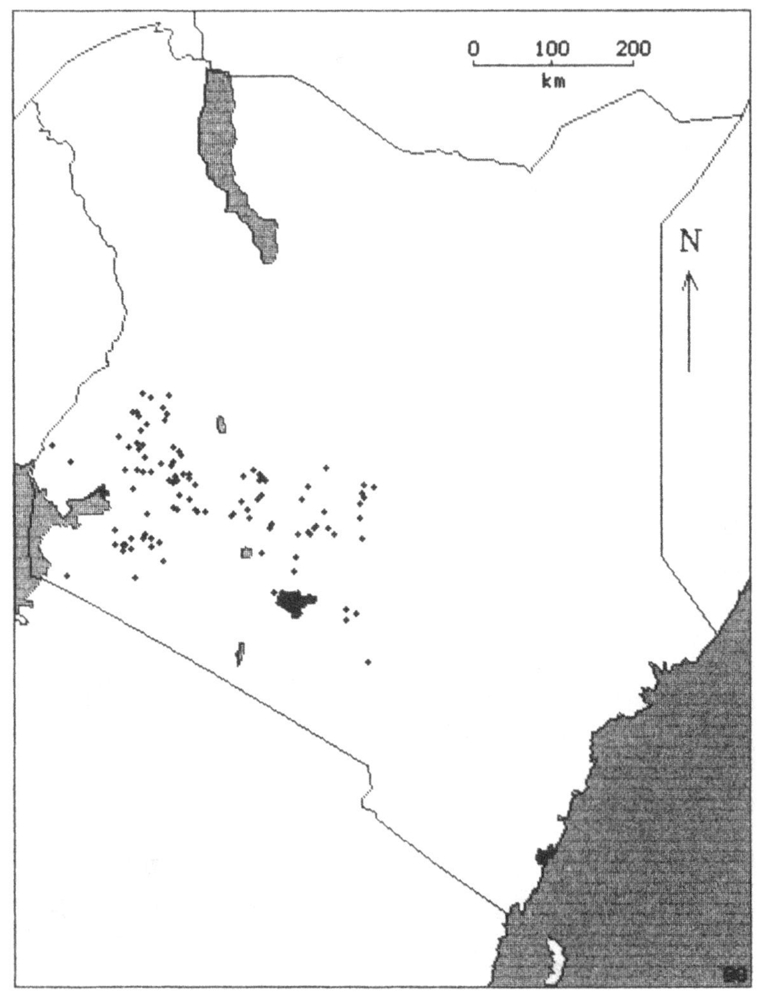


*Figure 4.32* Societies with average dairy deliveries/member < K.Sh. 1,000, 1983
*Source:* survey data

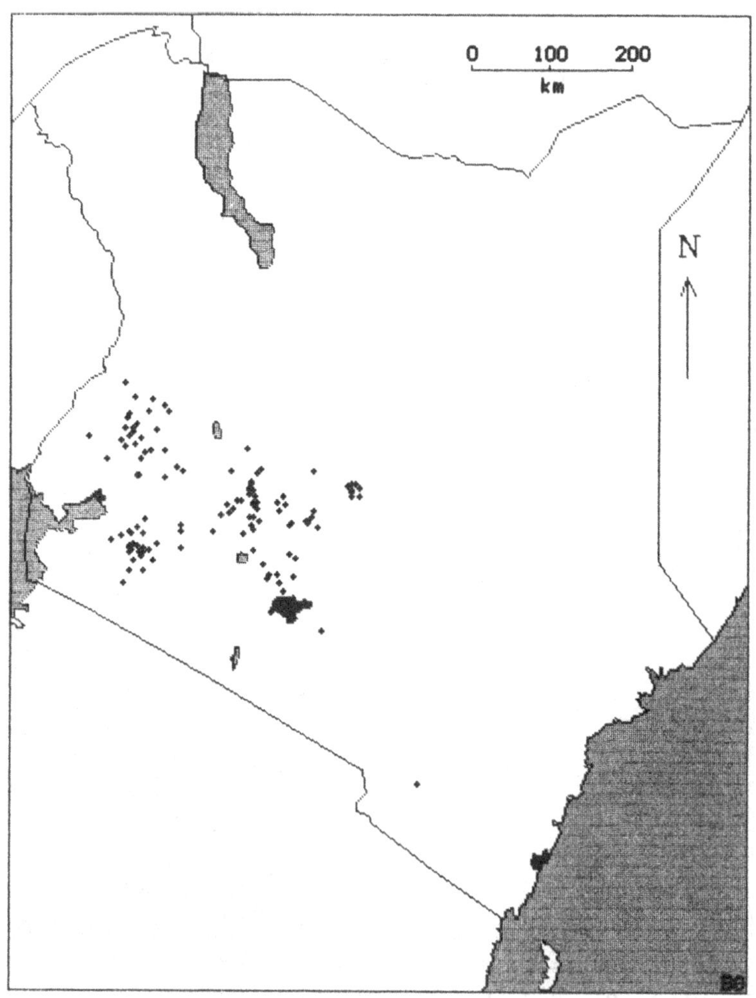


*Figure 4.33* Societies with average dairy deliveries/member in the range K.Sh. 1,000–4,000, 1983
*Source:* survey data

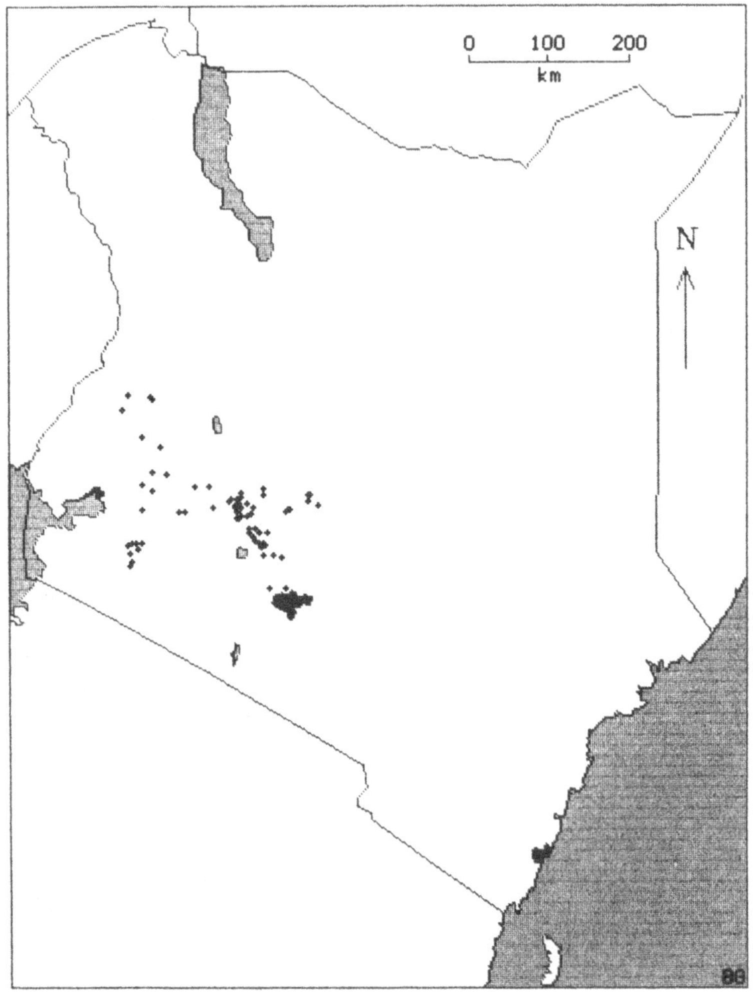


*Figure 4.34* Societies with average dairy deliveries ≥ K.Sh. 4,000, 1983
*Source:* survey data

3 size of the societies' respective areas of operation in combination with size of members' deliveries;
4 the quality of the local road network.

## Conclusions

It is commonly held that the small settlement societies in Rift Valley are managerially weak. However, given the environmental

*Table 4.25* Basic performance characteristics of dairy societies by district, taxonomized according to access to KCC-processing plants, 1982–83

| *District* | *Number of societies* | *Dairy sales (mill. Sh.)* | *No. of members* | *Average sales per member (Sh.)* | *Pay ratio (%)* |
|---|---|---|---|---|---|
| Kisii | 12 | 3.1 | 11.1 | 300 | 76 |
| Kericho | 36 | 20.4 | 10.5 | 1,900 | 81 |
| Uasin Gishu | 24 | 9.0 | 4.3 | 2,100 | 79 |
| Nandi | 19 | 22.8 | 9.8 | 2,300 | 86 |
| Trans-Nzoia | 9 | 7.8 | 1.6 | 4,900 | 89 |
| E. Marakwet | 9 | 2.8 | 3.9 | 700 | 82 |
| Nyeri | 23 | 48.8 | 38.3 | 1,300 | 76 |
| Nyandarua | 62 | 72.7 | 20.6 | 3,500 | 81 |
| Kiambu | 12 | 41.8 | 19.3 | 2,200 | 88 |
| Sub-total | *206* | *229.2* | *119.4* | *1,900* | *82* |
| S. Nyanza | 2 | 0.2 | 1.4 | 100 | 84 |
| Busia | 1 | <0.1 | 0.1 | 100 | 80 |
| Kakamega | 10 | 3.7 | 2.9 | 1,300 | 68 |
| Bungoma | 2 | 2.5 | 0.5 | 5,000 | 80 |
| Busia | 1 | 0 | 0.2 | N/A | N/A |
| Nakuru | 20 | 7.7 | 3.0 | 2,600 | 76 |
| Baringo | 7 | 14.0 | 3.9 | 3,600 | 76 |
| Laikipia | 11 | 1.5 | 1.7 | 900 | 73 |
| Narok | 2 | 0.6 | 0.5 | 1,200 | 70 |
| Kajiado | 2 | 1.6 | 0.7 | 2,300 | 81 |
| Muranga | 4 | 2.1 | 0.9 | 2,300 | 76 |
| Kirinyaga | 2 | 3.6 | 7.2 | 500 | 62 |
| Taita Taveta | 1 | 0.1 | 0.1 | 1,000 | 68 |
| Embu | 1 | 1.6 | N/A | N/A | 61 |
| Meru | 16 | 18.4 | 13.7 | 1,300 | 78 |
| Machakos | 5 | 0.9 | 7.1 | 100 | 76 |
| Sub-total | *87* | *58.6* | *43.9* | *1,300* | *75* |
| *Total* | *293* | *287.8* | *163.3* | *1,800* | *80* |

*Sources:* survey data and MOCD

conditions, the information at hand indicates that they perform their most essential function reasonably well. In this particular respect, many of the larger societies in the main smallholder areas actually seem to be worse off; to this has no doubt contributed long collection routes and mostly small deliveries per member. Additionally, it can be noted that the administration of the societies is demanding. Thus, we have on different occasions during 1983–85 observed serious shortcomings in the internal recording routines among dairy societies in Central province. Although the unions are doing the book-keeping, they have been

*Table 4.26* Basic performance characteristics of dairy societies, taxonomized according to access to KCC-processing plants, to category of environment and size of membership, 1982–83

| *KCC-area* | *Environm. category* | *Size categ. (members)* | *No. of soc.* | *Dairy sales (mill. Sh.)* | *No. of members* | *Sales/ member* | *Pay ratio (%)* |
|---|---|---|---|---|---|---|---|
| Kisii, Kericho, Nandi, U. Gishu, T. Nzoia, E. Marakwet, Nyandarua, Nyeri, Kiambu | | | | | | | |
| | C1 71–83 | < 499 | 21 | 16.7 | 4.7 | 3,500 | 80 |
| | | 500– 999 | 8 | 11.3 | 6.8 | 1,700 | 77 |
| | | 1,000–1,999 | 9 | 25.8 | 13.1 | 2,000 | 80 |
| | | 2,000–4,999 | 7 | 27.7 | 24.1 | 1,100 | 86 |
| | | >4,999 | 2 | 12.3 | 20.0 | 600 | 77 |
| | | | *47* | *93.8* | *68.7* | *1,400* | *81* |
| | C2 71–83 | N/A | 1 | 0.7 | N/A | N/A | 83 |
| | | < 499 | 77 | 62.5 | 15.4 | 4,100 | 81 |
| | | 500– 999 | 18 | 28.3 | 11.2 | 2,500 | 82 |
| | | 1,000–1,999 | 1 | 1.4 | 1.9 | 700 | 60 |
| | | 2,000–4,999 | 1 | 0.2 | 2.6 | 80 | 80 |
| | | | *98* | *93.1* | *31.1* | *3,000* | *81* |
| | C3 71–83 | N/A | 3 | 5.0 | N/A | N/A | 80 |
| | | < 499 | 45 | 26.9 | 8.9 | 3,000 | 84 |
| | | 500– 999 | 10 | 8.7 | 7.1 | 1,200 | 82 |
| | | 1,000–1,999 | 3 | 1.7 | 3.6 | 500 | 75 |
| | | | *61* | *42.3* | *19.6* | *2,200* | *82* |
| Subtotal | | | *206* | *229.2* | *119.4* | *1,900* | *82* |

| KCC-area | Environm. category | Size categ. (members) | No. of soc. | Dairy sales (mill. Sh.) | No. of members | Sales/ member | Pay ratio (%) |
|---|---|---|---|---|---|---|---|
| S. Nyanza, Siaya, Kakamega, Bungoma, Busia, Nakuru, Baringo, Laikipia, Narok, Kajiado, Muranga, Kirinyaga, Embu, Meru, Machakos, Taita/Taveta | | | | | | | |
| | C1 71–83 | < 499 | 13 | 4.5 | 2.6 | 1,700 | 74 |
| | | 1,000–1,999 | 1 | 1.3 | 1.2 | 1,100 | 62 |
| | | 2,000–4,999 | 2 | 3.7 | 7.2 | 500 | 62 |
| | | | *16* | *9.5* | *11.0* | *900* | *68* |
| | C2 71–83 | N/A | 2 | 5.6 | N/A | N/A | 72 |
| | | < 499 | 8 | 3.9 | 1.4 | 2,800 | 83 |
| | | 500– 999 | 6 | 2.3 | 4.1 | 600 | 76 |
| | | 1,000–1,999 | 11 | 11.7 | 15.4 | 800 | 77 |
| | | 2,000–4,999 | 1 | 0.1 | 2.0 | 50 | 65 |
| | | | *28* | *23.6* | *22.9* | *1,000* | *77* |
| | C3 71–83 | N/A | 1 | 1.5 | N/A | N/A | 79 |
| | | < 499 | 36 | 13.4 | 6.0 | 2,200 | 73 |
| | | 500– 999 | 1 | 6.7 | 0.7 | 10,000 | 81 |
| | | 2,000–4,999 | 1 | 1.7 | 2.1 | 800 | 81 |
| | | | *39* | *23.3* | *8.8* | *2,700* | *76* |
| | C4 71–83 | < 499 | 4 | 2.2 | 1.2 | 1,800 | 78 |
| Subtotal | | | *87* | *58.6* | *43.9* | *1,300* | *75* |
| Total | | | 293 | 287.8 | 163.3 | 1,800 | 80 |

*Sources:* survey data;
MOCD.

of little use in assisting affiliated societies. Practically all 'dairy unions' perform poorly and their assortment of service activities is too wide to be commercially viable. That is, the complexity of the administrative system and the range of service activities carried out are not warranted, considering their narrow economic base.

One major justification for the implementation of demanding administrative systems has been that marketing services have to be integrated with input and credit supplies. The latter, in turn, would be needed to offer members incentives to upgrade technologies and raise production. As seen here, these two factors (inputs and credit) mean little for the performance of dairy farmers compared to prices and the environmental considerations mentioned above (markets, processing, roads, extension services). It is probably more relevant to try to maximize payments to members by focusing on achieving cost-efficient collection, marketing and payment routines. For primary societies and their members, the present administrative system is unnecessarily costly and is linked to the maintenance of secondary societies of questionable value. In line with this, it can be noted that independent societies generally achieved a higher payment ratio in 1982/83 than those affiliated to unions. Apparently, it is also the case that most of the MOCD's staff time is spent on unions rather than on primary societies.

In summary, we may note that the existence of primary dairy societies means that smallholders have access to a market channel. In that sense, the cooperatives offer an incentive for commercialized dairy production. To achieve this, however, does not warrant the present type of cooperative organization because its administrative enlargement, intended to cater for a wide range of services, does not generate any essential incremental incentives. Instead the performance seems to be negatively affected, particularly among affiliated societies. As indicated above, promotion of dairy production would certainly comprise a variety of measures. One of these would have to be some kind of cooperative 'de-regulation'.

## 4.7 Other marketing activities

The societies belonging to this category do not represent more than 7–8 per cent of the total value of produce marketed by primary societies, and almost half of this share is taken by societies marketing sugar and cashew nuts. Excluding these latter types of produce, it is evident that remaining societies are of marginal importance. For most of the societies belonging to the category 'multipurpose', it has unfortunately not been possible to establish their main activity. It is likely however, that the majority of societies handle small surplus deliveries of staple crops.[33] The geographical distribution of the societies in Table 4.27 is given in Figures 4.35–40.

*Table 4.27* Basic performance characteristics of primary societies by type of produce marketed, 1983

| *Produce* | *Number of soc.* | *Sales (mill. Sh.)* | *Pay ratio (%)* | *Average sales/member (Sh.)* | *Number of members ('000)* | *Total produce sales (mill. Sh.)* |
|---|---|---|---|---|---|---|
| Cereals | 38 | 40.3 | 85 | 3,700 | 11.0 | 53.4 |
| Vegetables | 6 | 4.6 | 80 | 2,600 | 1.8 | 4.6 |
| Sugar cane | 54 | 79.2 | N/A | 2,900 | 27.7 | 84.7 |
| Cashew | 15 | 23.7 | 73 | 2,200 | 10.8 | 27.2 |
| Animals | 31 | 15.4 | 66 | 800 | 20.4 | 16.0 |
| Multipurpose | 89 | 24.7 | N/A | 500 | 47.1 | 44.3 |

*Source:* survey data

## *Sugar*

The societies are concentrated in the 'sugar belt', most of which falls in Kisumu district. Two categories of society can be defined. One is a combined production and marketing society, and the second a conventional marketing society linked to the Muhoroni settlement scheme. As regards the first category, members of the societies have contributed about one acre of land each to make possible cultivation of cane in large blocks. These collective operations are organized by the Sugar Belt Cooperative Union (SBCU) and are carried out either by the SBCU itself, or by private contractors, or by contractor groups at society level composed of individual members. The cane from these societies is delivered mainly to the Chemelil sugar factory, but also to Miwani. The societies also market members' privately grown cane. The settlement societies deliver the cane to the Muhoroni factory.

Seen over the period 1975–84, Kenya's production of refined (white) sugar has more than doubled. A peak was reached in 1980, after which total output decreased by about 10 per cent. In 1984, total production balanced domestic consumption (Figure 4.41). In the early 1970s, nucleus estates and large-scale farms accounted for most of the cane production. Cooperatively organized growers then accounted for about one-third of total deliveries. By 1983 their share had fallen to about 15 per cent. This development

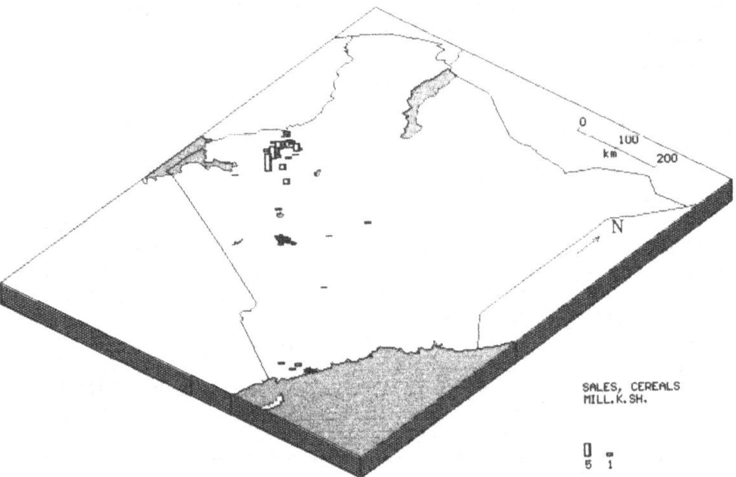


*Figure 4.35* Societies with cereals as main marketing activity, 1983
*Source:* survey data

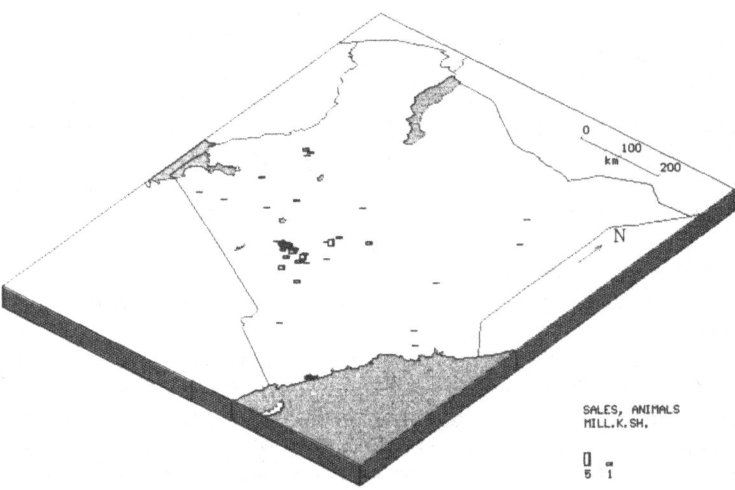


*Figure 4.36* Societies with animals as main marketing activity, 1983
*Source: survey data*

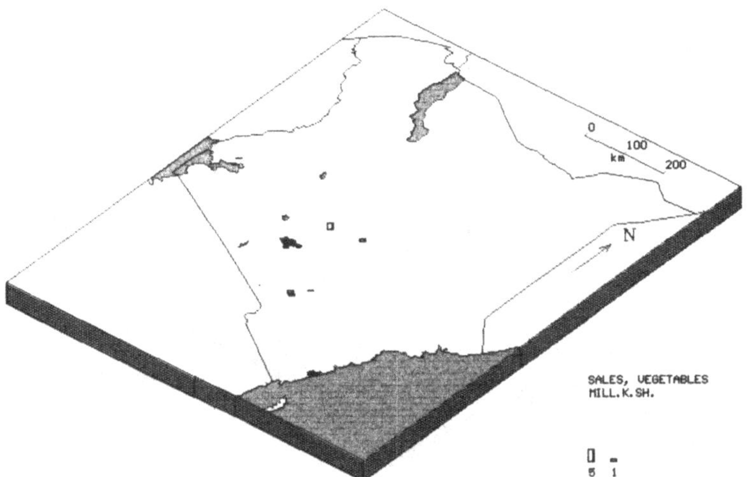


*Figure 4.37* Societies with vegetables as main marketing activity, 1983
*Source: survey data*

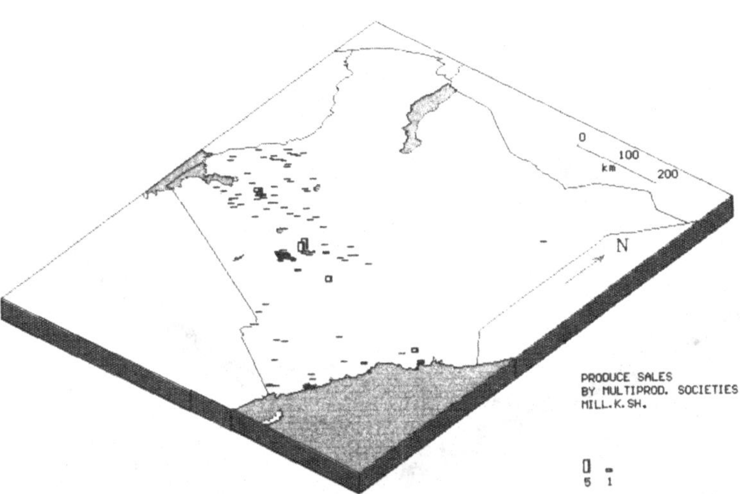


*Figure 4.38* Multiproduce societies, 1983
*Source: survey data*

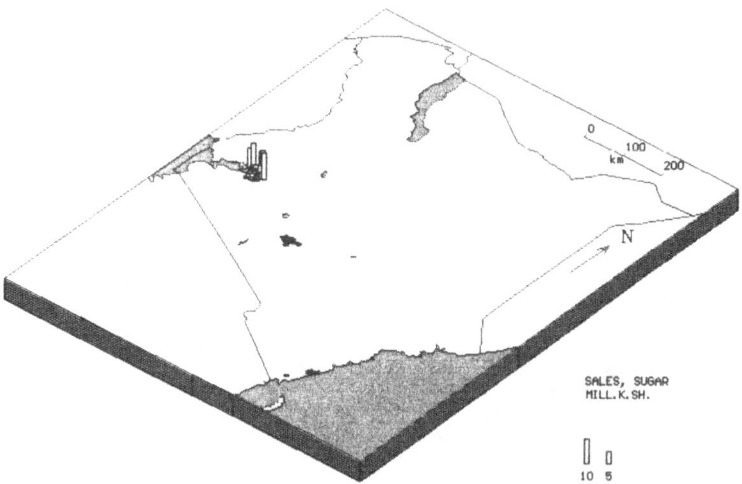


*Figure 4.39* Societies with sugar cane as main marketing activity, 1983
*Source:* survey data

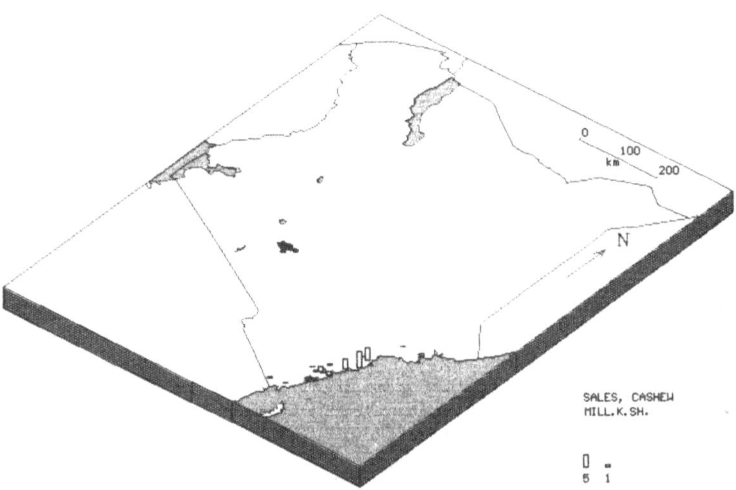


*Figure 4.40* Societies with cashew nuts as main marketing activity, 1983
*Source:* survey data

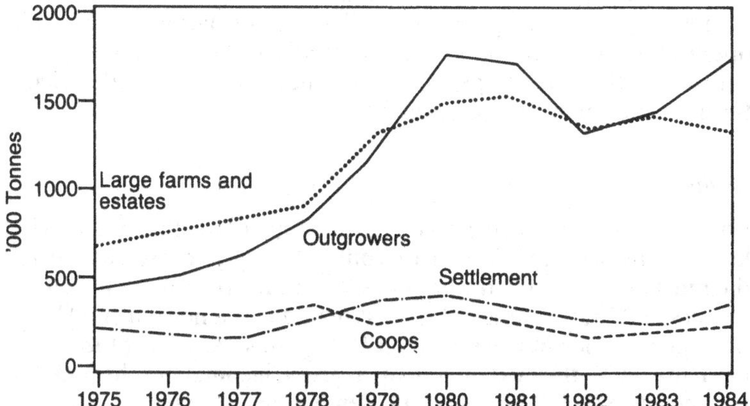


*Figure 4.41* Estimated production of sugar cane by category of producer, 1975–84
*Source:* survey data

primarily reflects a rapid expansion of the cultivated area. Three new sugar factories started operating in western Kenya in the 1970s (Mumias, Nzoia and Sony). The total area under cane grew from an estimated 38,000 ha (1976) to 95,000 ha (1984). Smallholders linked to outgrower schemes accounted for about two-thirds of this expansion. In the same period, the total acreage cultivated by cooperatively organized smallholders remained largely unchanged. Among societies linked to the SBCU, the cultivated area actually decreased during the first half of the 1980s.[34]

The overall average yield of cane per hectare was about 30 tonnes in 1983. On the production blocks and smallholdings which were linked to the SBCU through forty-seven primary societies, the yields seemed to be considerably lower. According to our estimates they were hardly more than half of the national average. The main reason for this was the generally poor management performance that has characterized both the SBCU and its affiliated societies. In the 1970s, assistance from external donors resulted in an operating subsidy which at the time covered up to two-thirds of current costs.[35] In spite of this, returns to growers/members have been meagre, and conditions evidently deteriorated in the early 1980s. At that time it was also clear that the introduction of production credit (CPCS) had resulted in substantial losses on loans.

As a result of the managerial and financial problems facing the SBCU and its affiliated societies, it has been very difficult to get access to adequate and reliable information about their operations. None the less, the information at hand supports the conclusion that the cooperatives have negatively affected agricultural development in the sugar belt.

### *Cashew*

Cashew is of importance as a cash crop along the coast. The kernels are used for dessert or confectionery purposes and from the nut shell is extracted a liquid used in industrial products such as plastics and brake linings.[36] It is estimated that a normal yield level from pure stands of trees is about 500 kg nuts per ha. At the prices paid in 1983, this would mean a gross income per hectare of between K.Sh. 1,600 and 2,200, depending on quality.

Along the coast, primary cooperative societies have long since been involved in the collection and delivery of cashew nuts to the National Cereals Board. In 1975, a processing plant was opened in Kilifi with Kilifi District Cooperative Union (KDCU) as co-owner. In 1976, the factory intake amounted to about 13,000 tonnes of raw nuts which was equivalent to 85 per cent of installed processing capacity. In the period 1981–84 production decreased. The factory then processed 8,000–9,000 tonnes annually.[37] Considering the capacity of the factory, it is apparent that production has not developed as anticipated.

Primary societies, affiliated to the KCDU, are intended to be the sole suppliers to the factory. In 1982/83, fifteen societies with approximately 11,000 members in Kilifi, Lamu and Kwale districts delivered raw nuts at a value of *c.*K.Sh. 24 million. It is not unlikely that the stagnating/decreasing production that can be observed for the period 1976–84 is related to the performance of the cooperative sector. Thus, in view of the fact that cashew nuts are easy to collect and handle, the marketing commissions deducted by the primary societies and the union are remarkably high. As an average, the net payment rate to members was only 73 per cent in 1982/83. At the same time, it can be questioned whether the services that the union performs are indispensable to the farmers. The main activities seem to be the provision of bags and transports. These activities can be as efficiently carried out or arranged by the primary societies themselves. A third, more demanding activity, is the provision of production credit. In our view, however, the nature of members' agricultural production is such that this kind of service on the whole seems expendable, i.e.

the cost of operating credit services cannot possibly be justified on grounds that it is of importance for members' production performance.

When it comes to actively promoting the economic interests of members of primary societies, most of whom have very small incomes, the contribution made by the union seems negligible. Although the whole cooperative set-up is based on the production of cashew, average yields of the cashew trees remain at a generally very low level (200–300 kg/ha). As cashew trees grow quickly and yield after just three years in the field, campaigns for planting of vegetatively propagated material could have given considerable results over a comparatively short period of time. Initiatives to that effect do not seem to have been taken, at least not by the KDCU. Instead, the union has made considerable financial losses through the investment of, at least, K.Sh. 6 million in a tourist hotel. Furthermore, while the union spent K.Sh. 66,000 on staff travel and K.Sh. 13,000 on entertainment in 1983/84, the less impressive amount of K.Sh. 565 was seen as affordable for member education activities.[38]

## 4.8 Unions

### *Credit services*

In the cooperative development strategy that evolved in the latter half of the 1960s,[39] district unions were seen as essential. This concept was based on the argument that cooperatives, to be able to contribute effectively to agricultural development, would have to provide at least two types of services in addition to marketing, namely production credit and inputs. In the 1960s and 70s, this was a stand favoured not only by politicians and planners in Kenya. Although rural credit had been used on a limited scale by colonial governments, it was now escalated into a major development tool.[40] Since the early 1970s, the international donor community, and not least the World Bank and FAO, had actively contributed to the introduction of credit programmes in many Third World countries.[41]

As noted by von Pischke *et al.*, one attractive feature of credit programmes is their 'appearance of offering fast relief for complex situations' (von Pischke 1983:2). They are easier and, not least, cheaper to introduce than land reforms, investments in infrastructure and other measures aimed at differentiation of the rural economy. To this may be added policy considerations whereby cheap credit can compensate at least the more important segments of the farming community for the effects of price controls and overvalued exchange rates.[42] Moreover, many policy-makers support the view that only through loans will farmers be able to adopt profitable new technology. A final, common feature of the 'credit paradigm' is that informal credit provided rather persistently by moneylenders and traders is seen as destructive in nature. In the building-up of supply systems, preference should therefore be given to government institutions or organizations which can be subjected to effective public control. This, it is argued, has the added advantage of making it possible to direct credit also towards vulnerable and poor strata of the rural population.[43]

The massive increase in the number and size of such programmes intervening in agriculture in Africa in the 1970s, has usually been backed by active political support. As argued by Bates, this can be explained by the fact that the nonmarket mechanisms (rationing) which follow this kind of direct intervention are politically much more useful than general development tools, for example pricing policies.[44]

Considerations of the nature referred to above have no doubt also played their part in Kenya.[45] Additionally, most agricultural credit intended for smallholders has been channelled through the cooperative structure.[46] The first major scheme to be introduced was CPCS. It covers primarily the coffee unions, although it is also used in cooperatives that market dairy, pyrethrum and sugar. In the coffee unions, CPCS was soon also linked to a savings scheme. It meant that 'banking sections' were established which facilitated a self-financed expansion of credit services. Continued expansion and diversification of the supply of credit was linked to support from donor agencies which also contributed technical assistance during the stage of implementation. The unions and their affiliated societies then basically were perceived as delivery systems.

Frequently, 'strings' were attached in the sense that the credit component was explicitly intended for farmers in less-developed areas and/or belonging to the poorer segments of the smallholder population. This usually meant that support was directed towards unions that were either operating outside the high potential areas or dealing with produce other than coffee. To ensure that the target groups actually would be reached, each credit scheme tended to adopt its own lending criteria and procedures. This obviously made the schemes administratively demanding both at central (Cooperative Bank) and union/society levels.

Another common feature was the concentration of financial and technical support given to the unions. In the major schemes, it included investments in storage facilities and stock, in improved offices, in vehicles, in staff training and also in subsidies to cover the increased costs incurred from a necessary expansion of the unions' administration and staff. Much of this support was provided as grants. Thus over a comparatively short period of time, from the late 1960s to the late 1970s, the service profile and administrative structure of the unions were given a new shape.

Even in the period 1975–80 it could be seen that this approach did not generate the anticipated positive effects on farm production. If members' deliveries accelerated at all, the growth was more often than not temporary in nature. In some cases the impact on production even seemed to be mainly negative. With the exception of the CPCS in coffee cooperatives, loan repayment levels generally were unacceptably low. In some cases it can be explained by crop failures and in others by too late a delivery of inputs. Further, farmers who did not realize sufficient yield increases to compensate for the credit received apparently tried to evade repayment. More importantly, this behaviour implies that many farmers did not see continued reliance on credit as a viable option, i.e. the potential returns achievable were not sufficient to compensate for the incremental time, costs and risks attached to the adoption of input-intensive technologies.

All systems based on rationing involve 'gate-keeping functions' and therefore offer built-in opportunities for corruption and favouritism, particularly under conditions of extreme resource scarcity. In this respect, credit schemes represent a case in point.[47] The flow of financial and other resources towards cooperatives thus makes them inordinately useful as nodes in local, regional and national networks of selective, political control. As a result the administratively distributed credit will tend to benefit other than officially identified smallholder strata, with consequences also for its end-use and for the commercial viability of cooperatives.

Most of these decidedly negative effects of credit programmes can be observed in Kenya, though their impact varies among both schemes and regions. The most serious problems can be found in Rift Valley, Western and S. Nyanza provinces. It should be stressed, however, that they are present in Central and Eastern provinces as well and even permeate the CPCS, which usually is referred to as a well-functioning scheme. A reflection of this is that in 1983–84, about 50 per cent of the total number of active members in societies linked to CPCS believed the loan-granting, decision-making process to be unfair and to favour influential people.[48]

An additional, fundamental reason behind the limited contribution of credit to agricultural development is that it has been unable to compensate for other, grave production disincentives. As discussed in earlier sections, one of these is the payment system. Prompt payment for crops has not been a pertinent feature of cooperatives and marketing boards. It may even be argued that the weak performance in this respect, in itself has generated a substantial need for credit.

### *Input supplies*

As regards the input supply activity, it can generally be argued that the performance of non-coffee unions has not favoured adoption. The siting of stores can in many instances be questioned as well as the assortment and pricing policies. With reference to the latter, the gross margin commonly is too low to cover the cost of the store operations. The transport activity has almost invariably been mismanaged. Under-utilization of lorries has been a consequence both of low levels of sales and of using them for other than commercial purposes. It has not been uncommon for revenue generated by input sales to be consumed by salaries and general running expenses. In view of the limited scale of operations, the staff deployment figures also indicate efficiency levels that leave much to be desired (Table 4.28).

Not all coffee unions are performing much better than 'non-coffee unions'. Four of them, however, undeniably play a dominating role. In 1982/83, they accounted for over 70 per cent of total cooperative input sales (excluding unaffiliated societies). Muranga union is the outstanding case, with sales that amount to almost half of the national total. Typically enough, the four unions are all located within a distance of 150 km from Nairobi and near railway stations. Agro-ecological conditions are predominantly favourable and the road transport network is well developed both at regional and local level. Furthermore, the distribution network used by the unions does not rely solely on union and society stores but extend down to the coffee factory level (Figure 4.42).

It is particularly interesting to note that the exceptional success of Muranga union as input supplier does not seem to depend primarily on the credit services provided. The decisive factors seem to be instead that prices are very competitive and that the inputs are easily accessible to most farmers. Linking this observation to the credit issue, it is interesting to note that the CPCS does not seem to have been a decisive determinant of the use of inputs among loanees.[49] In the same study, referring to the period 1975/76–80/81, is also concluded that the 'CPCS had virtually no demonstrable effect on the rate of growth or decline in mean produce deliveries by farmers' (Njonjo 1985:24).

The structure and operation of unions have clearly been derived from the assumption that tight coupling of organizations and workplaces at different hierarchical levels, and covering considerable geographical areas, would also generate economies of scale in input procurement and distribution. This obviously requires the different levels to be synchronized both at the stage of determining types and quantities of inputs and at the stage of actual distribution. Within the cooperative framework, it has generally not been possible to satisfy these basic logistical requirements. The observed exceptions (Muranga, Kirinyaga, Nyeri and Embu) are not simply due to a causal relation between credit and input usage levels but are also the result of an unusually favourable environment. In the other cases, the scale and mode of operation have been incompatible with geographical location and environmental conditions.

### *Performance profile*

Evidently the role assigned to unions was built on too-optimistic assumptions. These refer both to the expected effectiveness of credit and input supplies as incentives and to the ability of the unions to provide these and related services efficiently. In the absence of anticipated effects, administratively omnibus unions have run into financial and operational difficulties.

By 1983, practically all unions, except those based on coffee marketing, were playing a marginal role as suppliers of inputs. Ten coffee unions operating in environments 1 and 2 thus accounted for 85 per cent of the input sales and for two-thirds of total turnover. For most of the twenty-two non-coffee unions making a loss in 1982/83, the position was precarious (Tables 4.28–4.30 and Figure 4.43).

As illustrated in Table 4.30, these unions generally have been unable to accumulate their own capital. With a realistic assessment of the unions' assets, it actually seems clear that almost half of them should have been liquidated.[50] Continued survival has been made possible by *ad hoc* support from the government, the CBK and donor agencies. The value of assets specified in the accounts is grossly overvalued. This is primarily due to the credit activity. A major current asset of the unions thus consists of funds originally borrowed from the CBK for on-lending to affiliated primary societies and to members (cf note (I), Table 4.30). However, the

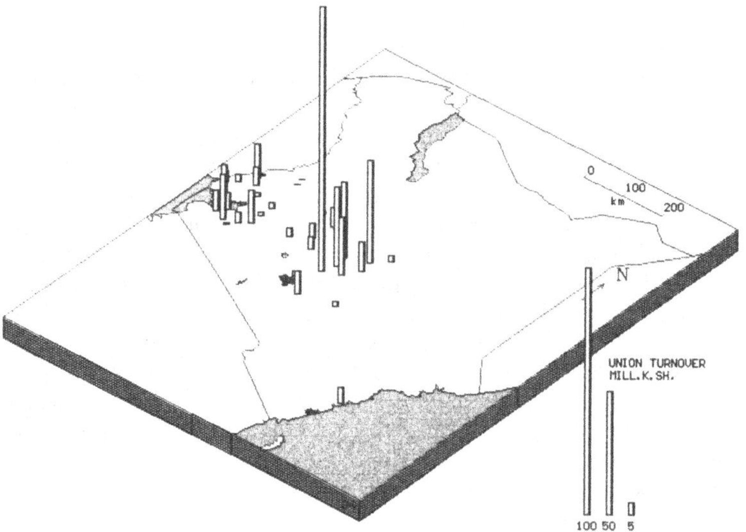


*Figure 4.42* Active cooperative unions, 1982–83
*Source:* survey data

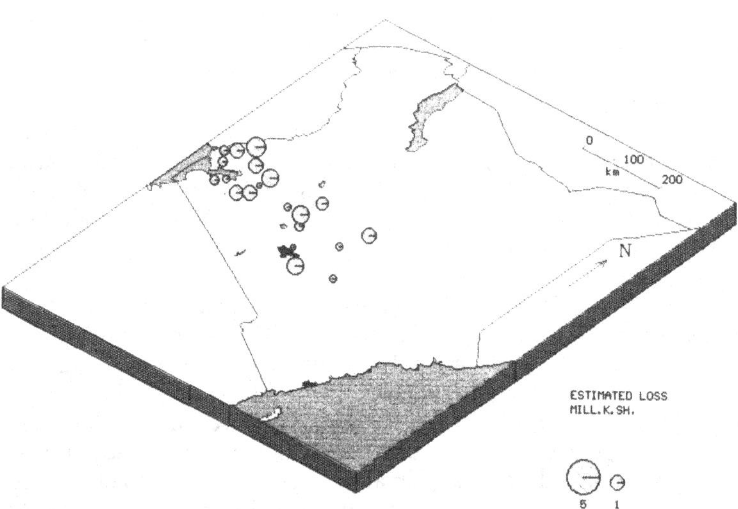


*Figure 4.43* Cooperative unions operating at a loss, 1982–83
*Source:* survey data

*Table 4.28* Basic features and performance characteristics of unions 1982–83, by result

| | *Profit 82/83* | *Loss 82/83* | *Total* |
|---|---|---|---|
| Number of unions covered[1] | 13 | 22 | 35 |
| Number of staff | 2,203 | 1,914 | 4,117 |
| Number of affiliated societies | 225 | 327 | 552 |
| Members of affiliated societies, '000 | 425 | 409 | 834 |
| Turnover, million K. Sh. | 252.3 | 147.5 | 399.8 |
| – Average per union, million K. Sh. | 19.4 | 6.7 | 11.4 |
| – Average per member of staff, K. Sh. | 114,500 | 77,100 | 97,100 |
| Sales of inputs, million K. Sh. | 134.2 | 42.9 | 177.1 |
| – Average per union, million K. Sh. | 10.3 | 2.0 | 5.1 |
| – Average per member of affiliated primary societies, K. Sh. | 320 | 110 | 210 |
| Percentage of main activities operated at profit | 46 | 36 | 40 |
| Result, million K. Sh. | 18.1 | –13.3 | 4.8 |

*Sources:* unions' annual accounts (1982/83);
survey data.

*Note*

1 The unions are: Kisii, Kimabu, Muranga, Kirinyaga, Nyeri, Masaba, Kakamega Sugar Belt, Muhoroni, Kiambu, Borabu, Kisumu, Bungoma, Embu, Meru North, Meru Central, Meru South, Kericho, Nyahururu-Makao, Kinangop, Ol'Kalou, Mt Elgon, Machakos, Siaya, Rachuonyo, Victoria, Luanda, Nambale, Malaba, Kilifi, Nakuru, Nandi, Kitui, West Pokot. In the case of Trans-Nzoia Union, annual accounts could not be made available.

repayment rate for production credits, as indicated above, has been extremely poor (for the various schemes usually in the range of 10–40 per cent). Moreover, as incomes generated from input supply and marketing services never evolved as anticipated, the unions developed considerable liquidity problems. As a consequence, sizeable portions of the funds borrowed from the CBK by non-coffee unions were not used as intended (i.e. for on-lending) but for covering their own operating expenses. The same thing happened in primary societies. According to a CBK estimation in 1983, referring to the provinces in western Kenya, the share of total loan funds that had been consumed in this way varied between 10 and 50 per cent, depending on district.

Considering the poor recording/administration of both individual credit and repayments and the very low levels of loan repayments, it may quite safely be concluded that the recoverable share of outstanding loans in reality represents only a fraction of the book value. Taking these adjustments into account, the assets of

*Table 4.29* Basic features and performance characteristics of unions 1982–83, by type of environment and main marketing activity

| | *Environment C1 71–83* | | *Environment C2 71–83* | | *Environment C3/4 71–83* | |
|---|---|---|---|---|---|---|
| | *Coffee* | *Other* | *Coffee* | *Other* | *Other* | *Total* |
| Number of unions[1] | 5 | 7 | 5 | 12 | 6 | 35 |
| Number of affiliated societies | 86 | 117 | 63 | 195 | 94 | 555 |
| Members of affiliated societies '000 | 291 | 117 | 178 | 207 | 41 | 834 |
| Turnover, million K. Sh. | 194.1 | 11.3 | 80.0 | 96.9 | 17.5 | 399.8 |
| – Average, million K. Sh. | 38.3 | 1.6 | 16.0 | 8.1 | 2.9 | 11.4 |
| – Average turnover/staff, K. Sh. | 131,600 | 39,000 | 92,400 | 73,900 | 100,600 | 97,100 |
| Sales of inputs, million K. Sh. | 121.5 | 1.7 | 28.4 | 16.7 | 8.8 | 177.1 |
| – Average, million K. Sh. | 24.3 | 0.2 | 5.7 | 1.4 | 1.5 | 5.1 |
| – Average, sales/member, K. Sh. | 420 | 10 | 160 | 80 | 220 | 210 |
| Percentage of main activities operated at profit | 52 | 38 | 41 | 37 | 29 | 40 |
| Result, million K. Sh. | 12.2 | –1.8 | 1.5 | –8.2 | 1.1 | 4.8 |

*Sources:* Unions' annual accounts (1982/83); survey data.

*Note*
1 See note, Table 4.28.

*Table 4.30* Financial performance indicators, unions 1982–83, by activity orientation and category of environment

| | *Environment C1 71–83* | | *Environment C2 71–83* | | *Environment C3/4 71–83* | |
|---|---|---|---|---|---|---|
| | *Coffee* | *Other* | *Coffee* | *Other* | *Other* | *Total* |
| Number of unions covered[1] | 5 | 7 | 5 | 12 | 6 | 35 |
| A) Total assets employed, million K.Sh. | 462.5 | 46.4 | 210.4 | 186.8 | 33.3 | 939.4 |
| – Average | 92.5 | 6.6 | 42.1 | 15.6 | 5.6 | 26.8 |
| B) Net capital employed,[2] Million K.Sh. | 105.4 | 2.3 | 66.4 | 34.9 | 23.4 | 232.4 |
| – Average | 21.1 | 0.3 | 13.3 | 2.9 | 3.9 | 6.6 |
| C) Net working capital[3] million K.Sh. | 58.7 | –2.3 | 1.6 | 22.9 | 17.2 | 98.1 |
| – Average | 11.7 | –0.3 | 0.3 | 1.9 | 2.9 | 2.8 |
| D) Own capital, million K.Sh. | 90.0 | 1.7 | 36.3 | 5.8 | 7.9 | 141.7 |
| – Average | 18.0 | 0.2 | 7.3 | 0.5 | 1.3 | 4.0 |
| E) CBK-loans, million K.Sh. | 20.9 | 47.1 | 15.9 | 133.3 | 25.5 | 242.7 |
| – Average | 4.2 | 6.7 | 3.2 | 11.1 | 4.3 | 6.9 |
| F) Result 82/3, million K.Sh. | 12.2 | –1.8 | 1.5 | –8.2 | 1.1 | 4.8 |
| Ratios: | | | | | | |
| G) Own capital/total assets (D) | 0.19 | 0.04 | 0.17 | 0.03 | 0.24 | 0.15 |
| H) Current liabilities/Total liabilities | 0.75 | 0.95 | 0.68 | 0.81 | 0.30 | 0.75 |
| I) Members' debts/total assets[4] | 0.41 | 0.56 | 0.30 | 0.42 | 0.32 | 0.39 |
| J) Members' deposits/members'[5] debts | 1.29 | 0.19 | 1.28 | 0.11 | 0.07 | 0.36 |

*Sources:* Unions' annual accounts (1982/83); Cooperative Bank, internal documentation; survey data.

*Notes*

1 Excl. Trans-Nzoia union.

2 Intangible and fixed assets less depreciation plus net current assets.

3 Current assets ./. current liabilities.

4 Credit and loans to affiliated societies and members.

5 Members' savings in unions with banking section/savings scheme.

non-coffee unions in environments 1 and 2 would not amount to more than 55–70 per cent of total liabilities.

Expectations regarding inputs sales and marketing have been based on the assumed critical role of credit. When organizational designs did not match expectations and credit apparently did not constitute the, assumed, binding constraint, the entire construct turned obsolete. This problem, unfortunately, is not limited to the unions as they are closely integrated with affiliated primary societies. As a result, the latter have largely lost their ability to operate as independently managed units. The stalemate characterizing the unions has therefore, in decisive respects, also immobilized affiliated primary societies.

Although coffee unions generally performed better than other unions, their position is not entirely satisfactory. In several cases, their liquidity position is unsatisfactory and too many activities (about 45 per cent) are operated at a loss. The unions seem to have a preference for getting involved in activities of limited relevance to their members. Like the non-coffee unions, their position is critically dependent on the soundness of loans to societies and members. Although the situation certainly seems to be better among coffee unions, it has not been possible for us to examine this matter more closely. Generally, however, it seems dangerous to operate savings services as one of several union activities. In situations where unions are making losses, it is at present far too easy to cover them with members' deposits. Consequently, the present banking sections should be separated from the unions and established as independent organisations dealing only with savings and credit services.

The MOCD's ability to supervise and direct the unions has generally been inadequate. Day-to-day intrusion in the already bureaucratic structure of unions and societies has little positive effect. Instead it contributes to a passive and indeterminate management climate.[51] The extremely limited possibilities for members to control the administration of unions also offer opportunities for collusion between government officers and cooperative staff/officials which not only results in irregularities but also causes the breakdown of supervisory and controlling functions.

Chapter five

# Impact

In the context of this study, impact may be perceived as the positive and negative results generated by a rural organization and by the specific policies on which it directly depends, seen in relation to the social and economic development objectives the organization is expected to fulfil. Impact indicators, in turn, denote variables assumed to adequately reflect these social and economic effects.

Considering the democratic and participatory characteristics usually associated with cooperative organizations, and which are also made explicit in Kenyan policy documents,[1] impact indicators reflecting these qualities obviously are essential. According to one definition, participation entails 'the creation of opportunities that enable all members of a community and the larger society actively to contribute to and influence the development process and share equitably in the fruits of development' (United Nations 1981:5). At a more general level, this formulation complies with the principal components of public good, usually referred to as being the basic recurrent concerns in policy decisions of governments, namely justice, liberty and welfare.[2]

Three aspects of participation, referring to scope, source and rules, may be seen as being of particular interest.[3] *Scope* of participation involves reach, functionality and reflection, where *reach* simply denotes to what extent an organization is linked to the population living within its area of operation. In our context, it may be operationalized to the relative share of rural households being members of agricultural service societies. *Functionality*, on the other hand, would indicate the degree to which those reached by an organization actually take part in its activities as economic actors, be it as buyers of inputs, loanees or as suppliers of produce.

Participation comprising only a functional dimension, i.e. taking part in activities possibly designed, induced, and controlled, by others, obviously is mechanical in character. A more comprehensive interpretation would need to take into consideration also a person's or group's ability to subordinate activities to conscious *reflection*. Reflection would constitute a motive force being integrated with an individual's or a group's actions. Consequently, the concept is meant to include 'all acts of mental labour such as thinking, deliberating, inquiring, researching, analysing, choosing, deciding, planning, etc.' (Rahman 1981:3). The structure and mode of operation of rural organizations may be more or less conducive to reflective participation. At the same time it is clear that the economic and socio-political environment may also condition the level of reflective participation.

Additionally, participation may be categorized according to its origin (*source*). A distinction then can be made between spontaneous, induced and coerced participation.[4] *Spontaneous* participation refers to voluntary and autonomous action or organizations unaided by government or other bodies, and is obviously closely related to reflective participation. *Induced* participation, i.e. sponsored, mandated and officially endorsed activity, is common, being typical of a variety of both community and cooperative organizations in developing countries. The development of cooperatives in Kenya belongs to this category, although both spontaneous and coercive features can be observed. *Coerced* participation (compulsory, manipulated and contrived) is characteristic of collective organizations such as communes, producer cooperatives and related forms of colletively organized agriculture, although elements of compulsion sometimes are also present in other types of rural organization, including agricultural service cooperatives.

The various types of concepts can be used as a point of departure for taxonomizing and examining some aspects of the impact generated by cooperatives in Kenya. In particular, we will pay attention to the earlier mentioned aspects of scope of participation in terms of their social and economic implications, and their relation to the induced mode of participation.

## 5.1 Scope of participation

### *Reach*

Total membership can be used as a measure of reach. With this definition, it seems evident that agricultural service societies considerably strengthened their position in rural areas in the period 1960–83 (Table 5.1). As also can be seen from the table, the increase in membership levelled off in the more favourable type of environment (C1) in the 1970s, while it accelerated in 'peripheral' smallholder areas. The latter phenomenon applies to Eastern, Rift Valley, S. Nyanza and Coast provinces. In Eastern province a major growth mechanism no doubt has been the lifting of the planting ban on coffee in the 1970s, while the expansion in S. Nyanza and Rift Valley has been linked to promotion of cotton and dairy, respectively.

With the exception of coffee, however, market (demand) factors played a limited role in the 1970s as compared to the member enrolment generated by induced changes in organization and service activities, i.e. the transformation of agricultural service cooperatives from dealing principally with produce marketing, as in the period 1963–73, towards that of encompassing the role of delivery system for farm inputs and producer credit.

This supply-oriented policy no doubt reflected the ambition of stimulating growth in areas with less developed smallholder agriculture, and, partly, also of reaching poorer smallholder strata (Table 5.2). The subsequent geographical dispersal of societies and membership is reflected in the Gini coefficient (members/ population by district) which decreased from 46.4 in 1970 to 38.5 in 1983. Even so, $G_{M83}$ indicates that the distribution of cooperative members deviates significantly from that of the rural population at large.

Thus, although a considerable dispersal in membership has taken place, Central province, with 17 per cent of the population, in 1983 still accounted for about one-third of the total membership. The total cooperative membership in this province then was equivalent to 70 per cent of the estimated total number of households. This figure, however, is somewhat misleading as it is inflated by the single-produce character of most active societies. Thus, in reality, the level of reach of cooperatives is 10–30 per cent lower, as households frequently are members of more than one society.

Individual districts displaying very high levels of reach (Nyeri, Kirinyaga, Meru, Kisii) thus have in common that they include densely populated areas with a high potential for production of several of the major types of 'cooperative produce'. In view of the fact that double and multiple memberships are more common in the major, ecologically favoured smallholder areas, it follows that the inter-district distribution of member households is more dispersed than that of the number of registered members, and that this pattern apparently has become more accentuated in the 1970s and early 1980s (Table 5.3).

With reference to the national level, exclusion of double and multiple membership implies that, at most, about 750,000 households are directly linked to agricultural service societies (as compared to the official figure of above 1.1 million and our revised gross figure as given in Table 5.1). Had it been possible to examine more systematically the member registers of societies, it would probably result in a further downward adjustment of total membership. Thus, in the cases where we have had the opportunity to examine the registers, they have been found to be poorly maintained, particularly with regard to terminated memberships.

The fact that households are reached by cooperative societies does not have to be of any social or economic consequence. It could been seen as a necessary but not sufficient condition for cooperatives to exercise a direct influence as a rural change agent. Even with this interpretation, it is necessary to consider the possibility that a sizeable proportion of the households are likely to be passive members, i.e. their activities as smallholders do not cause any social or economic interaction with their societies.

One reason for this can be that smallholders have joined societies in response to both locally and centrally engineered campaigns rather than with a serious intention of being active members; another that smallholders have 'withdrawn' due to poor marketing or business performance of their society (e.g. deficient collection routines, low or late payments, inadequate input supply services, etc.). Withdrawal has in many instances also been caused by the combination of coerced entry and economic obligations, as in the case of settlement societies. In the settlement schemes, membership of societies has been mandatory. The grounds for this were that the state had assigned these societies the responsibility of securing repayment of settlement loans through deductions from produce payments to members. As a result many settlers have avoided marketing their produce through cooperatives.

In other instances, registration as a member can be seen as an attempt to secure access to scarce resources, not least financial, which are supplied through cooperatives. This seems to have been a quite common phenomenon in those areas, particularly in the western parts of Kenya, where cooperatives have been used to introduce credit and input supply programmes. Due to deficiencies in the environment, adverse weather conditions, lack of information and proper extension services, poor society performance, etc. (see Chapter 4), distributed loan packages have in far too many instances failed to result in sufficiently raised output to faciltiate loan repayment. As in the case of settlement societies, a common response then has been that members try to avoid dealing with the society in order to circumvent repayment. To this could of course be added the cases where membership is simply seen as a means of getting access to rationed resources without any intention of ever making repayments. Thus, for a variety of reasons, a considerable proportion of the total membership is passive. Although the size of this stratum of the membership is very difficult to estimate, we reckon it to be about 100,000–150,000, i.e. equivalent to 12–15 per cent of the total number of member households.

Adding this to our earlier observations, reach in the sense of the number of *active* member *households*, would only amount to about 60 per cent of the officially recorded number of members of active primary societies, i.e. in the range of 600,000–700,000 members. Adjusting for the fact that not all rural households belong to the smallholder category, we arrive at the conclusion that the active membership in 1983 represented, at most, one-third of the total number of smallholder households. As noted earlier, though, the regional variations are considerable.

The high proportion of inactive members characterizing agricultural cooperatives is, to a significant degree, a direct result of the particular form of induced cooperative participation pursued by the government (see Chapter two and below). It has created the impression that it is through cooperatives that the state can make available scarce financial and material resources to smallholders. As a consequence, each individual member registration tends to be caused either because a cooperative holds an effective marketing monopoly or because the society may make it possible to secure access to financial and material resources. Few smallholders would have had reason to join as members if the decision had been governed only by the societies' level of cost efficiency and service quality.

### *Functional participation*

Functional participation is here defined as the degree to which smallholders reached by cooperatives interact with their societies as buyers of inputs, loanees and/or suppliers of produce for maketing. Accordingly, the concept applies primarily to those 600,000–700,000 households that are active members. The level of functional participation can be expected to be a vital determinant of a society's contribution to not only economic but also social development. As regards the latter aspect, it may thus be argued that only when a society directly and positively affects its members' income-earning capacity is there a potential for reflective participation. This latter factor, in turn, constitutes positive feedback by confirming that activity orientation, service quality and efficiency comply with member requirements.

*Table 5.1* Membership of agricultural service societies 1960, 1970 and 1983

| | | Membership ('000) | | | |
|---|---|---|---|---|---|
| *Environm.* | *District* | *1960* | *1970* | *1983* | *Diff. 60–83* |
| C1 71–83 | Nyeri | 13.1 | 47.8 | 92.6 | 79.5 |
| | Muranga | 6.2 | 45.4 | 84.6 | 78.4 |
| | Kiambu | 11.9 | 30.5 | 63.4 | 51.5 |
| | Kirinyaga | 4.8 | 26.3 | 47.0 | 42.2 |
| | Kisumu | 0.9 | 3.5 | 36.4 | 35.5 |
| | Kisii | 32.6 | 86.2 | 152.5 | 119.9 |
| | Kakamega | 2.5 | 7.6 | 12.1 | 9.6 |
| Sum | | *72.0* | *247.3* | *488.6* | *416.6* |
| C2 71–83 | Nyandarua | 0.0 | 11.4 | 20.9 | 20.9 |
| | Embu | 17.9 | 17.1 | 34.0 | 16.1 |
| | Meru | 30.0 | 57.4 | 129.5 | 99.5 |
| | Machakos | 5.4 | 20.5 | 91.6 | 86.2 |
| | Homa Bay | 1.1 | 5.9 | 31.0 | 29.9 |
| | Siaya | 0.2 | 2.0 | 19.7 | 19.5 |
| | Kericho | 0.3 | 6.6 | 14.6 | 14.3 |
| | Bungoma | 18.1 | 22.2 | 23.0 | 4.9 |
| | Busia | 0.0 | 1.6 | 11.5 | 11.5 |
| Sum | | *73.0* | *144.7* | *375.8* | *302.8* |
| C3 71–83 | Kilifi | 0.0 | 4.3 | 9.8 | 9.8 |
| | Kwale | 0.0 | 0.2 | 2.0 | 2.0 |
| | Lamu | 0.0 | 0.2 | 1.6 | 1.6 |
| | Taita | 2.9 | 3.9 | 6.2 | 3.3 |
| | Kitui | 0.0 | 1.4 | 3.6 | 3.6 |
| | Nakuru | 0.0 | 10.1 | 8.7 | 8.7 |
| | Baringo | 0.0 | 0.5 | 8.1 | 8.1 |
| | U. Gishu | 0.0 | 10.2 | 6.1 | 6.1 |
| | Nandi | 0.0 | 1.8 | 10.6 | 10.6 |
| | T. Nzoia | 0.0 | 0.0 | 4.6 | 4.6 |
| | Marakwet | 0.0 | 1.9 | 7.2 | 7.2 |
| | Laikipia | 0.0 | 1.6 | 3.2 | 3.2 |
| Sum | | *2.9* | *36.1* | *71.7* | *68.8* |
| C4 71–83 | Tana River | 0.0 | 0.0 | 0.9 | 0.9 |
| | Isiolo | 0.0 | 0.0 | 0.0 | 0.0 |
| | Marsabit | 0.0 | 0.0 | 0.0 | 0.0 |
| | Garissa | 0.0 | 0.0 | 0.6 | 0.6 |
| | Wajir | 0.0 | 0.0 | 0.2 | 0.2 |
| | Mandera | 0.0 | 0.0 | 0.0 | 0.0 |
| | W.Pokot | 0.0 | 1.6 | 1.5 | 1.5 |
| | Narok | 0.0 | 0.4 | 2.6 | 2.6 |
| | Kajiado | 0.0 | 0.2 | 2.6 | 2.6 |
| | Turkana | 0.0 | 0.0 | 0.0 | 0.0 |
| | Samburu | 0.0 | 0.0 | 0.0 | 0.0 |
| Sum | | *0.0* | *2.2* | *8.4* | *8.4* |
| Total | | 147.9 | 430.3 | 944.5 | 796.6 |

*Source* MOCD and survey data

One indicator that can be used to shed some light on members' functional participation is total turnover, including unions. In Table 5.4, differences between the relative distribution of turnover and population by the category of environment and district has been listed for 1970 and 1983. Already in 1970 a few districts, mainly in Central and Eastern provinces (C1/C2), held a dominating position. Six geographically contiguous districts then constituted a 'core region' that accounted for *c.* 63 per cent of total turnover (Kiambu, Muranga, Kirinyaga, Nyeri, Embu and Meru). The spatially biased distribution is reflected in the Gini coefficient ($G_{tp70}$=49.1). During the period 1970–83, this geographical concentration-domination was further accentuated. The core region referred to above, now generated 71 per cent of total cooperative turnover ($G_{tp83}$=51.6).

This development is quite remarkable considering that it runs counter both to the changes in the regional distribution of membership characterizing the period and to the intentions of the cooperative development strategy pursued by the government. The trend, though, is clearly in congruence with our findings in Chapter four on the performance characteristics of various segments of primary and secondary societies, and their critical dependence on the relation of organization-environment.

*Table 5.2* Changes in relative distribution of membership and population between 1970 and 1983, by category of environment[1]

| *Environm.* | *(A) % of total membership 1970* | *(B) % of distr. population 1970*[2] | *(C) Diff. (A)./.(B) 1970* | *(D) % of total membership 1983*[2] | *(E) % of total population 1983* | *(F) Diff. (D)./.(E) 1983* |
|---|---|---|---|---|---|---|
| C1 71–83 | 57.49 | 32.96 | 24.53 | 51.73 | 31.77 | 19.96 |
| C2 71–83 | 33.63 | 36.60 | −2.97 | 39.79 | 35.87 | 3.92 |
| C3 71–83 | 8.39 | 21.52 | −13.14 | 7.60 | 22.90 | −15.30 |
| C4 71–83 | 0.50 | 8.91 | −8.41 | 0.88 | 9.46 | −8.58 |

*Sources:* MOCD and survey data; Central Bureau of Statistics, Population Census 1969 and 1979, Vol. I.

*Notes*

1 For a specification by district, see Appendix.

2 Size of the population 1970 and 1983, is based on an assumed growth rate of 3.5% during 1969–70 and 1979–83.

Our data on total produce sales of primary societies can be used to examine further the level of functional participation in 1983 (Table 5.6). It then can be noted that primary societies in the core region[5] accounted for about 48 per cent of the total membership and a share of total sales equivalent to that of total turnover, i.e. *c.* 71 per cent.

*Table 5.3* Membership of agricultural service societies as a percentage of estimated number of rural households in 1983[1]

| *Environment* | *Member households (%)* |
|---|---|
| C1 71–83 | 56.10 |
| C2 71–83 | 39.70 |
| C3 71–83 | 11.20 |
| C4 71–83 | 3.10 |
| National average | 34.80 |

*Source*: MOCD and Population Census 1979, Vol. I.
*Note*
[1] See Appendix for specification by district.

*Table 5.4* Changes in relative distribution of turnover and population between 1970 and 1983, by category of environment[1]

| *Environm.* | *(A) % of total turnover 1970* | *(B) % of distr. population 1970*[2] | *(C) Diff. (A)./.(B) 1970* | *(D) % of total turnover 1983* | *(E) % of total population 1983*[2] | *(F) Diff. (D)./.(E) 1983* |
|---|---|---|---|---|---|---|
| C1 71–83 | 50.5 | 33.0 | 17.5 | 58.1 | 31.8 | 26.3 |
| C2 71–83 | 44.0 | 36.6 | 7.4 | 34.4 | 35.9 | −1.5 |
| C3 71–83 | 5.5 | 21.5 | −16.0 | 7.1 | 22.9 | −15.8 |
| C4 71–83 | 0.0 | 8.9 | −8.9 | 0.5 | 9.5 | −9.0 |

*Sources:* MOCD and survey data; Central Bureau of Statistics, Population Census 1969 and 1979 Vol. I.
*Notes*
[1] For a specification by district, see Appendix.
[2] Size of the population 1970 and 1983, is based on an assumed growth rate of 3.5% during 1969–70 and 1979–83.

*Table 5.5* Basic features of primary societies in western and central Kenya classified according to value of produce sales, 1982–83

| *Total* | *Region N/W/RV*[1] | *Region C/E*[2] | *Kenya* |
|---|---|---|---|
| Number of societies | 451 (100) | 293 (100) | 789 (100) |
| Total membership, '000(%) | 357 (100) | 566 (100) | 944 (100) |
| Total sales, K. Sh. Million | 444 (100) | 1,931 (100) | 2,431 (100) |
| Aver. sales/members, Sh. | 1,244 | 3,410 | 2,575 |
| *Society sales < 2.56 million* | | | |
| Number of societies (%) | 405 (90) | 293 (64) | 632 (80) |
| Membership, '000 (%) | 270 (75) | 149 (26) | 431 (46) |
| Sales, K. Sh. Million (%) | 209 (47) | 155 (8) | 384 (16) |
| Aver. sales/member, Sh. | 774 | 1,040 | 891 |
| *Society sales > 2.56 Million* | | | |
| Number of societies (%) | 46 (10) | 105 (36) | 157 (20) |
| Membership, '000 (%) | 87 (25) | 417 (74) | 513 (54) |
| Sales, K. Sh. Million (%) | 235 (53) | 1,776 (92) | 2,047 (84) |
| Aver. sales/member, Sh. | 2,701 | 4,259 | 3,990 |

*Source:* survey data.
*Notes*
[1] S. Nyanza, Western and Rift Valley provinces.
[2] Central and Eastern provinces.

*Table 5.6* Membership and produce sales; 'core' and 'periphery', 1982–83

| *Environment* | *District* | *Number of soc.* | *Members '000* | *Prod. Sales K. Sh Million* |
|---|---|---|---|---|
| *Core* | | | | |
| C1 71–83 | Nyeri | 27 | 92.6 | 332.2 |
| C1 71–83 | Muranga | 32 | 84.6 | 418.2 |
| C1 71–83 | Kiambu | 34 | 63.4 | 231.6 |
| C1 71–83 | Kirinyaga | 15 | 47.0 | 232.0 |
| C2 71–83 | Embu | 24 | 34.0 | 134.1 |
| C2 71–83 | Meru | 43 | 129.5 | 373.5 |
| Sub-total | | *175(22%)* | *451.1(48%)* | *1,721.6(71%)* |
| *Periphery* | | | | |
| C1 71–83 | Kisumu | 53 | 36.4 | 83.9 |
| C1 71–83 | Kisii | 62 | 152.5 | 105.3 |
| C2 71–83 | Homa Bay | 24 | 31.0 | 14.1 |
| C2 71–83 | Siaya | 11 | 19.7 | 4.1 |
| C2 71–83 | Kakamega | 22 | 12.1 | 23.8 |
| C2 71–83 | Bungoma | 28 | 23.0 | 49.5 |
| C2 71–83 | Busia | 9 | 11.5 | 0.2 |
| C3 71–83 | Nakuru | 41 | 8.7 | 15.7 |
| C3 71–83 | Baringo | 14 | 8.1 | 19.4 |
| C2 71–83 | Kericho | 54 | 14.6 | 38.5 |
| C3 71–83 | Uasin Gishu | 34 | 6.1 | 19.0 |
| C2 71–83 | Nandi | 22 | 10.6 | 38.7 |
| C3 71–83 | Trans Nzoia | 29 | 4.6 | 22.7 |
| C3 71–83 | Elgeyo Marakw | 15 | 7.2 | 4.9 |
| C3 71–83 | W. Pokot | 5 | 1.5 | 1.8 |
| C3 71–83 | Laikipia | 14 | 3.1 | 2.5 |
| C4 71–83 | Narok | 9 | 2.6 | 1.4 |
| C4 71–83 | Kajiado | 6 | 2.6 | 1.8 |
| C4 71–83 | Turkana | 1 | N/A | 0.5 |
| C2 71–83 | Nyandarua | 65 | 20.9 | 91.5 |
| C3 71–83 | Kilifi | 15 | 9.8 | 25.0 |
| C3 71–83 | Kwale | 6 | 2.0 | 3.8 |
| C3 71–83 | Lamu | 4 | 1.6 | 3.4 |
| C4 71–83 | Tana River | 2 | 0.9 | 6.6 |
| C3 71–83 | Taita Taveta | 9 | 6.2 | 3.5 |
| C3 71/83 | Kitui | 7 | 3.6 | 2.2 |
| C2 71–83 | Machakos | 47 | 91.6 | 125.5 |
| C4 71–83 | Garissa | 2 | 0.6 | 0.1 |
| C4 71–83 | Wajir | 3 | 0.2 | 0.0 |
| Sub-total | | *613(78%)* | *493.3(52%)* | *709.4(29%)* |
| Total | | 788 | 944.4 | 2,431.0 |

*Source:* survey data

*Table 5.7* Produce sales and member payments by category of environment,[1] 1982–83

| *Environment* | *Number of societies* | *Members ('000)* | *Produce sales K. Sh. Million* | *Payments K. Sh. Million* |
|---|---|---|---|---|
| C1 71–83 | 243 | 488.6 | 1,424.0 | 1,166.6 |
| C2 71–83 | 308 | 376.4 | 834.7 | 639.4 |
| C3 71–83 | 209 | 71.1 | 160.1 | 125.9 |
| C4 71–83 | 28 | 8.3 | 12.1 | 4.1 |
| Total | 788 | 944.4 | 2,430.9 | 1,936.0 |

*Source:* survey data
*Note*
[1] For a specification by district, see Appendix.

A further specification of variations in the level of functional participation can be arrived at by considering individual societies rather than districts. Ranking all societies by sales, we then find that 10 per cent of the total number of societies account for about one-third of the registered membership, and about one-tenth of the total number of smallholder households, but for not less than 70 per cent of total produce sales and for 73 per cent of total payments to members. The average sales/member in these seventy-eight societies, of which practically all are found in the 'core region', is about K.Sh. 5,000 as compared to K.Sh. 1,200 in other societies.

Ranking societies by sales also reveals distinct regional differences in structure and impact. In 1983, the top 20 per cent of all primary societies had sales exceeding about K.Sh. 2.6 million each. Their total number, membership and aggregated sales are shown in Table 5.5 for western and central Kenya, respectively.

As also illustrated by Table 5.7, the role of service cooperatives as marketing agents is evidently extraordinarily biased to the advantage of areas favoured in terms of ecology and infrastructure. The problem with this distribution, though, is not so much that some strata of the smallholder population have benefited from their membership but rather that cooperatives have proved largely unable significantly to influence market integration and income generation outside the most favoured agricultural regions.

Furthermore, even within the areas where cooperatives play a role, their impact is socially stratified. Available data on credit and input supply services in coffee production (see below) imply that a minority of the members economically dominate successful societies. A significant stratifying force, which certainly also plays a part in the more prosperous highland areas of Central and Eastern provinces, is the activity orientation or primary societies, in particular the way that the marketing profile of each individual society remains focused on one particular type of produce. This petrification, caused by excessive regulation both of agricultural market systems and of cooperatives, has as one obvious result that households producing food crops have no access to the cooperative marketing system.

The coffee boom in 1975–77 accentuated the favoured position of coffee-growers in the central highlands relative to other categories of members/smallholders. The government did not tax away this windfall which thus was left in the hands of the growers. As shown by Bevan, Collier and Gunning (1987) this had a significant and positive impact on income and employment, although about half of the income gains realized in 1977 (21 per cent) were eroded by accompanying inflation. The high price increases on non-food goods that followed the boom were obviously not limited to the tea- and coffee-producing 'core' regions and, hence, must have had a considerable negative impact on commercialized smallholders operating in other areas and with a different output mix. It is also interesting to note that, according to Bevan *et al.*, the biggest beneficiary of the coffee boom was the urban economy. As suppliers of non-food goods and as recipients of most of the investment boom following the windfall, urban areas increased their incomes much more than smallholders for the period 1977–83.

## Credit and inputs

From the beginning of the 1970s, the role of smallholder credit increased in importance and so too did the credit services provided by cooperatives. Whereas cooperatives received about one-fifth of the financial support extended by the government for this purpose in 1972/73, their share rose to about 50 per cent in the period 1974–81.[7] The principal credit programme has been the CPCS, which has been supplemented by 'special credit programmes' often aimed at reaching poorer smallholder strata and/or less developed argricultural areas (see Chapter three and Chapter 4.8). The membership and regional distribution of societies linked to the CPCS and the special credit programmes in 1983 are given in Table 5.8.

Thus, about 55 per cent of the total number of active primary societies were linked to one or more of these credit programmes. The fact that the societies represent about 85 per cent of the total registered membership, does not mean that the coverage of credit

*Table 5.8* Coverage of the CPCS and special credit programmes, 1982–83

| Province | CPCS No. soc. | Members | Special Progr.[1] No. soc. | Members | Total[2] No. soc. | Members |
|---|---|---|---|---|---|---|
| Central | 107 | 253,000 | 46 | 193,000 | 115 | 267,000 |
| Eastern | 56 | 191,000 | 59 | 178,000 | 81 | 222,000 |
| Coast | 1 | 4,000 | 18 | 11,000 | 19 | 15,000 |
| N. Eastern | 0 | 0 | 1 | 200 | 1 | 200 |
| Rift Valley | 13 | 4,000 | 66 | 25,000 | 74 | 27,000 |
| S. Nyanza | 80 | 161,000 | 50 | 111,000 | 115 | 219,000 |
| Western | 2 | 26,000 | 36 | 43,000 | 37 | 43,000 |
| Total | 280 | 639,000 | 276 | 561,200 | 442 | 793,200 |

*Source:* survey data

*Notes*

1 Includes 'Smallholder Production Services and Credit Scheme', 'Farm Input Supply Scheme', 'New Seasonal Credit Scheme', 'Integrated Agricultural Development Programme' (I and II), 'Smallholders' Coffee Improvement Programme', 'Machakos Integrated Development Programme' and 'German Agricultural Support Programme'.

The number of societies that have been linked to these programmes in the period 1970–83 is likely to be higher than the figure given in the table, as it only includes societies that were active in 1983.

2 The totals are adjusted for the fact that many societies (114) are linked both to CPCS and one or several of the special credit programmes.

services has been of a similar magnitude. On the contrary, the supply of credit has been decidedly selective in nature. Since the early 1970s, various 'special programmes' have channelled agricultural credit to the tune of K.Sh. 180 million to an estimated 120,000 members,[8] i.e. equivalent to something like 5–7 per cent of the total number of smallholder households. Probably about two-thirds of the total amount has gone to members of societies in Rift Valley and the western parts of the country. As depicted in Chapter four, practically all of these programmes display a poor record in terms of repayments. In 1983, for example, 79 per cent of the principal released under IADP(I) in 1977–80 had not been repaid, compared to 88 per cent for SPSCP and 70 per cent for FISS. Basically, the figures illustrate that the loans, and related measures, neither initiated sustained improvements of production technologies nor sufficiently raised output levels.

The insignificance or even absence of anticipated effects, in turn, were dependent on the presence of constraints that were more binding in nature than the lack of credit, and which constitute inherent features of the environment of most smallholder areas (Chapters three and four).

In these circumstances, the introduction of rationed material benefits of the type production/seasonal credit may actually have slowed down market integration of smallholder agriculture. The

*Table 5.9* Basic geographical characteristics of CPCS, 1983

| *Region* | *Number of CPCS societies* | *Total Member-ship* | *(%)* | *Number of loanees* | *(%)* | *Estim. Total Loans K.Shs mill* | *(%)* |
|---|---|---|---|---|---|---|---|
| 'Core'[1] | 111 | 383,000 | 60 | 58,000 | 72 | 175 | 82 |
| Other regions | 167 | 257,000 | 40 | 22,000 | 28 | 38 | 18 |
| Total | 278 | 640,000 | 100 | 80,000 | 100 | 213 | 100 |

*Sources:* MOCD, Rural Credit Section; MOCD, 'Statistics for Cooperative in Kenya 1981 and 1982'; Statistics Unit, MOCD, Nairobi, 1984; Table 3.6.

*Note*

[1] Covers the districts Kiambu, Muranga, Nyeri, Kirinyaga, Embu and Meru.

reason for this is two fold: first, because loan defaulters will try to avoid dealing with their societies, which in practice may mean that they cease to produce output dependent on this kind of marketing channel. Second, as a consequence of the poor performance of societies, unions and the MOCD in administering the loans, which also resulted in widespread irregularities, farmers' confidence in the ability of cooperatives to serve their interests is likely to have been seriously, and possible permanently, damaged.

The cooperative production credit scheme (CPCS) covered in 1982/83 about 280 societies with *c.* 640,000 members. A major difference between the CPCS and the special credit programmes is that the former is integrated with the administrative structure of primary societies and unions, and thus constitutes a regular service to members. Second, repayment is made through deductions from payments for produce marketed through the society and is thus bound to work for the types of produce in which cooperatives have been granted a monopoly, and for which alternative local markets are not readily available, such as coffee and pyrethrum. Moreover, in unions with banking sections, i.e. which provide members of primary societies with savings services, the CPCS is principally financed by societies and unions themselves.

Just as is the case with the special credit programmes, functional participation in the CPCS is selective in nature. Several circumstances contribute to the 'exclusiveness' of the scheme. When implementation of the scheme started in the late 1960s, priority was given, understandably, to the financially and managerially stronger segments of the cooperative sector, i.e. primarily to coffee societies and unions in Central and Eastern provinces. Since then the scheme has been implemented also in most pyrethrum, dairy and sugar societies. With the exception of sugar-cane societies, this means that the scheme is restricted geographically to the highland regions. In addition, it is mainly in the financially stronger coffee societies in Central and part of Eastern provinces that the CPCS has come to play a significant role (Table 5.9).

In relation to the total number of member households estimated earlier – i.e. 600,000–700,000 – the level of 'annual' functional participation is in the range of 12–15 per cent. In the 'core region' the level would be about twice as high as the average for other smallholder areas. Using the member household estimates this would mean 10–12 and 20–22 per cent, respectively.

A question of significance in this context is of course the distribution of loans among members. If it is approximately the same members that, seen over a 5–10 year period, have had access to CPCS loans, the impact of the scheme obviously would be confined to a very small portion of both member and smallholder households. On the other hand, if CPCS loans continuously are offered to new, eligible members, the scheme's effectiveness in influencing prevailing production technologies may be jeopardized. Not unexpectedly, available evidence seems to indicate that the lending practices fall somewhere in between these extremes. Thus, in a sample of societies and unions studied by Njonjo *et al.*[9], it was found that about 27 per cent of the members had received CPCS loans during 1975–81. Applying this finding to the national level, it may be inferred that something like 200,000–250,000 members would have utilized CPCS loans in the period 1970–1983, of whom about three-quarters were members of societies in the Central and Eastern provinces. Hence, in this 'core region' about 50–60 per cent of the members at any time would have functionally participated in the scheme as compared to about half of that level in other CPCS areas.

As regards the CPCS' contribution to raised agricultural production, the picture is ambiguous. Although loanees rather consistently seem to record higher yield levels than non-loanees, it is not possible to claim that this difference is due to the CPCS. Njonjo thus notes that 'CPCS loanees had consistently higher mean deliveries and consumed relatively higher volumes of inputs than non-loanees, before during and after acquisition of CPCS loans' (Njonjo 1985:28). Furthermore, for the principal types of produce – coffee, dairy and pyrethrum – average annual growth rates over a six-year period were found to be practically identical for both non-loanees and loanees. In the same study, it was also found that about 60 per cent of the loanees did not use the loans for procurement of inputs; neither had the loans resulted in any measurable degree of differentiation of agricultural production.

The officially stated, more specific, objectives of the CPCS have been to enable smallholders to:

(i) increase their existing volumes of production and sales of the produce handled by their societies;
(ii) diversify the agricultural product mix;
(iii) increase their consumption of farm inputs and services;
(iv) raise their agricultural incomes.

With reference to the observations above, it seems unlikely that the CPCS has contributed significantly to any of these objectives. Seen in the context of not only households linked to service co-operatives but also the smallholder sector at large, it may be seen as a device that has made financial resources available to a narrow, already favoured stratum of the farming population. Apparently, these resources have only to a limited extent been used directly in agriculture.

In the main coffee-producing areas, particularly in Central province, the most common mode of providing production credit has been the 'store credit'. This rather flexible service simply entails that member households can collect inputs, primarily fertilizers and insecticides, at their society store up to a predetermined limit, usually a certain percentage of expected deliveries. Although this so-called store credit is not officially recognized, i.e. by the MOCD, it seems to be the most efficient means of providing credit so far available.

In conclusion, the benefits of credit to smallholders are not very clear. First, the integration of credit with marketing and input supply services add considerably to the administrative complexity and costs of societies and unions. These disadvantages affect not only loanees but all members. It is not unlikely that prompt payments for crop deliveries are a partial substitute for credit. The frequently late payments have been a serious disincentive to production for example of cotton and pyrethrum, and thus obviously also contributed to create a need for credit. In coffee societies, on the other hand, payments seem too frequent. Apart from escalating administrative costs, they consist of a mixture of advances and crop payments which, due to foregone interest, reduces the value of payments. In many instances the individual payments get very small and the mixing of advance and crop payments is not easy to interpret and therefore causes misunderstanding among members. It would seem reasonable to cut this procedure by making only two payments a year; the first would be an advance payment timed to fit farmers' procurement of inputs. If combined with well-functioning savings services, this could reduce both credit requirements and the costs of the present system.

## Input supplies

Although sales of inputs largely reflect the distribution of credit among societies and regions, it does not necessarily mean that there is a general causal relation between them (Njonjo, 1985). Particularly in western Kenya and Rift Valley, cooperative input sales play a minor role in spite of a range of measures, including targeted credit services, aimed at inducing more input-intensive farm technologies. Not only the special credit programmes but also the CPCS seem to have been of limited value. On the other hand, the more informal 'store credit', mainly offered by coffee societies in Central province, seems to have played a more important role in establishing sustained changes of crop husbandry practices. This kind of change is dependent on the prevalence of a basic capacity to generate a stable surplus production, which largely is governed by local agro-ecological conditions and the level of development of public and commercial infrastructure. Variations within these more favoured settings, in turn, seem to be influenced by a range of other interrelated circumstances such as the smallholder's output mix, level of education and access to information (extension services). In the case of cooperatively organized smallholders, it seems clear that a more significant and regular use of inputs is largely confined to about 250,000–300,000 coffee farmers in Central and Eastern provinces (Table 4.28).

In summary, in terms of functional participation, cooperatives are serving – though to varying extents and degrees of success – the requirements of relatively privileged strata of smallholders. Consequently, they do not constitute foci for the provision of a wider range of services in rural areas that could meet the requirements of broader smallholder strata. This is likely to affect negatively not only food production and poorer smallholder strata but also the participation of women in cooperative organizations. Improvement in the position of women with regard to access to marketing and other services is certainly no matter of marginal significance. On the contrary, as women are likely to account for the major portion of agricultural output in Kenya, support in these and related respects (e.g. extension services) is likely to be of instrumental importance for the pace and pattern of agricultural development. In the major coffee-producing areas, women today play a dominant role but only as agricultural labourers. This primarily means the picking of cherry, the carrying of cherry to the factory and sorting of parchment coffee at the factory site.[10] In terms of functional and reflective participation, however, their importance is negligible. Except for rare cases where the head of a household is a woman, practically all transactions between the society and households are controlled by the male members.

### *Reflective participation*

The vertical interdependencies following from the state's ambition to promote, supervise and control the development of agricultural cooperatives has at local level resulted in petrified organizations and limited member influence. Even the narrow margin of freedom left for members' decision-making and their right to get information about society operations has been implicated by rather complex administrative systems and the mode of communication established between on the one hand state/cooperatives and, on the other, the membership. Hence, members have to meet considerable requirements in terms of knowledge and levels of education to understand and judge the operations and management of their societies and unions.

Given the overall cooperative development policy, it is hardly surprising that the state initially gave member education low priority compared to management training of society/union employees and government staff. It was apparently felt that by promoting professionalism, it would be possible to achieve efficient management within a reasonable time-span. Thus, not until 1971 were more systematic measures taken to expose members to the kind of information needed for them to exercise a controlling influence on their societies.

In 1974, these intentions were translated into a nationwide programme for member and committee member education. Apart from a study carried out in 1980/81,[11] no systematic attempt has been made to assess its impact or more generally to determine members' and committee members' knowledge about cooperatives, and hence their ability reflectively to participate in the activities of their societies.

According to Standa and Maranga (1981), most committee members do not know even the essentials, such as which documentation is mandatory for a cooperative society, the role of budgets, and basic techniques of administering financial transactions. Interestingly enough, some committee members also tend to consider employees of their societies and unions as leaders and, even, as 'officials'.[12] Apparently, the relations between these two categories often are very poor, and this evidently does not further the committee members' access to information about the operations of their society. Tensions are common also among the committee members themselves. This has obvious consequences for locally arranged education activities among ordinary members, for which the committees have been assigned a main responsibility.

The smallholders' principal sources of information about their rights and obligations as members appear to be committee members and staff from the ministry. However, most members have little formal education, if any, and as the member education material is written in English and Kiswahili, the delivery of information is subjected to at least one stage of transformation when translated to a vernacular. The latter is often the only possible mode of disseminating information if the intention is to reach all members. Further, as literacy levels are far from satisfactory, many members have to rely on their oral memory when information is disseminated. When a speaker translates from one of the official languages to a vernacular, there is obviously a risk that information is both 'sifted' and that, in the case of technical terms, that they cannot be meaningfully translated. Thus, even when members are exposed to educational activities, the information received is likely to be selective and fragmented, and most members can never get access to or utilize printed reference material.

In addition to these problems, most member education activities at society level are a sporadic rather than a regular phenomenon and they are arranged as general meetings which are often poorly attended. All this clearly indicates that few members are effectively reached by information about the cooperative mode of organization, their rights and obligations as members and how these rights can be exercised.

This conclusion is supported by Standa *et al.*, who found that while most members seem to be aware of their right to elect a committee, one-third of the members covered by the study were not aware of the powers of the Annual General Meeting (AGM), i.e. they did not know the extent to which the AGM could influence the management of their society. Hence, they did not know how to handle commonly felt problems, such as high deductions, late payments and various procedural anomalies.[13] Moreover, in spite of the fact that members generally were aware of their right to elect the committee of the society, few knew its technical duties. Most members also seem to have scant knowledge about the role and operations of the unions and it was observed that as many as two-thirds of the members were unaware of the existence of the Kenya National Federation of Cooperatives. Interestingly enough, the KNFC is one of the bodies in charge of organizing member educational activities.

State-administered cooperative support has resulted in societies and unions with often complex administrative structures and procedures. For members to be able to judge and possibly influence the operation of their societies, evidently requires quite ambitious member education activities. However, in Kenya their organization and content leave much to be desired. Seen in combination with a generally low level of education, their positive impact on the general level of cooperative knowledge among members ought to have been close to negligible. Even with good intentions, state-administered support apparently has created an institutional set-up sufficiently complex to allow most vital decision-making to be appropriated by government officers, personnel linked to donor agencies, union and society staff, and a narrow stratum of well-educated, articulate and influential rural households.

## 5.2 Source of participation

### *Central level*

With reference to sources of the predominantly induced mode of participation, one aspect of interest is to identify conditions that have influenced the design of cooperative strategies and also how adopted strategies have affected central institutions directly concerned with their realization. As regards the latter aspect, it has earlier been shown that the core institutions at central level, increased considerably both in size and complexity in the period 1963–83 (Table 5.10)

*Table 5.10* Staff changes in government and central cooperative bodies, 1963–73

| | *Number of permanent staff* | | |
|---|---|---|---|
| | *1963* | *1973* | *1983* |
| Dep./Min. of Coop. Dev. | 163 | 619 | 1,869 |
| KNFC | 10 | 28 | 130 |
| CBK | – | 16 | 219 |
| Coop. College | – | 28 | 148 |
| Coop. Insurance Soc. | – | – | 43 |
| Total | 173 | 691 | 2,409 |

*Sources:* Min. of Cooperative Development, Coop. Bank of Kenya, Kenya National Federation of Cooperatives; internal documentation

Evidently the growth cannot be linked singularly to agricultural cooperatives, as urban savings and credit societies developed rapidly in the 1970s. Even so, it is clear that the expansion of the latter category of societies can explain only a minor part of the changes.[14]

The growth of the superstructure seems to have been generated by three principal forces, namely (i) national development policies, (ii) cooperative policies and legislation, (iii) cooperative development support.

Within the framework of a mixed economy, national development policies came to focus on modernization and a high rate of economic growth. It resulted in concentrating resources on the urban–industrial segment of the economy. Most rural regions have rather consistently been starved of public investment. To the benefit of the urban population, price controls on food crops have been maintained as well as overvalued currencies and high protective tariffs on manufactured goods, which have all contributed to turn the rural–urban terms of trade against agricultural producers.

In the 1960s and early 1970s, a high rate of agricultural growth and national economic growth was no doubt achieved. In important respects, though, this growth can be seen as an effect of the correction of imbalances that prevailed during the colonial period. Thus, most of the expansion of agricultural production in this period can be linked to areal expansion of cash crops, which previously smallholders were not allowed to grow, and to the expansion of smallholder agriculture in formerly alienated areas. In the highland areas the effects of easing this restriction were further accentuated by the land-saving innovation of hybrid maize.

In an agricultural economy, the primary sector has to be instrumental in contributing to economic transformation. In the Kenyan context, attempts to direct this process have resulted in far-reaching government control of agricultural markets. As prices and cost of production generally moved to the disadvantage of the smallholder sector, a mode of selective incentive in the form of subsidized inputs and credit services has been seen as essential to ensure high growth rates in the export-oriented, and politically and economically influential segments of the rural economy.[15] Within this context, cooperatives apparently were perceived as representing a feasible mode of ensuring a stable and rising production of high-value cash/export crops. However, with the provision of credit, inputs and technical assistance, there also followed a machinery for government supervision/control and development support.

The obsession with securing export revenues or saving foreign exchange through cooperatives is clearly reflected both in the types of produce given priority and in the activity orientation of individual primary societies. Although called 'multiproduce', their organization and administrative structure in high-potential smallholder areas have almost without exception been geared towards the handling of one of the specific types of produce given priority. It is not possible to detect any serious intention to use cooperatives as a means of more generally meeting the service requirements of the total smallholder population.

To ensure compliance with the intentions behind the cooperative portion of the agricultural development strategy, new legislation was promulgated which, as earlier shown, gave the government far-reaching powers to direct and control the development of cooperatives. In the early 1970s, the biased economic growth pattern, which had characterized the first ten years of independence, resulted in policy changes. These changes which assigned cooperatives a prominent role were, however, more drastic in formulation than in actual deed.

There were few other surprises. The prevailing national development strategy had already generated an omnibus, regulation-prone and influential polity, increasingly permissive to vested interests. It was not prepared seriously to promote economic liberalization or a more substantial priority/resource shift to the advantage of rural areas. The solution arrived at thus came to replicate the selective delivery system approach already tried mainly in the central parts of the country.

Extension of this strategy, however, required the introduction of relatively complex, albeit homogeneous, cooperative organizations and administrative procedures that had to precede economic growth. As earlier shown, this supply-side approach neglected both the role of the market system and the completely different environmental conditions facing marginalized smallholders. The target groups themselves had little, if any, influence on the orientation and design of the support programmes. In addition to deficiencies in implementation, the widened application of the cooperative as an agent for rural and agricultural change failed.

Subsequent to the intensified and geographically spread nature of cooperative promotion which characterized the period 1973–83, a more profound change was the increased itemization of development support in the form of projects and programmes.[16] Its most visible, concrete effect was an expansion in the number of societies and members, and in the size of the central administration, including the CBK and the KNFC. In the latter half of the 1970s, this expansion continued seemingly unabated, even in the face of a stagnating agricultural sector. The main contributing factors were that both the state and the donor agencies contributed to the resources required for the maintenence of the strategy. The growth of the government bureaucracy was also inflated by accentuated employment problems among young, educated people. The protected, highly capitalized industrial sector, given so high a priority in the national development strategies, had by then proved its inability to absorb more than a fraction of the annual addition to the labour force.

In the process of itemization and bureaucratic growth, there followed a widened appropriation by central bodies of decision-making functions at primary society and union levels. While their ability to interfere in operations and to change decisions, activities and organizations increased, their ability positively to influence the performance of societies/unions remained limited. Induced participation, relying mainly on various forms of subsidies and development support, clearly also gave way to more coercively flavoured modes of promotion. These repressive tendencies[17] reflect both the poor performance of most cooperatives in the 1970s and early 1980s, and the stagnation of the economy as a whole. Eventually, the economic stagnation reduced the resources available to the central bodies to pursue their increasingly complex supervisory, controlling and promotional roles. As a consequence, the state's mode of implementing its cooperative policies deteriorated into what can be called 'casual micro-regulation'.

We thus can discern a trend towards the development of a central bureaucracy that, seen in relation to its officially proclaimed role in national and cooperative policies, is largely defunct and a cooperative sector which, apart from a core of coffee societies and unions, displays much the same symptoms. The operational constraints facing the government bureaucracy may of course be interpreted as a largely positive development as it may give local cooperatives a certain degree of freedom. Unfortunately, this is not the case as more basic constraints to more flexible operations are still at work. We then refer not only to the cooperative legislation, but also to the wider and more intricate cobweb of laws, regulations and other institutions established to control the agricultural and national economy.

The privileges this system generates for a predominantly urbanized political, bureaucratic and commercial elite are increasingly dependent upon a patrimonial and politically repressive rule. As is well known, this kind of setting is typically linked not only to coercion, but also has to rely on personal loyalty and patron-client relations.[18] This, in turn, is surely a good way of bolstering corruption and incompetence 'not only' in the bureaucracy but also in activities and organizations dependent on government. For the cooperative movement, the implications of this decay are obvious, and its consequences are in part reflected in the results achieved both by the delivery system approach and the performance of societies and unions.

### *Donor agencies*

An additional question of interest in this context is how donor agencies have affected the structure and position of cooperatives and the central bureaucracy, respectively.

As shown in earlier chapters, donor agencies have played a significant role in the development of the cooperative sector in Kenya. For example, in one of the major development programmes, the total input of expatriate staff amounted to about 600 man-years over the period 1968–83. Generally, their influence can be seen both in the administrative structure of agricultural cooperatives, in the kind of service activities offered, and in the promotion of cooperatives in disadvantaged regions.

One question that needs to be asked when considering the orientation and scope of donor assistance to cooperatives is why projects and programmes have not been appraised and evaluated more systematically in relation to the broader policy and development contexts in which they are supposed to be implemented. In Kenya, one aspect that should have deserved more attention is the official strategy of cooperative development in relation to sectoral and national development policies. Others include, *inter alia*, the strategies devised for agricultural/rural/regional development, and the degree and nature of direct state intervention, including regulation of markets and prices.

Taken together, these kinds of assessments could offer an indication regarding the likelihood of rural organizations such as cooperatives playing a meaningful role in agricultural development. Additionally it would have been necessary to pay more attention to the regional and local environments in which support for cooperative organizations is intended or planned, and, hence, to establish the compatibility of suggested support with local conditions in terms of agro-ecology, landownership, infrastructure, education and, not least, farmers' preferences and priorities.

The superficial treatment of these aspects seems to be linked to a myth regarding the unique qualities of what is perceived as the cooperative mode of organization. This ideologically justified trust in cooperatives has, rather uncritically, spilled over to encompass a faith in their effectiveness as social and economic agents of change. Given these assumed qualities, assistance has tended to confine itself to finding technically rational solutions to intra-organizational issues. Thus, a common belief seems to be that administrative and organizational engineering will not only ensure rational service activities but also externalise the inherent qualities of cooperatives.

However, when, for these reasons, 'social intelligence' is low in demand, it tends to sustain an oversimplified view of the nature of social and economic conditions both at national and local levels. As a consequence, it easily reproduces a 'donor culture' infatuated by the perception that cooperatives in major respects are able to create the conditions required for their own success. It thus easily generates inflated expectations and wholesale solutions.

Paradoxically enough, and as shown earlier in this study, donor agencies' promotion of cooperatives in Kenya has also built on an excessively paternalistic philosophy that runs counter to what could be expected to constitute cooperative development. The legitimacy assumed to follow from channelling support through the state machinery may of course have been seen as less dispensable than cooperative ideals. The partnership has no doubt ensured that target groups and institutions comply with introduced measures, and, hence, also prompt implementation.

This behaviour, however, contradicts basic cooperative ideals as, in reality, it has contributed to the creation of a structure in which societies and unions are reduced to mere appendices of a central government bureaucracy. The latter, in turn, is permeated by influential, factional forces and interests that frequently run counter to the, earlier mentioned, basic components of public good. Another paradox is that many donor agencies, in spite of this, persist in maintaining, at least to their audiences at home, that the development support rendered to what they call co-operatives constitutes a meaningful way of promoting not only rural development but also local participation and the building of democratic institutions.

Chapter six

# Summary and conclusions

## 6.1 Summary

After their inception in the mid-1940s, agricultural cooperatives were used by the state as an instrument for promoting agricultural and rural development. The spread pattern in the colonial period clearly reflects the ability of the more commercialized, affluent and/or loyal sectors of the smallholder population to grasp economic opportunities offered by the administration. The imprint of state interference is also seen in the structure that developed after independence. New cooperative legislation, promulgated in 1966, gave the government extensive powers to intervene directly in cooperative organizations. In the 1970s, in response to decelerating growth and increasing regional inequalities, the role of cooperatives was redefined and widened. Increasing emphasis now was laid on their role as a delivery system for the channelling of production credit and farm inputs, with the intention of contributing to the spread of more input-intensive technology and the revitalization of the agricultural economy.

Available data on the expansion pattern characterizing the cooperative sector in the period 1946–83, support the following general observations.

### Activity orientation

A decisive factor conditioning the registration of societies has been government regulations stipulating that smallholders – below a specified size of holding – had to be members of cooperative societies in order to have access to market channels for certain types of produce. This has applied to coffee, pyrethrum, sugar, cotton (this condition was abolished in the early 1980s), and to a certain extent, dairy produce. The adoption of any of these activites thus had to be anteceded by the registration of a primary cooperative society. A second type of state-instigated registration has been the settlement society. In this case, however, the main concern behind the ordinance was not so much promotion of commercialized agriculture as the orderly repayment of settler loans. In addition to these regulation-induced registrations of societies, there have also been the more 'genuine' cases. Judging from available data, though, these constitute but a small share of the total number of registrations.

## Phasing

Periods with high frequencies of registration are all characterized by specific government initiatives: these were the late 1940s, the second half of the 1950s, the mid-1960s and the late 1970s. The first peak was largely a result of campaigns carried out by the Registrar of Cooperatives in areas west of Rift Valley; a second wave of registrations resulted from the implementation of the Swynnerton Plan; a third from the government's settlement programme; and the latest from the introduction of input-intensive technology and a reorientation of development support towards smallholder areas with low income levels and/or stagnating agriculture. It can be noted that variations in registration frequency do not in any systematic manner follow the growth performance of the agricultural economy.

A variety of means have been used for inducing or persuading smallholders to join societies, including campaigns, crop-specific conditions, loan regulations (settlement), and access to credit and farm inputs. The considerable effectiveness of these measures, in terms of generating society registrations, implies a responsiveness among smallholders to opportunities perceived to contribute to improved material conditions. Hence, the manner in which cooperatives have been promoted is likely to have effectively cultivated the view among smallholders that the major benefit of cooperatives has been their access to resources provided by the state.

## Geographical distribution

The ecological limits for the types of produce made dependent on cooperative marketing have determined the basic geographical pattern of registrations. Changes in spread profile over time thus are a function of this factor, in combination with specific government initiatives. Before independence, registrations were concentrated in campaign areas and in the major coffee zones east and west of Rift Valley. In the 1960s, the pattern became more dispersed, reflecting both the implementation of settlement programmes and the 'cooperativization' of the cotton industry in the Lake Victoria region. At the same time, registration densities were increasing in all major smallholder areas. After the mid-1970s, the pattern became even more dispersed, reflecting active state support directed towards economically lagging smallholder areas, including ecologically more marginal lands.

*Survival*

In the period 1946–83, the survival rate of societies rose continuously, from 41 per cent in 1946–62 to 67 per cent in 1963–70, and 72 per cent in 1971–83. Prior to 1971 a clear relation could be observed between survival rates and regional variations in 'operational environment'. The latter concept denotes variations in conditions that influence the prospects of commercial agricultural production. These include ecology, land tenure, density of transport network, levels of education, population density, and degree of economic differentiation. Thus, in environments favoured in terms of agro-ecology and infrastructure, cooperatives generally displayed lower mortality rates. Survival was also influenced by the kind of produce handled by the societies. Cooperatives which enjoyed a local marketing monopoly for specific types of produce generally displayed higher survival rates.

In the period 1971–83, the relationship between environment and survival became insignificant; the effect of produce orientation also became more ambiguous. These changes can be explained by the drastically increased government control, supervision and promotion made possible by the new cooperative legislation. A related cause was the shift in promotional policies from marketing services towards provision of credit and the supply of farm inputs.

The strengthened role of the state, in combination with a shift in policy towards supply functions and the rural periphery, resulted in a considerable expansion of the Ministry of Cooperative Development and related bodies at central level. Evidently, the state, with the support of donor agencies, has managed to build an organizational infrastructure that also extends to less developed areas. The mere existence of societies and union does not, of course, necessarily mean that they, as marketing and supply organizations, contribute in any meaningful way to agricultural and rural development.

### *Performance*

This argument is supported when examining the societies' efficiency and quality of service. Although survival rates generally improved during 1971–83, it is clear that the same trend did not apply to their performance characteristics. Instead, for each main activity (produce orientation), the conditioning influence of the environment is again confirmed. It is also worth noting that, generally, farmers seem to aptly respond to changes in produce prices. Obviously this contributes to an accentuation in the deterioration of societies once they are unable to maintain acceptable levels of efficiency and quality of service.

Between 1971 and 1983, cooperatives lost ground as marketing organizations. Their combined share of smallholders' value of gross marketed production fell from 48 to 43 per cent. For types of produce other than coffee, the position has deteriorated quite dramatically, that is from 25 to about 10 per cent. The fact that this contraction has taken place in a context where the agricultural sector as a whole suffered from decelerating growth, further underlines the generally poor performance of agricultural service societies.

Considering primary societies by activity, coffee cooperatives have increased their economic dominance in the period 1971–83. However, also within this segment of the cooperative sector, performance is closely dependent on the operational environment in terms of ecology, land tenure, infrastructure and economic differentiation. The societies' ability autonomously to influence these basic determinants of their own success is apparently very limited.

Their principal contribution seems to be to maintain a reasonable level of cost efficiency and quality of service. Their ability in these respects is basically governed by the relations between, on the one hand, environmental conditions and, on the other, transaction costs. The latter, in turn, are in essential respects a function of the organizational structure of societies and the institutional network of supervision, control and promotion of which they constitute a part. Environments that are less favourable in terms of infrastructure, ecology and productivity are largely unable to support the scale requirements and rigidity of this organizational set-up. This incompatibility characterizes most coffee cooperatives outside Central and parts of Eastern provinces.

The performance record of cotton societies illustrates the combined impact of adverse environmental conditions and state intervention. The latter feature, reinforced by support from donor agencies, has taken the form of organization-building and a subsequent introduction of a widened range of supply-side services, principally credit and inputs. This mode of intervention may actually have retarted development in some areas, mainly in the Lake Victoria region. What remains are administratively inflated cooperatives, of which most have practically ceased to operate, a considerably enlarged regional government bureaucracy and indebted smallholders.

According to the official view, cooperatives and farmers are to blame for the failure. We have arrived at the opposite conclusion. That is, physically, technologically and economically the environment in which cotton-producing smallholders in western Kenya operate is too rudimentary to allow the expected levels of agricultural output. The expected achievements become even more unrealistic when considering also the potential of the environment to support the kind of omnibus and petrified organizational set-up characterizing the cooperatives.

In the case of pyrethrum societies, the influence of excessive state interference is most clearly visible. Pyrethrum is grown in a more favourable environmental setting than cotton. Furthermore, the produce is simple to handle, process and transport. It requires few inputs except labour. In the early 1980s, production collapsed with serious social consequences, particularly for smallholders in Kisii, in the western part of Kenya.

This development is the result of a range of circumstances, but with the decisive one being the price and marketing policies of the Pyrethrum Board. The effects were aggravated by the Board's arrogance and negligence in its dealings with the cooperatives. The latter, in turn, were largely unable to articulate their members' interests, while the MOCD continued to concern itself mainly with supervisory routines.

In dairy marketing, performance seems inversely related to the size of societies. Evidently, performance is also affected by their mode of administration, as societies affiliated to unions generally display a poorer record. As regards both sugar cane and cashew societies, available evidence indicates deficient performance. This applies in particular to the unions, which seem to have constituted more of a burden then an asset to the smallholders concerned.

## Unions

The centrally invented and implemented organizational structure of unions has relied on too-optimistic assumptions regarding the effectiveness of intervention and administratively rationed incentives. In the absence of anticipated effects, omnibus unions have run into financial and operational difficulties.

By 1983, practically all unions, except those based on societies marketing coffee, played a marginal role as suppliers of inputs. Ten coffee unions which operated in environments favoured in terms of agro-ecology and infrastructure, then accounted for 85 per cent of total cooperative input sales and for two-thirds of total turnover.

Most of the twenty-two non-coffee unions operated at a loss in 1982/83, and generally their position was precarious. Commonly, they have been unable to accumulate their own capital. With a realistic assessment of the unions' assets, it seems clear that almost half of them should have been liquidated. Continued survival has been made possible by *ad hoc* support from the government and donor agencies.

Although coffee unions performed better than other unions, their position was not entirely acceptable. In several cases their liquidity position was unsatisfactory, and generally too many activities were operated at a loss (about 45 per cent). The unions also seemed to have a preference for getting involved in activities of limited relevance to affiliated societies and their members.

Generally, it is here concluded that the cooperative set-up is mostly incompatible with local conditions. Only environments that are decidedly favoured in terms of agro-ecology, infrastructure and economic differentiation have the capacity to support the cooperative mode of organization, as it has been applied in Kenya.

## *Impact*

### Scope of participation

To indicate the influence of cooperatives on production and on the living conditions of smallholders, three concepts have been used, namely (i) reach, (ii), functional participation and (iii) reflective participation. Reach simply denotes the extent to which a cooperative organization is linked to households within its area of operation. In the context of this study, it is defined as the number of rural households that are active members of service societies. Functional participation indicates the degree to which those reached by societies actually take part in its activities as economic actors. By reflective participation is meant the subordination of society activities to members' conscious reflection and decision-making. Finally, the profile of the cooperative sector in the above respects is linked to the source of participation. Of three main categories – spontaneous, induced and coerced – the two latter are predominant in Kenya.

### Reach

An estimation of the actual number of active households has to take into account the magnitude of double and multiple memberships as well as the number of members who, although, being registered, are no longer active. We then arrive at a total reach of agricultural service societies in the range of 600,000–700,000 households, i.e. around one-third of the estimated total number of smallholder households. This evidently is considerably less than the officially stated membership of approximately 1.1 million. Geographically, the distribution of members is more concentrated than that of the total rural population. This feature, however, became less distinctive in the 1970s and early 1980s as a result of the expansion of cooperatives in more peripheral areas.

### Functional participation

Both in terms of turnover and produce sales, six districts in the Central and Eastern provinces constitute a core region. With less than half of the membership, they accounted for over 70 per cent of turnover and produce sales in 1982/83. Thus, while the changes in membership in the period 1970–83 were characterized by geographical dispersal, the economic dominance of the core regions increased markedly. With reference to the size of societies, it is also clear that relatively few societies were of dominating importance. Thus, ranking all societies by sales, we find that the top 10 per cent (78 societies) accounted for almost three-quarters of total produce payments to members. This represented, however, only one-third of the total membership and an estimated one-tenth per cent of the total number of smallholder households. The average sales per member in these societies, of which practically all are found in the core region, was in 1983 about K.Sh. 5,000 as compared to K.Sh. 1,200 in other societies.

This bias to the advantage of the privileged strata of smallholders is further accentuated when credit and input supply services are taken into account. In the case of 'special credit programmes' we estimate that they have reached something like 5–7 per cent of the smallholder households. The figure for the Cooperative Production Credit Scheme is in the range of 15–20 per cent, though with large regional variations. In some basic respects, sales of inputs reflect the distribution of credit among societies and regions. It does not necessarily mean, however, the presence of a straightforward causal relation between credit services and sales of inputs. This is particularly clear in western Kenya, and in the case of the CPCS the relation is rather ambiguous. A more significant and regular use of inputs is largely confined to about 250,000–300,000 coffee-growers in Central and Eastern provinces.

### Reflective participation

The cooperative legislation constitutes the main institutional means of ensuring that members' ability to control their societies has remained limited. Contrary to officially stated intentions, these rights have been confined further in the 1970s and 1980s. Members' and committee members' knowledge about the structure and basic management features of their societies and their rights and obligations as members can, none the less, be used to indicate their general ability constructively to exercise the rights still remaining. Available evidence then indicates that most committee members do not know the essentials about the management of their societies. As regards ordinary members, few are effectively reached by relevant information. Owing to this, and to a generally low level of education, most members have a very poor knowledge about how to exercise their rights and thus influence society operations.

### *Source of participation*

With reference to sources of the predominantly induced mode of participation, one aspect of interest is to identify conditions that have influenced the design of cooperative strategies and also how adopted strategies have affected the institutions directly involved in their realization. As regards the latter aspect, it is clear that the number of central bodies as well as their size and complexity have increased considerably. In terms of employment, the combined size of the staff establishment has grown from less than 200 at independence to over 2,400 in 1983. The growth of this superstructure seems to have been generated by three principal forces, namely: national development policies; cooperative policies and legislation; and cooperative development support. As regards the first of these, the high propensity of state intervention in economically important segments of the agricultural sector, partly through cooperatives, certainly has a political rationale.

Promotion of development has been perceived as equivalent to advancing industry and the urban sector together with the economically and politically most vital segments of the smallholder sector. A central function of the latter would then be to contribute to the foreign exchange earnings required for modernization. This element of the strategy, geared towards the promotion of 'progressive' smallholder strata, has resembled the philosophy already introduced by the colonial government in the context of the so-called Swynnerton Plan. In addition, the post-independence strategy has been a prerequisite for facilitating a more general and profound extraction of a surplus from agriculture.

The wide-reaching powers assumed by the government bureaucracy through a new cooperative legislation, would ensure that the anticipated agricultural growth pattern was realized. This ambition is reflected in the produce orientation, organization and administrative structure of the societies that were given priority. In the 1960s, the serious stratification mechanisms contained by these policies were concealed by the growth generated by 'structural' changes in smallholder agriculture in the form of introduction of earlier prohibited cash crops, the settling of smallholders in formerly alienated areas, and the introduction of hybrid maize.

Since the early 1970s, though, the transformation process has been faltering. Agricultural production and the rural economy has stagnated. Urban growth has been fuelled more by bureaucratic proliferation than by industrial expansion. In the absence of major forces of growth in secondary and tertiary industries in the private sector, and in order to maintain the political support of an increasingly influential urban population, policies with a bias against rural areas in general and smallholder agriculture in particular have continued. Given a rather weak political base, it has at the same time been necessary to maintain a network of allies in rural areas. One way of contributing to this has obviously been through a selective distribution of benefits and subsidies, for which purpose the cooperative infrastructure has also played a role.

The prinicipal function of agricultural service cooperatives within the framework of national development policies thus has been to secure high growth rates for export produce that can earn foreign currency. In addition it has facilitated a selective distribution of subsidies and benefits. Since the mid-1970s, the subsidization aspect has grown in prominence as reflected in a widened application of cooperative 'supply-side' approaches. While this increased 'itemization' has left rather few imprints in terms of increased agricultural production, it has had an effect on the number both of societies and of members and, in particular, on the size and complexity of the central bureaucracy. For the polity, promotion of cooperatives along these lines has had the added advantage of giving an impression of progressive rural development effort while constituting a cheap substitute both for land reforms and for critically needed public investment in infrastructure.

In the wake of itemization and bureaucratic proliferation has followed a continued appropriation by the central bodies of the decision-making functions at primary society and union levels. The means to interfere directly in operations and decision-making thus were strengthened, and even tended towards more coercively slanted modes of promotion. However, the government's ability positively to influence the performance of cooperatives has remained limited. In the 1980s, this ability has been further restricted by the stagnation of the national economy. Eventually this also forced the central bodies to cut their budgets. As a consequence, the government's mode of implementing its complex supervisory, controlling and promotional obligations has deteriorated into what can be called 'casual micro-regulation'.

## Donor agencies

Since a few years after independence, donor agencies have played an essential role in the development of the cooperative sector in Kenya. Generally, their influence can be seen both in the administrative structure of agricultural cooperatives, in the kind of services offered, and in the promotion of cooperatives in disadvantaged regions.

Their acceptance of cooperatives as the appropriate object of support seems to be nurtured by a myth regarding the unique qualities of this mode of organization. Apart from the fact that in Kenya they are cooperative only in a semantic sense, this ideologically and morally justified trust in cooperatives has, rather uncritically, spilt over to encompass a faith in their effectiveness as social and economic agents of change.

The fact that cooperatives in Kenya have very little in common with conventional service societies thus seems to have been of little concern. Actually, donor agencies' promotion of cooperatives in Kenya has been built on an excessively paternalistic philosophy which runs counter to the very meaning of cooperative development. Possibly, the legitimacy assumed to follow from channelling support through the state machinery has been judged as less dispensable than cooperative ideals. The partnership has no doubt ensured that target groups and institutions had to comply with introduced measures and hence, also, an acceptable implementation record. In terms of impact rather than implementation performance, however, the longer-term achievements leave much to be desired. As a matter of fact, the main contribution of the support rendered seems to have been to strengthen an institutional set-up in which primary societies have been reduced to mere appendices to central and regional bureaucracies.

Apart from direct resource transfers, assistance has tended to confine itself to finding technically feasible solutions to administrative and organizational issues. Within this context, high priority has been given 'supply-side strategies'. Lack of credit and inputs has been perceived as a critical constraint to the growth of agricultural production. As noted by van Pischke *et al.* one attractive feature of credit programmes is their 'appearance of offering fast relief for complex situations' (von Pischke 1983:2). They are easier and, not least, cheaper to introduce than land reforms, investments in infrastructure and other measures aimed at raising the production capacity of the rural economy.

That the bureaucratic, government-controlled mode developed for introducing input-intensive technology would eventually become defunct could have been anticipated, had social information been gathered and used more systematically. Thus a common feature of external assistance is that it has not been preceded by sufficiently serious attempts to appraise the social and economic implications of (i) new national development policies and (ii) the strategies and institutional machinery devised for rural, agricultural and cooperative development. Prior to the design of supporting measures, it would of course in most cases also have been necessary to examine the local environments in which support was intended with regard to agro-ecology, infrastructure, landownership, education and, not least, farmers' preferences and priorities.

## 6.2 Conclusions

First it can be noted that our empirical findings rather consistently support the conclusion that smallholders are responsive to economic incentives. The problem is that these incentives are a function not only of prices and competition, but also of 'residual' circumstances which profoundly affect conditions of both production and consumption. Kenya represents a case where both markets and 'residual' factors have been subjected to a combined mode of state intervention that has seriously distorted the development of smallholder agriculture.

The role of cooperatives, as it has evolved since independence, can be seen as one of the changes in rural and agricultural development policies which have been sanctioned not only by the government but also by major donor agencies. In this respect Kenya conforms to a pattern which is generally applicable to sub-Saharan Africa. As observed by Uma Lele, with reference to the World Bank's activities in the region, it has involved a major shift, 'from upstream activities, such as investments in human capital and infrastructure, to the more downstream efforts to immediately influence development outcomes' (Lele 1987:326). For example, while the transport and education sectors accounted for almost two-thirds of the Bank's loans and credits to Africa in the 1960s, their share had decreased to less than one-third in the 1970s. Instead multisectoral, rural development projects ('integrated projects'), of which cooperatives usually constituted one component, absorbed an increasing share of the resources made available. Thus in the early 1980s, this kind of project accounted for 24 per cent of the capital assistance to African agriculture.[1]

According to a World Bank estimation, donor agencies were deploying a total of about 80,000 technical assistance staff in sub-Saharan Africa in the early 1980s at a cost of about US$ 4 billion annually.[2] It may be assumed that a sizeable portion of these staff requirements has been generated by the priority given the kind of organizationally complex development projects mentioned above which, in turn, are likely to have contributed to the rapid expansion of the government bureaucracy noticeable in most African countries. In Kenya, these trends are clearly observable. Further the neglect of the need for infrastructural support has resulted in inadequate and regionally biased investments in public goods with consequences both for the production capacity of agriculture and the performance of supporting marketing and supply activities.[3]

Second, partly as a consequence of the priority given downstream activities, government has permeated the expanding market system with an inordinate range of laws, regulations and administrative structures. In rural environments characterized by low productivity and high distance friction, the structure and behaviour prescribed for cooperatives have created unrealistic threshold requirements and made their management excessively dependent on spatially extended networks of decision-making and supervision. It has not only seriously obstructed the democratic features usually associated with cooperatives but has also largely eliminated essential ingredients of entrepreneurship such as creativity, flexibility and adaptability.

A continued and widening mismatch between environmental requirements and the prescribed mode of cooperative organization can be expected. Shortage of arable land in combination with rapid population growth will perpetuate land fragmentation. In this setting, the cost of supplying services through administratively demanding cooperatives will turn prohibitive. Given basic social and economic characteristics of the rural environment, a shortcoming of state-administered cooperatives, in particular, is thus their high 'transaction frequency'. The concept is here used to denote a specific administrative characteristic, namely that the exchange of goods and services between a member and his society practically always generates documents and a number of recordings. Basically, the total volume of such transactions is determined by the size of the functional membership of a society, and the number of exchanges each of them generates, *not* by total turnover or sales.

As noted earlier in this study, the average size of smallholdings is already limited, and with continued rapid population growth, land fragmentation is bound to continue. Even if households then give priority to covering their subsistence requirements, produce is still likely to enter the market. Assuming intensified land use and technological progress, the marketed volume may remain stable. However, this surplus will be divided between a growing number of producers and thus result in a gradually widening mismatch between the cooperatives' mode of organization and environmental requirements. Thus, if societies are used as the predominant marketing channel and distribution system, the increasing number of members *and* produce lots will substantially increase both the total number of transactions and, subsequently, the administrative costs. However, this cost inflation will not be accompanied by a corresponding expansion of the total volume and value of handled goods and services. The increasing cost of services supplied has principally to be paid by the farmer and, hence, will negatively affect production and income generation.

In industrialized countries on the other hand, the growing importance of cooperatives was accompanied by an *increase* in the average size of holdings. Thus, improved infrastructure and production technologies set a development path characterized by a decreasing number of members. Most of the remaining individual members were rapidly increasing both deliveries to and procurements from their societies. In this context, then, it was possible to reap scale economies and maintain competitive overhead costs. When this model is not only implanted in African agriculture, with its completely different structure and development trends, but is also overburdened and petrified by omnibus administrative procedures and obligations, the dismal results achieved are not really surprising. Hence societies will cease to operate, or will have to depend increasingly on government subsidies, or they will confine their services to narrow strata of commercial farmers.

State intervention has also come to play the additional twin roles of facilitating appropriation/diversion of financial resources for the benefit of privileged strata, and of facilitating political control. These features have become more pronounced following the reorientation of agricultural service cooperatives towards 'supply-side' functions, i.e. the administered provision of credit and farm inputs.

Through the mono-produce orientation of individual societies and their focus on export/industrial crops, they mainly serve the requirements of relatively privileged strata of smallholders. This also has a negative effect on the social and economic conditions of women. At present, women's role in terms of functional and reflective participation is negligible. Except for cases where the head of household is a woman, practically all transactions are controlled by male members. Usually women participate only as agricultural labourers. Improvement of their position with regard to access to marketing and other services is certainly no matter of marginal significance. On the contrary, as women are likely to account for the major portion of agricultural output in Kenya, support in these and related respects – for example extension services and improved local infrastructure – is likely to be of instrumental importance for the pace and pattern of agricultural development.

Large portions of the cooperative structure thus can be seen as part of a cobweb of legitimized privileges that cause petrification of the role cast and the social reproduction process of the economy at large. Hence it effectively contributes to exclude private initiatives that, in minor or major ways, are threatening established political or economic interests. What would be the remedy? If one accepts the constraints of the existing system, the answer would be some kind of 'muddle-through' strategy. The following rectifying measures then would have to be considered:

1 Liberalize national marketing systems for agricultural produce;
2 Reorganize primary and secondary societies;
   (a) Abolish the present administrative system which integrates marketing, credit and input supplies. It is administratively costly and managerially petrifying, while generating few of its intended effects (cf. J.D. von Pischke 1983). Hence, also abolish credit sales to individual members.
   (b) Separate savings/credit activities from unions. Allow

independent cooperative organizations to deal with these services.

(c) Give priority to efficient marketing services at primary level, with emphasis on collection, delivery and payments. Stimulate the establishment of multiproduce societies and, in particular, the inclusion of marketing services for staple (food) produce.

3 Intensify, and decentralize, management training of committee members and union/society staff;
4 Reorganize and intensify member/committee member education;
5 Revise/liberalize the cooperative legislation;
6 These measures will have to be preceded or at least combined with radically raised public investment in infrastructure, including rural service centres.

As regards the list of needed changes in the cooperative sector, it could certainly be made both longer and more detailed. The catch, however, is that in the medium term the suggested measures are constrained by the mode of cooperative development of which they now constitute part. Thus, even if implementation succeeds, basic stratification mechanisms may not be affected.[4] Additionally, if the present legislation is not changed, possible positive impacts would be neutralized by a sustained dysfunctionality between commercial efficiency requirements and state administration. In this respect, organization theory supports our conclusion that multi-level organizational structures cannot accommodate both differentiation among base units and a high degree of vertical interdependence.[5]

Hence, there is little reason to be very optimistic about the outcome of a revised cooperative development strategy. There is an obvious risk that the present development strategy, with its reliance on bureaucratic superstructures and administrative engineering, would largely remain intact. Within this context, incremental benefits are likely to be appropriated by the establishment and narrow strata of the smallholder population, on terms determined by the former. To most smallholders it would mean continued limited access to adequate production and marketing services, and both in terms of efficiency and allocation the national economy would make losses.

If briefly one considers changes that could be advantageous to the rural economy in general and smallholders in particular, rather than having the overriding ambition of keeping cooperatives alive at any cost, a different set of measures seem to be needed, *inter alia*:

1 abolish licence arrangements and monopolies in wholesale and manufacturing;
2 deregulate the national market system for agricultural produce and inputs;
3 vitiate, or at least drastically reduce, the role of national marketing boards;
4 revoke local monopolies, including those of cooperatives, i.e. allow private traders to participate freely in marketing and input supply activities;
5 replace the present cooperative law with legislation that protects cooperative societies from government intervention.

As in the case of the 'muddle-through' scenario above, a drastic reorientation of priorities regarding public investment in infrastructure to the advantage of rural areas and smallholder agriculture would be necessary. This would include investments in transports, rural service centres, extension services, research focusing on the requirements of smallholders, water supplies, health, education, land rehabilitation and conservation. Government thus should attend to its conventional *raison d'être*, namely to the provision of public utilities.

As seen here, it would also be within this realm that donor agencies could make useful contributions. Donor agency interventions through integrated rural development programmes conventionally involve resource transfers of 'private goods' character. These, however, have to be avoided as they typically result in market distortions and social anomalies.[6]

Arguments in favour of economic liberalization and deregulation are thus not simply a matter of competition and prices, although those aspects in themselves are important.[7] The decisive importance of liberalization lies probably in the fact that it is not easily compatible with political repression, and therefore will enhance raised levels of social activity, including intensified circulation of information and economic interaction. Hence, it will also release/develop resources in the form of initiative, knowledge, experience and ambitions among ordinary people who, under the present system, are petrified by fear, apathy and defeatism.

The impact of these changes can be expected to be significant. At least in the short or medium term, one effect would be a drastically reduced number of active agricultural service societies. In the new setting, most of the marketing and input supply services would probably be taken over by more efficient and flexible private enterprises. These effects would directly benefit the smallholder. With the consequences of changed legislation, the role of the ministry and central appendices would diminish. The role of the government bureaucracy could be confined to what traditionally is expected of a 'Registrar of cooperatives', i.e. registration and liquidation of societies, and a general control that cooperatives operate in accordance with basic laws of book-keeping.

How then would the suggested changes affect smallholders in terms of bargaining position and democratic participation? As regards the latter aspect, it is clear that within the present institutional setting the influence of members/smallholders on cooperatives is minimal. This is directly attributable both to the bureaucracy and regulations emanating from the cooperative legislation, and to the political and economic system of which they constitute part. Liberalization of the economy would probably strengthen individual freedom and, hence, facilitate increased voluntary participation in local associations, farmers' unions, etc.

Thus, if a liberalized market leads to cartelization and generally unfavourable bargains for farmers in their dealings with the commercial sector, they have in the new context an option that does not exist today, namely that of utilizing organizational means for strengthening their position. These means include not only farmers' unions but certainly also the establishment of service cooperatives. As distinct from the present situation, they would then be cooperative not only in name but also in nature by emanating from local, commonly felt needs.

# Appendix 1

Environmental indicators; reference period 1963–70

| *Distr.* | *Name* | *DENS70* | *ADJ71* | *ENROLM69* | *RDCOV70* | *HIGH6370* | *EMPLOY69* | *SURV6370* |
|---|---|---|---|---|---|---|---|---|
| 2 | Kisumu | 197 | 7 | 34 | 64 | 61 | 14 | 74 |
| 3 | Kisii | 316 | 156 | 27 | 51 | 98 | 3 | 94 |
| 4 | S. Nyanza | 120 | 100 | 29 | 33 | 25 | 2 | 67 |
| 6 | Siaya | 156 | 55 | 28 | 44 | 50 | 1 | 75 |
| 10 | Kakamega | 229 | 196 | 33 | 36 | 83 | 3 | 67 |
| 11 | Bungoma | 115 | 167 | 39 | 34 | 78 | 3 | 80 |
| 12 | Busia | 126 | 115 | 39 | 34 | 25 | 3 | 40 |
| 20 | Nakuru | 43 | 16 | 33 | 26 | 27 | 36 | 44 |
| 21 | Baringo | 16 | 57 | 10 | 10 | 44 | 4 | 100 |
| 22 | Kericho | 101 | 105 | 29 | 12 | 78 | 17 | 76 |
| 23 | U. Gishu | 52 | 0 | 35 | 4 | 100 | 28 | 68 |
| 24 | Nandi | 78 | 63 | 23 | 33 | 94 | 14 | 90 |
| 25 | T. Nzoia | 52 | 0 | 10 | 30 | 91 | 38 | 89 |
| 26 | Marakwet | 60 | 48 | 21 | 26 | 57 | 3 | 86 |
| 27 | W. Pokot | 17 | 0 | 8 | 14 | 100 | 5 | 50 |
| 28 | Laikipia | 7 | 0 | 62 | 7 | 56 | 36 | 38 |
| 29 | Narok | 7 | 199 | 18 | 3 | 11 | 2 | 0 |
| 30 | Kajiado | 4 | 386 | 19 | 7 | 9 | 7 | 11 |
| 50 | Nyeri | 113 | 80 | 46 | 36 | 97 | 10 | 38 |
| 51 | Muranga | 185 | 154 | 42 | 65 | 70 | 9 | 63 |
| 52 | Nyandarua | 52 | 154 | 43 | 36 | 89 | 15 | 98 |
| 54 | Kiambu | 200 | 96 | 42 | 66 | 79 | 20 | 59 |
| 55 | Kirinyaga | 156 | 82 | 33 | 44 | 81 | 4 | 87 |
| 66 | Kilifi | 26 | 0 | 17 | 8 | 56 | 4 | 86 |
| 67 | Kwale | 26 | 6 | 9 | 10 | 47 | 6 | 46 |
| 69 | T. River | 1 | 0 | 7 | 1 | 0 | 4 | 33 |
| 70 | Taita | 7 | 9 | 41 | 5 | 71 | 17 | 43 |
| 80 | Embu | 68 | 61 | 33 | 36 | 68 | 5 | 71 |
| 81 | Meru | 62 | 117 | 28 | 14 | 85 | 4 | 86 |
| 82 | Isiolo | 1 | 0 | 11 | 6 | 0 | 12 | 0 |
| 83 | Kitui | 12 | 0 | 20 | 8 | 0 | 2 | 18 |
| 84 | Machakos | 51 | 52 | 29 | 12 | 69 | 5 | 79 |
| 85 | Marsabit | 1 | 0 | 8 | 2 | 0 | 3 | 0 |
| 95 | Garissa | 2 | 0 | 4 | 10 | 0 | 3 | 0 |
| 96 | Wajir | 2 | 0 | 5 | 0 | 0 | 1 | 0 |

*Sources:* Population Census 1969, Vol. I and statistical abstract, Min. of Works and Min. of Coop. Development (internal documentation); district surveys.
*Notes*
DENS70: population per sq. km (1970).
ADJ71: adjudicated area, '000 HA (1971).
ENROLM69: ratio tot no. children aged 5–14/children aged 5–14 in school (1969).
RDCOV70: Kilometres of classified roads per 100 sq.km (1970).
HIGH6370: percentage of societies located in areas with high agro-ecological potential (in register 63–70).
EMPLOY69: percentage of population of working age (15–55) employed in the modern sector (1969).

# Appendix 2

Environmental indicators; reference period 1971–83

| *Distr.* | *Name* | *DENS83* | *ADJ81* | *ENROLM79* | *RDCOV83* | *HIGH7183* | *EMPLOY79* | *SURV7183* |
|---|---|---|---|---|---|---|---|---|
| 2 | Kisumu | 252 | 55 | 78 | 67 | 55 | 15 | 77 |
| 3 | Kisii | 433 | 218 | 76 | 70 | 95 | 5 | 95 |
| 4 | S. Nyanza | 156 | 313 | 75 | 34 | 25 | 3 | 53 |
| 6 | Siaya | 205 | 170 | 75 | 47 | 44 | 1 | 67 |
| 10 | Kakamega | 320 | 309 | 70 | 45 | 85 | 7 | 48 |
| 11 | Bungoma | 179 | 228 | 73 | 33 | 83 | 6 | 45 |
| 12 | Busia | 200 | 170 | 73 | 34 | 33 | 4 | 83 |
| 20 | Nakuru | 81 | 16 | 69 | 22 | 33 | 26 | 69 |
| 21 | Baringo | 21 | 116 | 56 | 14 | 44 | 5 | 87 |
| 22 | Kericho | 142 | 247 | 69 | 35 | 85 | 21 | 87 |
| 23 | U. Gishu | 87 | 0 | 70 | 25 | 100 | 18 | 83 |
| 24 | Nandi | 119 | 134 | 73 | 32 | 93 | 20 | 74 |
| 25 | T. Nzoia | 115 | 0 | 56 | 29 | 88 | 20 | 62 |
| 26 | Marakwet | 60 | 80 | 65 | 21 | 59 | 6 | 82 |
| 27 | W. Pokot | 34 | 245 | 25 | 20 | 100 | 3 | 71 |
| 28 | Laikipia | 15 | 27 | 65 | 11 | 78 | 13 | 56 |
| 29 | Narok | 12 | 682 | 31 | 11 | 0 | 3 | 70 |
| 30 | Kajiado | 8 | 1617 | 33 | 8 | 10 | 6 | 60 |
| 31 | Turkana | 3 | 0 | 10 | 4 | 0 | 2 | 33 |
| 32 | Samburu | 4 | 0 | 18 | 6 | 0 | 5 | 0 |
| 50 | Nyeri | 162 | 136 | 77 | 45 | 95 | 12 | 73 |
| 51 | Muranga | 286 | 154 | 70 | 69 | 68 | 11 | 71 |
| 52 | Nyandarua | 72 | 157 | 71 | 33 | 90 | 12 | 99 |
| 54 | Kiambu | 306 | 96 | 70 | 64 | 84 | 25 | 64 |
| 55 | Kirinyaga | 221 | 89 | 68 | 46 | 77 | 7 | 94 |
| 66 | Kilifi | 38 | 124 | 41 | 11 | 38 | 7 | 94 |
| 67 | Kwale | 38 | 171 | 38 | 13 | 56 | 6 | 56 |
| 68 | Lamu | 7 | 44 | 48 | 6 | 0 | 9 | 100 |
| 69 | T. River | 3 | 0 | 29 | 3 | 0 | 5 | 50 |
| 70 | Taita | 9 | 15 | 68 | 6 | 50 | 17 | 90 |
| 80 | Embu | 106 | 100 | 68 | 33 | 65 | 8 | 91 |
| 81 | Meru | 91 | 130 | 65 | 18 | 87 | 6 | 76 |
| 82 | Isiolo | 2 | 0 | 35 | 6 | 0 | 9 | 0 |
| 83 | Kitui | 17 | 49 | 57 | 9 | 0 | 4 | 54 |
| 84 | Machakos | 79 | 156 | 70 | 19 | 59 | 7 | 89 |

| *Distr.* | *Name* | *DENS83* | *ADJ81* | *ENROLM79* | *RDCOV83* | *HIGH7183* | *EMPLOY79* | *SURV7183* |
|---|---|---|---|---|---|---|---|---|
| 85 | Marsabit | 1 | 0 | 10 | 2 | 0 | 4 | 0 |
| 95 | Garissa | 3 | 0 | 7 | 4 | 0 | 5 | 60 |
| 96 | Wajir | 3 | 0 | 7 | 3 | 0 | 2 | 100 |
| 97 | Mandera | 4 | 0 | 8 | 5 | 0 | 2 | 0 |

*Sources:* Population Census 1979, Vol. I and statistical abstract; Min. of Works and Min. of Coop. Development (internal documentation); district survey.

*Notes*

DENS83: population per sq.km (1983).

ADJ81: adjudicated area. '000 HA (1981).

ENROLM79: ratio tot no. children aged 5–14/children aged 5–14 in school (1979).

RDCV83: kilometres of classified roads per 100 sq. km (1983).

HIGH7183: percentage of societies located in areas with high agro-ecological potential (in register 71–83).

EMPLOY79: percentage of population of working age (15–55) employed in the modern sector (1969).

# Appendix 3

Membership by district and province, 1960, 1970 and 1983.

| *Area* | *1969* | *1970* | *1983* |
|---|---|---|---|
| Kisumu | 937 | 3547 | 36378 |
| Kisii | 32612 | 86227 | 152462 |
| S. Nyanza | 1111 | 5898 | 31027 |
| Siaya | 234 | 2036 | 19746 |
| *Nyanza* | *34894* | *97708* | *239613* |
| Kakamega | 2509 | 7592 | 12120 |
| Bungoma | 18052 | 22218 | 22985 |
| Busia | 0 | 1585 | 11450 |
| *Western* | *20561* | *31395* | *46555* |
| Nakuru | 0 | 10111 | 8686 |
| Baringo | 0 | 540 | 8135 |
| Kericho | 272 | 6646 | 14638 |
| U. Gishu | 0 | 10161 | 6139 |
| Nandi | 0 | 1750 | 10562 |
| T. Nzoia | 0 | 0 | 4638 |
| Marakwet | 0 | 1913 | 7239 |
| W. Pokot | 0 | 1595 | 1453 |
| Laikipia | 0 | 1636 | 3153 |
| Narok | 0 | 388 | 2573 |
| Kajiado | 0 | 160 | 2567 |
| Turkana | 0 | 0 | 0 |
| Samburu | 0 | 0 | 0 |
| *Rift Valley* | *272* | *34900* | *69783* |
| Nyeri | 13079 | 47798 | 92632 |
| Muranga | 6241 | 45393 | 84572 |
| Nyandarua | 0 | 11393 | 20872 |
| Kiambu | 11938 | 30496 | 63445 |
| Kirinyaga | 4781 | 26339 | 46952 |
| *Central* | *36039* | *260030* | *308473* |
| Kilifi | 0 | 4301 | 9839 |
| Kwale | 0 | 207 | 1960 |
| Lamu | 0 | 171 | 1642 |
| T. River | 0 | 0 | 894 |
| Taita | 2886 | 3904 | 6193 |
| *Coast* | *2886* | *8583* | *20528* |

| *Area* | *1969* | *1970* | *1983* |
|---|---|---|---|
| Embu | 17946 | 17106 | 33950 |
| Meru | 30002 | 57360 | 129481 |
| Isiolo | 0 | 0 | 0 |
| Kitui | 0 | 1365 | 3585 |
| Machakos | 5362 | 20463 | 91637 |
| Marsabit | 0 | 0 | 0 |
| *Eastern* | *53310* | *96294* | *258653* |
| Garissa | 0 | 0 | 598 |
| Wajir | 0 | 0 | 185 |
| Mandera | 0 | 0 | 0 |
| *North Eastern* | *0* | *0* | *783* |
| *Total* | *147962* | *430299* | *944388* |

*Sources:* DOCD, annual report 1960, append. III Colony and Protectorate of Kenya, 1961.
DOCD, report for the years 1968–70, Table 1. Rep. of Kenya, 1971.
Min of Coop. Development, internal records.

# Appendix 4

**Registrations by province, 1932–83**

Nyanza province

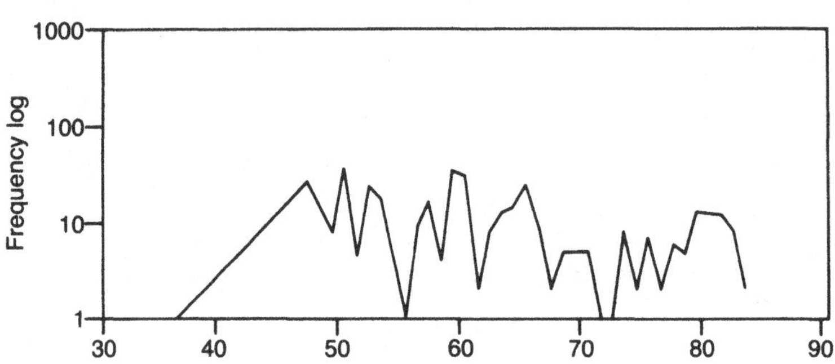


Western province

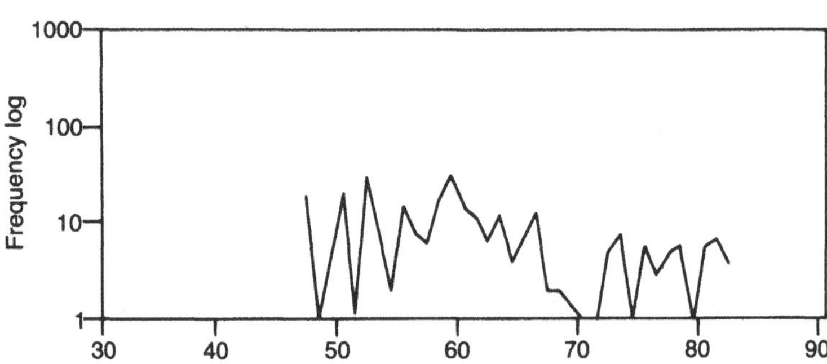


Rift Valley province

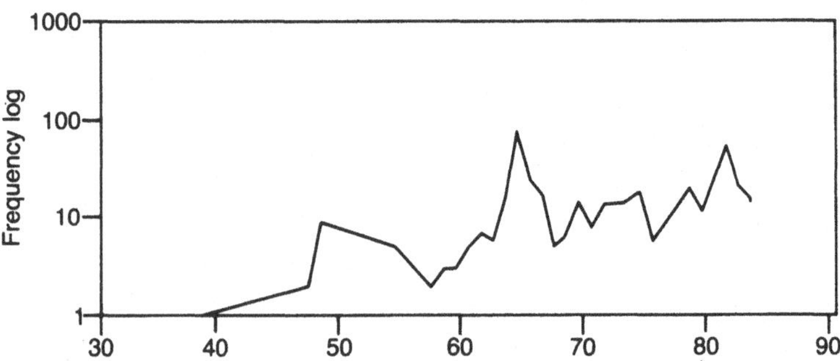

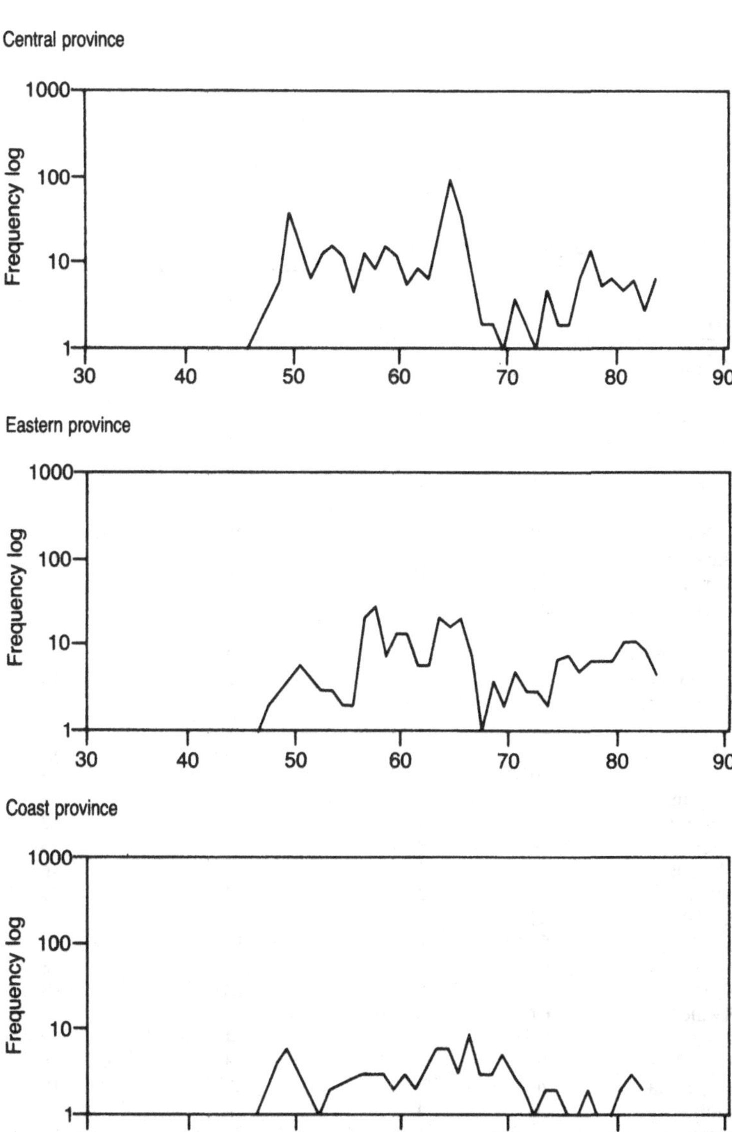
Central province
1000
100
10
1
Frequency log
30
40
50
60
70
80
90
Eastern province
1000
100
10
1
Frequency log
30
40
50
60
70
80
90
Coast province
1000
100
10
1
Frequency log
30
40
50
60
70
80
90

# Appendix 5

MOCD staff by district, 1973 and 1983.

| *District* | | *Prov.* | *Total 1973* | *Total 1983* |
|---|---|---|---|---|
| Kisumu | 2 | 6 | 20 | 58 |
| Kisii | 3 | 6 | 18 | 52 |
| S. Nyanza | 4 | 6 | 13 | 61 |
| Siaya | 6 | 6 | 8 | 41 |
| Kakamega | 10 | 8 | 6 | 64 |
| Bungoma | 11 | 8 | 15 | 61 |
| Busia | 12 | 8 | 9 | 50 |
| Nakuru | 20 | 7 | 27 | 47 |
| Baringo | 21 | 7 | 1 | 12 |
| Kericho | 22 | 7 | 19 | 29 |
| Uasin Gishu | 23 | 7 | 29 | 25 |
| Nandi | 24 | 7 | 5 | 20 |
| Trans. Nzoia | 25 | 7 | 14 | 26 |
| E. Marakwet | 26 | 7 | 2 | 18 |
| W. Pokot | 27 | 7 | 4 | 15 |
| Laikipia | 28 | 7 | 0 | 17 |
| Narok | 29 | 7 | 5 | 18 |
| Kajiado | 30 | 7 | 6 | 19 |
| Turkana | 31 | 7 | 3 | 11 |
| Samburu | 32 | 7 | 3 | 12 |
| Nyeri | 50 | 2 | 11 | 46 |
| Muranga | 51 | 2 | 16 | 46 |
| Nyandarua | 52 | 2 | 9 | 43 |
| Kiambu | 54 | 2 | 21 | 46 |
| Kirinyaga | 55 | 2 | 10 | 35 |
| Mombasa | 65 | 3 | 8 | 18 |
| Kilifi | 66 | 3 | 10 | 18 |
| Kwale | 67 | 3 | 6 | 19 |
| Lamu | 68 | 3 | 4 | 10 |
| Tana Triver | 69 | 3 | 3 | 8 |
| T. Taveta | 70 | 3 | 7 | 16 |
| Embu | 80 | 4 | 19 | 29 |
| Meru | 81 | 4 | 17 | 52 |
| Isiolo | 82 | 4 | 0 | 25 |

| District | | Prov. | Total 1973 | Total 1983 |
|---|---|---|---|---|
| Kitui | 83 | 4 | 6 | 15 |
| Machakos | 84 | 4 | 18 | 67 |
| Marsabit | 85 | 4 | 0 | 11 |
| Garissa | 95 | 5 | 0 | 15 |
| Wajir | 96 | 5 | 0 | 0 |
| Mandera | 97 | 5 | 0 | 8 |

*Source:* Min. of Coop Development
*Notes*
Province codes: 2=Central; 3=Coast; 4=Eastern; 5=N. Eastern; 6=Nyanza; 7=Rift Valley; 8=Western.

# Notes and references

## 1 Introduction

1 McCall, M. K., 'The significance of distance constraints in peasant farming systems with special reference to sub-Saharan Africa', in *Applied Geography* (1985), 5, pp. 325–45.
2 Antle, J. M. 'Third World economic development and its consequences for agriculture', pp. 1–17 in *US Agriculture and Third World Economic Development: Critical Interdependency*, National Planning Association, Food and Agriculture Committee, Washington DC, 1987.
3 Johnston, B. F., Kilby, P., 'Unimodal and bimodal strategies of agrarian change', pp. 50–65 in J. Harris (ed.) *Rural Development. Theories of Peasant Economy and Agrarian Change*, Hutchinson Univ. Library, London, 1982.
4 Hydén, G., *Efficiency versus Distribution in East African Cooperatives. A Study in Organizational Conflicts.* East African Literature Bureau, Nairobi, 1973. Livingstone, I., Ord, H. W., *Economics for Eastern Africa*, Heinemann, London, 1980.
5 Worsley, P., (ed.) *Two Blades of Grass. Rural Cooperatives in Agricultural Modernization*, Manchester University Press, 1971, p. 37.
6 Okafor, F. O., 'Socio-economic criteria for evaluating cooperative efficiency in Nigeria', pp. 255–68 in *Review of International Co-operation*, vol. 72 no. 4, ICA, London 1979.
7 Munkner, H.-H., 'Problems of co-operative management in Africa', pp. 127–47 in H.-H. Munkner (ed.) *Credit Union Development in Africa*, Institut für Internationale Solidarität, St. Augustin, 1978. Nouyrit, H., 'The agricultural cooperative between member participation, vertical organization building and bureaucratic tendencies', pp. 447–57 in E. Dulfer and W. Hamm (eds) *Cooperatives in the Clash between Member Participation, Organizational Development and Bureaucratic Tendencies*, Quiller Press, London, 1985.
8 Munkner, H.-H, 1978, op. cit., p. 129.
9 Anangisye, E. M., 'Important experiences of African co-operatives' in *Review of International Co-operation* vol. 76, no. 2, pp. 38–44. Copac, *Cooperative Information Note No. 30. Republic of Senegal*, Rome, 1985. Sarré, E., *Cooperative Information Note No. 9. Republic of Upper Volta.*

10 Copac, 1985, op. cit., p. 1.
11 Munkner, H.-H., 'Practical problems of law reform in Africa – with particlar reference to co-operative laws', pp. 51–71 in *Year Book of Agricultural Co-operation 1982*, the Plunkett Foundation, Oxford, 1983.
12 Bezzabeh, M., 'A review of the recent trends in agrarian reform and rural development in tropical Africa', in *Land Reform, Land Settlement and Cooperatives,* no. 1/2, FAO, 1981, pp. 2–19.
13 Gyllström, B., 'Fattigdom och förtryck: Om jordbruks-kooperationens utvecklingsbetingelser i Afrika', *Svensk Geografisk Årsbok 1985*, Gleerup, Lund, 1986, pp. 44–62.
14 Asthana, M. M., *Cooperative Information Note No. 12. Ghana,* Copac, Rome, 1982.
15 Dadson, J. A, *The Need for Cooperative Reorientation – The Ghanian Case.* Paper presented at the seminar 'Cooperatives Revisited', Scandinavian Institute of African Studies, Uppsala, 1986.
16 Munkner, H.-H., (ed.), 'Introduction', pp. 7–15 in *Towards Adjusted Patterns of Cooperatives in Developing Countries.* Results of a symposium on 'Ways towards an African Cooperative', Friedrich-Ebert-Stiftung, Bonn, 1984.
17 Asthana, M. M., *Cooperative Information Note No. 11. Ghana*, Copac, Rome, 1982.
18 World Bank, *Accelerated Development in sub-Saharan Africa. An Agenda for Action*, Washington DC, 1981.
19 Illy, H. F., 'How to build in the germs of failure: credit cooperatives in French Cameroon', pp. 75–85 in H.-H. Munkner (ed.), *Towards Adjusted Patterns of Cooperatives in Developing Countries.* Results of a symposium on 'Ways towards an African Cooperative'. Friedrich-Ebert-Stiftung, Bonn, 1984.
20 Grönberg, E-B., Johansson, M., 'Zambian women and the cooperative movement. A case study of Nachikungu MPC Society Ltd.' *Rapporter och Notiser No. 85*, Department of Social and Economic Geography, University of Lund, 1988. Ncube, P. D. and Aulakh, H. S. *Co-operative Organization in Zambia with Special Focus on Rural Development – Problems and Prospects.* Paper presented at the seminar 'Cooperatives Revisited', Scandinavian Institute of African Studies, Uppsala, 1986.
21 Internal documentation, Dept of Cooperative Development, Harare.
22 Bryceson, D., 'Second thoughts on marketing co-operatives in Tanzania. Background to their reinstatement', *Plunkett Development Series 5*, the Plunkett Foundation, Oxford.
23 Ståhl, M., 'Capturing the peasants through cooperatives – the case of Ethiopia', in B. Gyllström (ed.), *State, Cooperatives and Rural Change in Africa*, Lund Studies in Geography, Series B., Dept of Social and Economic Geography, University of Lund, 1988.
24 Ståhl, M., 1985, op. cit.
25 UNRISD, *Rural Co-operatives as Agents of Change, Rural Institutions and Planned Change*, vol. VII, Geneva, 1975. Harvey, C., Jacobs, J.,

Lamb, G. and Schaeffer, B., *Rural Employment and Administration in the Third World. Development Methods and Alternative Strategies*, Saxon House, 1979. Hydén, G., 'Cooperatives and the poor. Comparing European and Third World experience', in *Rural Development Participation Review*, vol. II, no. 1, 1980, pp. 9–12. Robertson, A. F., *People and the State. An Anthropology of Planned Development*, Cambridge University Press, 1984. UNDP, *Rural Cooperatives*, (stencil), 1984.

26 Cited from Stettner, L., 'Co-operation and egalitarianism in the developing countries' in *Review of International Co-operation* vol. 66, no. 6, p. 3.

27 See for example, Copac, 'Rural cooperatives: some lessons and suggestions from a UNDP evaluation study' in *Cooperative Programme Note*, Copac, Rome, 1983. Dadson, J. A., 1986, op. cit. Westergaard, P. W., 'Co-operatives in Tanzania as economic and democratic institutions', pp. 121–52 in C. G. Widstrand (ed.) *African Co-operatives and Efficiency*, the Scandinavian Institute of African Studies, Uppsala, 1972.

28 For a discussion of these aspects, see: Worsley, P. (ed.), *Two Blades of Grass: Rural Cooperatives in Agricultural Modernization*, Manchester University Press, 1971, pp. 1–40; Hedlund, H., *A Cooperative Revisited in Kenya*; paper presented at the seminar 'Cooperatives Revisited', Scandinavian Institute of African Studies, Uppsala, 1986.

29 Widstrand, C. G., 'Problems of efficiency in the performance of co-operatives', pp. 9–31 in C. G. Widstrand, (ed.), *African Co-operatives and Efficiency*, the Scandinavian Institute of African Studies, Uppsala, 1972. Kasfir, N., 'Organizational analysis and Uganda co-operative unions', pp. 203–7, in C. G. Widstrand (ed.), 1972, op. cit.

30 Hydén, G. and Karanja, E., 'Agriculture and co-operatives in Kenya', pp. 158–220 in R. Apthorpe (ed.) *Rural Cooperatives and Planned Change in Africa*, vol. IV, UNRISD, Geneva, 1970. Hydén, G., *Efficiency versus Distribution in East African Co-operatives*, East African Literature Bureau, Nairobi, 1973. See also: Hydén, G., 'Co-operatives and their socio-political environment', pp. 61–80 in C. G. Widstrand (ed.), 1972, op. cit; Hydén, G., 'Cooperatives and the poor: comparing European and Third World experience', in *Rural Development Participation Review*, vol. II, no. 1, Fall 1980.

31 Hydén, G., *No Shortcuts to Progress: African Development Management in Perspective*, Heinemann, London, 1983.

32 Hedlund, H., *A Cooperative Revisited in Kenya*, paper presented at the seminar 'Co-operatives Revisited', The Scandinavian Institute of African Studies, Uppsala, 1986, p. 30. See also: Hedlund, H., *Kaffe, kooperation och kultur. En studie av en kooperativ kaffeförening i Kibirigwi, Kenya*, Nordiska Afrikainstitutet, Uppsala, 1986.

33 Interestingly enough, part of Hydén's field data from the late 1960s refers to the same society as the one covered by Hedlund in 1984. In view of this, the diverging conclusions reached by Hydén and Hedlund may seem puzzling. However, since the late 1960s, Kirinyaga district

has experienced a rapid development of smallholder agriculture, of physical and social infrastructure, and of commercial activities. These developments are due to a rare combination of favourable factors of ecological, political and economic nature.

34 Apthorpe, R., 'Some problems of evaluation', pp. 209–29 in C. G. Widstrand (ed.), 1972, op. cit.

35 Bager, T., *Marketing Cooperatives and Peasants in Kenya*, Scandinavian Institute of African Studies, Uppsala, 1980.

36 Laut, P., *Agricultural Geography*, vol. 1, Systems, subsistence and plantation agriculture. Nelson, Melbourne, 1974, pp. 75–80.

37 Apthorpe, R., 1972, op. cit., p. 222.

38 Bates, R., *Markets and States in Tropical Africa: The Political Basis of Agricultural Policies*, University of California Press, Berkeley, 1981. Bates, R., *Essays on the Political Economy of Rural Africa*, Africa Studies Series 38, Cambridge University Press, Cambridge, 1983. Bates, R., 'The politics of agricultural policy – a reply', in *IDS Bulletin*, vol. 17, no. 1, 1986, pp. 12–15.

39 Smith, W. E., Lethem, F. J. and Thoolen, B. A., *The Design of Organizations for Rural Development Projects – A Progress Report*, World Bank Staff Working Papers No. 375, Washington, 1980.

40 Ncube, P. D. and Aulakh, H. S., *Co-operative Organization in Zambia with Special Focus on Rural Development – Problems and Prospects*. Paper presented at the seminar 'Cooperatives Revisited', Scandinavian Institute of African Studies, Uppsala, 1986.

41 Gyllström, B., *Government vs. Agricultural Marketing Cooperatives in Kenya. Some Observations on Modes and Consequences of State Intervention*. Paper presented at the seminar 'Cooperatives Revisited', The Scandinavian Institute of African Studies, Uppsala, 1986. Ståhl, M., 'Capturing the peasants through cooperatives – the case of Ethiopia', in B. Gyllström (ed.), *State, Cooperatives and Rural Change in Africa. Lund Studies in Geography, Ser. B.*, Dept of Social and Economic Geography, University of Lund, 1988. Gyllström, B., 'Administered interdependencies vs. spatial integration. The case of agricultural service cooperatives in Kenya', in B. Gyllström (ed.), *State, Cooperatives and Rural Change in Africa. Lund Studies in Geography, Ser B.*, Dept of Social and Economic Geography, University of Lund, 1988.

42 Friedman, J., 'The Spatial organization of power in the development of urban systems' in *Economic Development and Cultural Change*, vol. IV, no. 3, pp. 12–50. Gyllström, B., *The Organization of Production as a Space-Modelling Mechanism in Underdeveloped Countries: The Case of Tea Production in Kenya*, CWK Gleerup, Lund, 1977. Gyllström, B., 1986, op. cit.

43 Hedlund, H., (ed.) 'Introduction', in *A Cooperative Revisited in Kenya*, Scandinavian Institute for African Studies, Uppsala, 1988.

## 2 Spread

1 Leys, C., *Underdevelopment in Kenya. The Political Economy of Neo-Colonialism 1964–71,* Heinemann, London, 1975, Ch. 2.
2 Leo, C., *Land and Class in Kenya*, University of Toronto Press, Toronto, 1984.
3 Soja, E. W., *The Geography of Modernization in Kenya. A Spatial Analysis of Social, Economic and Political Change,* Syracuse University Press, 1968.
4 Soja, E. W., op. cit., pp. 27–47.
5 Soja, E. W., op. cit., pp. 18–19.
6 van Zwanenberg, R. M. A., *An Economic History of Kenya and Uganda*, the Macmillan Press Ltd., London 1975, p. 37.
7 Leys, C., op. cit., p. 40.
8 Mosley, P., *The Settler Economies. Studies in the Economic History of Kenya and Southern Rhodesia 1900–63*, Cambridge University Press, Cambridge, 1983.
9 Kitching, G., *Class and Economic Change in Kenya. The Making of an African Petite-Bourgeoisie*, Yale University, 1980, Ch. 2.
10 van Zwanenberg, R. M. A., op. cit. Wafukho, J. and Wanjohi, M., *Historical Background of Co-operative Movement in Kenya (before) up to 1945.*. Kenya National Federation of Cooperatives, Nairobi (undated stencil).
11 Karanja, E., 'The development of cooperative movement in Kenya', Ph.D. thesis, University of Pittsburg, 1974.
12 Kitching, G., op. cit., p. 62.
13 Kitching, G., op. cit., p. 61.
14 Holmquist, F. W., *Peasant Organization, Clientelism and Dependency: A Case Study of an Agricultural Producers Cooperative in Kenya*, Indiana University, 1975; Ch. II.
15 van Zwanenberg, R. M. A., op. cit., p. 41.
16 Kitching, G., op. cit., p. 28.
17 Lavrijsen, J. S. G., *Rural Poverty and Impoverishment in Western Kenya*, Geografisch Instituut, Rijksuniversiteit Utrecht, 1984.
18 Kitching, G., op. cit., p. 41.
19 Kitching, G., op. cit., p. 76.
20 Kitching, G., op. cit., pp. 74–77.
21 Soja, E. W., op. cit., pp. 24–25.
22 Kitching, G., op. cit., p. 29.
23 Kitching, G., op. cit., p. 38.
24 Kitching, G., op. cit., p. 64
25 Holmquist, F., op. cit., p. 86.
26 Kitching, F., op. cit., p. 179.
27 Holmquist, F., op. cit., p. 87.
28 Maitha, J. K., *Coffee in the Kenyan Economy. An econometric analysis*, East African Literature Bureau, Nairobi, 1974.
29 Leo, C., op. cit., p. 56.
30 Colonial Office, circular with memorandum as enclosure, London, 20 March 1946.

31 Ouma, S., *A History of the Co-operative Movement in Kenya*, Bookwise Ltd, Nairobi, 1980, p. 39.
32 Karanja, E. op. cit., p. 56.
33 Hydén G., *Efficiency vs. Distribution in East African Co-operatives. A study in Organizational Conflicts*, East African Literature Bureau, Nairobi, 1973.
34 Swynnerton, R. J. M., *A Plan to Intensify the Development of African Agriculture in Kenya*, Government Printer, Nairobi 1954.
35 Freeman, D. B., 'The importance of being first: preemption by early adopters of farming innovations in Kenya' in *Annals of the Association of American Geographers*, vol. 75, no. 1, pp. 17–28.
36 Department of Coop. Development, *The Role of District Cooperative Unions in Kenya's Development Efforts*, Nairobi, 1976 (stencil).
37 Ouma, S. J. op. cit., pp. 48–49.
38 Hydén, G. op. cit., p. 149.
39 Freeman, D. B., op. cit., p. 23.
40 van Zwanenberg, op. cit., p. 49–50.
41 Stewart, F., 'Kenya strategies for development', pp. 75–89 in T. Killick (ed.) *Papers on the Kenyan Economy. Performance, Problems and Policies*, Heinemann, Nairobi, 1981.
42 Lamb, G., 'Government, cooperatives and peasant agriculture in Kenya', pp. 25–36 in *Institute of Development Studies Bulletin*, vol. 6, no. 1, 1974.
43 Sharpley, J., *Economic Policies and Agricultural Performance. The Case of Kenya*, Development Centre Papers, OECD, Paris, 1986.
44 World Bank (b), *Kenya. Growth and Structural Change*, vol. I, Washington DC, 1983.
45 Leo, C., op. cit., Part II. Leys, C., op. cit., Ch. 3.
46 Njoroge, L. O., *Cash Crop Substitution in South Kinangop Settlement Scheme, Nyandarua District*, Department of Geography, University of Nairobi, Nairobi, July 1980.
47 Hydén, G., 1973, op. cit., Chs 2 and 4. Karanja, E., 1973, op. cit., pp. 78–79.
48 Brett, E. A., 'State power and economic inefficiency: explaining political failure in Africa', in *IDS Bulletin* vol. 17, no. 1, pp. 22–30.
49 Ilchman W. F. and Bhargava R. C., 'Balanced thought and economic growth', pp. 26–44 in C. K. Wilber (ed.) *The Political Economy of Development and Underdevelopment*, Random House, New York, 1973. Robertson, A. F., *People and the State. An Anthropology of Planned Development*, Cambridge University Press, Cambridge, 1984, pp. 26–43.
50 Hydén, G., op. cit., p. 176.
51 Cooperative Bank of Kenya, *Manual on Cooperative Banking*, 1971. Department of Cooperative Development Audit and Accounts Division, *Manual on the HT-Coffee System*, Nairobi, 1973.
52 Cooperative Bank of Kenya, Annual Report and Statement of Accounts, 1968/69–1971/72.
53 Muliro, M., *Cooperative Message to Kenyan Cooperators on the 50th*

*International Cooperative Day*, Min. of Cooperatives and Social Services, Nairobi (stencil).

54 DOCD (a), *Plan for Cooperative Development in Kenya with Nordic Assistance, 1972–77*, Nairobi, 1971.

55 Rep. of Kenya, *Cooperative Development Policy for Kenya*, Sessional Paper No. 8, 1970, Government Printer, Nairobi.

56 Freeman, D. B., op. cit., p. 23.

57 Rundquist, F-M., *Hybrid Maize Diffusion in Kenya*, CWK Gleerup, Lund, 1984.

58 World Bank (b), op. cit.

59 World Bank (a), *Kenya: into the Second Decade.* Johns Hopkins Univ. Press, Washington DC, 1975.

60 Rep. of Kenya, Economic Survey 1981, Central Bureau of Statistics, Nairobi.

61 Rep. of Kenya, Economic Survey 1984, Central Bureau of Statistics, Nairobi.

62 Sharpley, J. op. cit., pp. 23–31.

63 Sharpley, J. op. cit., p. 35.

64 Sharpley, J. op. cit., Table 2.10.

65 Sharpley, J. op. cit., pp. 32–42.

66 World Bank (b), op. cit.

67 Sharpley, J., 'Resource transfers between the agricultural and non-agricultural sectors: 1964–77', pp. 311–19 in T. Killick (ed.) *Papers on the Kenyan Economy. Performance, Problems, Policies*, Heinemann, Nairobi, 1981.

68 Here defined as the total population less children (0–14) and persons above 60 years of age.

69 Rep. of Kenya, *Statistical Abstract 1974*, Table 231, and *Statistical Abstract 1983*, Table 211.

70 Henin, R. A. 'The characteristics and development implications of a fast growing population', pp. 193–207 in T. Killick (ed.), *Papers on the Kenyan Economy*, Heinemann, Nairobi, 1981.

71 Hunt, D., *The Impending Crisis in Kenya. The Case for Land Reform*, Gower, Hampshire, 1984.

72 Leys, C., op. cit. World Bank (a), op. cit. ILO, *Employment, Incomes and Equality*, Geneva, ILO, 1972.

73 Bigsten, A., *Regional Inequality and Development. A Case Study of Kenya*, Dept. of Economics, University of Gothenburg, 1978.

74 House, W. J. and Killick, T., 'Social justice and development policy in Kenya's rural economy', pp. 31–69 in D. Ghai and S. Radwan, (eds) *Agrarian Policies and Rural Poverty in Africa*, ILO, Geneva, 1983.

75 House, W. J. and Killick, T., op. cit., pp. 40–41. Households classified as poor had less than K.Sh. 2,200 to meet total consumption needs.

76 World Bank (b), op. cit., Annex I.

77 House, W. J. and Killick, T., op. cit., p. 41.

78 House, W. J. and Killick, T. 'Social justice and development policy in Kenya's rural economy', pp. 31–63 in D. Ghai and S. Radwan, *Agrarian Policies and Rural Poverty in Africa*, ILO, Geneva 1983.

79 Livingstone, I., *Rural Development, Employment and Incomes in Kenya*, report prepared for the ILO's Jobs and Skills Programme for Africa, ILO, Addis Ababa, 1981, p. 12.27.
80 Hunt, D., op. cit.
81 Hunt, D., op. cit., p. 273.
82 ILO, *Employment, Incomes and Equality: A Strategy for Increasing Productive Employment in Kenya*, Geneva, ILO, 1972.
83 These projects/programmes were:
   1 Smallholder Production Services and Credit Programme (SPSCP), financed by USAID.
   2 Integrated Agricultural Development Project (IADP), Phases I and II, financially supported by the World Bank.
   3 Farm Input Supply Scheme (FISS), financed by Danida.
   4 Machakos Integrated Development Programme (MIDP), financed by the EEC.
   5 Smallholder Coffee Improvement Programme (SCIP), financially supported by the World Bank.
   6 Arid and Semi-Arid Lands Development Programme (ASAL). Source: MOCD, Research and Evaluation Section, Report no. 1, 1979
84 MOCD, 1979, op. cit., p. 33.
85 Lamb, G., 'Government, co-operatives and peasant agriculture in Kenya' in *Institute of Development Studies Bulletin*, Vol. 6, No. 1, Sept. 1974, pp. 25–36.
86 Hydén, G., 1983, op. cit.

**3 Survival**

1 Societies in register were defined as follows: (i) for the period 1946–62, those registered 1946–60, (ii) for 1963–70, societies registered 1946–60 and being active 1963 plus societies registered 1961–68, and (iii) for 1971–83, societies being registered 1946–68 and being active 1971 + those registered 1969–80.
2 Gyllström, B., 'Befolkningstillväxt och ekonomisk utveckling i Kisii, Kenya' in *Geografiska Notiser* Nr 4, pp. 155–62, Lund, 1975.
3 Epstein, T. S., 'Differential access to markets and its impact on agricultural development', pp. 221–34 in ICRISAT, *Agricultural Markets in the Semi-arid Tropics*, ICRISAT Centre, Patancheru, 1985. Lundahl's (1979) description of peasant behaviour in regions of Haiti where 'urban' crops are grown is in this particular respect strikingly similar to what can be observed in Kenya. In the latter case, it may be noted that both Muranga and Kiambu are situated close to Nairobi. See, Lundahl, M., *Peasants and Poverty. A Study of Haiti*, Croom Helm, London, 1979, pp. 125–26.
4 Kitching, G., 1980, op. cit., p. 127.
5 Kinyanjui, K., *Regional and Class Inequalities in Provision of Primary Education in Kenya, 1968–73: A Historical and Socio-Economic Background*, occasional paper no. 37, IDS, Nairobi, undated.
6 Cf. Lundahl, 1979, op. cit., pp. 595–96. Maranga, J. S. and Standa, E.

M., *The Co-operative Member and Committee Member Education Programme*, report on a pilot evaluation. Report no. 7, Research and Evaluation Unit, Min. of Coop. Development, Nairobi, 1981.

7 For further specifications, see Appendix.

8 District surveys were carried out during 1984–85 which included determining the physical location of all primary and secondary societies. These data have been checked against information about agro-ecological conditions as given in Rep. of Kenya, *Integrated Rural Survey 1974–75*, Appendix 1 and World Bank, *Second Integrated Agricultural Development Project*, map on ecological zones, 1979.

9 Estimations for 1970 and 1983, based on the Population Census 1969 and the Population Census 1979, respectively.

10 Based on internal records, Min. of Transport.

11 Rep. of Kenya, *Population Census 1969*, vol. 1 and *Statistical Abstract 1971*, Table 204, and for 1979, *Population Census 1979* and *Statistical Abstract 1983*, Table 215.

12 Rep. of Kenya, *Population Census 1969*, Vol. 1 and *Population Census 1979*, vol. 2.

13 Rep. of Kenya, *Statistical Abstract 1972*, Tables 4, 5 and *Statistical Abstract 1983*, Tables 4, 5. To the adjudicated area has been added the area covered by smallholder settlement programmes.

14 Hydén, G., *Efficiency versus Distribution in East African Cooperatives. A Study in Organizational Conflicts*, pp. 19–27, East African Literature Bureau, Nairobi, 1971. Karanja, E., *The Development of the Co-operative Movement in Kenya*, pp. 78–79, Ph.D. study. University of Pittsburgh, 1973.

15 World Bank, *Kenya. Growth and Structural Change*, vol. 1, Table 7.2, Washington DC 1983. Rep. of Kenya, *Statistical Abstract 1984*, Table 74(b), Government Printer, Nairobi, 1985.

16 This concern was first voiced in the now famous ILO report (1972) on 'Income, Employment and Inequality', op. cit.

17 World Bank, *Kenya into the Second Decade,* pp. 33–34, Washington DC, 1975.

18 Rep. of Kenya, *Development Plan 1974–78*, Part I, Nairobi, 1974. World Bank, 1975, op. cit.

**4 Performance**

1 Coffee, pyrethrum, cotton, sugar, dairy, cashew.

2 Rep. of Kenya, *Sessional Paper No. 8*, Government Printer, Nairobi, 1970.

3 Dep. of Cooperative Development, Commissioner's Circular 2/1972.

4 Dep. of Cooperative Development, Commissioner's Circular 10/1972.

5 Min. of Cooperative Development, Commissioner's Circular, 1980.

6 Min. of Cooperative Development, pub/1/vol. V/182, 1982.

7 Min. of Cooperative Development, pub/1/vol. VI(18), 1984.

8 Acland, J. D., 'An introduction to the production of field and plantation crops in Kenya, Tanzania and Uganda, in *East African Crops*, Longman, London 1971., pp. 59–93.

9 De Graaf, J., *The Economics of Coffee*, Pudoc, Wageningen, 1986., pp. 183–84.
10 de Graaf, J., op. cit., 1986., pp. 189–93.
11 Freeman, D. B., 'The importance of being first: preemption by early adopters of farming innovations in Kenya', pp. 17–28 in *Annals of the Association of American Geographers*, 75(1), 1985.
12 The price paid by marketing boards, i.e. before deduction of processing and handling costs by KPCU, unions and primary societies.
13 Gyllström, B., 'The case of tea production in Kenya' in *The Organization of Production as A Space-Modelling Mechanism in Underdeveloped Countries*. CWK Gleerup/Lund University, 1977.
14 Bates, R. H., 'T... political basis of agricultural policies' in *Markets and States in Tropical Africa*, University of California Press, Los Angeles, 1981, p. 28.
15 Graaf, J. de, *The Economics of Coffee*, Koninklijk Inst. voor de Tropen, Amsterdam, 1986, pp. 199–200.
16 Whitaker, M. J., 'Supply of inputs to smallholder coffee farmers through the cooperative distribution system in Kenya from 1981 to 1983' in *Kenya Coffee*, Jan./Feb. 1985, pp. 279–90.
17 Unless otherwise stated, data on cotton production, prices and commissions have been obtained from the Cotton Lint and Seed Marketing Board (internal documentation), and through interviews (in 1985) of members of a committee appointed by the CLSMB, MOCD, KNFC, and CBK to examine the technical efficiency of ginneries and to determine an appropriate ginning fee.
18 KNFC, 'A survey of structure, costs and margins for seed cotton buying, ginning and related activities' in *The Cotton Industry*, Price Monitoring and Analysis Section, Nairobi, 1981.
19 ILO, 1981 (Livingstone).
20 Interviews of staff (1985) at the District Cooperative Office, Homa Bay; Lake Victoria Union, Rachuonyo Union and the Provincial Cooperative Office, Kisumu.
21 Circular MOCD/AGR/7/VOLIX/57.
22 See note (1) above.
23 The MIDP is financed by the EEC and comprises a wide range of efforts aimed at improving the socio-economic conditions in Machakos district. Of the total programme cost for the period 1978–82, estimated at Sh. 200 million, about 50 per cent was earmarked for agriculture. MIDP (I) i.e. 1978–82, also included a credit programme with a total fund of Sh. 20 million, to be administered by cooperatives, and direct support to unions and societies that amounted to Sh. 6.2 million.
24 Machakos District Cooperative Union, 'Start period of the project' (stencil), 1984.
25 *SPSCP* (Smallholder Production Services and Credit Programme). USAID-supported programme (1976–80) aimed at providing seasonal credit to small farmers with less than Sh. 1,000 in net farm income. Apart from the credit component, the SPSCP supported the operations of financially weak cooperative unions and assisted in the

financing of construction of stores. Provisions were also made for expenditure on staff salaries, vehicles, office supplies, etc. The total budgeted cost for the programme was Sh. 101 million. However, probably not more than half of this amount was released.

*IADP(I)* (Integrated Agricultural Develoment Project). World Bank supported project (1977–82) with an estimated total cost of Sh. 150 million. The project's main stated objective was to enable the extension and cooperative services effectively to develop their role of supervising and co-ordinating agriculture. As regards its activity orientation, it was strikingly similar to that of the SPSCP. Admittedly, there was also an 'infrastructural' component but of negligible magnitude.

*FISS* (Farm Input Supply Scheme) financed by Danida (1976–84). The scheme provided bulk credit to unions/societies in marginal areas for the purpose of stockholding/resale of farm inputs. The principal difference between the FISS and the SPSPC/IADP is that the former gives less weight to seasonal credit. For the period 1979–84, the total cost of FISS was estimated at Sh. 31 million. See further: MOCD, *Priority Areas for Research and Evaluation Activities*, Report no. 1, Research and Evaluation Section, Nairobi, 1979.

26 Acland, J. D., 1973, op. cit, pp. 152–63.

27 Rep. of Kenya, *Economic Survey*, 1973, pp. 62–63.

28 Information about the activities of the Masaba union were collected on three different occasions during 1983–85. The main source of information was the union's internal documentation. In addition, interviews were held with the union staff, the union committee, committees of selected primary societies (Keroka, Gesima, Eronge) and with staff at the district office of the Ministry of Cooperative Development. In 1984, similar, though less detailed information, was gathered during visits to Kiambu Dairy/Pyrethrum Union and Nyaharuru Union (Central province).

29 Kitching, G., op. cit., p. 318.

30 Copac, *Cooperative Information Note Republic of Kenya*, pp. 13–14, Rome, 1984.

31 Kenya Cooperative Creameries Ltd., *Annual Report 1983–84*, Nairobi, 1984.

32 Finnagro, *Rural Dairy Development Project – Phase I*. Annual Report for 1983, Finnagro Oy, Feb. 1984 (stencil).

33 Adding the number of societies marketing the various types of produce considered in the preceding sections does not reconcile with the total number of active societies. This is simply because in those instances societies classified as 'multiproduce' market one of the major types of produce, *but not as the major activity*: they have been included both in the 'produce specific' tables and Table 4.26 above.

34 Sugar Board 1986, internal documentation.

35 Copac, op. cit., p. 10.

36 Acland, J. D., op. cit., p. 29.

37 Kenya Cashew Nuts Ltd, annual accounts 1981/82–83/84.

38 Kilifi District Cooperative Union, annual accounts 1983/84.

39 Republic of Kenya, *Cooperative Development Policy for Kenya*, Sessional paper No. 8, 1970. Government Printer, Nairobi.
40 One particularly influential article, originally published in 1966, was that of H. T. Patrick, 'Financial development and economic growth in developing countries', pp. 50–57 in J. D. von Pischke *et al.*, *Rural Financial Markets in Developing Countries: Their Use and Abuse*, Johns Hopkins University Press, London, 1983.
41 von Pischke *et al.*, op. cit.
42 Bates, R., *Markets and States in Tropical Africa: The Political Basis of Agricultural Policies*, University of California Press, Berkeley, 1981.
43 von Pischke *et al.*, op. cit.
44 Bates, R. H., 1981, op. cit., pp. 3–5.
45 Repub. of Kenya, 1970, op. cit.
46 Repub. of Kenya, *The Role of District Cooperative Unions in Kenya's Development Efforts*, Dep. of Cooperative Development, Nairobi, 1976 (stencil).
47 von Pischke *et al.*, op. cit.
48 Njonjo, A. L., Chege, F., Kimenye, D., Ng'ang'a, A. and Cookson, F., *Cooperative Production Credit Study*, Vol. 1, p. 30, Business and Economic Research Bureau, Nairobi, 1985.
49 Njonjo, A. L., *et al.*, 1985, op. cit.
50 These unions are Masaba, Kisumu, Kakamega, Bungoma, Sugarbelt, Muhoroni, Kiambu, Kericho, Siaya, Rachuonyo, Victoria, Luanda, Nambale, Malaba, Nyahururu-Makao, Nakuru.
51 Gyllström, B., 'Government vs. agricultural marketing cooperatives in Kenya. Some observations on modes and consequences of state intervention', in H. Hedlund, *Cooperatives Revisited*, Scandinavian Institute for African Studies, Uppsala, 1988.

## 5 Impact

1 Republic of Kenya, *Cooperative Development Policy for Kenya*, Sessional Paper No. 8, Nairobi, 1970. In the policy paper it is argued that 'government has no intention of either killing the initiative in the spontaneous leadership, or of permanently interfering with the endeared cooperative principles of democratic control' (p. 7).
2 Finsterbusch, K., 'Evaluation methods', pp. 285–311 in Finsterbusch, K., Llewellyn, L. G. and Wolf, C. P., *Social Impact Assessment Methods*, Sage, London, 1983.
3 Gyllström, B., 'Participation and rural development', in *Review of International Co-operation*, vol. 76, no. 1, pp. 18–24, International Cooperative Alliance, Geneva, 1983.
4 United Nations, *Popular Participation as a Strategy for Promoting Community Level Action and National Development*. New York, 1981, p. 8.
5 Kiambu, Muranga, Nyeri, Kirinyaga, Embu and Meru.
6 Bevan, D., Collier, P. and Gunning, J., 'Consequences of a commodity boom in a controlled economy: accumulation and redistribution in

Kenya, 1975–83', in *The World Bank Economic Review*, vol. 1, no. 3 (May), 1987.

7 Njonjo, A. L., Chege, F., Kimenye, D., Ng'ang'a, A. and Cookson, F., *Final Report on Cooperative Production Credit Scheme Study*, Business and Economic Research Co. Ltd., Nairobi, 1985.

8 MOCD, *Statistics for Cooperatives in Kenya*, Table 3.8., Min. of Cooperative Development, Nairobi, 1983. The figures in the table have been adjusted by exluding loans released under the GMR scheme.

9 Njonjo, A. L., 1985, op. cit.

10 Hedlund, H., 'A cooperative revisted in Kenya', in H. Hedlund (ed.) *Cooperatives Revisited*, Scandinavian Institute of African Studies, Uppsala, 1988 (forthcoming). Samuelsson, M., *Women's Ability to Participate Actively in Cooperatives*, Uppsats (60p). Department of Social and Economic Geography, University of Lund, 1987.

11 Standa, E. M and Maranga, J. S., *The Cooperative Member and Committee Member Education Programme*, report No. 7, Research and Evaluation Unit, Development Planning Division of the Min. of Cooperative Development, Nairobi, 1981.

12 Standa, J. M., *et al.* 1981, op. cit., p. 28.

13 Standa, J. M., *et al.* 1981, op. cit., pp. 37–38.

14 Gyllström, B., *Government vs. Agricultural Marketing Cooperatives*, Scandinavian Institute for African Studies, Uppsala, 1986.

15 Cf. Bates, R. H., *Markets and States in Tropical Africa. The Political Basis of Agricultural Policies*, University of California Press, Berkeley, 1981.

16 Harvey, C., Jacobs, J., Lamb, G. and Schaeffer, B., *Rural Employment and Administration in the Third World. Development Methods and Alternative Strategies*, Saxon House, 1979.

17 In the field of cooperative development, similar tendencies have been reported by Verhagen with reference to Sri Lanka. See, Verhagen, K., *Co-operation for Survival*. An analysis of an experiment in participatory research and planning with small farmers in Sri Lanka and Thailand, Royal Tropical Institute, Amsterdam, 1984, Ch. 7.3.

18 Sandbrook, R., *The Politics of Africa's Economic Stagnation*, Cambridge University Press, Cambridge, 1985.

## 6 Summary and conclusions

1 Lele, U., op. cit., p. 328.

2 Lele, U., op. cit., p. 329.

3 For a more general discussion, see D. Elz, 'Agricultural marketing policies and development', pp. 5–13 in D. Elz (ed.) *Agricultural Marketing Strategy and Pricing Policy*, World Bank, Washington DC, 1987.

4 Leys, C. *Underdevelopment in Kenya. The Political Economy of Neo-Colonialism 1964–71*, Heinemann, London, 1975.

5 Lorsch, J. W. and Allen, III S. A., *Managing Diversity and Interdependence*, Harvard University, Boston, 1973.
6 Berg, E., 'Obstacles to liberalizing agricultural markets in developing countries', pp. 22–27 in D. Elz (ed.) *Agricultural Marketing Strategy and Pricing Policy*, World Bank, Washington DC, 1987.
7 Bale, M. D., 'Government intervention in agricultural markets and pricing', pp. 98–103 in D. Elz (ed.) *Agricultural Marketing Strategy and Pricing Policy*, World Bank, Washington DC, 1987.

# Bibliography


Acland, J. D., *East African Crops. An Introduction to the Production of Field and Plantation Crops in Kenya, Tanzania and Uganda*, Longman, London, 1971.

Anangisye, E. M., 'Important experiences of African Cooperatives' in *Review of International Cooperation* 76(2), pp. 38–44.

Antle, J. M., 'Third World economic development and its consequences for agriculture', pp. 1–17 in *US Agriculture and Third World Economic Development: Critical Interdependency*, National Planning Association, Food and Agriculture Committee, Washington, 1987.

Apthorpe, R. (ed.) *Rural Cooperatives and Planned Change in Africa*, vol. IV, UNRISD, Geneva, 1970.

Apthorpe, R., 'Some problems of evaluation', pp. 209–29 in C. G. Widstrand (ed.) *African Cooperatives and Efficiency*, The Scandinavian Institute of African Studies, Uppsala, 1972.

Asthana, M. M., *Cooperative Information Note No. 11. Ghana*, Copac, Rome, 1982.

Asthana, M. M., *Cooperative Information Note No. 12. Ghana*, Copac, Rome, 1982.

Bager, T., *Marketing Cooperatives and Peasants in Kenya*, Scandinavian Institute of African Studies, Uppsala, 1980.

Bale, M. D., 'Government intervention in agricultural markets and pricing', pp. 98–103 in D. Elz (ed.) *Agricultural Marketing Strategy and Pricing Policy*, World Bank, Washington DC, 1987.

Bates, R., *Markets and States in Tropical Africa: The Political Basis of Agricultural Policies*, University of California Press, Berkeley, 1981.

Bates, R., *Essays on the Political Economy of Rural Africa*, Africa Studies Series 38, Cambridge University Press, Cambridge, 1983.

Bates, R., 'The politics of agricultural policy – a reply', in *IDS Bulletin*, vol. 17, no. 1, 1986, pp. 12–15.

Berg, E., 'Obstacles to liberalizing agricultural markets in developing countries', pp. 22–27 in D. Elz (ed.) *Agricultural Marketing Strategy and Pricing Policy*, World Bank, Washington DC, 1987.

Bevan, D., Collier, P. and Gunning, J., 'Consequences of a commodity boom in a controlled economy: accumulation and redistribution in Kenya, 1975–83' in *The World Bank Economic Review*, vol. 1, no. 3 (May), 1987.

Bezzabeh, M., 'A review of the recent trends in agrarian reform and rural development in tropical Africa', in *Land Reform. Land Settlement and Cooperatives*, no. 1/2, FAO, 1981, pp. 2–19.

Bigsten, A., *Regional Inequality and Development. A Case Study of Kenya*, Dept of Economics, University of Gothenburg, 1978.

Brett, E. A., 'State power and economic inefficiency: explaining political failure in Africa', in *IDS Bulletin* vol. 17, no. 1, 1983, pp. 22–30.

Bryceson, D., 'Second thoughts on marketing co-operatives in Tanzania. Background to their reinstatement', *Plunkett Development Series 5*, the Plunkett Foundation, Oxford.

Collier, P. and Lal, D., 'Poverty and growth in Kenya', *Studies in Employment and Rural Development*, no. 55, IBRD, May 1979, mimeo. Cited in D. Hunt, *The Impending Crisis in Kenya. The Case for Land Reform*, Gower, Aldershot, 1984, table 3.6.

Colonial Office, Circular with memorandum as enclosure. Colonial Office, Downing Street, London, 20 March 1946.

Cooperative Bank of Kenya, *Annual Report and Statement of Accounts*, 1968/69–1971/72.

Copac, 'Rural cooperatives: some lessons and suggestions from a UNDP evaluation study', *Cooperative Programme Note*, Copac, Rome, 1983.

Copac, *Cooperative Information Note No. 30. Republic of Senegal*, Rome, 1985.

Copac, *Cooperative Information Note Republic of Kenya*, pp. 13–14, Rome 1984.

Copac, *Cooperative Programme Note. Rural Cooperatives: Some Lessons and Suggestions from a UNDP Evaluation Study*, p. 3, Copac, Rome, 1983.

Copac, *The Role of Government in Cooperatives*, Rome, 1984 (stencil).

Dadson, J. A., *The Need for Cooperative Reorientation – The Ghanaian Case*, paper presented at the seminar 'Cooperatives Revisited', Scandinavian Institute of African Studies, Uppsala, 1986.

DOCD (a), *Plan for Cooperative Development in Kenya with Nordic Assistance, 1972–77*, Nairobi, 1971.

DOCD, *The Role of District Cooperative Unions in Kenya's Development Efforts*, Nairobi, 1976 (stencil).

Dulfer, E. and Hamm, W., (eds) *Cooperatives in the Clash between Member Participation, Organizational Development and Bureaucratic Tendencies*, Quiller Press, London, 1985.

Elz, D., (ed.) *Agricultural Marketing Strategy and Pricing Policy*, World Bank, Washington DC, 1987.

Elz, D., 'Agricultural marketing policies and development', pp. 5–13 in D. Elz (ed.) *Agricultural Marketing Strategy and Pricing Policy*, World Bank, Washington DC, 1987.

Epstein, T. S., 'Differential access to markets and its impact on agricultural development', pp. 221–34 in *ICRISAT, Agricultural Markets in the Semi-arid Tropics*, ICRISAT Center, Patancheru, 1985.

Finnagro, *Rural Dairy Development Project – Phase I. Annual Report for 1983*, Finnagro Oy, Feb. 1984 (stencil).

Finsterbusch, K., 'Evaluation methods', pp. 285–311 in Finsterbusch, K., Llewellyn, L. G. and Wolf, C. P., *Social Impact Assessment Methods*, Sage, London, 1983.

Finsterbusch, K., Llewellyn, L. G. and Wolf, C. P., *Social Impact Assessment Methods*, Sage, London, 1983.

Freeman, D. B., 'The importance of being first: preemption by early adopters of farming innovations in Kenya', pp 17–28 in *Annals of the Association of American Geographers*, 75(1), 1985.

Friedman, J., 'The spatial organization of power in the development of urban systems', in *Economic Development and Cultural Change*, vol. IV, no. 3, 1985, pp. 12–50.

Ghai, S. and Radwan, S., (eds) *Agrarian Policies and Rural Poverty in Africa*, ILO, Geneva, 1983

de Graaf, J., *The Economics of Coffee*, Koninklijk Inst. voor de Tropen, Pudoc, Wageningen, 1986.

Grönberg, E-B. and Johansson, M., 'Zambian women and the cooperative movement. A case study of Nachikungu MPC Society Ltd', in *Rapporter och Notiser No. 85*, Department of Social and Economic Geography, University of Lund, 1988.

Gyllström, B., 'Befolkningstillväxt och ekonomisk utveckling i Kisii, Kenya' in *Geografiska Notiser Nr 4*, p. 155–62, Lund, 1975.

Gyllström, B., *The Organisation of Production as a Space-Modelling Mechanism in Underdeveloped Countries. The Case of Tea Production in Kenya*, CWK Gleerup, Lund, 1977.

Gyllström, B., 'Fattigdom och förtryck: Om jord-brukskooperationens utvecklingsbetingelser i Afrika' in *Svensk Geografisk Årsbok 1985*, Gleerup, pp. 44–62, Lund, 1986.

Gyllström, B., 'Government vs. agricultural marketing cooperatives in Kenya. Some observations on modes and consequences of state intervention'. Paper presented at the seminar 'Cooperatives Revisited', the Scandinavian Institute of African Studies, Uppsala, 1986.

Gyllström, B., 'Administered interdependencies vs. spatial integration. The case of agricultural service cooperatives in Kenya', in B. Gyllström (ed.), *State, Cooperatives and Rural Change in Africa*, Lund Studies in Geography, Ser B., Dept of Social and Economic Geography, University of Lund, Lund, 1989.

Harris, J. (ed.) *Rural Development. Theories of Peasant Economy and Agrarian Change*, Hutchinson University Library, London, 1982.

Harvey, C., Jacobs, J., Lamb, G. and Schaeffer, B., *Rural Employment and Administration in the Third World. Development Methods and Alternative Strategies*, Saxon House, 1979.

Hedlund, H., *A cooperative revisited in Kenya*, paper presented at the seminar 'Cooperatives Revisited', Scandinavian Institute of African Studies, Uppsala, 1986.

Hedlund, H., *Kaffe, kooperation och kultur. En studie av en kooperativ kafféförening i Kibirigwi, Kenya*, Nordiska Afrikainstitutet, Uppsala, 1986.

Hedlund, H., (ed.) 'Introduction', in *A Cooperative Revisited in Kenya*, Scandinavian Institute for African Studies, Uppsala, 1988.

Henin, R. A., 'The characteristics and development implications of a fast-growing population', pp. 193–207 in T. Killick (ed.), *Papers on the Kenyan Economy*, Heinemann, Nairobi, 1981.

Holmquist, F. W., *Peasant Organization, Clientelism and Dependency: A Case Study of an Agricultural Producers' Cooperative in Kenya*, Indiana University, 1975.

House, W. J. and Killick, T., 'Social justice and development policy in Kenya's rural economy', pp. 31–69 in S. Ghai and S. Radwan. (eds) *Agrarian Policies and Rural Poverty in Africa*, ILO, Geneva, 1983.

Hunt, D., *The Impending Crisis in Kenya. The Case for Land Reform*, Gower, Hampshire, 1984.

Hydén, G. and Karanja, E., 'Agriculture and Cooperatives in Kenya', pp. 158–220 in R. Apthorpe (ed.) *Rural Cooperatives and Planned Change in Africa*, vol. IV, UNRISD, Geneva, 1970.

Hydén, G., 'Cooperatives and their socio-political environment', pp. 61–80 in C. G. Widstrand (ed.), *African Cooperatives and efficiency*, the Scandinavian Institute of African Studies, Uppsala, 1972.

Hydén, G., *Efficiency versus Distribution in East African Cooperatives. A Study in Organizational Conflict*, East African Literature Bureau, Nairobi, 1973.

Hydén, G., 'Cooperatives and the poor. Comparing European and Third World experience' in *Rural Development Participation Review*, vol. II, no. 1, 1980.

Hydén, G., *No Shortcuts to Progress. African Development Management in Perspective*, Heinemann, London, 1983.

ICRISAT, *Agricultural Markets in the Semi-arid Tropics*, ICRISAT Center, Patancheru, 1985.

ILO, *Employment, Incomes and Equality: A Strategy for Increasing Productive Employment in Kenya*, Geneva, ILO, 1972.

Ilchman, W. F. and Bhargava, R. C., 'Balanced thought and economic growth', pp. 26–44 in C. K. Wilber (ed.) *The Political Economy of Development and Underdevelopment*, Random House, New York 1973.

Illy, H. F., 'How to build in the germs of failure: credit cooperatives in the French Cameroon', pp. 75–85 in H.-H. Münkner (ed.), *Towards Adjusted Patterns of Cooperatives in Developing Countries*, results of a symposium on 'Ways towards an African Cooperative'. Friedrich-Ebert-Stiftung, Bonn, 1984.

Johnston, B. F. and Kilby, P., 'Unimodal and bimodal strategies of agrarian change', pp. 50–65 in J. Harris (ed.), *Rural Development. Theories of Peasant Economy and Agrarian Change*, Hutchinson University Library, London, 1982.

KNFC, *The Cotton Industry*, 'A survey of structure, costs and margins for seed cotton buying, ginning and related activities'. Price Monitoring and Analysis Section, Nairobi, 1981.

Karanja, E., *The Development of Cooperative Movement in Kenya*, Ph.D thesis, University of Pittsburg, 1974.

Kasfir, N., 'Organizational analysis and Uganda cooperative unions', pp. 203–7, in C. G. Widstrand (ed.), 1972, op. cit.

Killick, T. (ed.), *Papers on the Kenyan Economy. Performance, Problems, Policies*, Heinemann, Nairobi, 1981.

Kinyanjui, K., *Regional and Class Inequalities in Provision of Primary Education in Kenya, 1968–73: A Historical and Socio-Economic Background*, occasional paper no. 37, IDS, Nairobi, undated.

Kitching, G., *Class and Economic Change in Kenya. The Making of an African Petite-Bourgeoisie*, Yale University, 1980.

Lamb, G., 'Government, co-operatives and peasant agriculture in Kenya', pp. 25–36 in *Institute of Development Studies Bulletin*, vol. 6 no. 1, 1974.

Laut, P., *Agricultural Geography*, vol. 1 'Systems, subsistence and plantation agriculture', Nelson, Melbourne, 1974.

Lavrijsen, J. S. G., *Rural Poverty and Impoverishment in Western Kenya*, Geografisch Institut, Rijksuniversiteit Utrecht, 1984.

Lele, U., 'Growth of foreign assistance and its impact on agriculture', p. 326 in Mellor, J. W., Delgado, C. L. and Blackie, M. J., (eds) *Accelerating Food Production in Sub-Saharan Africa*, pp. 321–42, Johns Hopkins University Press, Baltimore, 1987.

Leo, C., *Land and Class in Kenya*, University of Toronto Press, Toronto, 1984.

Leys, C., *Underdevelopment in Kenya. The Political Economy of Neo-Colonialism 1964–71*, Heinemann, London, 1975.

Livingstone, I. and Ord, H. W., *Economics for Eastern Africa*, Heinemann, London, 1980.

Livingstone, I., *Rural Development, Employment and Incomes in Kenya*. Report prepared for the ILO's Jobs and Skills Programme for Africa, ILO, Addis Ababa, 1981.

Lorsch, J. W., Allen, III S.A., *Managing Diversity and Interdependence*, Harvard University, Boston, 1973.

Lundahl, M., *Peasants and Poverty. A Study of Haiti*, Croom Helm, London, 1979.

MOCD, *Statistics for Cooperatives in Kenya*, Ministry of Cooperative Development, Nairobi, 1983.

Maitha, J. K., *Coffee in the Kenyan Economy. An Econometric Analysis*, East African Literature Bureau, Nairobi, 1974.

Maranga, J. S. and Standa, E. M., *The Co-operative Member and Committee Member Education Programme. Report on a pilot evaluation*. Report no. 7, Research and Evaluation Unit, Ministry of Coop. Development, Nairobi, 1981.

McCall, M. K., 'The significance of distance constraints in peasant farming systems with special reference to sub-Saharan Africa', in *Applied Geography* (1985), 5, pp. 325–45.

Mellor, J. W., Delgado, C. L. and Blackie, M. J., (eds) *Accelerating Food Production in Sub-Saharan Africa*, Johns Hopkins University Press, Baltimore, 1987.

Mosley, P., *The Settler Economies. Studies in the Economic History of Kenya and Southern Rhodesia 1900–1963*, Cambridge University Press, Cambridge, 1983.

Muliro, M., *Cooperative Message to Kenyan Cooperators on the 50th International Cooperative Day*, Ministry of Cooperatives and Social Services, Nairobi (stencil).

Münkner, H.-H. (ed.) *Credit Union Development in Africa*, Institut für Internationale Solidarität, St. Augustin, 1978.

Münkner, H.-H., 'Problems of cooperative management in Africa', pp. 127–47 in H.-H. Munkner (ed.) *Credit Union Development in Africa*, Institut für Internationale Solidarität, St. Augustin, 1978.

Münkner, H.-H., 'Practical problems of law reform in Africa – with particular reference to cooperative laws', pp. 51–71 in *Year Book of Agricultural Co-operation 1982*, the Plunkett Foundation, Oxford, 1983.

Münkner, H.-H., (ed.), 'Introduction', pp. 7–15 in *Towards Adjusted Patterns of Cooperatives in Developing Countries*. Results of a symposium on 'Ways towards an African Cooperative', Friedrich-Ebert-Stiftung, Bonn, 1984.

Nash, M., (ed.) *Essays on Economic Development and Cultural Change* in honor of Bert F. Hoselitz, University of Chicago Press, 1977.

Mcube, P. D. and Aulakh, H. S., *Co-operative Organization in Zambia with Special Focus on Rural Development – Problems and Prospects*. Paper presented at the seminar 'Cooperatives Revisited', Scandinavian Institute of African Studies, Uppsala, 1986.

Njonjo, A. L., Chege, F., Kimenye, D., Ng'ang'a, A. and Cookson, F., *Cooperative Production Credit Study*, vol. 1, Business and Economic Research Bureau, Nairobi, 1985.

Njoroge, L. O., *Cash Crop Substitution in South Kinangop Settlement Scheme*, Nyandarua District. Department of Geography, University of Nairobi, Nairobi, July 1980.

Nouyrit, H., 'The agricultural cooperative between member participation, vertical organization building and bureaucratic tendencies', pp. 447–57 in E. Dulfer and W. Hamm (eds) *Cooperatives in the Clash between Member Participation, Organizational Development and Bureaucratic Tendencies*, Quiller Press, London, 1985.

Okafor, F. O., 'Socio-economic criteria for evaluating cooperative efficiency in Nigeria', pp. 255–68 in *Review of International Cooperation*, vol. 72, no. 4, ICA, London, 1979.

Ouma, S., *A History of the Co-operative Movement in Kenya*, p. 39, Bookwise Ltd, Nairobi, 1980.

Patrick, H. T., 'Financial development and economic growth in developing countries', pp. 50–57 in von Pischke, J. D. *et al.*, (eds), 1983.

von Pischke, J. D. *et al.*, *Rural Financial Markets in Developing Countries. Their Use and Abuse*, Johns Hopkins University Press, London, 1983.

Rahman, M. A., 'Participation of the poor in rural development. Concept of an inquiry', in *Development – Seeds of Change, Village through Global Order*, 1981, no. 1.

Ranis, G., 'Development theory at three-quarters century', pp. 254–69 in M. Nash (ed.) *Essays on Economic Development and Cultural Change* in honor of Bert F. Hoselitz, University of Chicago Press, 1977.

Republic of Kenya, *Population Census 1969*, Central Bureau of Statistics, Nairobi.

Republic of Kenya, *Cooperative Development Policy for Kenya*, Sessional Paper No. 8, 1970, government printer, Nairobi.

Republic of Kenya, *Plan for Cooperative Development in Kenya with Nordic Assistance, 1972–77*, Dep. of Cooperative Development, Nairobi, 1971.

Republic of Kenya, *Development Plan 1974–78, Part I*, Nairobi, 1974.

Republic of Kenya, *Cooperative Development Policy for Kenya*, Sessional Paper no. 14 of 1975.

Republic of Kenya, *Integrated Rural Survey 1974–75*, Central Bureau of Statistics, Nairobi.

Republic of Kenya, *The Role of District Cooperative Unions in Kenya's Development Efforts*, Department of Cooperative Development, Nairobi, 1976 (stencil).

Republic of Kenya, *Population Census 1979*, Central Bureau of Statistics, Nairobi.

Republic of Kenya, *Economic Survey*, various issues 1968–83, Central Bureau of Statistics, Nairobi.

Republic of Kenya, *Economic Survey*, various issues 1968–84, Central Bureau of Statistics, Nairobi.

Robertson, A. F., *People and the State. An Anthropology of Planned Development*, Cambridge University Press, Cambridge, 1984.

Rundquist, F.-M., *Hybrid Maize Diffusion in Kenya*, CWK Gleerup, Lund, 1984.

Samuelsson, M., *Women's Ability to Participate Actively in Co-operatives*, Department of Social and Economic Geography, University of Lund, 1987 (stencil).

Sandbrook, R., *The Politics of Africa's Economic Stagnation*, Cambridge University Press, Cambridge, 1985.

Sarré, E., *Cooperative Information Note No. 9. Republic of Upper Volta*, Copac, Rome, 1981.

Sharpley, J., 'Resource transfers between the agricultural and non-agricultural sectors: 1964–1977', pp. 311–19 in T. Killick (ed.) *Papers on the Kenyan Economy. Performance, Problems, Policies*, Heinemann, Nairobi, 1981.

Sharpley, J., *Economic Policies and Agricultural Performance. The Case of Kenya*, Development Centre Papers, OECD, Paris 1986.

Smith, W. E., Lethem, F. J. and Thoolen, B. A., *The Design of Organizations for Rural Development Projects – A Progress Report*, World Bank Staff Working Papers no. 375, Washington, 1980.

Soja, E. W., *The Geography of Modernization in Kenya. A Spatial Analysis of Social, Economic and Political Change*, Syracuse University Press, 1968.

Ståhl, M., 'Capturing the peasants through cooperatives – the case of Ethiopia', in B. Gyllström (ed.), *State, Cooperatives and Rural Change in Africa*, (forthcoming in Lund Studies in Geography, Ser B., Dept of Social and Economic Geography, University of Lund).

Standa, E. M. and Maranga, J. S., *The Co-operative Member and Committee Member Education Programme*, Report No. 7, Research and Evaluation Unit, Development Planning Division, Ministry of Cooperative Development, Nairobi, 1981.

Stettner, L., 'Co-operation and egalitarianism in the developing countries', in *Review of International Cooperation* 66(6).

Stewart, F., 'Kenya strategies for development', pp. 75–89 in T. Killick (ed.) *Papers on the Kenyan Economy. Performance, Problems and Policies*, Heinemann, Nairobi, 1981.

Swynnerton, R. J. M., *A Plan to Intensify the Development of African Agriculture in Kenya*, Government Printer, Nairobi, 1954.

UNDP, *Rural Cooperatives*, (stencil), 1984.

UNRISD, *Rural Cooperatives as Agents of Change, Rural Institutions and Planned Change*, vol. VII, Geneva, 1975.

UNRISD, *Rural Cooperatives as Agents of Change: A Research Report and a Debate*, Geneva, 1975.

United Nations, *Popular Participation as a Strategy for Promoting Community Level Action and National Development*, New York, 1981.

Verhagen, K., *Co-operation for Survival. An Analysis of an Experiment in Participatory Research and Planning with Small Farmers in Sri Lanka and Thailand*, Royal Tropical Institute, Amsterdam, 1984.

Wafukho, J. and Wanjohi, M., *Historical Background of Cooperative Movement in Kenya (before) up to 1945*, Kenyan National Federation of Cooperatives, Nairobi (undated stencil).

Westergaard, P. W., 'Co-operatives in Tanzania as economic and democratic institutions', pp. 121–52 in C. G. Widstrand (ed.) *African Co-operatives and Efficiency*, the Scandinavian Institute of African Studies, Uppsala, 1972.

Whitaker, M. J., 'Supply of inputs to smallholder coffee farmers through the cooperative distribution system in Kenya from 1981 to 1983', in *Kenya Coffee*, Jan./Feb. 1985, pp. 279–90.

Widstrand, C. G. 'Problems of efficiency in the performance of co-operatives', pp. 9–31 in C. G. Widstrand (ed.) *African Co-operatives and Efficiency*, the Scandinavian Institute of African Studies, Uppsala, 1972.

Wilber, C. K., (ed.) *The Political Economy of Development and Underdevelopment*, Random House, New York, 1973.

World Bank, *Kenya: into the Second Decade*, Johns Hopkins University Press, Washington DC, 1975.

World Bank, *Accelerated Development in Sub-Saharan Africa. An Agenda for Action*, Washington DC, 1981.

World Bank (b), *Kenya. Growth and Structural Change*, vol. 1, Washington DC, 1983.

Worsley, P. (ed.), *Two Blades of Grass. Rural Cooperatives in Agricultural Modernization*, Manchester University Press, 1971.

van Zwanenberg, R. M. A., *An Economic History of Kenya and Uganda*, The Macmillan Press Ltd., London, 1975.

# Index

Printed in the United States
by Baker & Taylor Publisher Services